Beyond and Before

"Examining every aspect of progressive rock – words and music, theatre and politics – Hegarty and Halliwell deftly unpick the tangled threads of tradition and radicalism that make up the genre's tapestry. In addition to shedding vital new light on an often maligned and misunderstood phase in rock's history, this probing and incisive study tracks prog's continued and unexpected reverberations through popular music long after punk had supposedly vanquished and banished it."

Simon Reynolds, author of *Retromania: Pop Culture's Addiction to Its Own Past* (2011) and *Rip It Up and Start Again: Postpunk 1978–84* (2005)

"*Beyond and Before* is a wonderful account of both the rich legacy and the ongoing story of progressive rock in all its forms. At last, here is a book that gives prog its due respect as a vital part of the history of rock music, without tying it to a simplistic narrative of over-ambition, decadence and decline. The best thing about the book is its comprehensive, nuanced definition of what counts as progressive. In Hegarty and Halliwell's capable hands we journey from such unlikely precursors of the concept album as Frank Sinatra and Duke Ellington, through the 1970s Golden Age of Jethro Tull, Genesis and Pink Floyd to contemporary exponents as various as Spock's Beard, Porcupine Tree and The Decemberists."

Greg Walker, Regius Professor of Rhetoric and English Literature at the University of Edinburgh

"This is a great book. Hegarty and Halliwell have rescued progressive rock from the condescension of history by crafting a work that is smart, sympathetic, and impressively sweeping in its coverage of a much derided, yet enormously diverse and influential transnational music. Whether your taste is Porcupine Tree or Pink Floyd, Epica or ELP, Mike Oldfield or Midlake, there is plenty to admire and ponder in this ambitious and compelling account. By offering an expanded definition of prog rock in terms of its roots, musical and lyrical characteristics, geographic sources, artwork, performance practices, and legacies, *Beyond and Before* offers an exhilarating read."

Brian Ward, Professor of American Studies at the University of Manchester

Beyond and Before

Progressive Rock since the 1960s

Paul Hegarty and Martin Halliwell

continuum

2011

The Continuum International Publishing Group
80 Maiden Lane, New York, NY 10038
The Tower Building, 11 York Road, London SE1 7NX

www.continuumbooks.com

Copyright © Paul Hegarty and Martin Halliwell

Library of Congress Cataloging-in-Publication Data
A catalog record for this book is available from the Library of Congress.

ISBN: HB: 978-0-8264-4075-4
PB: 978-0-8264-2332-0

Typeset by Pindar NZ, Auckland, New Zealand
Printed and bound in the United States of America

Contents

Acknowledgements

The roots of this project lie in the mid-1990s, when we were both living in Nottingham, facing one of the lowest points in the critical reception of progressive rock. The realization of this book has been a long time coming, but it has benefited from a number of important studies published in the late 1990s and from the dramatic resurgence of progressive rock albums and performances, in their many guises and forms, since the millennium. We would like to thank Ben Andrews, Colin Harrison and, particularly, Michael Hoar for helping sow the seeds for this project, and for being there to witness its growth over the last fifteen years. We would also like to thank David Barker, editorial director at Continuum, for being such a supportive and accommodating editor, our universities in Cork and Leicester, and all the artists and bands whose artwork and stills feature in this book for being so generous with permissions.

We want to thank, separately, a number of friends and colleagues who have helped, either tangibly or tangentially, to bring *Beyond and Before* to fruition. Martin would like to thank Luke Boudour, Sue Currell, Nick Everett, Corinne Fowler, Jonathan Heath, Andrew Johnstone, George Lewis, Catherine Morley, Andy Mousley, Joel Rasmussen, Mark Rawlinson, Phil Shaw, Adam Siviter and Gary Slater. He also wishes to thank Mark Halliwell, Kathryn Ward (1969–2010), his families in Derby and Leicester and, especially, Laraine for all her support and for putting up with writing sessions that lasted far longer than the most excessive 1970s drum solo. Paul would like to thank John Byrne, Patrick Crowley, Gary Genosko, Claire Guerin, Greg Hainge, Jim Horgan, Kevin Kennedy, Ronan Lane, Vicky Langan, Rosa Menkman, Dave Murphy, Brian O'Shaughnessy, Eamonn O'Neill, Mick O'Shea, Alex Rose, Stephen Roggendorff, David Tibet, Albert Twomey and Steven Wilson. Thanks to Wölf for constant inspiration since the project began in mid-2008.

Illustration Credits

Chapter 2
Still from *Pink Floyd: London 1966/1967* (2005) © Peter Whitehead.
Cover of The Moody Blues, *In Search of the Lost Chord* (1968). Artwork by Phil Travers
© The Moody Blues.

Chapter 3
Ian Anderson and Clive Bunker of Jethro Tull at the Isle of Wight Festival (August 1970).
Photograph by David Redfern/Redferns.
Pentangle performing in 1967. Photograph by Brian Shuel/Redferns.

Chapter 4
Cover art for King Crimson, *The Court of the Crimson King: An Observation* (1969).
Artwork by Barry Godber © Robert Fripp. Courtesy of DGM Ltd. on behalf of King Crimson.
Peter Gabriel as the Slipperman, *The Lamb Lies Down on Broadway* tour, Copenhagen, Denmark
(January 1975). Photograph by Jorgen Angel/Redferns.

Chapter 5
Cover of Rush, *A Farewell to Kings* (1977). Art direction and graphics © Hugh Syme.
Cover of Hawkwind, *Warrior on the Edge of Time* (1975). Art Direction by Pierre D'Auvergne
© Hawkwind.

Chapter 6
Soft Machine outside the Albert Hall in London (12 August 1970). Photograph by
Keystone/Getty Images.

Chapter 7
Still from *Pink Floyd: Live at Pompeii* (Adrian Maben, 1972). Bayerische Rundfunk/Ortf/
The Kobal Collection.
Still from *The Song Remains the Same* (Peter Clifton/Joe Massot, 1976).
Starmavale/Swan Song/The Kobal Collection.

Chapter 8

Genesis, *Selling England by the Pound* (1973). Painting by Betty Swanwick © Genesis.
Yes recording *Fragile* at Advision Studios in London (September 1971).
Photograph by Michael Putland/Getty Images.
Rush recording *Permanent Waves* in Le Studio, Quebec (October 1979).
Photograph by Fin Costello/Redferns.

Chapter 9

Publicity still of Emerson, Lake and Palmer (c. 1970).
Photograph by Michael Ochs Archives/Getty Images.
This Heat in performance, Cold Storage (c. 1980). Photograph by Lesley Evans.
Cover of King Crimson, *Discipline* (1981). Knot logo by Steve Ball © Robert Fripp.
Courtesy of DGM Ltd. on behalf of King Crimson.

Chapter 10

Cover art for Marillion, 'Assassing' single (1984) © Mark Wilkinson,
www.the-masque.com/shadowplay
Cover art for Marillion, *Script for a Jester's Tear* (1983) © Mark Wilkinson,
www.the-masque.com/shadowplay
Cover art for IQ, *The Wake* (25th Anniversary Edition, 2010). Artwork by Peter Nicholls © IQ.

Chapter 11

Kate Bush's Tour of Life, Carré Theatre, Amsterdam (29 April 1979).
Photograph by Rob Verhorst/Redferns.

Chapter 12

Cover of Talk Talk, *Spirit of Eden* (1988) © James Marsh, www.jamesmarsh.com
Cover of Talk Talk, *Laughing Stock* (1991) © James Marsh, www.jamesmarsh.com

Chapter 13

Artwork for Current 93, *Earth Covers Earth* (1988). Artwork by Ruth Bayer © Current 93.
Cover of Midlake, *The Courage of Others* (2010) © Midlake.
Cover art for Joanna Newsom, *Ys* (2006) © Benjamin Vierling, www.bvierling.com

Chapter 14

Mike Portnoy of Dream Theater performing at Fields of Rock, The Netherlands (June 2007).
Photograph by Paul Bergen/Redferns.
Cover of Porcupine Tree, *Fear of a Blank Planet* (2007).
Photography by Lasse Hoile. Design by Carl Glover.

Coda

Porcupine Tree in concert, New York (September 2010). Photograph Claudia Hahn © Porcupine Tree.

Front cover image

Cover of The Mars Volta, *Frances the Mute* (2005). Artwork by Storm Thorgerson © Hipgnosis.

Introduction

Progressive Rock since the 1960s

'Ever get the feeling you've been cheated?' asked John Lydon, on stage at Winterland, San Francisco, in January 1978, in his last days as Johnny Rotten. The dream of the Sex Pistols to break free from rock cliché was over, ended in a farce of hype, self-indulgence and musical stasis. Punk was born in 1976 from a fury of destruction and renewal, and its principal target was progressive rock, whose alleged self-indulgence and pretension would be brought to a close by the fresh and angry authenticity of a newly stripped-down version of rock, invigorated through simplicity.

The dominant discourse in music history is that progressive rock was victim to punk's return to basics, albeit a basis that imagined it needed to destroy all that had gone before in order to proclaim a new beginning. In practical terms, nothing of the sort happened. The rock bands that were commercially successful remained so, and some, such as Genesis and Rush, increased in popularity during the late 1970s. Critically speaking, though, progressive rock remained doomed, as a generation of supporters of punk, particularly in Britain and centred on the weekly music paper the *New Musical Express*, moved into academia (with the growth of cultural studies) and into the mainstream press. To this day, a suspicion lingers over anything that recalls the experimentation practised by 1970s progressive rock bands. For example, in 1998, the *Observer* ran an article, 'Oh No, It's Yes: Where Even Irony Fears to Tread', which noted the rise of nostalgia for the 1970s but claimed that progressive rock remains 'utterly unforgiven' in media circles.[1] The article's author, David Thomas, goes on to say that in 1973–4

> many of us huddled against the cold of the power cuts and the three-day week in Afghan sheepskins, earnestly debating the secret meaning of the latest progressive rock concept album and pondering great questions of life like, who was the best bass player, Greg Lake or John Paul Jones?[2]

Although Thomas here recoils from a formative phase of his musical education, the limits of this kind of discourse have been, to our mind, fatally exposed, primarily because since the late 1990s progressive rock has renewed itself as a major cultural force without recourse to the musical vocabulary assumed to be the staple of all progressive styles.[3]

The obvious approach to a new study of progressive rock is to pretend that its hostile reception around the time of punk simply never occurred. Yet this might lead to a wistful or nostalgic view of 1970s progressive rock, cut dead in its prime by the assault of punk or undone from within by the excesses of the rock industry. This book wishes to avoid such nostalgia by pursuing two other aims: we focus on the long and varied musical history of progressive rock, first, to counter recent social histories of 1970s Britain that marginalize its existence as a major musical form, and, second, to problematize the received orthodoxy that punk did away with prog.[4] Such strategies enable us to examine how progressive rock works across its cultural, historical and musical range, rather than attempting to justify or deny a single generation's hostile interpretation of prog.

This is not to resurrect prog at the expense of punk, though. The punk attack on progressive and stadium rock undeniably occurred, and it would be true to say that the inspiration created by punk – to open music up to all, rather than its being the province of musical virtuosos – was significant, creative and powerful. It is also true that the rock criticism emerging as a serious force in the late 1970s had much to say, notably on what Theodor Adorno and Max Horkheimer in the mid-1940s called 'the culture industry', which, after World War II, increasingly replaced cultural creativity with standardized products that have only surface attraction or 'style'.[5] For all the virtues of *Listening to the Future: The Time of Progressive Rock* (1998), Bill Martin is wrong to caricature punk as an example of cynical music for a cynical society that totally rejected the utopianism of the mid-1960s and its bearing on the youth cultures of the 1970s.[6] Above all, though, we cannot write off the historical reception of progressive rock; Martin joins Edward Macan, author of the other major book on progressive rock, *Rocking the Classics: English Progressive Rock and the Counterculture* (1997), in acknowledging the power of that critical paradigm. They each do so largely unconsciously, and they effectively accept the characterization of progressive rock offered by its critics. In this book, we realize the need to accept the reality of 'punk criticism', but without believing all of it to be true.

The problem is not that punk-inspired criticism is entirely wrong or misguided. The fault lies in the limited view of what progressive rock actually was – and still is. To this day, mention the words 'progressive rock' and many will conjure images of long solos, overlong albums, fantasy lyrics, grandiose stage sets and costumes, and a dedication to technical skill bordering on the obsessive. A few moments in its history have come to represent the whole, such as the much repeated image of the massive tour buses that Emerson,

Lake and Palmer used to carry around the band's vast array of musical and stage equipment in the mid-1970s, or Led Zeppelin's luxuriously fitted Starship One aeroplane used for the band's 1975 US tour. But these images tend to be a spurious metonymy of convenience. If we move up a notch in 'what was wrong with prog', we still encounter a range of references limited to Yes, Genesis, Jethro Tull, and Emerson, Lake and Palmer (ELP). Although these bands have certainly been responsible for melodramatic moments in their histories, even the most virulent opponent could not deny that they were highly popular in the 1970s and, for the most part, experimental in their compositions, albums and performances.

Beyond these nemeses of authentic rock lie the more interesting cases of King Crimson, Soft Machine and Van der Graaf Generator, bands that never received the same amount of vitriol as the aforementioned foursome, with Lydon himself keen on Van der Graaf Generator and its portentous singer Peter Hammill in particular (much to the disgust of Sex Pistols' manager, Malcolm McLaren). What is curious is that Martin and Macan use the same categorization to defend and explicate progressive rock. We will argue throughout this book, in different ways according to the type of progressive rock discussed, that prog is an incredibly varied genre based on fusions of styles, approaches and genres, and that it taps into broader cultural resonances that link to avant-garde art, classical and folk music, performance and the moving image. One of the best ways to define progressive rock is that it is a heterogeneous and troublesome genre – a formulation that becomes clear the moment we leave behind characterizations based only on the most visible bands of the early to mid-1970s. To do this, we need to explore the roots and sources of progressive rock; earlier examples of the concept album and song-cycle; the incredible variety of prog during the 1970s; and its legacies and parallels in rock music since the late 1970s, including neo-progressive and post-progressive revivals in the 1980s and late 1990s and the immense sprawl of metal into progressive methods, styles and forms.

Over the last ten to fifteen years, groups that update progressive rock have been massively successful – think of Radiohead, Tool, Muse, The Mars Volta and Porcupine Tree, among other innovative bands that have helped to resuscitate its long-lost credibility. We could say that the question of credibility no longer applies. In addition to sales, concert attendance and internet activity, the resurgence of interest among fans and practitioners of progressive rock can be seen in the now regular publication of *Classic Rock Presents Prog* magazine, launched in spring 2009: an offshoot of *Classic Rock* that focuses on the history of the genre and the rich diversity of prog across Europe and North America in the present. Other signs of this resurgence can be seen in the mainstream press. An article on contemporary music styles covered by the *Sunday Times* in January 2009 makes the claim that watching and listening to bands such as Radiohead, Muse and The Secret Machines is 'to witness all the mad splendour of prog rock, alive and well three decades after its heyday (and apparent death at the hands of punk)'.[7] Bemoaning the stereotyping of prog bands and style, the article continues:

> Back in the days before prog and art rock were seen as two separate entities, the best practitioners not only justified their mission – to make music of a greater complexity and inventiveness than the standard rock song format allowed for – with some superb albums, they also pointed the way towards the music of similarly unfettered and adventurous contemporary bands.[8]

Leaving aside the uncritical celebration of 'unfettered and adventurous' music, it is clear that progressive rock has equally complex legacies and genealogies, as explored in a *Guardian* feature in July 2010 that coincided with the inclusion of a dedicated progressive rock stage at that year's High Voltage festival in Victoria Park, London.[9]

As well as expanding on the *what* of progressive rock, we will extend the *when*. As the title of this book suggests, we are interested in the 'before' and 'beyond' of prog, as well as its high phase, from the late 1960s to the mid-1970s. This explains the two sections of the book: the first part deals with the 'before' and 'during' of progressive rock, tracing its conceptual and historical roots up to 1976–7, while the second part looks at the 'beyond', including responses to punk, a renegotiation of the legacy of prog, and the renewal of musical possibilities over the last thirty years. Our title, *Beyond and Before*, indicates that time features in many intersecting ways: the temporal reach of progressive rock; its interest in experimental time signatures; and time as a recurring theme in lyrics, song-cycles and concepts, such as Rush's 2010–11 Time Machine tour. In addition, we will expand on the *where* of prog. Bill Martin notes that prog was the first 'world music', because of its synthesizing of non-European elements with the already semi-global European classical music and English rock.[10] We want to make the case that it is literally a global music, spreading rapidly beyond England, crisscrossing the Atlantic and emerging in various European countries including Germany, Italy, the Netherlands and Sweden, and building on (but also complicating) the countercultural moves for individual and social freedoms that became visible in so many places in 1968.

This book will argue strongly for a highly diverse and open-ended idea of what progressive rock is, not out of a fashionable belief in political or cultural difference but because openness and extreme diversity (even within a single track) are key characteristics of progressive rock, its sources and its later forms. Nevertheless, a model is needed to avoid arguing that every interesting rock album that produces something new is somehow progressive. It would be accurate to say that any such album is a candidate for being thought of as progressive. Equally, it is important to avoid an overly reductive definition in terms of period or style. Bill Martin in *Music of Yes* (1996) and *Listening to the Future* proposes a set of guidelines for what progressive rock is and how it works.[11] For us, this model is too reductive if taken as a definitive paradigm; but used in combination with many ideas Martin offers as being of secondary importance, it is a productive way of beginning to think analytically and expansively about progressive rock.

Martin outlines three dominant characteristics of prog, which he then moulds into a four-point model. First, he writes of progressive rock being a true synthesis of different musical forms. Whereas The Beatles, along with many other 1960s bands, included elements of classical music or music from outside European traditions,

> in full-blown progressive rock, the synthesis is much more complete in the following way: when we hear the presence and juxtaposition of harpsichord and sitar [in progressive rock tracks], this sounds much more like something that has been part of the music all along.[12]

This interpretation means that diverse forms are integrated rather than acting as texture or ornamentation. The second key element of a progressive rock genre is musical virtuosity. This is controversially used, as Martin acknowledges, to exclude Pink Floyd, among others, a group that many regard as not only progressive in style but also very keen on musical skill.[13] His point is a subtle one; if we include all bands on this basis, we would have to include many rock records far outside what is usually thought of as progressive rock – a direction this book embraces by tracing the complex roots and multiple directions of the concept album. Third, for Martin, progressive rock is inherently, if not permanently, English in origin: that is, it derives from a particular collision of influences in English culture, such as religious dissenting, class as a determining social factor, a nationalistic sense of heritage, and a critique of social convention. In Martin's model, all progressive bands follow on from these national origins, as progressive rock 'sets sail from England'.[14] We will return to this idea after a quotation that incorporates the three strands of Martin's model:

> As a style of music progressive rock has five specific traits: 1) it is visionary and experimental; 2) it is played, at least in significant part, on instruments typically associated with rock music, by musicians who have a background in rock music, and with the history of rock music itself as background; 3) it is played, in significant part, by musicians who have consummate instrumental and compositional skills; 4) it is a phenomenon, in its 'core', of English culture; 5) relatedly, in significant part, it is expressive of romantic and prophetic aspects of that culture.[15]

These are not quite the same points identified in Martin's earlier list of key elements, but they need to be considered together with them. The first part of the definition is essential: for Martin, progressive rock is a type of utopianism interested in social change, even when it seems furthest from concrete political concerns (and especially so in the music of Yes). Furthermore, it is the pinnacle of rock 'n' roll's nascent avant-gardism. Martin's model is as much about exclusion as inclusion: music after the 'time of progressive rock', in 1978, could not attain the critical function of its high phase because society had lost its utopianism and had descended into social cynicism linked to a more brutal form of capitalism.[16] Following Edward Macan, another way of describing this moment is the splintering of the late 1960s counterculture into a series of fragmented subcultures, of which punk would be one example. For Martin, punk is merely the most blatant example of cultural cynicism (with the exception of Sex Pistols' 1977 album *Never Mind the Bollocks*, which conveys authentic musicalized anger). Ironically, this attempt to recover a politically progressive music resulted in his adopting a highly conservative position, paralleling the critical views of postmodernism that emerged in the 1980s and 1990s.

Martin follows a line that characterizes the moment in which he is writing: bemoaning (or half-heartedly praising) the end of the avant-garde in a manner that was common at the time of Fredric Jameson's *Postmodernism, or the Cultural Logic of Late Capitalism* (1991). Because of an over-emphasis on Jameson's notion of the 'waning of affect' through commodity production, this text is often misread as a blanket condemnation of contemporary aesthetics. Jameson explains the postmodern turn as the endpoint of exhaustion of modernism, cutting across diverse cultural forms:

> This break is most often related to notions of the waning or extinction of the hundred-year-old modern movement [. . .] Thus abstract expressionism in painting, existentialism in philosophy, the final forms of representation in the novel, the films of the great *auteurs*, or the modernist school of poetry . . . all are now seen as the final, extraordinary flowering of a high-modernist impulse which is spent and exhausted with them. The enumeration of what follows, then, at once becomes empirical, chaotic, and heterogeneous: Andy Warhol and pop art, but also photorealism, and beyond it, the 'new expressionism'; the moment, in music, of John Cage, but also the synthesis of classical and 'popular' styles found in composers like Phil Glass and Terry Riley, and also punk and new wave rock.[17]

Here, diversity rather than agonistic cultural trends mark a break from the modernist tradition in the 1960s and 1970s. Just like the 'end of history', which returned in the late 1980s (alongside the apparent end of ideology), the end of the avant-garde through the rejection of modernism is meaningful, but perhaps signals only the end of a particular Hegelian or Marxist notion of progression. If this particular conception is only part of a multi-dimensional progression, as opposed to progress as an inevitable upward or rising movement, then it cannot go away but only change configuration. We would argue that this occurred in what comes 'after' progressive rock in more and increasingly diverse forms. Developing Jameson's point about the diversity of postmodern cultures, rather than adopting the view of the dominance of a singular musical expression that plugs into a certain historical moment (psychedelic rock in 1967 or punk in 1976), Andreas Huyssen points towards the various competing 'phases and directions' of modernist culture running through the 1960s and 1970s, not all of which were moving in the same direction. The problem for Huyssen is that one version of modernism became 'domesticated in the 1950s'.[18] An 'adversary culture' that had marked earlier twentieth-century modernism still existed after mid-century, but it was overshadowed by a Cold War critical consensus and an academic emphasis on the text divorced from its material mode of production and its circulation in the marketplace. Similarly to Jameson, in *After the Great Divide* (1986) Huyssen suggests an alternative narrative of modernist culture, not as monolithic but as mobile and porous.

These views help us to understand the diversity of progressive rock, but we also need to step backwards to consider popular music before prog and its relation to the avant-garde. Chapter 2 examines the roots of progressive rock in the mid-1960s, but we need to explore whether or how rock relates to different models of the avant-garde in order to complete and broaden our reading of Martin's typology. Can we say with him, for example, that rock 'n' roll had any musical claims to being an avant-garde? If it did, was this more through its social impact or its inspiration for future musical experimentation?

Michael Nyman distinguishes between avant-garde music as that which is programme-based and functions within the orchestra or composer or musical-score genre, and experimental music where the status of music itself is questioned (by John Cage or La Monte Young or the international Fluxus project) or where its seriousness as high art is replaced by the repetitions and non-European influences of minimalism.[19] Although this is a tidy distinction, it differs from the usual understanding of the avant-garde in visual art, where a succession of aesthetic innovations gave rise to an avant-garde in the form of Dadaism, which did precisely what interests Nyman in experimental music, only fifty years earlier: unleashing a succession of early twentieth-century avant-gardes that questioned the basis of art.

Italian theorist Renato Poggioli's 1962 book *Teoria dell'arte d'avanguardia* (translated as *The Theory of the Avant-Garde* in 1968) historicizes the concept within the framework of modernity, and argues that avant-garde art itself can arise only when the idea of an avant-garde is present. The key seems to be that anything avant-garde cannot be judged on formal grounds alone. This is also true for two subsequent books: Peter Bürger's 1974 study *Theorie der Avantgarde* (translated as *Theory of the Avant-Garde* in 1984) and Rosalind Krauss's *The Originality of the Avant-Garde and Other Modernist Myths* (1985). For Krauss, the avant-garde artist imagines his or her self to be a new origin for art (which applies equally to modernist conceptions of time and history); having emerged parthenogenetically, the artist can pass on craft, lore or inspiration to the generations that follow. Krauss defines this as the 'myth of the avant-garde', which postmodernist practitioners attempt to dispose of with their lack of belief in autonomous originality.[20]

For us, progressive rock is both formally and socially avant-gardist, even if the latter becomes harder to see in the mid-1970s and might not be the case for all of its early twenty-first-century versions. In terms of Nyman's instrumentalist distinction between 'avant-garde' and 'experimental', we note that prog does both: it crosses this divide even if its critics might imagine that the grandiose musical ambitions of The Nice or Emerson, Lake and Palmer were to be surpassed by more directly authentic music. Martin's argument about rock 'n' roll being avant-garde from the start targets critics of progressive rock who claim that it is a perversion of rock, and that its authenticity can be restored only through the new simplicity of punk. In this respect, Martin is right to argue against a primal authenticity that validates certain forms of music and denigrates others. But Martin overstates the formal radicalism of rock 'n' roll by claiming that it was always hybrid and always innovative, particularly when formally it simplified blues structures and historically it developed in the 1950s alongside more radical musical forms: the emergence of free jazz, mathematical programme music, and the avant-gardism of the Black Mountain College in North Carolina.[21]

To understand whether this makes progressive rock avant-gardist requires further detail. Formally, although rock 'n' roll might have brought innovations to popular music, it would seem that if it ever thought of avant-garde music, it was to react against it, in a bid to speak to the 'real world' of young Americans. But what if the *audience* was avant-garde? Beyond the negative reception by panicky holders of power in the US in the mid-1950s (repeated slightly later in Britain), open-minded listeners keen on social, cultural and artistic change were successors to the original black audiences for so-called 'race music' in the 1940s or jazz in the pre-World War II period, for whom rock 'n' roll was no bolt from the blue but an organic outcrop of existing musical forms.[22] But this would not necessarily have been a conscious avant-gardism, at least not until the mid-1960s; as Charlie Gillett notes, 'few people in the rock 'n' roll audience deliberately or consciously considered music' intellectually.[23] Much of what white listeners in the 1950s heard as rock 'n' roll would have seemed exotic, but for black listeners its rhythm and blues elements were unremarkable and simply a phase in organic musical development.[24] Furthermore, rock 'n' roll audiences, according to sociologist David Riesman, were often elective communities formed around an awareness of new sounds, clubs, fashions and slang:

> There were still other ways in which the minority may use popular music to polarize itself from the majority group, and thereby from American popular culture generally: a sympathetic attitude or even preference for Negro musicians; an equalitarian attitude toward the roles, in love and work, of the two sexes; a more international outlook [and] a feeling that music is too important to serve as a backdrop for

dancing, small talk, studying, and the like; a diffuse resentment of the image of the teen-ager provided by the mass media.[25]

This audience helped to produce the musicians of 1960s and 1970s rock who became self-aware avant-gardists, purposely trying to introduce greater formal innovation into a rock format that still conveyed the excitement, rebellion and creative inspiration of rock 'n' roll. The promise or threat of social change and the formal structure of rock 'n' roll – simple lyrics, vocal mannerisms, and repetitive beats, chords and song structures – were easily and rapidly assimilated by the music industry that would triple its sales in the US between 1954 and 1959. It was precisely the affirmative elements of rock 'n' roll that made it so malleable, and progressive musicians of the 1960s would reintroduce complexity into rock, as a way of maintaining rebellious individuality and group identity alike in the face of massive capitalist and cultural recuperation of youth culture.[26]

The second trait that Martin identifies – that prog contains rock elements – is unarguable, although we will be discussing music that has gone a long way from the 1960s and 1970s rock template. If 'progressive' is to mean anything, it has to include the sense of referring to previous musical styles, whether those are progressive or not. When looking beyond the 1970s, Martin identifies only bands that refer specifically to the narrowly defined progressive rock style of the 1970s, whereas we would see 'progressive' as being meaningful only if it does more than that – although, as we discuss in Chapter 10, 'neo-progressive' music exists as a direct reference to the history of prog, often to the exclusion of other musical reference points. King Crimson's Robert Fripp identified this as a problem with what was termed progressive rock as far back as 1973, but this was part of Fripp's attempt to distance himself from the broader movement of prog. This is one reason we use the term 'prog' interchangeably with 'progressive rock' in this book. Initially, prog was just a shorthand for the progressive rock style, but recent years have seen it become a transferrable adjective, and it suggests a wider palette than that drawn on by the most popular 1970s bands.

The question of virtuosity is a vexed one for those who want progressive rock to be more than the self-indulgence for which prog is criticized. It is undeniable that many progressive rock musicians, especially in the 1970s, were talented, skilful and creative. The question is whether this hindered or helped musical creativity, particularly as progressive bands were interested in different ways of writing and performing as a group and of developing ideas into integrated concept albums, rather than filling out albums and concerts with tracks featuring virtuoso solos. Martin is correct to argue that Yes has always been an astonishingly skilful musical group, with its individuals incredibly inventive in ways that foster communal creativity, often in the form of what seems to be five musicians all playing lead at the same time. King Crimson has the same level of skills in all areas of music-making, but in very different ways from Yes. However, there are two problems with the use of virtuosity as a defining feature of progressive rock.

First, virtuosity was often praised for its very existence, hence the move to painfully long concert solos in the 1970s as an extension of jazz group practice. The 1970s music media were full of polls for best bass player and who could sustain the longest drum solo, with an increasing sense that personal technique could override band creativity (and often led key figures to release solo albums during sabbaticals from their bands). To balance this view, it is worth noting that Yes pursued virtuosity only for its own sake to a moderate degree on certain concert tours, and King Crimson almost never did. The worst offenders would be rock bands that did not receive the critical derision levelled at prog – bands who had stayed with a more blues-based style, and who were also filling stadia (such as The Who and Led Zeppelin, with John Bonham's 20-minute live drum solos filling out the latter's 1969 track 'Moby Dick').

Second, and more significantly, it is simply not true that progressive rock either required or always had very skilled musicians. More folk-based prog bands would have had little need for it, while still creating records we would recognize as progressive rock (see Chapters 3 and 13). Other bands would work at complex structures made up of simple elements. The music known as *kosmische* or Krautrock would often be highly repetitive. And did Hawkwind ever care about being virtuoso? Bill Martin would exclude space rock, just as he excludes Frank Zappa, funk (he refers to 'progressive soul' in passing), and the raft of 1970s groups that were not technically brilliant, such as the Irish band Horslips.[27] Early neo-prog, the most genre-referential type of prog, was often musically limited when it started out in the wake of punk and heavy metal in late 1970s Britain.

One dimension of Martin's point about the Englishness of progressive rock is uncontroversial in terms of the English poetic tradition in which it can be placed, which includes the Romantic poets, William Blake, John Milton, and traditional folk ballads and tales.[28] Macan echoes these points but takes a more pragmatic line: 'the genre originated in England and achieved its "classic" form at the hands of English bands during the early 1970s; even the neo-progressive revival of the early 1980s began in England'.[29] Once we factor in folk music, progressive folk, psychedelia and neo-progressive bands such as Pallas, then we are talking not about England but about all of Britain and Ireland, so the broader point about progressive rock being essentially English requires further comment. Prog rock emerged in Britain when the music industry was successful to the point it could countenance highly experimental music as a potentially viable commercial proposition, which linked together rock, jazz and folk scenes in which the musical and cultural exchange across regions and national borders was an implicit feature.[30]

The insistence on the Englishness of prog works only in relation to English progressive bands (and the encouragement of prog by English labels, including early independent labels Charisma and Virgin and the offshoots of major companies such as Harvest, Vertigo and Deram). Other than the largely unexplained inclusion of Magma (Germany) and PFM (Italy), all prog has to be English for Martin. We contend, and will argue later, that as progressive rock emerges from more specific musical trends, moments, locations and social conditions than an amorphous and peculiarly ahistorical Englishness, it cannot be reduced to being inherently English. Its influences in jazz, folk and classical, let alone in, say, Asian music, make this a much more complex picture, although England did produce a larger number of groups in the formative moments of progressive rock. In short, although progressive rock arises in England, it comprises elements that arrive from elsewhere; it is built in a specific historical musical phase; and it very quickly travelled across Europe and the Atlantic and, more recently, to other areas of the world such as China, with the Shanghai band Cold Fairyland influenced equally by Jethro Tull and Chinese folk music.

So much for where progressive rock might arise. Before we return to this question in Chapters 1 and 2, we will adapt one further idea from Bill Martin: that of 'stretching out'. The most well-known characteristic of progressive rock, for fans and detractors alike, is the length of songs, solos, albums and concerts. To a large extent, there is no such thing as progressive rock without extended form, which is the term we will largely use, but 'stretching out' gives the sense of how extended form arises. The stretch is not just of time but also of practice, recombining different genres and bringing in sounds, ideas and styles that would normally be beyond rock: 'though the phrase suggests longer works, the idea has more to do with stretching beyond established boundaries'.[31] This means that in this book we include The Beatles, The Beach Boys, The Doors, The Pretty Things, The Zombies, The Byrds, The Grateful Dead and Pink Floyd not merely as precursors of prog but as essential developments of progressiveness in its early days. Martin delineates two types of stretching out, based on his two exemplars of progressive rock – Yes and King Crimson:

> One form of stretching out is akin to jazz, while the other is more akin to Western classical music. One might think of the way King Crimson, for example, has definite affinities with avant-garde jazz, while Yes has affinities with twentieth-century classical music.[32]

The implications of Martin's perspective need pursuing, and not just into the extended jams of the space rock of Hawkwind, for example. Once we have identified 'stretching out' as a characteristic of prog, we can then extend it backwards; it can be identified in the free jazz of Ornette Coleman and John Coltrane, the sprawl of Karlheinz Stockhausen's electronic music, and Duke Ellington's 1943 concept piece *Black, Brown and Beige* (see Chapter 1). Stretching out connects to the need for prog to reference rock and other musical styles, and it helps us identify progressive rock as being involved in a process that is properly avant-garde and experimental. From the late 1960s onwards, progressive rock functioned, more often than not, as a self-conscious avant-garde, formally and socially. In so doing, as a musical genre it eludes the 'myth of the avant-garde' that the world has been reborn for the first time, and instead adopts the properly modernist attitude of referencing its precursors in continued innovation. We, as listeners, readers and critics, see a continuum of avant-gardes as if this was how it happened, because now it has always already happened.

The question of rock 'n' roll being avant-garde is relevant only once the question can be posed of post-1965 rock music, because a key part of an avant-garde is to have a movement for which it is the vanguard: rock 'n' roll can be read as a form of avant-garde free from content and devoid of formal complexity and experimentation. This, in turn, propelled the formless fuzz of psychedelia that gradually uncurled jams, solos and the literal stretching of tunes, and gave rise to the first moments of full-blown prog at the very end of the 1960s.[33] Prog did this, according to Macan, as an active response to the total environment and sensual overload of psychedelia, and the tools it used derived from classical music both in the guise of a more narrative version of extension and in terms of structure:

> Progressive rock was able to solve yet another challenge posed by the psychedelic jam – how to create a sense of direction – by drawing on nineteenth-century symphonic music's fondness for building up tension until a shattering climax is reached, abruptly tailing off, and then starting the process anew.[34]

In fact, classical music would be what distinguished prog from other forms of rock, even though Macan admits the multiple influences on and within progressive rock.[35] Not only that, but classical music is used as a means to buttress highly speculative, while notionally empirical, claims about church music in England: namely, that choral Anglican music was important in England over several centuries, and was a key part of the musical backdrop for members of progressive groups in the late 1960s and 1970s, some of whom would have been participants in that scene through their childhood upbringing or their adult practices.[36] There might be some peripheral value here, but Macan is more persuasive when claiming that English composer and collector of folk music Ralph Vaughan Williams was a catalyst for combining classical music forms and a particularly English Romantic sensibility.

Among the various styles of prog, only a handful of groups could be said to be intent on emulating or citing classical music. On *Ars Longa Vita Brevis* (1968), The Nice followed hard on the heels of Procol Harum's borrowing of Johann Sebastian Bach in 'A Whiter Shade of Pale' (1967). The Nice reworked classical pieces and wrote in a classical style, such as pieces in sonata form divided into movements. Keith Emerson pursued this vein in Emerson, Lake and Palmer during the 1970s, while longer pieces by Yes sought to emulate the sonata form. This classical tradition is to some extent present in many bands, if only through the simulating warmth of the Mellotron, which bands started to use after 1965 as a sample-playback keyboard that gives a layered texture and richness to the recorded sound. But the sonata form is one among many other elements even when actual orchestras were used, such as in Deep Purple's collaboration with the Royal Philharmonic Orchestra, released as *Concerto for Group and Orchestra* in 1969.

We will develop these formal and historical features of progressive rock in the following chapters. However, in addition to the above elements, there is a further essential component of progressive rock that introduced highly developed form and content: innovations in musical technology, the creative use of the studio, and new recording techniques. As Chapters 1 and 2 discuss with reference to Britain and the United States, this is a stretching out that stretches back to the 1950s, in the shape of a growing understanding of the possibilities of 'the album' and the recording process itself, and crystallized in 1967, with the release of some key albums in the emergence of progressive rock.

Notes

1. David Thomas, 'Oh No, It's Yes: Where Even Irony Fears to Tread', the *Observer*, Review (8 March 1998), 5.

2. Ibid., 5.

3. Thomas notes that the release of Radiohead's *OK Computer* in 1997 might signal 'a triumphant return for all things prog' (5). This view might have been stimulated by the publication of two books on progressive rock: Edward Macan's *Rocking the Classics: English Progressive Rock and the Counterculture* (New York: Oxford University Press, 1997) and Paul Stump's *The Music's All That Matters: A History of Progressive Rock* (London: Quarter Books, 1997). Stump's book gave rise to a *Guardian* review in defense of prog rock, even while acknowledging that it was sometimes 'bloated and overblown' – Adam Sweeting, 'The Hair's Apparent', the *Guardian* (2 May 1997), 4.

4. Dominic Sandbrook's *State of Emergency: The Way We Were: Britain, 1970–1974* (London: Allen Lane, 2010) contains a few references to progressive rock, but Andy Beckett's *When the Lights Went Out: Britain in the Seventies* (London: Faber, 2009) has almost none. For a third social history of 1970s Britain in which music is unevenly represented, see Alwyn W. Turner, *Crisis? What Crisis? Britain in the 1970s* (London: Aurum, 2008).

5. A similar process had already occurred in the 1960s, observed George Melly in *Revolt into Style: The Pop Arts in Britain* (Harmondsworth: Penguin, 1970).

6. Bill Martin, *Listening to the Future: The Time of Progressive Rock, 1968–1978* (Chicago and La Salle: Open Court, 1998).

7. 'Your Definitive Guide to Today's Music Scene', the *Sunday Times*, Culture (11 January 2009), 26–7.

8. Ibid., 27.

9. 'Prog Rock: The Music that Refused to Die', the *Guardian*, Film and Music (23 July 2010), 4. For other recent appraisals see Greg Walker, 'Grand Masters of Vinyl', *Times Higher*

Education (11 September 2008), 41–4 and Will Romano, *Mountains Come Out of the Sky: The Illustrated History of Prog Rock* (Milwaukee, WI: Backbeat Books, 2010).

10. Martin, *Listening to the Future*, 41, 295–6.

11. See Bill Martin, *Music of Yes: Structure and Vision in Progressive Rock* (Chicago and La Salle: Open Court, 1996).

12. Martin, *Listening to the Future*, 100.

13. Ibid., 102–3.

14. Ibid., 104.

15. Ibid., 121.

16. An example of this can be seen in *Red Riding: In the Year of Our Lord 1974* (2009), the Channel 4 adaptation of David Peace's novel *1974* (1999), in which listening to King Crimson is a symbol of the gloomy cynicism and introspection of the mid-1970s.

17. Fredric Jameson, *Postmodernism, or, the Cultural Logic of Late Capitalism* (London: Verso, 1991), 1.

18. Andreas Huyssen, *After the Great Divide: Modernism, Mass Culture and Postmodernism* (London: Macmillan, 1986), 190.

19. See Michael Nyman, *Experimental Music: Cage and Beyond*, 2nd edn (Cambridge: Cambridge University Press, [1974] 1999), 1–30.

20. Renato Poggioli, *The Theory of the Avant-Garde* (Cambridge, MA: Belknap, 1968); Peter Bürger, *Theory of the Avant-Garde* (Minneapolis: University of Minnesota Press, 1984); Rosalind Krauss, *The Originality of the Avant-Garde and Other Myths* (Cambridge, MA: MIT Press, 1985), 151–70.

21. Martin, *Listening to the Future*, 34–7.

22. This is the argument developed by Jacques Attali in *Noise: The Political Economy of Music* (Minneapolis: University of Minnesota Press, [1977] 1985). Attali's broad argument is that 'noise' is deemed unacceptable by mainstream policed society and its 'guardians' (moral or armed), and that musicians have often been the heralds of social change, demonstrated in the reaction of political and religious authorities to them.

23. Charlie Gillett, *The Sound of the City* (London: Sphere, 1971), 291.

24. Ibid., 42.

25. David Riesman, 'Listening to Popular Music', in *Mass Culture*, ed. Bernard Rosenberg and David Manning White (Glencoe: The Free Press, 1957), quoted in Gillett, *Sound of the City*, 14.

26. Such a claim is not to resist rock 'n' roll as a style, as it features throughout Gillett's *Sound of the City* and in places in Glenn C. Altschuler's *All Shook Up: How Rock 'n' Roll Changed America* (New York: Oxford University Press, 2003). Altschuler describes the assimilation of black music as rock 'n' roll increased in popularity: 'For African Americans, rock 'n' roll was a mixed blessing. At times a force for integration and social respect, rock 'n' roll was also an act of theft that in supplanting rhythm and blues deprived blacks of appropriate acknowledgement, rhetorical and financial, of their contributions to American culture' (Altschuler, *All Shook Up*, 34). This appropriation cannot be disputed, but Gillett notes the multiple sources of rock 'n' roll, including country rock and a range of black popular music styles that varied from city to city, so it is perhaps spurious to talk of a singular or homogeneous 'black' culture.

27. Martin, *Listening to the Future*, 41.

28. Ibid., 114–21.

29. Macan, *Rocking the Classics*, 10.

30. Martin even acknowledges this point, but does not incorporate it into his model

(*Listening to the Future*, 137). Gillett goes so far as to claim that Jimi Hendrix is the pivotal figure in the English music scene (*The Sound of the City*, 329).

31. Martin, *Listening to the Future*, 180.

32. Ibid., 74.

33. Macan and Martin agree that King Crimson's *In the Court of the Crimson King: An Observation* (1969) is the first fully fledged example of a 'mature' progressive rock style.

34. Macan, *Rocking the Classics*, 44.

35. Ibid., 30.

36. Ibid., 40, 147–8.

PART 1

Before and During

Chapter 1

Extended Form

Progressive rock needs time: time to arrive, time to develop, time in which specific pieces of its music can work through musical content and form. This is no different to any form of music on one level; music is a sequence of time defined by organized sounds occurring within it. But progressive rock is acutely aware of this status, unlike rock 'n' roll, surf music and pop, with their more or less uniform sense of how long a piece of music should be and predictably structured sequences of verse, chorus, verse, chorus, break or bridge, chorus. The relation of progressive rock to the time and history of popular music is to be its avant-garde, to look to the future even as it looks to the past by mobilizing traditional forms such as folk music. If progressive rock loses this impetus, it becomes a 'style', arguably the exact opposite of 'progressive'. Even here, in this book, we would have to concede that progressive rock had just such a loss of self-awareness for much of the period between the mid- to late 1970s and the mid-1990s, while the spirit of prog rock moved into other musical forms.

Chapter 2 discusses the specific moment of arrival of progressive rock between 1965 and 1970, but this gestation can be seen in the following features: the extension of rock songs into longer pieces; the linking of these pieces into song suites and concept albums; and the increased use of the studio as an integral part of the creative process of music-making, rather than being a mechanical and ancillary part of it. For critics and advocates alike, this combination of elements demonstrated not only the individual maturity of performers such as The Beatles in the mid-1960s but also the maturing of rock as a genre. By the end of the late 1960s, the idea that rock was capable of replicating earlier forms of Western classical music seemed not only feasible but also desirable. Virtuosity and the value accorded to 'classically trained' musicians in the 1970s would seem to support this, and lent credence to the attempts of mid-1970s journalists to retrieve an authenticity that had been lost in rock music. However, while musical authenticity was contested in the mid-1970s when punk aggressively pitted itself against all established forms of rock music, creativity was at the heart of progressive rock, particularly in the creative use of the studio, extended forms that enhanced the possibilities of 'the album', and aesthetic connections with earlier attempts to develop sustained album-length concepts.

The album goes back further than we might suspect – to 1909, in fact. But in its recognizable form, the term was not much used until the late 1940s. This is principally because the 78 rpm shellac discs that were the industry standard could hold only about 3 minutes of sound. So an album would have to be made of several discs, with a 20-minute sonata needing at least three. Apart from some recordings of classical music, albums were mainly compilations of children's songs and collections of highlights of either several artists, or, less often, one artist. The gradual shift to vinyl records as the norm meant there was a clear distinction between 45 rpm, 7-inch singles, which contained a similar amount of music to 78s, and albums that played at 33 rpm and came in either 10- or 12-inch forms. In between was the 'extended play' 7-inch record, usually featuring four pieces. Rock music discovered in the mid-1960s that an album could be more than a collection of unconnected songs, or songs arranged according to quality (with the singles or better tracks on the A-side of an album), but jazz was already there in the late 1950s, most notably on albums by Duke Ellington, Ornette Coleman and Frank Sinatra.

The use of the studio increasingly became a key part in developing the album through multitracking, inserts, different takes, effects, and recording strategies such as positioning of microphones or players. But of equal material significance was the vinyl form itself, which from 1948 (after a false start in the early 1930s) allowed up to 40 minutes' play, with 20 minutes per side. That records were somehow treated naturalistically prior to The Beatles' *Sgt. Pepper's Lonely Hearts Club Band* (1967), often taken to be the first concept album (see Chapter 2), is an interesting but fundamentally flawed myth. Similarly, the idea of 'extended form' was not restricted to classical music or to live performance. Extended form, it should be noted, is not just about length but specifically the extension of form beyond the industry standard. For example, jazz composer Duke Ellington would make a series of thematically linked albums from the late 1950s, but he had already dispensed with the conventional meeting of content and form on the 78 rpm record with his *Reminiscing in Tempo* (1935). This release extended over two 78 records and is 13 minutes long. The title and its music perform a self-referential awareness of time and its constraints enacted through sound recording.[1] Like Bertolt Brecht, Kurt Weill and other writers of musicals, Ellington thought that music has the power to convey social meaning through experimentation with both content and form, and it could do this through a focusing of lyrical and musical themes in popular or hybrid idioms. This suspicion reached fruition, albeit slowly, in his visionary extended releases *Black, Brown and Beige* (1943) and *New World A-Coming* (1945).

In 1943, Duke Ellington played his musical rendering of the African

American historical experience, *Black, Brown and Beige*, to a not particularly receptive crowd. After a few nights' performance at the Carnegie Hall in Manhattan, it was shelved for fifteen years, although selections were played as part of concerts. In 1958, Ellington revisited the piece, cutting and refocusing it, notably on variations of the theme song 'Come Sunday'. This song alternates with the theme of 'The Work Song' (Sunday being the only time that the people 'imported' from Africa had time to rest and reflect instead of being worked through slavery), and it concludes with a recital of the Christian Psalm 23. The whole is a piece in six numbered parts, three per side of the vinyl album.[2] There is a clear divide between the two sides, with only side two featuring the voice of gospel singer Mahalia Jackson. This movement suggests the coming to being through a Hegelian dialectic awareness of oppression. Hegel's famous master–slave dialectic is rendered material in actual slavery, but the central part of Hegelian thought involves the internal struggle that is a coming to consciousness either of the individual, the group, or humanity as a whole, thereby combining the metaphysical with the material and historical.[3]

Side two of *Black, Brown and Beige* illustrates the transition from victimhood to active freedom (still only aspirational in 1958, even after *Brown versus the Board of Education* in 1954 made segregation unconstitutional) without minimizing the suffering that black people still had to endure (hence the 'and though I walk in the shadow of death' line of Psalm 23). Parts one to three on side one are highly thematic, almost repetitive, whereas side two (parts four to six) offers more direct content, including Mahalia Jackson's two sung sections. But the abstraction of side one plays a formal strategy beyond its harmoniousness, as Ellington moves from a situation where African Americans exist only as abstraction towards tangible being on side two. In a 1957 essay, 'The Race for Space', Ellington argued that the extended jazz form was not just an expression of creative freedom but the key to racial harmony. He asserted that 'music is bigger' than race, skin colour and language, and that the ensemble jazz band functions by combining sounds and harmonies out of 'a polyglot of racial elements'. The extended form finds full expression in this essay, which closes with a universalist clarion call for 'a new sound' to pave the way for 'harmony, brotherly love, common respect and consideration for the dignity and freedom of men'.[4]

In *Black, Brown and Beige*, Ellington produces a clear example of modernist narration, where form becomes expression and content beyond the notes themselves. In between the original performance of 1943 and its appearance on record in 1958, Ellington continued to work on lengthy pieces that paralleled the European symphonic tradition, and in *A Drum is a Woman* (1957) he produced an album that replicated in its form the history of jazz.[5] *A Drum is a Woman* was conceived as a TV special including dance, performance and narration – a multimedia yet populist work. At one level, it tells the story of jazz, but it is how this is enacted that makes it part of conscious avant-gardism; its aim is not to relate but to be 'a tone parallel to the history of jazz'.[6]

In fact, what makes this album worthy of reference here is not its contribution to avant-gardism as such, but how its structure prefigures that of progressive rock concept albums. It features two protagonists, Carribee Joe and Madam Zajj (perhaps a precursor of Peter Gabriel's 'Rael' on Genesis's 1975 double concept album *The Lamb Lies Down on Broadway*). As we move swiftly from Africa into the twentieth-century American South, the two figures reappear through the album, either being narrated or narrating themselves. The whole is structured into four parts with recurrent motifs, each then subdivided; the principal narrator's parts eventually meld the work into a structured piece, the musical narration emerging only gradually over time.

It might seem less evident that Ornette Coleman's *Free Jazz* (recorded 1960, released 1961) works as a pre-empting of progressive rock, but it is important insofar that it is a purposive attempt to rethink the form of the genre within the form of the piece itself. Ellington replicates the classical tradition by other means, using clearly defined movements, reprises, and thematic connectivity in lyrics and music, but he does so without parroting that tradition. Instead, he moves on from it, and thereby moves jazz on, just as progressive rock bands would do with rock music a few years later. Ellington's bid to narrate through form in a way that is socially constructive is not only modernist; it was echoed in folk revivals of the early to mid-1960s and the utopianism of late 1960s rock. Both Ellington and Coleman consciously attempted to extend the vocabulary and performance of jazz, in line with music critic William Cameron's argument in 'Is Jazz a Folk Art?' (1958) that jazz 'thrives on invention and change', driven not only by urban energies but also by folk melodies 'constructed from bits and snatches of previous ones', and by licks and riffs that 'add sparkle and continuity to . . . personal ideas'.[7] This can be seen in Coleman's music, which extends jazz – and experimental music in general – through improvised synchronous invention. The interplay between improvisation and orchestration had characterized jazz from its early days at the beginning of the twentieth century, but *Free Jazz* was a programmatic statement, one that had greater import than jazz cornetist Don Cherry's and saxophonist John Coltrane's take on Coleman in *The Avant-Garde* (1960).

There were earlier experiments with free improvisation feeding into what was later identified as the 'free jazz' of Lennie Tristano or bebop, but Coleman's *Free Jazz* was 37 minutes of ensemble improvisation. Although solos were allocated, the rest of the double quartet (one quartet recorded in each channel) was not supposed to tread water; the solo had to be a group effort and not just an individual run. Within this structure, the solo deviates from being a personal expression (letting one of the stars of the band have their moment) to being about expression itself: the content of free jazz is its production, and the expression is at group level. It would no longer be possible for one performer to be expressive while the others supported; instead of replicating race and class divisions, the jazz ensemble was for Ellington a model of 'a new sound' and a utopian social formation. In this rethinking of jazz, we can see the embryonic purpose and role for group composition and improvisation in prog.

Jazz itself divides into a heritage or classic version, which maintained the separation between the lead and supporting musicians, and an increasingly aesthetically and politically avant-garde version, which during the 1960s pushed jazz further from its conventions. John Coltrane, Pharoah Sanders and Chicago's Association for the Advancement of Creative Musicians (AACM) would bring back the possibility of an individual channelling expressivity, but it would be in tandem with advances of the group dynamic. Coltrane himself moved towards a modernist version of spirituality, via Ravi Shankar's popularizing of Indian classical music, substantial drug intake and, above all, the notion that music could be forced to a position where it would enact ecstasy, not just show it. Like Jackson Pollock's painterly abstractions, Coltrane's *Sun Ship* (1965) and *Interstellar Space* (recorded in 1967, released posthumously in 1972), in particular, signalled this shift. In the definitive 1960s statement of free jazz, the eleven-piece *Ascension* (1965), Coltrane not only aims for ecstatic release but tries to lose this release – attaining, briefly, almost insensibly, a moment of nothing. While Miles Davis's early genre-crossing directly influenced many progressive rock musicians, a more accurate signal of what was to come was evident in albums such as *Free Jazz* and *Ascension*, which develop over a long period of time and offer the prospect of limitless music.

The blues revival musicians of the early 1960s, who would feed into heavy rock and progressive rock, not only worked through the palette of Muddy Waters or Fats Waller but also looked to jazz as a method that culminated in Jimi Hendrix's stretching of the idea of the solo.[8] On the face of it, Hendrix's lengthy solos appear to be a step back from free jazz, as Hendrix becomes the solitary hero exploring the boundaries between music and self, supported by his trusty sidekicks. This would be to underestimate the contribution made, particularly by drummer Mitch Mitchell, to a group dynamic of improvisation in The Jimi Hendrix Experience (which formed in London in 1966), but the key is to look at the moment within rock history that gave rise to Hendrix and British blues guitarists such as Eric Clapton and Peter Green. For all the eventual cross-pollination of genres, it seems that internally each one followed a path of development towards increased complexity and a potentially radical awareness of pushing the limits of established musical forms.[9] As the next chapter develops within the cultural context of late 1960s Anglo-American musical exchange, rock music was still a recent phenomenon and quickly proliferated as a number of different musical styles. The different directions of rock music in the mid- to late 1960s signalled that generic progression in popular music was accelerating. Even from within this musical climate, Hendrix's solos are much more an exploration of possibility, along with a loss of self in that possibility, than those of other solo guitarists of the time. Hendrix steps apart from the group and crowd to bring back the moment of his stepping away, trying to create something like an 'electric church'.[10]

The blues revival and boom that Hendrix surpassed had already been in swing in London since the late 1950s. It initially revolved around the reception and replication of American blues and 'race music', and as British musicians came into contact with established blues performers the revival became more of a process of translation and transformation.[11] Blues was not purist in the way fans had taken it to be, but it was just as much a formal approach or set of methods used to convey authenticity. This creative rethinking of what the blues meant formally (as opposed to its just being an expression of authenticity) freed up early rock musicians to move beyond what on record seemed like fixed templates and 4/4 rhythms – a development that can best be seen through flexible British blues groups such as Alexis Korner's Blues Incorporated (formed in 1961), John Mayall's Bluesbreakers (1963–7), and early Jethro Tull recordings from 1967 to 1969. As part of this freeing-up process, rock bands moved from playing covers to writing songs, and shifted from pure performance to singles and albums. Progressive rock would not be a full rejection of blues-based rock, particularly as with hindsight we can see the experimentation of the late 1960s flowed directly from the translation of blues and jazz into rock. Ultimately, the early 1960s rock version of the blues (as seen in London) remained a potential source for progressive rock, with Hendrix, Clapton and Keith Emerson consolidating the relevance of musical virtuosity on the back of blues. What differentiates blues from prog rock is that, for progressive groups, blues was just one genre or resource among many others, to be merged into something new.

By 1966–7, rock performances were elongating under the influence of cannabis and LSD. Psychedelic music emerged as a response to the effects of LSD; it tried not simply to emulate drug-taking or provide a background to consumption but rather to replicate the sensory experience of a trip by creating a total environment. This can be seen across a musical spectrum, including blues-based recordings and short tracks by Fleetwood Mac, such as the psychedelic breaks that punctuate the melodic 'Man of the World' (1969) and the lyrics of the blues-rock hybrid 'The Green Manalishi (with the Two-Prong Crown)' (1970). Fleetwood Mac did not experiment with the extended form as much as other blues musicians (the segues between tracks on The Jimi Hendrix Experience's final 1968 recording, *Electric Ladyland,* provide a good example of extended form); but between the expansion of the blues form into nascent rock music and the use of drugs that suggested a longer format for songs, rock literally expanded in time from the mid-1960s onwards. Even before this, popular music was expanding and stretching vertically into complexity, incorporating non-Western or non-rock forms. It did this through the fuzz of psychedelic music, literal referencing (as on The Beatles' 1965 album *Revolver*), an interest in Asian music and mysticism (George Harrison's sitar songs), or a heightening of content as a formal strategy (as with The Kinks' take on middle England on *The Village Green Preservation Society* of 1968).[12]

Before tracks stretched in terms of length, individual notes and chords expanded. Guitar playing in the 1950s and the early 1960s exploited the newly commercially available electric guitar through solos and overdriving of amplifiers. The distortion and fuzziness of sound that had once been seen as a problem was now what Michael Hicks calls 'the essence of the sound [and] that essence signified raw power, survivability in the face of interference'.[13] Deep Purple's Ritchie Blackmore and The Kinks' Ray Davies are among many who purposely damaged amplifiers to produce a fuzz-driven sound, and effects boxes were purpose-built for such outcomes.[14] Although it might be imagined that garage and American psychedelia were in some way the scuzz to prog rock's clean sound, in the late 1960s Keith Emerson would overdrive amps as a central part of sound in his band The Nice, and the first track, '21st Century Schizoid Man', on King Crimson's debut album from 1969 is awash with distortion on voice and guitar alike.

With feedback and other effects, rock simultaneously expanded the reach of its music in terms of volume and its range of instrumentation, as even a trio could now produce a wide array of sound live. This expansion became infinite once the studio was mobilized, particularly via multitracking but also by structuring a recording to provide a band with its own individual sound. Studios were key players even in the 1950s, helping to create distinctive sounds in order to trade singers and bands on authenticity (for example, the 'slap-back' echo effect practised at the Sun Studio in Memphis), whereas producers had to work out how to record feedback and distortion as they 'wanted to faithfully document the distorted sound of the *guitars*, rather than distort the *recording* by overdriving the microphones'.[15] The major change in the mid-1960s was the ownership of the studio process, related closely to machine-led sounds in live performance achieved by the manipulation of amplifiers and effects pedals.[16]

The translation of live music through technologies of studio fidelity was matched in the mid-1960s, with a move to record the lengthened versions of songs that bands were now playing in concerts. Early 1960s rock bands, jug bands and hippie jam bands were all stretching out tracks through solos, mirroring the way jazz appropriated (and retrospectively created) musical standards. It is misleading to infer that the length of those jams is in itself a precursor or early moment of prog. Just as it was the control of the studio by artists or by chosen producers that defines the move to progressive rock, the decision to *record* these lengthened tracks as part of an album proved crucial. An album had to be more explicitly constructed and was no longer seen as an inferior index to the 'true' performance of the elongated form. It also became clear that an album had two sides. This realization gave groups the opportunity to create different moods on each side, or to have more commercial songs on one side and extended jams or compositions on the other.[17]

The earliest long tracks were jam-based extensions of songs, replicating the live versions of those tracks; lengthier composed tracks did not appear until the late 1960s, although even on albums such as *Sgt. Pepper* the pop song is on occasion relatively long for the period and rock genre. The Dutch Nederbeat or freakbeat band Q65 ended its 1966 album *Revolution* with a 13-minute version of Chicago bluesman Willie Dixon's 'Bring It On Home'. The simple musical vocabulary is pushed through many permutations, with the guitar sound alternating between a wide range of styles and sustained periods of fuzzed riffing; the refrain of 'bringing it home' is literally replicated as the vocals continually circle around the title line. Experimentation, though, is at a premium – occasional bursts of reverb and a short burst of Maurice Ravel's *Boléro* (1928) are exceptions. Equally, 'Revolutions' is not a track about virtuosity on the model of Cream's blues workouts, but its presence on an album makes it more than a typical live jam. In the context of the overall psychedelic restlessness of Q65's sound, nor does the track perform the same work as the brutal minimalism of The Velvet Underground's 'Sister Ray' (1968), with its 10 minutes of percussive chords, extended to over 25 minutes in later performances.

Also recorded in 1966, but released in 1967, was 'Revelation', the first side-long rock track – by Los Angeles rock band Love, on its second album, *Da Capo*. Although the band subsequently expressed its dissatisfaction with the track on the grounds that it was not long enough, at 18:55 there is more than enough of it. The argument was that in concert 'Revelation' would be a vehicle for lengthy jamming and solos, but it had to be dramatically shortened for the recording. Unlike the band's inventive singles, there is little development on this track, although occasionally a rock-funk freak-out threatens to erupt (as in the section with saxophone, from 12:30 to around 16 minutes). Again, despite the track's untypical conservatism, Love makes a strong statement that goes beyond the track itself. As extended tracks on 1967 concept albums by The Pink Floyd and The Moody Blues demonstrate (see Chapter 2) there need not be temporal or sonic limits to rock songs or albums.

In 1968, The Nice produced a side-long track in the form of the title track to *Ars Longa Vita Brevis*, which aspired to be a reformulation of the symphonic form in rock terms. Already, the band's first album, *The Thoughts of Emerlist Davjack*, released the previous year, had featured music from a range of styles, notably classical and jazz. The latter style is directly represented by 'Rondo', based on a Dave Brubeck piece, but elsewhere there are moments of jazz playing by Keith Emerson. Classical music also features explicitly on these two albums, with versions of works by Leoš Janáček, Jean Sibelius and Johann Sebastian Bach. Although this might seem the height of pretension in a rock context (and the symphonic side of *Ars Longa Vita Brevis* is unsure how to combine the two forms into 'classical rock'), the attempt to create something outside of existing genres is a radical move that replicates developments in jazz. Rather than being a cosy meeting of different sectors of high culture, the genres collide, the sounds are often overdriven and, as with much of British progressive rock, the album also features the 'low music' of music hall.[18] The most innovative stretch by The Nice, though, is its version of Leonard Bernstein's 'America'. Bernstein's track was a centrepiece of the 1961 musical *West Side Story*, and The Nice released its 6-minute instrumental version of it as a single in 1968. The song is dissected by Emerson's dissonant keyboard rendering of variations on the main melody. The utopian promise of the United States is sonically shredded, just as it would be by Jimi Hendrix's deconstruction of the American national anthem, 'The Star-Spangled Banner', at the Woodstock Festival the following year (see Chapter 3). The Nice's take on 'America' closes with a child's voice, which reinforces the critical purpose of this reworking: 'America is pregnant with promises and anticipation, but is murdered by the hand of the inevitable'.

Yes also adapted Bernstein, covering 'Something's Coming' (1969) for an early B-side, drawn out to 6:55 in length. In addition to meandering around the themes of the song, the complex drumming and the non-subservience of any instrument make this more of a pointer to the ensemble ethic of Yes than much of their first album from the same year (which features a lengthened take on The Beatles' 1964 song 'Every Little Thing'). It also refers to the song 'America', as did the group's later version of Paul Simon's 'America' (1971). Yes's version, at 10:40, represents a high point of pushing a song beyond its limits: the original floats in the centre and is preceded by a long instrumental passage that uses both Simon's and Bernstein's songs for material. Although not having the politically radical purpose of The Nice's 'America', this track expands on a vision of what America might be, as the personal geography of Simon's song is placed in the midst of a wide expanse of music. This is an ever-broader America, full with the notion that there is always more to discover, to explore and to understand, emphasized by the song's breaking up into different guitar styles.

The authentic extended rock composition appears in the form of side two of Procol Harum's *Shine on Brightly* (1968), and does not quite fill a side. But at 17:27 and divided into five parts (with further subsections), it develops the full potential of the lengthened rock track into a complex and meaning-ful form. Procol Harum had already rethought the possibilities of the rock single, with their borrowing of Bach for 'A Whiter Shade of Pale' (1967), but whereas that track shuffles through an impressionistic surrealism, 'In Held 'Twas in I' takes the drug culture and Eastern mysticism spreading through 1968 as content and driver of musical form. Edward Macan has argued that progressive rock used classical music as a means of 'solving the problem' of psychedelia, insofar as psychedelic music took up a lot of time but did not really progress.[19] This is an important insight but needs modifying: The Grateful Dead, for example, the epitome of psychedelic jamming music, released a track, 'That's it for the Other One', on *Anthem of the Sun* (1968) that, although only 7:40 long, is divided into four parts and is free of the aimlessness psychedelic music is presumed to have once it pushes beyond the garage-style singles of the mid-1960s. 'That's it for the Other One' is not as organised and developmental as 'In Held 'Twas in I', which is a fully formed progressive sonata-type piece, but both are psychedelic. What differentiates Procol Harum's track, and makes it a type of progressive rock along with bands such as Rare Bird, is that it takes a position on psychedelic experience by using its music as a resource.

Procol Harum's track follows a spiritual journey from the seeking of enlightenment, through madness (not only signified by the lyrics but also announced by a carnival section, the breaking down into micro-sections around the 'Autumn of my Madness' lyrical part, and the unmooring of that section) and through spacey slow organ and guitar that move towards a reflective wisdom. Although the attainment of self-knowledge is uncertain (the narrator may be a fool for thinking himself wise), a lengthy choral and then instrumental finale signals resolution. 'In Held 'Twas in I' is more than a personal reflection or the capturing of an individual experience, through its exploration of the psychedelic fusion of mind and spirit and the hippie interest in holistic experience. This is signalled by the change of musical styles and the early incorporation of drones and sitar, which suggest the descent of the mind-expanding quest into formalism without criticizing the hippie venture. The track is, then, meta-psychedelic in commenting on psychedelia by using its own methods; it works as a synecdoche of the move from psychedelic rock to progressive rock, even as it reveals their connectedness. Ultimately, as the following chapters explore, the alteration in the idea of recording or composition is not possible without a radical rethinking of what the studio is, of what a band should do with an album, and the notion that rock should be more than entertainment with a ready recourse to the familiar and the everyday.

Notes

1. Duke Ellington had already pushed the boundary of the single 78 rpm record towards the way classical music was presented on 'Creole Rhapsody' in 1931, filling both sides of the record. The year 1937 also saw another piece, 'Diminuendo and Crescendo in Blue', fill two 78s.

2. The work was originally designed to represent a tripartite history of the black experience in America. Subsequently, isolated parts appeared both live and on record. Mike Levin summarizes the mixed reception of *Black, Brown and Beige* as a performance, and concludes that the resistance was due to its refusal of generic restraint and its scale: Levin, 'In *Downbeat*', in *The Duke Ellington Reader*, ed. Mark Tucker (New York: Oxford University Press, 1993), 166–70. For a musicological reading of *Black, Brown and Beige*, see Brian Priestley and Alan Cohen, '*Black, Brown and Beige*', in the same volume (185–204), and for Ellington's utopianism, see Graham Lock, *Blutopia: Visions of the Future and Revisions of the Past* (Durham, NC: Duke University Press, 1999), 108–18.

3. See G. W. F. Hegel, *Phenomenology of Spirit* (Oxford: Oxford University Press, [1807] 1977), 104–38.

4. Duke Ellington, 'The Race for Space' (1957), in *The Duke Ellington Reader*, 296.

5. The sexist connotations of the title *A Drum is a Woman* are well-matched in the 'exotic and erotic' lyrical direction of the album.

6. Duke Ellington, quoted by Bernard Lee, liner notes to *A Drum is a Woman* (2008 edition).

7. William Cameron, 'Is Jazz a Folk Art?', *The Second Line*, 9 (1–2) (January–February 1958), 13.

8. The same can be said of Bert Jansch and other guitarists within the folk revival, which was not just about resuscitating a tradition, but about renovation and combination with other musical approaches. For a clear expression of how folk and blues revivals were close together in aspiration and how they related to one another, see Colin Harper, *Dazzling Stranger: Bert Jansch and the British Folk and Blues Revival* (London: Bloomsbury, 2006).

9. This is not to imply that genres simply mature and that progressive rock stood as a highpoint of this generic maturity. It is to make the point that without establishing forms it is impossible to establish a genre: in this case, rock 'n' roll succeeded by rock.

10. See Paul Gilroy, 'Soundscapes of the Black Atlantic', in *The Audio Culture Reader*, eds Michael Bull and Les Back (Oxford and New York: Berg, 2003), 381–95.

11. For a detailed account of the presence, reception and mobilization of blues in Britain in the 1950s and 1960s, see Roberta Freund Schwartz, *How Britain Got the Blues: The Transmission and Reception of American Blues Style in the United Kingdom* (Burlington, VT: Ashgate, 2007).

12. We would argue that the long development of modernism in the visual arts is accelerated in the rock music of the 1960s. So the incorporation of narrative content by The Kinks, with its focus on everyday British society, can be equated with the nineteenth-century painterly realism of Gustave Courbet or with postwar neo-realism in cinema.

13. Michael Hicks, *Sixties Rock: Garage, Psychedelic and Other Satisfactions* (Urbana and Chicago: University of Illinois Press, 1999), 13.

14. Ibid., 17–18.

15. Ibid., 14. For a discussion of Sun Studio's slap-back effect, see Greg Milner, *Perfecting Sound Forever: The Story of Recorded Music* (London: Granta, 2009), 150–2.

16. Early examples of this are The Beatles' 'Tomorrow Never Knows' on *Revolver*, and The Yardbirds' 'Happenings Ten Years Time Ago' (1966). The Yardbirds' single includes feedback, reversed tapes of guitars and a muffled voiceover from Jeff Beck in its instrumental section; it tightly integrates guitar through electrical and recording technologies rather than simply using them as ornamentation.

17. Noted by Martin, *Listening to the Future*, 153.

18. Since the 1930s, Duke Ellington had been moving jazz towards classical approaches. Miles Davis's *Sketches of Spain* (1960), which focuses on Rodrigo's *Guitar Concerto*, also took classical music out of its fixity. Neither goes as far as The Nice in incorporating different genres (including classical music) while maintaining the audibility of those genres clearly within the new work.

19. Macan, *Rocking the Classics*, 43–4.

Chapter 2

The Roots of Progressive Rock

The history of a musical movement is often told as a series of dramatic beginnings, when disparate musical and social trends come together in a moment of creative fusion. These moments are usually mythologized and are very often established well after the fact. The recording of Elvis Presley's first single for Sun Records in Memphis in 1954, for example, is often used as a metonym for the birth of rock 'n' roll. This particular beginning makes sense only retrospectively, though, in light of Elvis's growing celebrity of 1956, and by ignoring the intersecting currents of regional and race music that preceded it. As such, the nineteen-year-old Elvis is a symbol of a more complex cultural history, which incorporates the commercial repackaging of 'race music', social and political tensions in the South, the growth of mass culture after World War II, and the entrepreneurialism of Sam Phillips at Sun Records. Although it is unhelpful to read back the emergence of a progressive rock style into mid-1950s rock 'n' roll – a task that Bill Martin attempts by locating a 'synthesis of simplicity and complexity' in the songs of Chuck Berry, Little Richard and Jerry Lee Lewis – the notion of fusion, on both social and musical levels, undergirds most interpretations of progressive rock.[1] Carrying forward this reading, we argue that the traditional starting point of progressive rock in 1967–8 needs to be placed within a much broader cultural context, as indicated in the previous chapter.

The birth of progressive rock is frequently traced back to the release of The Beatles' 1967 album, *Sgt. Pepper's Lonely Hearts Club Band*, for a number of different reasons. The year 1967 was the high point of both psychedelic culture and the impact of the hippie experience on both sides of the Atlantic. More specifically, *Sgt. Pepper* was the first rock release, arguably, to weave a concept through a song-cycle that encompasses a whole album, and to make the concept integral to the cover art. The concept is embedded in the title of the album; developed most explicitly in the two versions of the 'Sgt. Pepper' song (at the beginning and towards the end of the album) that invite the reader into the album's sonic world; and is symbolized by The Beatles' brass-band costumes on the sleeve, surrounded by a cast of diverse cultural and historical figures. The cover, by British pop artist Peter Blake, and directed by modern-art champion Robert Fraser, fuses both high and low culture – from Sigmund Freud, Karl Marx and Oscar Wilde to Stan Laurel, Bob Dylan and Marilyn Monroe – and is developed through the use of a brass band on the album, mixed with what Jonathan Gould sees as a parody of 'Tin Pan Alley, Denmark Street and Broadway' which 'drift[s] from track to track, exploiting the same sorts of incongruity between style, form, and content' that could be detected on tracks from the band's previous albums *Rubber Soul* (1965) and *Revolver* (1966).[2] Despite parodic and jocular elements and the retrieval of bygone popular motifs drawn from vaudeville, circus and music-hall traditions, tracks such as the acronymic 'Lucy in the Sky with Diamonds' and the concluding and elegiac 'A Day in the Life' make *Sgt. Pepper* into an emphatic statement that not only was The Beatles now a serious band but that its members had tapped into an underground music scene at one remove from, or even in direct opposition to, the cultural and commercial mainstream.

The countercultural impulse in the second half of the 1960s – particularly 1967 – is one of the major reasons why critics such as Clinton Heylin look back to *Sgt. Pepper* as a dramatic moment of emergence.[3] The experimental use of sampling and recording techniques make it a very innovative album: the wide range of instrumentation included woodwind, brass, organ, harpsichord, sitar and tambora; new sound effects were made possible by the use of the polyphonic Mellotron keyboard; and a multitrack environment was created in Abbey Road Studios to manipulate recording speed and echo. The technical qualities of the album are its hallmark, but in other respects the composition is more elusive, particularly the album's concept, which is little more than a loose theme captured by the cover art, picked up in the opening track and then reprised briefly towards the end. There is no real conceptual unity, only a 'feeling of continuity' created by minimizing the gap between each track to create an impression of flow. One argument is that the 'illusion of a concept' was added after recording, engineered by producer George Martin rather than by the musicians, but the intention to unify the album thematically and visually is nevertheless embedded in both music mythology and studio reality.[4]

Gould calls one of the continuous threads on the album 'theatricality and eclecticism', which is signalled by the band's costumes and woven musically and lyrically through the song-cycle.[5] This mode of performativity is made explicit on the cover, which is at once both beguiling and elusive. The cover can be read either as a celebration of cultural history, with a huge cast of characters brought together across the barriers of space and time, or as the band's personae mourning their own passing: a funeral for the four moptops, 'dressed for eternity in their dark suits, their faces aglow with the embalmed look of wax effigies', attended by their historical ancestors.[6] This narrative of transformation goes beyond the cover: the gatefold sleeve opens to show the four musicians in their old-time Sgt. Pepper's guise against a bright yellow backdrop, a blank colour field for this new musical departure; and on the back cover, for the first time in popular music, the lyrics are printed like a literary work on a red background superimposed over a view of the band. This theme of disappearance (McCartney looks away on the back cover) and emergence (the band reborn on the front cover) links to Joan Peyser's reading of the record as oscillating between the modalities of illusion and revelation, exemplified by the selection of songs on each side of the album.[7] These themes are also integral to the mystique created by the album, which aided its status as a breakthrough release, not only within The Beatles' career but also as a transformative moment in the history of popular music, where a complex set of cultural themes, the extended song-cycle and intriguing visual motifs took prominence over the commercial 3-minute single.

Despite the iconic status of Sgt. Pepper, it is important to remember that The Beatles had been musically innovative since 1965. Across the Atlantic, The Beach Boys were inspired by Rubber Soul to modulate their surf-and-sun California songs, creating Pet Sounds in 1966 as a musically and harmonically rich song-cycle. On Pet Sounds, singer-songwriter Brian Wilson used an eclectic mixture of instruments, echo, reverb and innovative mixing techniques learnt from Phil Spector to create a complex soundscape in which voice and music interweave tightly. The cover art of Pet Sounds, showing the band at San Diego Zoo, does not signal the album's conceptual unity, but the textures, melodies and harmonies of the songs and the running themes of emotional fragility, loss and striving give a more sonically organic impression than the eclecticism of Sgt. Pepper. Whereas Sgt. Pepper explores the relationship between past and present, between metaphysical and material worlds, and between fantasy and reality, in a manner that foreshadows the temporal and narrative expansion of progressive bands from the late 1960s and 1970s, the personal intimacy of Pet Sounds sets it at a slight remove from the psychedelic culture that informed the San Francisco sound of 1966–7. Nevertheless, the trippy feel of Pet Sounds related directly to Brian Wilson's experimentation with LSD; Wilson had stopped touring with The Beach Boys in 1964 and took acid a year later, claiming that his trips took him 'to the gates of consciousness, and then on to the other side . . . On acid, I saw myself stretched out from conception to death, the beginning to the end'.[8]

In many ways, Pet Sounds takes the listener on a psychological journey far from the cultural engagement of the Sgt. Pepper album cover. The importance of cultural reference is reinforced by Lennon and McCartney's interest in everyday life (on 'Fixing a Hole', 'She's Leaving Home', 'A Day in the Life') and the exploration of intersecting worlds: what Steve Turner describes as the higher world of 'visionary ecstasy' (on 'Lucy in the Sky with Diamonds') and the lower, earthy world (on 'Strawberry Fields Forever', released early in 1967), which both inform the 'middle world' of everyday life.[9] While The Beatles were sometimes introspective (the Eastern mysticism of George Harrison's 'Within You Without You', for example), the more inward-looking quality of *Pet Sounds* characterized Brian Wilson's next and (until recently unreleased) project *Smile*, which he abandoned in May 1967, when his clinical paranoia become too intense for him to function as a musician or producer.

The fact that comparable experiments were happening on both sides of the Atlantic between 1966 and 1968 suggests that the roots of progressive rock cannot simply be found in English culture, such as the Canterbury scene in South East England, which both Edward Macan and Bill Martin see as the driving force in its formative years. As discussed in Chapter 1, extended tracks, the interweaving of themes through a song-cycle, experimental recording techniques and expansive use of cover art all mark an engagement in, but also a movement beyond, psychedelic culture. Psychedelia was in many ways a self-referential cultural mode, celebrating the experience of sensual absorption: it offers a total experience for the listener, but often at the expense of the contemplative and cerebral spaces that would characterize progressive rock.

But this does not mean psychedelic music was monolithic in character. The complex intersection between American and British culture in the mid-1960s is important here, particularly in terms of musical crossovers and the exchange of ideas: for example, folk rock band The Byrds played in London in July 1965, and The Beatles visited David Crosby and Roger McGuinn in Los Angeles before the band's Hollywood Bowl concerts in August that year. The opening of Barry Miles' Indica Bookshop in Mayfair saw a regular stream of American underground writing into London (Paul McCartney was a regular visitor to Indica), and the International Poetry Incarnation at the Royal Albert Hall cemented the links between beat culture and the London scene by showcasing Allen Ginsberg and Lawrence Ferlinghetti (the founder of San Francisco's City Lights bookshop in 1953). Technological innovations such as the Mellotron and the Moog (the latter of which was first used on a commercial release on Walter Carlos's *Switched on Bach* in 1967) were also important in creating the signature sound of 1967. By the mid-1960s, American music had stronger commercial impetus than any European national music industry, but British acts such as The Beatles and The Rolling Stones were central to the American popular music scene, as was Jimi Hendrix's schooling in the underground clubs of London and The Who's emergence as a transatlantic phenomenon in 1967. It is important not to overlook parallel emergences in Europe in the 1960s, such as musical innovations by German composer Karlheinz Stockhausen (one of the figures on the cover of *Sgt. Pepper*) and the European avant-garde interest in the mixing of cultural forms and pushing concepts to the limit, as practised by neo-Dadaist Yves Klein in the late 1950s and early 1960s. These same energies led Joan Peyser, in 1968, to comment that 'the best rock is moving with unprecedented speed into unexpected, more artistically interesting areas [where] the boundaries between art [music] and rock music are becoming less defined'.[10] The blurring of what Peyser calls the 'intramusical' elements (which interested composers such as Stockhausen and Cage) and 'extramusical' elements (narrative, cover art, performance, drugs, mysticism) made 1967 a crossroads in rock music.

For all these reasons, it is difficult to dislodge *Sgt. Pepper* as the iconic album that opened up the sonic and thematic possibilities for progressive music and, according to Jonathan Gould, was the 'catalyst for an explosion of mass enthusiasm for album-formatted rock that would revolutionize both the aesthetics and the economics of the record business'.[11] We need to position the emergence of the concept album, however loose the concept, alongside other cultural events. If *Sgt. Pepper* is the defining album of 1967, then the pivotal moment of the underground scene of that year was the 14 Hour Technicolour Dream at Alexandra Palace, London, on 29 April. Not only did the Technicolour Dream stage the symbolic coming together of John Lennon and Yoko Ono (they had met a year earlier and did not start a relationship until spring 1968), but the closing act, The Pink Floyd (soon to drop the 'the'), emphasized the importance of this underground event for providing a showcase for new, expansionist music. The Technicolour Dream was organised by Barry Miles and John 'Hoppy' Hopkins, editors of the underground paper *International Times* – a concrete realization of the 'happening', as Allan Kaprow had dubbed the total aesthetic experience in the late 1950s. It was far from just being a musical event, though, with light-shows, poetry readings, experimental films and performance art creating a multimedia experience that invited the audience inside the circle of experimentation. An important figure drawn inside this circle was documentary filmmaker Peter Whitehead, who saw in Pink Floyd's long jazz-rock improvisations new possibilities for film and image. From its opening in late 1966, the UFO Club pioneered light shows and introduced recently formed bands, many of which had played at Alexandra Palace in April, such as Procol Harum, Soft Machine, Tomorrow and The Incredible String Band. In his memoir *White Bicycles* (2006), Joe Boyd claims that 'the sixties' peaked at dawn on 1 July 1967, when Tomorrow was playing at the UFO Club, featuring Steve Howe on lead guitar, who was to join Yes in 1970.[12]

Peter Whitehead has spoken about his attraction to the dark side of pop music, which he saw inhabited not by The Beatles but by The Rolling Stones, whom he had filmed in 1965. Whitehead detected in environments such as UFO the possibility for exploring the 'dislocation of consciousness' embedded in psychedelic music.[13] Whitehead wanted to shift filmmaking away from linear narrative and character development, to explore looser sonic and visual arrangements in which subjective experiences, symbols and cosmic themes could coexist. Whitehead's interest in the technical aspects of filmmaking (he often appears as a figure in his own films) is mirrored by the technical virtuosity of Pink Floyd's performances and the complex textures of the band's instrumentation, including Syd Barrett's tape-echo device, Binson Echorec, with its multiple inputs, subtle changes of speed, and sound-delay functions.

Pink Floyd: London 1966/1967 (Peter Whitehead, 2005).

Whitehead filmed The Pink Floyd playing its 17-minute psychedelic song 'Interstellar Overdrive' and an improvised piece called 'Nick's Boogie', and featured them in his 1967 film *Tonite Let's All Make Love in London*, alongside images of 'Swinging London'; interviews with Michael Caine, Mick Jagger and Vanessa Redgrave; and a poetry reading by Allen Ginsberg. Ginsberg's appearance provided a direct connection to the San Francisco psychedelic scene, which was experiencing its 'summer of love' in 1967, when numerous events and happenings were held in Haight-Ashbury – including the Human Be-In, in Golden Gate Park in January, following the Love Pageant Rally of the previous October, which marked the day when LSD became illegal.[14] Summer 1967 brought thousands of visitors to San Francisco from across the US and the Atlantic to experience the highpoint of the psychedelic movement, following two years of concerts at the Fillmore Auditorium by The Grateful Dead, Jefferson Airplane, Big Brother and the Holding Company, and The Great Society, together with soul and blues acts. Throughout 1967–8, the West Coast hippie movement gathered momentum down to Los Angeles and up to Portland, Oregon. But darker currents were circulating: despite the Aquarian enthusiasm for Eastern mysticism, LSD and communal living, new journalists Hunter S. Thompson and Joan Didion were pointing to the destructive side of the drugs subculture that linked closely to the underground music scene, and Charles Manson (an advocate of LSD) claimed that the murder spree he led in summer 1969 was inspired by *The Beatles* (also known as 'The White Album').

The drugs scene reflects the other, less euphoric side of underground music culture. While Acid Tests were moving through California, a drugs bust at the UFO Club put John Hopkins in jail for nine months, and Keith Richards' house was raided in June 1967. When UFO was forced to move from its basement on Tottenham Court Road, producer Joe Boyd recalls that 'the *agape* spirit of '67 [had] evaporated in the heat of ugly drugs, violence, commercialism and police pressure'.[15] Shifting his focus from London,

Whitehead took his experimental filmmaking to the US, with his new project *The Fall* (1968), which explores the rising student protests at Columbia and Berkeley Universities, mounting violence during a pivotal moment of the Vietnam War, the assassinations of Martin Luther King Jr and Robert Kennedy, and student activism in May 1968. Whitehead uses The Nice's rendition of 'America' in the title sequence of *The Fall* to accompany the filmmaker's descent of a Manhattan skyscraper and his movement around the city's streets, forming an audio-visual prelude to 'the fall' of spring 1968. If the social tumult documented in Whitehead's films and as experienced at UFO meant that music was 'on the way down' in 1967–8, as Boyd describes it, then it also pointed the way forward for progressive rock bands in exploring the tensions between escape and authority, between the dislocation of consciousness and its re-engagement through complex music patterns, and between the theatricality of the avant-garde and the politics of everyday life.

What emerged from the underground scenes of London and San Francisco was a desire to link music, performance and art, and to make more complex music than the commercial industry permitted. Basement clubs and communal houses formed fresh spaces in which improvisation and experimentation could flourish, while an interest in mythology and altered states of consciousness offered new themes for musicians to tell stories through their music. The narrative dimension of progressive music was not about storytelling in the classic realist mode but about a modernist fusion of myth and reality; the dislocation of a single narrative perspective; and a theatricality that takes its spirit from the modernist avant-garde and found new outlets in the postwar years through abstract art, happenings and the multimedia movement Fluxus. This avant-garde energy is often overlooked when recounting the development of 1960s music, but it is important for understanding both the cultural environment of progressive music and the fusion of high and popular culture embodied in *Sgt. Pepper*.

The late 1950s in the United States was a much more eclectic time for drama and performance than in Britain, where working-class kitchen-sink drama dominated much of the decade. According to drama critic Richard Kostelantz, the late 1950s in the US represented a shift towards a 'theatre of mixed-means', as new performance spaces off-Broadway allowed dramatists to experiment with the length and genre of their performances and to rid themselves of the fourth-wall convention of classical playwriting.[16] To this end, Allan Kaprow was calling in 1958 for 'total art', which was as 'open and fluid as the shapes of our everyday experience'.[17] Inspired by Jackson Pollock, Kaprow wanted artists to use any material that came to hand and not be constrained by convention:

> Pollock, as I see him, left us at the point where we must become preoccupied with and even dazzled by the space and objects of our everyday life [. . .] We shall utilize the specific substances of sight, sound, movements, people, odors, touch. Objects of

every sort are materials for the new art. [. . .] All of life will be open to [these artists]. They will discover out of ordinary things the meaning of ordinariness. They will not try to make them extraordinary but will only state their real meaning. But out of nothing they will devise the extraordinary and then maybe nothingness as well. People will be delighted or horrified, critics will be confused or amused, but these, I am certain, will be the alchemies of the 1960s.[18]

This recommendation was populist (an attack on the elitism of the art academy) and encouraged resourcefulness, if not a new type of virtuosity, in the alchemical creation of new art out of ordinary objects. This was embodied by Kaprow's *18 Happenings in 6 Parts* at the Reuben Gallery in Manhattan in autumn 1959, which linked together performance and film, sounds and art, recording and improvisation. This created an environment in which it became impossible to detach the experience of the artwork from the artwork itself. Other mixed-media experiments with sound, lighting, engineering and theatre, such as Lucinda Childs' *Vehicle*, performed in Manhattan in 1966, revealed different directions for the happening.[19]

Kaprow's work was largely in the sphere of performance, whereas the champion of underground film Jonas Mekas was energized by short experimental films in which, as Kaprow describes, the viewers 'enter, are surrounded, and become part of what surrounds us'.[20] Mekas was interested in flicker techniques (such as those favoured by Peter Whitehead), which leave the viewer disorientated and exposed to 'a new spiritualized language of motion and light'.[21] Kaprow's work dovetailed with that of John Cage, whose class he had attended in the New School in Greenwich Village. While Cage's influence on popular music can most easily be seen in the work of Brian Eno and in the early soundtracks of Michael Nyman, his disregard for conventional time signatures and his willingness to use found noises, chance operations, silence and indeterminacy not only opened up a new soundscape, but also meant that each performance was a new artwork and demanded that the listener participate actively to make sense of the music. Although Cage is often interpreted as a grand formalist, preoccupied by the operational side of music, Kaprow argues that there is an anti-formalist side to Cage: not only do his compositions have 'no definite frame' (rather like Jackson Pollock's paintings) 'so that the sounds and silences . . . could be continued indefinitely', but that 'musical sound and noise' and 'art and life' are fused in Cage's music.[22] This was the case for Cage's 1967 book *A Year from Monday*, in which unstructured sentences and typographical variations explore musical, aesthetic and philosophical correspondences.

Neither Kaprow nor Cage explicitly influenced the development of psychedelic music – even though Paul McCartney had been listening to Cage and Stockhausen in 1967 and, according to George Martin, had expressed his desire to Lennon to produce an avant-garde instrumental section for *Sgt. Pepper*, 'a spiralling ascent of sound' starting 'with all instruments on their lowest note and climbing to the highest in their own time.'[23] But Cage and Stockhausen shifted the horizon of what was sonically possible; this was the most obvious tip of the avant-garde iceberg and helped to break down perceived barriers between serious and popular music. It is useful to trace this avant-garde musical lineage, as it suggests that cultural innovation in the mid- to late 1960s had a broad palette and cannot be reduced to the study of a single cultural form. This palette was epitomized by Fluxus art, which flourished at the same time as pop art: in this respect, Yoko Ono (a member of Fluxus and a growing influence on John Lennon) emerged at the same time as Peter Blake, the artist behind the *Sgt. Pepper* cover art.

Also inspired by Jackson Pollock (and by art critic Harold Rosenberg's claim in 1952 that 'what was to go on the canvas was not a picture but an event') and the transatlantic avant-garde practised by the likes of Marcel Duchamp, Fluxus was a mixed group of artists who moved fluidly between theatre, performance, film, music, graphics and poetry.[24] Fluxus flourished in Manhattan and San Francisco between 1957 and 1964, but its genesis was in Wiesbaden, West Germany, where thirty or so artists came together at Fluxus Internationale Festspiele Neuester Musik in 1962. The following year, a manifesto was released that followed the spirit of Kaprow's happenings in stressing that life and art are inseparable – what the artist George Maciunas called a mixture of 'chance operations, concept art, anti-art, indeterminacy, improvisation, meaningless work, natural disasters' in the form of 'plans of action, stories, diagrams, music, dance constructions, poetry, essays, compositions, mathematics'.[25] While we might be tempted to read Fluxus as a disintegration of the modernist tradition of experimentation into a collection of meaningless ephemera, it is better to interpret it as a practical application of Kaprow's artistic vision, in which cultural forms intersect in ways that implicate the viewer's subjectivity in the art object.

There is a direct relationship between such experiments and those that emerged in the psychedelic club scene in London and San Francisco that link, via Stockhausen and Fluxus, to the Central European avant-garde. By 1967, these avant-garde impulses had become more diffuse, but through the likes of Whitehead and Ono, plus the desire of guitarist Bob Weir to tape the sound of 'thick air' during the recording of The Grateful Dead's second album, *Anthem of the Sun*, we can see direct lines of impact. The lines are mixed, though: we can clearly see John Lennon's interest in the experience of everyday life (before he had met Yoko Ono) in the lyrics to 'A Day in the Life' on *Sgt. Pepper*, while Lennon's diaries from 1968–9 (when he would have been influenced by Ono) show him immersing himself in, if not parodying, the philosophy of 'the everyday'.[26] Whether or not we are drawn towards tracing specific influences, it is clear that within these multiple emergences was a strong cultural impetus to break down the relationship between the subject and object of art and to fuse distinct cultural modes, both intra-musical and extra-musical, to create a holistic experience. This fits in with what Fluxus artist Dick Higgins calls the 'post-cognitive' moment in 1960s culture. Rather than interpreting reality and its origins directly on a cognitive level, a post-cognitive mode 'plays the game rather than determin[ing] who made the rules or where they come from' to create 'novel realities'.[27]

Psychedelic music is clearly in the post-cognitive mode in which time is elongated and guitar riffs are not bound to any specified time sequence. The 'dislocation of consciousness', as Whitehead calls it, is brought about by the enveloping quality of the music, evidenced by the complex musical patterns, the nature of the performance itself, and the use of oil wheels and coloured filters to distort visual acuity. The use of reverberation and echo also created distorted sonic effects that prevent the listener from standing back from the music. Allied to this, within the underground culture of UFO and Haight-Ashbury, the politics of everyday experience gave its practitioners an artistic rationale to reject mainstream culture. Arguably, psychedelic music often lacked the kind of unifying concept that enabled *Sgt. Pepper* to stand out from other key releases of 1967: The Grateful Dead's eponymous first album; Country Joe and the Fish, *Electric Music for Mind and Body*; The Jimi Hendrix Experience, *Are You Experienced*; The Moody Blues, *Days of Future Passed*; and The Pink Floyd's *Piper at the Gates of Dawn*. These last two albums (Pink Floyd's first album was recorded at Abbey Road Studios at the same time as *Sgt. Pepper*) proved to be a more of a part of early progressive music, partly because The Moody Blues and Pink Floyd made more innovative use of keyboards, were less bound by generic constraints (reflected in the country rock of The Grateful Dead and Country Joe), and were less steeped in blues rock than Cream or The Jimi Hendrix Experience.

Both *Piper at the Gates of Dawn* and *Days of Future Passed* move beyond the idea of psychedelic music being its own content in their interest in the narrative (horizontal) and symbolic (vertical) dimensions of music. Both albums can be seen as 'post-cognitive' in the ways that they help to reshape emotions and ideas. Neither album peddles a fully blown concept, but both use temporality ('dawn' and 'the future') as a floating signifier of transcendence in which time periodically expands and contracts. The title of *Piper at the Gates of Dawn* is drawn from Kenneth Grahame's 1908 children's story *The Wind in the Willows* (in a chapter featuring an elusive piper, alluded to as Pan), and *Days of Future Passed* uses an Everyman journeying from dawn to night as a narrative patterning device for a symphony in which classical orchestration and rock music play equal roles. While Pink Floyd's first album has come to represent the culmination of the British psychedelic experience (this was the band's only full album release before Syd Barrett was forced to leave after his excessive use of LSD), the poetic and narrative aspects of *Days of Future Passed* push it towards being a fully fledged concept album.

This difference is also signified by the album covers. Whereas *Piper at the Gates of Dawn* depicts the four band members in a fractured swirl, with long hair and psychedelic clothing, as a backdrop to the distorted pink lettering

of the band's name (the album title did not appear on the cover), the cover of
Days of Future Passed depicts an abstract psychedelic watercolour by David
Anstey, in which a distorted rainbow blends into the earth and sea, with fragments of human faces overshadowed by the sands of time and the threatening
night. There is no centre to either image: the viewer's gaze shifts across the
fractured faces and clothing of the four members of Pink Floyd; and on *Days
of Future Passed*, the land mass in the middle provides no stable point of
focus, bleeding into the sea on one side and hemmed in by the night on the
other. The contrast to the cover of The Moody Blues' next album, *In Search
of the Lost Chord*, is stark. Philip Travers, who collaborated regularly with the
band in the late 1960s and early 1970s, provides a more obviously psychedelic
image for *In Search of the Lost Chord*. Here a meditating figure is positioned
in the lower middle of the cover, between an oversize skull and foetus, but
his hood is pulled upwards into the energy of the sun, where a celestial face
blurs into the band's name and outstretched arms meld into the album title.
Whereas *Days of Future Passed* plays on the idea of a lack of centre, the cover
of *In Search of the Lost Chord* creates multiple centres that move outwards into
a life cycle, into the mystical elements, and into the music itself.[28]

The Moody Blues, *In Search of the Lost Chord* (1968). Artwork by Phil Travers.

The swirl of images on the cover of *Piper at the Gates of Dawn* links closely to the swirl of electronic and natural sound effects and radio interference on the album, juxtaposed with the heavy bass on 'Interstellar Overdrive', the simple percussion on the gothic fairy stories 'The Gnome' and 'The Scarecrow', and the sitar on 'Chapter 24'. The album is as eclectic musically and lyrically as *Sgt. Pepper*, but the imagery is more disturbing because everyday experiences mix with broader natural and cosmological themes, offering no stable reality. The lyrics are both simple and obscure, and the ethereal dreamscape of 'Flaming' jostles with the experience of illness in 'Take Up Thy Stethoscope and Walk'. At times, the album is both tender and grotesque; simple activities such as cycling are imbued with symbolic qualities (referencing the father of LSD Albert Hoffman's acid bike ride of 1943); surrealist and nonsense lyrics complicate dangerous relationships that periodically emerge in relation to cats, mothers and gnomes; and temporal patterns are distorted and opaque, such as the Eastern mysticism of 'Chapter 24', which juxtaposes sunset and sunrise.

The enveloping soundscape and driving drumbeat draw the listener inside *Piper at the Gates of Dawn*. However, the chaos of the album means that it is hard to establish any overall pattern – the swirl of the cover image mirrors the swirling sensation of listening to the album, echoing Barrett's performances of 1967 in which he raised his arms like a pantomime actor, 'wringing increasingly amazing sounds from his Telecaster, which was covered with mirrors to reflect the swirling light show'.[29] It is hard, as Jim DeRogatis concurs, not to read the album as Barrett's project, in which the listener can detect the singer losing his grip on reality. If anything, then, *Piper at the Gates of Dawn* seems too sonically experimental, thematically unstructured and lyrically overdetermined to represent a prototypical example of progressive rock. To this end, Macan reads Pink Floyd's second album, *A Saucerful of Secrets* (released in 1968 after Barrett had left the band), as a better proto-progressive example, in which, a year before the moon landings, the band (with David Gilmour replacing Barrett) explores the nature of space travel extended through 'several distinct [musical] movements that attempt to convey an extramusical source of inspiration'.[30] Given their background as architecture students, Pink Floyd's members became increasingly interested in extended, intricate and architectural modes of composition, and, as Nicolas Schaffner detects, reveals interesting musical reference points, such as the track 'A Saucerful of Secrets', which echoes the New York electronic composer Jacob Druckman's *Animus* series (1966–9) for woodwind instruments and tape recorder.[31]

Despite a similar preoccupation with time, *Days of Future Passed* is a very different type of album. It represented a departure from the view of The Moody Blues' record label, Deram, that the band should showcase the studio's new recording technique, advertised at the top right of the album cover as Deramic Sound System. Rather than following Deram's suggestion to record a rock version of Antonin Dvořák's *Symphony No. 9* (or the *New*

World Symphony), the band produced seven tracks that span the course of a day, from dawn to dusk, linked by orchestral passages from the London Festival Orchestra and arranged by composer Peter Knight.

Psychedelic elements weave through the album, from echoes and harmonies on 'Tuesday Afternoon' to drug lyrics such as 'The smell of grass/Just makes you pass/Into a dream' on 'Dawn is a Feeling'. Rather than the full immersion in a subjective experience, or the recounting of an individual's intimate story, the narrative relates a cultural journey in which children, pensioners and the haunting image of the white night riders all play key roles. Significantly, the mode of address constantly changes: 'The Day Begins' is abstract and cosmological; the listener is addressed directly as 'you' in the yearning 'Dawn is a Feeling'; the exuberance of childhood is represented by sleigh bells and the play-world lyrics of 'Another Morning'; the first-person experiences of the working-day 'Lunch Break: Peak Hour' and 'The Afternoon' suggest tasks to be done; the transitional 'Evening' blends first-person experience with the diurnal pattern of the sinking sun; and the album closes with the transcendent 'Nights in White Satin', before the 'cold-hearted orb' of the spoken poem 'Late Lament' ends the song-cycle by taking the listener back to the first three words of the album. Time furnishes the overarching structure of the album and the dominant theme running through each song. Time stands still for the children of 'Another Morning'; extends to make the day last a 'thousand years' in 'Dawn'; accelerates on 'Peak Hour', where problems need solving and 'time cannot be run'; and transports the listener to the relaxed reflections of late afternoon and evening and to the timeless dreamscapes of a night that will never end. The songs provide the time for both endeavour and contemplation, while the passing of the day is both intensely real and illusory: the time discovered during 'Peak Hour' slips away at twilight and enters a timeless realm of night riders.

If 1967 was a moment of emergence for progressive rock and the year that marked the release of at least three significant albums – *Sgt. Pepper, Piper at the Gates of Dawn* and *Days of Future Passed* – then it was also a year in which different musical energies and cultural synergies came together. Although all three albums are artefacts that combine intra- and extra-musical elements and tap closely into the psychedelic drug scene, the long improvised performances of Pink Floyd at UFO and the Roundhouse and the simplistic lyrics of Barrett's songs are far removed from the refined poetry and symphonic structure of *Days of Future Passed*. These three albums explore the fluidity of time in different ways: The Beatles' alter-ego, The Lonely Hearts Club Band, retrieves both a lost North and a transnational cultural history while exploring the permeable membrane between outer and inner experiences; Pink Floyd gestures mythically towards Pan but also to outer space and the dream world of childhood; and night-time visitations transform Everyman's daily cycle for The Moody Blues. All three albums demonstrate different ways of composing, conceptualizing, narrativizing and visually representing music, and offer alternative modes of understanding how Kaprow's 'total experience' could be translated into the album form. If the moment of punk in 1976–7 looked back on the previous ten years and saw a monolithic musical form, then it clearly overlooked the multiple directions of progressive music from its very beginnings.

Notes

1. Bill Martin, *Listening to the Future*, 31.

2. Jonathan Gould, *Can't Buy Me Love: The Beatles, Britain and America* (London: Portrait, 2007), 390.

3. See Clinton Heylin, *The Act You've Known for All These Years* (Edinburgh: Canongate, 2007).

4. Ibid., 175.

5. Gould, *Can't Buy Me Love*, 390.

6. Ibid., 392.

7. See Joan Peyser, 'The Music of Sound, or The Beatles and The Beatless', in *The Age of Rock*, ed. Jonathan Eisen (New York: Vintage, 1969), 126–34.

8. Brian Wilson and Todd Gold, *Wouldn't it Be Nice: My Own Story* (London: Bloomsbury, 2002), 205.

9. Steve Turner, *The Gospel According to The Beatles* (Louisville: Westminster/John Knox Press, 2006), 6.

10. Peyser, 'The Music of Sound', 136.

11. Gould, *Can't Buy Me Love*, 418.

12. Joe Boyd, *White Bicycles: Making Music in the 1960s* (London: Serpent's Tail, 2006), 1.

13. See Peter Whitehead, ''60s Experience' on *Pink Floyd: London 1966/1967* DVD (2005).

14. For more detail, see the website of Allen Cohen, one of the organizers of the Love Pageant Rally and the Human Be-In: s91990482.onlinehome.us/allencohen/be-in.html.

15. Boyd, *White Bicycles*, 6.

16. Richard Kostelantz, *The Theatre of Mixed-Means* (New York: R. K. Editions, [1968] 1980), 3.

17. Allan Kaprow, 'Notes on the Creation of a Total Art' (1958), in *The Blurring of Art and Life*, ed. Jeff Kelley (Berkeley, CA: University of California Press [1993] 1996), 12.

18. Kaprow, 'The Legacy of Jackson Pollock', in *The Blurring of Art and Life*, 7–8.

19. Lucinda Childs, *Vehicle*, performed as part of *9 Evenings: Theatre and Engineering*, the 69th Regiment Armory, New York City, 16–23 October 1966: www.fondation-langlois.org/html/e/page.php?NumPage=1734.

20. Kaprow, 'Notes on the Creation of a Total Art', 12.

21. Jonas Mekas, 'Movie Journals', *Film Culture: Expanded Arts*, 43 (Winter 1966), 10–11.

22. Kaprow, 'Formalism: Flogging a Dead Horse', in *The Blurring of Art and Life*, 160.

23. Quoted in Heylin, *The Act You've Known for All These Years*, 124.

24. Harold Rosenberg, 'The American Action Painters', *Art News*, 51 (December 1952), 22.

25. La Monte Young, *An Anthology* (New York: Young & Mac Low, [1963], 1970), n. p.

26. See Craig Saper, 'Fluxus as Laboratory', in *The Fluxus Reader*, ed. Ken Friedman (Chichester: Academy Editions, 1998), 136–51.

27. Saper, 'Fluxus as Laboratory', 148.

28. For artist Philip Travers' discussion of the artwork for *In Search of the Lost Chord*, see rockpopgallery.typepad.com/rockpop_gallery_news/2008/03/.

29. Jim Derogatis, *Kaleidoscope Eyes: Psychedelic Music from the 1960s to the 1990s* (London: Fourth Estate, 1996), 66.

30. Macan, *Rocking the Classics*, 21.

31. Nicholas Schaffner, *Saucerful of Secrets: Pink Floyd Odyssey* (London: Helter Skelter, [1991] 2005), 142.

Chapter 3

Out of the Garden

Two major concept albums discussed in Chapter 2 – The Moody Blues' *Days of Future Passed* and The Pink Floyd's *The Piper at the Gates of Dawn* – provide divergent trajectories for considering the place of nature in progressive rock. The cyclical narrative of *Days of Future Passed* begins and ends in nature; the hectic pace of working life is a brief interlude in a diurnal cycle, overlooked by the 'cold-hearted orb' of the opening and closing lyrics. David Anstey's psychedelic watercolour on the album cover transforms nature into a swirl of light and brooding darkness, draping human life with dreamlike abstractions and indistinct colour fields. The melodic and orchestral flow of *Days of Future Passed* contrasts with the quasi-gothic, staccato pattern of *The Piper at the Gates of Dawn*. In the first lines of 'Astronomy Domine', the 'lime and limpid green' of nature is thrown into conflict with 'the blue you once knew'. There is no pastoral meditation here. 'Astronomy Domine' pulses out into outer space and down to the 'icy waters underground'; the drumbeat is insistent, underpinning guitars that meander through spaces beyond the visible and the recognizable. This is a planetary version of nature in which terra firma and reassuring natural textures are more radically transformed than on *Days of Future Passed*, into disorientating colours, optics and sounds. On *The Piper at the Gates of Dawn*, nature constantly dissolves and then reappears in the guise of creaturely oddities (a Siamese cat, a gnome and a scarecrow) and kinetic transportations ('night prowling sifting sand', dreaming on an eiderdown of clouds, adventures in the grass, and the changes of the winter solstice) that rarely give the reassurance that The Moody Blues locate in nature. The visitation of the Nights in White Satin is a sublime phenomenon to behold, whereas the interstellar soundscapes of Pink Floyd's album transport the listener into sonic energy fields that beguile and entice but also disorientate and disrupt.

The lyrical and musical differences between these two albums reveal a sustained ambivalence towards nature in rock music produced in the late 1960s and early 1970s. Nature is rarely a sustained utopia for progressive bands, even if it contains utopian and transcendental possibilities and acts as a source of imagination and creativity. Some early 1970s songs adopted an explicitly ecological approach to nature, attuned to a hippie sensibility: for example, Yes and Crosby and Nash would both sing about the perilous plight of whales. More often, nature is a liminal space of possibility and experience, dangerous at times but usually a better alternative to the town or city. Nature at first seems abundant and triumphant, but tensions between technological processes and traditional instrumentation, the commodification of nature, nostalgia for more authentic times and places, and the quest for alternative lifestyles and habitats all problematize the natural world in progressive rock. Even when nature is seen as a positive resource, it is often presented in conflict with mainstream politics, 'straight' attitudes, or intractable problems arising from mass-populated urban environments.

These tensions are borne out in the fate of the outdoor music festivals in the late 1960s and very early 1970s, which followed in the wake of the jazz and folk festivals of the 1960s and the pastoral setting of the Golden Gate Park for San Francisco's Summer of Love. In June 1967, a few days before the Monterey Pop Festival, the Fantasy Fair and Magic Mountain Music Festival took place at Mount Tamalpais in northern California and epitomized the idea of a rural utopia. Set on the south face of the mountain, the festival featured Jefferson Airplane, Moby Grape, The Byrds, The Doors, and Country Joe and the Fish, many of them dressed in medieval costume. The brochure gave license for the audience to explore the adjoining woods and fields, stating that 'you will immediately [be] surrounded by color and motion, the good vibrations of thousands of people flowing with the natural beauty of Mt. Tamalpais'. Britain held its own three-day outdoor music festival in August 1967, at Woburn Abbey, dubbed the 'Festival of the Flower Children', and the following year Hyde Park, London, was the venue for a series of free summer concerts up to 1971. DJ John Peel claimed that the concert of June 1968, featuring Pink Floyd, Jethro Tull and Tyrannosaurus Rex, was the best he had ever attended, writing:

> I hired a boat and rowed out and I lay in the bottom of the boat, in the middle of the Serpentine and just listened to the band play . . . it was like a religious experience . . . they just seemed to fill the whole sky and everything. And to coincide perfectly with the lapping of the water and the trees and everything.[1]

In July the following year, the pastoral backdrop of Hyde Park (a bounded oasis set in the heart of London's West End) formed the perfect setting for The Rolling Stones to release one thousand white doves during Mick Jagger's recital of Percy Bysshe Shelley's elegiac poem of 1821, 'Adonais', in memory of Brian Jones, who had died two days earlier.

While these festivals celebrate a Romantic version of 'Nature', the Woodstock Music and Art Fair (15–17 August 1969) and the sequence of three Isle of Wight Festivals (August 1968 to 1970) hint at a darker relationship with the natural world – a place of liberation but also a resource for commercial exploitation. The Woodstock Festival, held at White Lake in upstate New York (seventy miles from Woodstock), attracted an audience of four hundred thousand over four days. Like the Monterey Pop Festival, Woodstock concentrated on folk, blues and rock, featuring many of the bands that played at Monterey, together with Joan Baez, Joe Cocker, Crosby, Stills and Nash, Arlo Guthrie, and Richie Havens, all of whom feature in Michael Wadleigh's film *Woodstock: 3 Days of Peace & Music* (1970), as well as Ravi Shankar, The Grateful Dead and The Band. Wadleigh intended to depict the festival as a contemporary version of *The Canterbury Tales*: a pilgrimage for hippies seeking the communal expression of music and love. The film begins with the bucolic setting of White Lake; the camera cuts between pastoral images and the building of the enormous concert stage, switching its angle from ground level to helicopter-eye views. The film's visual style derives from the editing work of Thelma Schoonmaker and the young Martin Scorsese, particularly the use of split screens to incorporate extra concert footage, to emphasize the concert's massive scale, and to juxtapose the arriving audience and live performances with the construction and logistics of running the festival. The gathering of so many people suggests, as Sheila Whiteley argues, that the festival's triumph was to engender 'participation rather than passivity' in the audience.[2]

Although Wadleigh's choice of footage focuses more closely on anti-war and political songs than on ballads or more progressive music, the film is not simply an untrammelled representation of a pastoral idyll set against the backdrop of race riots, political assassinations and the Vietnam War. Echoing the electric and ideological distortions of The Nice's version of Bernstein's 'America' (see Chapter 1), the most politicized of all songs at Woodstock was Jimi Hendrix's version of 'The Star-Spangled Banner', in which he distorted the national anthem by making use of the 'noise elements' of his guitar with 'evocations of bombs falling and exploding, the screaming of sirens, the howls of the victims'.[3] Hendrix followed this with 'Purple Haze', played at 6.30 a.m. on the final morning of the festival to a near-deserted site. In the film, the camera pans around to the heaps of debris left behind by the audience; the team of helpers clearing up garbage, food and human remains suggests that Wadleigh and his editing team sought balance and took care not to over-romanticize the festival.

The promoters of Woodstock clearly targeted the audience as consumers, but the logistics of the event were not carefully controlled: the audience was vastly greater than expected, it was impossible to control tickets and many avoided paying.[4] The film and album were part of a US$1,500,000 media package (offsetting US$3,400,000 spent on or after the festival), and glimpses of the tensions between the free festival that Woodstock became (many of the audience were in the grounds long before the organizers) and the economics of the event can be glimpsed in Wadleigh's film. Not apparent, though, were the five thousand medical cases and three deaths (two by drug overdoses and one by a tractor) of audience members. This darker undercurrent affected many of the rock festivals in the late 1960s and early 1970s, arising most dramatically in the stabbing of a black teenager at the hands of the Hells Angels at the free Altamont Festival held in December 1969, but also in the commercial tensions of the Isle of Wight Festivals. The Isle of Wight's local paper, the *Islander*, commented on the 'rolling green hills and bright, bright sunshine' of the 1968 Isle of Wight Festival, but noted that the enclosure 'looked very much like a prison camp, a detention compound. An area all round the billowing black PVC walls was marked off with wire, and patrolled by a Security man holding an alsatian on a tight lead'.[5] The documentary *Message to Love: The Isle of Wight Festival* depicts the organizational chaos of the third festival in 1970 and a discontented audience, many of whom refused to pay the entrance fee (Hawkwind were the driving force in staging an alternative, free festival beyond the perimeter). Both films offset the musical exuberance of the performers with the logistical problems of running such events, as muddy roads, congested campsites, lack of adequate facilities and electrical problems hampered the filming.

One moment during the 1970 Isle of Wight Festival symbolized the tensions between the garden festival as a rural idyll and more disruptive forces that continued to punctuate the pastoral leanings of many progressive bands. During Joni Mitchell's set, just as she was finishing a rendition of 'Woodstock', an acid-tripping hippie 'chillingly reminiscent of Charles Manson' stumbled on stage with 'a very important message' for the people of Devastation Row (a section of the audience shut outside the confines of the concert); he claimed he had an agreement to meet Mitchell on stage and afterwards proclaimed that her lyrics of trying 'to get back to the garden' were both prophetic and a personal message to him. The organizers were deeply concerned by this invasion. A tearful Mitchell broke off her set to rebuke the audience, unfavourably contrasting them to a Hopi Indian ceremony she had recently visited and accusing them of being 'tourists' because of their lack of respect.[6] Concerns that the pastoral ideal of 1967 was becoming increasingly compromised by festival management led Isle of Wight 1970 to be dubbed 'the last great festival', owing to the rather ineffectual corrugated-metal fences around the venue (making it look like a 'psychedelic concentration camp') that did not prevent audience members entering without payment.[7] Nevertheless, others saw in the communal kitchens and the presence of voluntary caring organizations an example of what outdoor festivals could be, while the 1969 festivals marked an important year for the full emergence of progressive rock, as it blended with folk, blues, jazz and psychedelia. King Crimson and Family supported the Rolling Stones in the Hyde Park concert; the 1969 Newport Jazz Festival featured rock bands for the first time, including Jethro Tull and Led Zeppelin; the Isle of Wight Festival in 1969 included The Nice,

Family, The Who, The Moody Blues and The Third Ear Band, alongside the progressive folk of Pentangle, Indo-Jazz Fusions, The Band and Bob Dylan; and the following year's festival featured Supertramp, Jethro Tull, Family, The Doors, Jimi Hendrix, and the first appearance of Emerson, Lake and Palmer, all of whom were experimenting with extended song structures.

Despite these increasing tensions within the organization of outdoor festivals, it is instructive to explore the different strains of pastoral that emerged within the music of the late 1960s and early 1970s, many of which echo the desire to return to a mythical agrarian past contrasted with present realities. This tension is well illustrated on Jethro Tull's early albums. Although it took them until 1971 to release an extended concept album, the band's first two albums, *This Was* (1968) and *Stand Up* (1969), blend British blues with jazz riffs often overlaid by lead singer Ian Anderson's signature flute, a sound best illustrated by 'Serenade for a Cuckoo' on *This Was*. Jethro Tull eschewed the total experience of psychedelic light-shows and, when they started playing at the Marquee in 1967, offered a pared-down, rootsy sound that Anderson described in 1968 as 'a sort of progressive blues with a bit of jazz'.[8] The blues track 'Beggar's Farm' is a good example of improvisation; two-thirds of the way through (2:40), Anderson's flute breaks away from the band's 4/4 metrical arrangement, suddenly increasing the tempo through a sustained crescendo, rejoining the drum and bass again, and then breaking away for a breathy coda. The lyrics on the early albums improvise on blues themes of sadness, betrayal, leave-taking and time passing with extended instrumental passages that link a DIY approach to composition with forays into the reworking of classical pieces, such as a 'cocktail jazz' approach to Bach's 'Suite in E Minor For Lute' on 'Bourée'. Seasonal change and ruptures in natural rhythms provide the backdrop to many early songs: the sun ceases to shine on 'Some Day the Sun Won't Shine for You', 'Beggar's Farm' promises destitution, 'A New Day Yesterday' sees flirtatious games among the trees, summer is elusive on 'Look into the Sun', and the fears of getting old in wintertime trouble the singer on 'We Used to Know'. Nature does not figure explicitly on the album's out-take single, 'Living in the Past', but the song's irregular 5/4 time signature jars with its potential nostalgia, and the lyrics suggest that retreating into the past 'while others shout of war's disaster' might prove blind during a moment of social tumult.

Ian Anderson's bizarre stage persona of eccentric tramp-cum-minstrel with unkempt hair and dressed in a long coat signalled the odd combination of sonic and lyrical elements in Jethro Tull's music and foreshadowed the emphasis on theatricality in the performances of Yes, Genesis and Rush in the mid-1970s. Anderson's flute technique, involving grunts and snorts, not only exaggerated his pantomimic facial gestures, obvious on early television performances (such as a 1970 performance of 'Witches Promise' on BBC's *Top of the Pops*), but also furnished the band with a theatrical style suited to larger venues. Andrew Blake categorizes early Jethro Tull as a version

Ian Anderson and Clive Bunker of Jethro Tull at the 1970 Isle of Wight Festival.

of 'electric folk', alongside Pentangle and Fairport Convention, particularly Anderson's vocal technique, which harked back to medieval minstrelsy by offering 'a vocalisation worlds away from the fuller sound of the blues singer, and full-throated scream of emergent heavy metal or the delicate, understated humour of the singer/songwriter'.[9] The combination of Anderson's 'Anglicised folk-song voice' and lyrics that steered a course between topicality, tradition and escape was not unique at the time. But Anderson's flute gave Jethro Tull a distinctive sound, and guitarist Martin Barre offered further progressive possibilities when he joined the band in 1969.

A harder, rockier sound enhanced by the use of electronic organ and Mellotron on *Benefit* (1970) and *Aqualung* (1971) was balanced by the band's interest in European folk and its use of traditional instruments including mandolin, bouzouki, balalaika and harmonica. Distinct musical strains are harder to distinguish on *Benefit*, and time is favoured over nature as a primary theme; there is never enough time 'to do what must be done' ('Play in Time') and there is 'no time for everything' ('A Time for Everything?'), but fleeting moments of triumph over time are still possible, as the 'glad bird' shakes its wings on 'To Cry You a Song'. Coinciding with the demise of the rural folk festival, during the early 1970s the natural world fades from view in Jethro Tull's lyrics, surfacing only occasionally in the pastoral strains of *Thick as a*

Brick (1972) and the whimsical interlude 'The Story of the Hare Who Lost His Spectacles' on *A Passion Play* (1973). Nature returns explicitly, though, in *Minstrel in the Gallery* (1975), *Songs from the Wood* (1977) and *Heavy Horses* (1978), as an enchanted place, a better alternative to the class-ridden values and heartache of urban Britain. These folk-rock albums resuscitate nature as a place of magic, 'full of dragons and beasties' ('Lullaby') and of music and laughter ('Songs from the Wood'), a place for renewal ('Moths', 'Cup of Wonder'), for making love ('Acres Wild') and of honest toil ('Heavy Horses'). Perhaps arising from the industrial misery of Britain in the mid-1970s (and reflecting Anderson's decision to move to the country), these albums replace the indifference of nature on the early blues albums with pastoral renewal, where May Day and the winter solstice are transformational moments in the shepherd's calendar. But on the longer tracks, such as the 8-minute 'Heavy Horses', lyrical passages punctuate the rhythmic drive of the chorus, which emphasizes the toil required to cultivate the earth. Taken as a pair, *Songs from the Wood* and *Heavy Horses* contrast with the sterility, weariness and 'crazed' social institutions of the band's previous album *Too Old to Rock 'n' Roll: Too Young to Die* (1976), offering a pastoral alternative to bureaucratized society – a pastoral full of creaturely transformations, musical wonderment and agrarian pleasures that is less a retreat into the past and more a positive embracing of alternative lifestyles.

Although it took a decade for Jethro Tull to fully celebrate nature, developments in the folk-rock scene at the turn of the 1970s provide a broader range of musical expressions. Ronald Cohen reads the promotion of folk rock in California in the mid- to late 1960s as a means to buoy up the popularity of folk festivals, with the organisers of the Berkeley Folk Festival in 1965 recruiting Jefferson Airplane and Country Joe and the Fish to play alongside more traditional folk acts.[10] This story suggests that after the folk revival of the early 1960s, rock began to supplant folk, symbolized by Bob Dylan's turning to his electric guitar and eschewing his earlier socially engaged songs in favour of poetic introspection and psychic exploration. However, folk rock had many musical routes, blending personal and social lyrics, literary and mythic subject matter, the use of acoustic and electrical instruments, and the celebration of nature and political critique. If nature for The Beatles in the late 1960s was multilayered (the lower level of 'Strawberry Fields Forever' clashing with the higher level of 'Lucy in the Sky with Diamonds'), then for many bands at the turn of the 1970s nature operated on an ambivalent middle level; bands tended to reject the naive utopian version of nature but did not want to give up on a pastoral-acoustic mode or the possibilities of social renewal.

The folk rock of The Byrds, for example, epitomized on the album *The Notorious Byrd Brothers* (1968), linked in one direction to the hippie culture of Laurel Canyon ('Tribal Gathering'), alternative sexual experiences (the David Crosby out-take 'Triad') and Vietnam protest ('Draft Morning'), and in the other direction to a loose layering of folk, jazz and raga rhythms, interspersing sitars with electric and steel guitars, and interleaving vocal harmonies with feedback loops. That the band, which came to prominence in 1965 with covers of Bob Dylan's 'Mr Tambourine Man' and 'All I Really Want to Do', were close to collapse in 1968, as members pulled in different musical directions (evident on the album cover, where a horse's head appears in the fourth window of a logger's cabin where Crosby's face should have been), is less important than the album's celebration of a cosmically charged natural world. The fullest expression of this is 'Goin' Back', which retreats into the past to rediscover the wisdom of youth, and ends with the singer finding in the present the courage to fully appreciate nature. As with the 1967 albums by The Moody Blues, Pink Floyd and The Beatles already discussed, nature for The Byrds can be positively transformed not only through drugs ('Artificial Energy') but also through spiritual enlightenment and sexual freedom. Beyond everyday perceptions, the lyrics and music reveal magical landscapes that fuse with the cosmos, especially on the album's final track, 'Space Odyssey' (based on Arthur C. Clarke's science-fiction story 'The Sentinel'), which pairs a futuristic Moog drone with chanted lyrics that link the discovery of an ancient pyramid on the moon in the year 1996 to utopian possibilities for human evolution.

The English folk tradition was quite distinct from the West Coast celebration of nature, particularly the psychedelic turn of Californian folk rock in the mid-1960s, exemplified by The Grateful Dead's fifth studio album, *American Beauty* (1970), particularly the tracks 'Box of Rain' and 'Ripple'.[11] Folk elements are evident on early Moody Blues albums in the celebration of an English pastoral that inflected one branch of the Anglo-folk tradition rooted in an agrarian version of Olde England, where class-bound loyalties revolve around tales of impossible love and challenges to feudal authority. Ewan McColl in London and Pete Seeger in New York State continued to write and perform politically engaged pure folk into (and beyond) the 1960s, but Bob Dylan's hybrid folk-rock fusions inspired a number of bands to take folk music in alternative directions in the second half of the decade. Fairport Convention is the best case of a folk band that experimented with progressive forms, concepts and instrumentation in its late 1960s albums. Emerging from the psychedelic tinges of Fairport's debut album of 1968, progressive elements are evident on the third album, *Unhalfbricking* (1969), which mixes American folk influences (three tracks were written by Dylan) with the extended 11-minute track 'A Sailor's Life', adapted from the nineteenth-century popular song, merging the contemplative depth of Sandy Denny's vocals with musical virtuosity (Fairport named this track the 'first proper step into the genre that would become known as British folk-rock').[12] Other shorter tracks on *Unhalfbricking*, 'Genesis Hall', 'Autopsy' and 'Who Knows Where the Time Goes', move beyond traditional folk to differing degrees. 'Autopsy' (4:22), for example, adopts a four-part structure: the first part follows a jazz rhythm in 5/4, before switching at 1:20 to a slower, drum-led section in 4/4, followed by a blues instrumental by guitarist Richard Thompson (varying between 4/4 and 6/4), and then returns at 3:06 to the 5/4 jazz rhythm in the closing part. Denny's vocals soar to begin with and then become breathier, switching pathos for a meditation on lost time, before the instrumental break takes the listener back to an autopsy of regret, ending with the lyrics 'Crying the hours into tears/Crying the hours into years'.

This progressive shift was exemplified on the following album, *Liege and Lief* (released December 1969 in the UK, and July 1970 in the US), which developed a distinctive Anglo-folk rock, blending traditional and electric instrumentation to revisit mythical stories from the past. The album focused more intently on natural themes than the previous two albums *What We Did on Our Holidays* (1969) and *Unhalfbricking*, the covers of which both depicted town life (albeit slightly surreally), in contrast to the otherworldly quality of *Liege and Lief*, with its sepia tones, distinctive title graphics and dreamy portraits of the six band members.

Liege and Lief has more electric elements than the previous albums, but it also contains folk ballads – newly written ('Come All Ye') and traditional ('Reynardine') – and a four-part 'Medley' combining reels and jigs. The final track, 'Crazy Man Michael', echoes the unfulfilled pastoral life of William Wordsworth's poem 'Michael' (1800), but it is the two new arrangements of traditional songs – the first from seventeenth-century England, 'Matty Groves', and the second a Scottish bewitching ballad, 'Tam Lin' – that best illustrate Fairport's blend of electric folk. At over 8 minutes and blending acoustic and electric guitars, drums and fiddle, 'Matty Groves' relates a love affair between the peasant worker of the song title and a fair lady, whose husband, Lord Donald, returns from his travels to challenge Matty Groves to a duel. Gallantly, Lord Donald offers his adversary the best weapon and the first strike, but Matty is no match for his aristocratic opponent. Lord Donald kills a second time when his wife rejects him, but he has the gallantry to bury the two lovers together, with the lady at the top – 'for she was of noble kin'. Less a natural tale than one of domestic adultery and jealousy across class lines, the song segues into a long instrumental passage for the last three and a half minutes, increasing in tempo through a violin-led section, which seems to celebrate Matty Groves' life after the metrical arrangement of the first section of the song. 'Tam Lin' (7:13) begins much more dramatically with drums and bass, which play at the end of each of Sandy Denny's couplets, except for two instrumental breaks – the first led by a violin and the second an electric guitar – which punctuate the tightly structured song. 'Tam Lin' and 'Matty Groves' embody a creative tension between acoustic and electric music in progressive rock, using tightly structured narratives juxtaposed with freer instrumental sections in which musical virtuosity comes to the fore.

Fairport Convention experimented with the concept album *Babbacombe Lee* in 1971, based around the story of John 'Babbacombe' Lee, the nineteenth-century English criminal who survived being hanged three times, and they continued to blend rearranged traditional songs with new compositions. But, after Sandy Denny left in 1970 to join Fotheringay, the band arguably failed to advance the blending of folk and rock elements of *Liege and Lief*. Other late 1960s folk bands reflected these fusions, such as the psychedelic folk of The Incredible String Band; the jazz, blues and folk musical fusions of Pentangle; and the acid folk of Comus, which ranged from the rough psychedelic blues of its 1971 single 'Diana' to the pagan pastoral of the 7-minute 'Song to Comus' (influenced by John Milton's Comus masque from 1634) on *First Utterance* (1971), an album Jeanette Leech calls 'the most radical acid-folk album of them all'.[13] *First Utterance* is a much darker affair than most folk rock, but taps into a seam of the folk revival by exploring the folk song as a location of protest, violence and sexual licence, and connecting these back to nature. The Watersons' thematic song-cycle *Frost and Fire: A Calendar of Ritual and Magical Songs* (1965) brought together these phenomena to show that the cycles of nature are those with which humanity should commune, even to the point of human sacrifice as a means of ensuring fertility. Encompassing every type of activity and emotion in a celebration of rural life, the song-cycle is also about work as a means of engaging with the land. Music archivist A. L. Lloyd, the writer of the liner notes to *Frost and Fire*, asserts that 'it's due to their relation with economic life, not to any mystical connection, that these song-customs have persisted right up to our own time'. This is a well-developed reflection, but it sidesteps the dark content of the songs for the overly determined idea that the economy drives everything.

Comus did not look to traditional songs, and reflected a move away from folk rock towards a progressive folk that did not refer to the folk music tradition, but the band twisted traditional instrumentation into an ecstatic, mounting discordance where a lost, sexual and often deadly nature could be summoned. This pastoral is about an unleashing of energy that taps into a host of pagan gods and stories, so as to signal a deep relationship to the land or nature in the abstract, rather than the specific locatedness of the folk revival and folk rock. Similarly, The Incredible String Band seemed to be neither folk nor prog, while also being both. The band's milieu was neither the history of Albion nor a newly invented tradition but the psychedelic festival and event. Although the group went on to make the side-long (and derivative) track 'Ithkos' on *Hard Rope and Silken Twine* in 1974, traces of prog can be found in 'the jerky raucousness' of its first self-titled album (1966) and *The Hangman's Beautiful Daughter* (1968), especially the nine-part and 13-minute track 'A Very Cellular Song', with its insistent refrains foreshadowing the release offered by long prog tracks of the 1970s.[14] The Incredible String Band mined the concerns of folk rock in the rediscovery of traditional instruments and references to gardens, nature, freedom and play, but viewed them through the twin lenses of drugs and whimsy, akin to Syd Barrett-era Pink Floyd, Caravan and Soft Machine.

More broadly, the *Bumpers* compilation album released by Island in 1970 blended blues (Jethro Tull, Traffic, Free), folk (John and Beverley Martin, Fairport Convention, Fotheringay) and progressive rock (King Crimson, Renaissance), while Transatlantic Records not only promoted British folk music during the 1960s and early 1970s but also encouraged heavy and soft rock, with bands such as Stray and Unicorn on its label. This eclecticism was mirrored by Pentangle, a band that featured prominently on a 1972 Transatlantic Records compilation album.[15] Formed from a collaboration between folk guitarists John Renbourn and Bert Jansch, but relying heavily on Danny Thompson's jazzy double-bass playing, the group's first three albums, *The Pentangle* (1968), *Sweet Child* (1969) and *A Basket of Light* (1969), present original compositions; reinterpretations of traditional songs and jazz styles (for example, of Charlie Mingus on *Sweet Child*); and experiments with extended form, notably the 18-minute 'Jack Orion' on the 1970 album *Cruel Sister* (stretched from its 9:50 on Jansch's 1966 album *Jack Orion*). Nature emerges periodically in Pentangle's songs, such as the bluesy 'Far Behind the Sun' on *The Pentangle*, the contemplative 'The Trees They Do Grow High' on *Sweet Child*, and the pastoral 'A Cuckoo' on *A Basket of Light*. Pentangle often explored the complex relationship between nature and time, most evident in the titular pun of the old English folk song 'Let No Man Steal Your Thyme' (exploring the garden of female virginity), the cyclical changes of 'Springtime Promises', and the ethereal visions of the 7-minute 'Pentangling'. This is also evident in the band's unusual time signatures, inflected by Jacqui McShee's layered voice, which is both wistful and hopeful.

Pentangle performing in 1967.

This type of folk-rock fusion was important for progressive rock bands, because it allowed them to mediate between the outlaw pose of the blues-rock singer and the folk desire for union with a homely version of nature. Such musical and lyrical fusion also facilitated complexity, which was very important for bands that wanted to move away from the short, tightly con-strained song structure of the pop single. Folk rock was not only a mediating form; it bound together the seemingly separate genres of the blues and folk, completing the work of the 1960s revivals of those forms in Britain. One band to continue this trend of the recombination of styles is Genesis, which in the late 1960s was a fledging progressive band from Charterhouse School in Surrey. Although most of the tracks on the first album, *From Genesis to Revelation* (1969), had concise pop structures, the three tracks for a Night Ride session for BBC Radio in February 1970 – 'Shepherd', 'Pacidy' and 'Let Us Now Make Love' – tightly weave pastoral and lyrical elements, signalling more complex song structures to come. Genesis was less influenced by blues than Jethro Tull, but minstrelsy is evoked by the timbre of Peter Gabriel's vocals, through Gabriel's flute (used less sparingly and more melodically then Ian Anderson's flute) and in the mythological figures that populate the band's early songs. 'Shepherd', for example, begins with a dramatic bardic opening, 'Rise up! Take your lyre and sing/Listen! To the news I bring', and then transports the listener to a fairytale world of dreams and imagination. The search for sexual union of the 6-minute 'Let Us Now Make Love' is also a meditation on time, emphasized through the acoustic and vocal folk harmonies of the chorus: 'let us make love until the end of time – now and forever'. But just as the imaginative freedom of 'Shepherd' is constrained by the coming of the dawn, so 'Let Us Now Make Love' promises consummation, only for the passage of time to threaten to keep the shepherd-like singer from his beloved. The rising pitches, rests and undulations of Gabriel's voice mingle elation and melancholy, as if time can never be outrun and union lies just beyond earthbound possibilities. There is an ethereal quality to early Genesis tracks, an interest in pastoral acoustic instrumentation and an enthrallment with natural cycles, but this is tempered by stories in which the pastoral ideal is glimpsed only fleetingly or might exist only in dreams.

Nature as a guiding reference point is developed to a further level of complexity on Genesis's second studio release, *Trespass* (1970), depicted on the album cover as a well-cultivated valley surrounded by mountains, seen from afar by two courtly figures from a grand arched window. The inside illustration of the gatefold sleeve reinforces the pastoral aspects of the album, in its depiction of a pleasant wooded glade in the foreground and a picturesque vista of river and sky beyond. The medieval script, gargoyle and cherub on the front cover and pale-blue foreground reinforces the benign, otherworldly qualities of the album, but this jars with the transgressive encroachment upon hidden truths in the title *Trespass*. These darker themes are dramatically emphasized by the image of a bejewelled knife, which slices into the back sleeve cover, scarring a line that cuts across the pastoral vista and courtly scene on the front cover. Paul Whitehead used a razor blade to slash the image where the knife goes in, to emphasize the border-crossing theme of the album, and a smaller image of the back-cover knife can be seen in a tree trunk in the near left of the inside illustration.

Trespass makes extensive use of acoustic guitar and flute, which reinforces the band's folk-rock reverence for nature; but the theme of trespassing weaves through the six songs, revealing the natural world to be more varied and treacherous than in earlier Genesis songs. On the second track, 'White Mountain', for example, the young wolf Fang defies the 'laws of the brethren' to journey through forests, snowstorms and 'jungles of ice' in search of the 'sacred haunts of the dead'. The song depicts Fang as a trespassing creature who desires new knowledge but is pursued by a wolf pack led by the old war hero One-Eye. The third (and last) verse adopts the perspective and voice of One-Eye, who slays Fang to retain his crown and laurels, causing the young wolf's blood to turn the white mountain red. The brethren's authority is thus preserved, but the imaginative scope of the song belongs to Fang and his journey to the white mountain.

The third track, 'Visions of Angels' – which has a more conventional verse-chorus structure than the first two tracks, 'Looking for Someone' and 'White Mountain' (perhaps because it was written earlier) – promises imaginative ecstasy within a sunny forest, but the song actually reinforces melancholy and existential doubt because the singer reveals his loved one to be out of reach, transported to the celestial sphere. 'Dusk', the fifth track, develops the theme of transportation as the singer's hand moves magically of its own accord, 'touching all the trees' as 'once it touched love's body', but the dreamlike harmonies reveal 'angry tigers' that threaten the beauty of dusk.

Positioned between 'Visions of Angels' and 'Dusk' is the track 'Stagnation', which best foregrounds the album's ambivalence towards nature, as well as the band's storytelling interests, which emerge through phases and episodes rather than verse-chorus repetition.[16] 'Stagnation' begins with a benign red sky and peaceful hills; the first word of the second verse, 'Wait', shifts the tone to a figure haunted by unspoken sins of the past and the image of an 'ice-cold knife' that decorates the dead. Despite a friendly moon, the singer is isolated in a stagnant pool, where he is forced to feed off 'bitter minnows'. Spiritual thirst makes him increasingly desperate in the closing section of the song; Gabriel's voice becomes feverish as he tries to rid himself of the 'filth that lies deep in his guts'. Although we are not told what kind of trespass led to this isolation, the juxtaposition of benign nature and human desperation characterizes *Trespass* and feeds thematically into the epic closing track, 'The Knife'. Nature and the acoustic elements fade away in 'The Knife' to leave an ugly human world full of loss, violence and transgression, emphasized by fast-tempo keyboards, bass, electric guitar, heavy drums and heroic-revolutionary lyrics, in which it is impossible to determine whether the new regime spreading bloody 'kindness' is any better than the old world full of evil and lies.

This theme of transgression is more specific on the band's next release, *Nursery Cryme* (1971), where it is bounded by a Victorian sense of propriety and normalized morality, symbolized by a well-tended garden – perhaps referencing an earlier incarnation of the band, The Garden Wall. The 'cryme' of the album title not only takes an archaic spelling but also links to the disjointed world of Paul Whitehead's artwork, which spans the front and back of the album cover and principally links to the 10-minute opening track, 'The Musical Box'. It depicts a surreal Alice figure playing croquet on a newly cut lawn, with a number of severed heads rather than croquet hoops; Alice casts a dark, grim reaper-like shadow, which spills over onto the back cover, where we see a grand Victorian hall. The parallel lines of the cut grass form a series of diagonals on the front cover, meeting at a vanishing point high on the horizon, blending with a green sky and threatening clouds. The lyrics of 'The Musical Box' help explain the cover, by relating the tale of a Victorian girl, Cynthia, who removes her brother's head with a croquet mallet.[17] The rest of the song occurs indoors, as if the natural order has been broken by the murderous act. When Cynthia opens her dead brother's musical box, the tune of 'Old King Cole' brings Henry back to life, but he swiftly transforms into a lascivious old man who unnaturally lusts after Cynthia: a transformation dramatized by the old-man costume worn by Gabriel for live performances in 1972. Although Cynthia's nurse (who is also depicted on the album cover, on wheels and carrying a stick) kills the old man by throwing the musical box at him, the themes of infanticide and incestuous desires mark 'The Musical Box' as one of the band's most challenging and disturbing songs.

Nursery Cryme can be read as a countercultural attack on authority, but it is less specific in its social focus than many releases of the late 1960s and does not seek to offer cultural alternatives. Instead, the reader is presented with a series of tangled tales and mythologies that critique respectability but do not provide easy answers. On the third track, 'The Return of the Giant Hogweed', for example, the hogweed located by a Victorian explorer in a Russian marsh is brought back to Kew Gardens and grows so rapidly that it overruns London and eventually threatens the whole of humankind. This invasion narrative is tinged with Cold War threats (the Soviet Union versus the West), but the song does not push any allegorical dimension, except perhaps in relation to class consciousness: a rampant natural life-form transplanted for the pleasure of royalty seeks revenge against the imperialist, leisure-seeking English social set. That the hogweed is given its own voice in the last verse, and on the inside gatefold sleeve, as it towers with mythological stature over the image of a well-heeled Victorian girl, suggests that the song is, perhaps, sympathetic to a botanical life-form that is 'immune to all our herbicidal battering' – at a moment when conservation was arriving on national agendas.

Nature becomes ever more entangled on later Genesis albums, with the following two studio albums, *Foxtrot* (1972) and *Selling England by the Pound* (1973), exploring the complex relationship between social and natural worlds (depicted by the quasi-pastoral cover of *Selling England*), before entering the urban labyrinth of Manhattan on *The Lamb Lies Down on Broadway* (1974). These albums (discussed in the next two chapters) marked a distinct movement away from the folk-rock pastoral of early Genesis, perhaps because guitarist Anthony Phillips left the band after *Trespass* and took with him a pastoral sensibility that featured on his first solo release, *The Geese and the Ghost* (1977), the cover of which depicts a natural valley (and a ghostly fairy) not dissimilar to the pastoral glade on the inside gatefold of *Trespass*. Nevertheless, Genesis albums continued to include quasi-pastoral songs: 'Horizons' (on *Foxtrot*); 'Dancing with the Moonlight Knight' (on *Selling England*); 'Ripples' on the 1976 album *A Trick of the Tale* (following Peter Gabriel's departure a year earlier); and the cover art of *Wind and Wuthering* (1977), which references Emily Brontë's gothic novel *Wuthering Heights* (1847), with images of fluttering moths and 'soft wind breathing through the grass'.

Rather than simply celebrating a hippie version of the natural world, Genesis used myth and storytelling and unusual 'note clusters' (which created new chord sequences) to explore the complexity and transformations of nature.[18] Other bands discussed in the next two chapters, such as Yes on *Close to the Edge* (1972), Wishbone Ash on *Argus* (1972), and Rush on *Caress of Steel* (1975) and *Hemispheres* (1978), moved pastoral themes away from folk roots into territories where spiritual awakening and fond memories intertwine with decay and violence. This is a very different take on progressive rock than the one suggested by Andrew Blake in *The Land Without Music* (1997). Blake contrasts the Romanticism of the rock singer with a formal, systems-based version of progressive rock: 'of rationality, or argument, of development, rather than formula and repetition'.[19] Even though progressive bands were very interested in musical form, as this chapter has indicated, they not only explored the natural world in more nuanced ways than rock bands, but the organic fusions of musical styles and motifs pushed these groups closer to the actual and metaphorical edges of nature.

The English progressive tradition arguably stayed closer than North American bands to a recognizable version of pastoral. Pink Floyd, between Syd Barrett's departure in 1968 and the release of *The Dark Side of the Moon* in 1973, consciously looked to natural settings, sounds, concepts and locations as a reaction to the culture industry the band was soon to plentifully feed. *Ummagumma* (1969) contains 'Grantchester Meadows'; the unmarked cover of *Atom Heart Mother* (1970) features a cow, with its languid title track filling side one; and side two of *Meddle* (1971) is filled by the slow and sumptuous 'Echoes', its lyrics rapt by the beauty of nature. This move to the extended meditation on the landscape is perhaps best illustrated by Mike Oldfield's instrumental albums from the mid-1970s – *Hergest Ridge*

(1974) and *Ommadawn* (1975) – which represent striking examples of the persistence of the pastoral in progressive music. On both albums, Oldfield explored the real and mythical topography of Offa's Dyke, on the boundary of England and Wales, as a touchstone for his multi-instrumental composition, as a therapeutic retreat from the demands of the music industry, and as a place of pastoral and spiritual renewal.[20] Oldfield was drawn to Celtic tunes and traditional instruments, as well as orchestral scale and arrangements. He later reflected on the moment of first hearing Jean Sibelius's *Fifth Symphony* (1915–19) at school as the opening up of a musical vista 'of pine forests and mountains, it had such a feeling of enormous space and motion, huge and great in its momentum and intricacy'.[21]

Oldfield took these grand musical vistas into his second album, *Hergest Ridge*, which is calmer and more meditative than its predecessor, *Tubular Bells*, its progression through different motifs tempered. Transcendent passages (starting at 5 and 18 minutes) shade into more languorous phases using chimes and oboe, but a 6-minute dissonant keyboard and guitar sequence shakes up the second half of the album (to suggest that all is not well in the garden) before sinking into a gentle closing vocal-acoustic-vocal. The female vocals of Clodagh Simonds (of Mellow Candle) and Sally Oldfield are used among a plethora of instruments on the two albums as part of their layered textures, but the closing segment of *Ommadawn* offers a more straightforward and homely view of nature. On this album, Oldfield shifts away from parameters of extension and breadth to close with a short vocal-acoustic piece, 'On Horseback', which focuses on the genteel pastoral retreat of Hergest Ridge. The song is whimsical in its conception (the horse is a 'little brown beastie' and a child's choir is used towards the end) and provides a more reassuring sense of nature compared to the disorientations and metamorphoses of *Piper at the Gates of Dawn* or the pagan view of nature of Comus and The Incredible String Band. As such, 'On Horseback' is an existential meditation about living on safe terra firma, where horse-riding is not only a retreat from technology and urbanism but also preferable to the psychedelic freedom of 'flying through space'.

Closer to the recognizable mode of 1970s progressive rock – between folk rock, psychedelic folk, and the expanding vistas of Pink Floyd and Mike Oldfield – is Gentle Giant. The band's name is reflected in the big-eyed, red-haired but balding giant on its debut album of 1970, which stands in for mythical figures, archetypes and stories that structure a rural tradition disowned by modernity. Folk inflects the band's sound, from instrumentation that combines traditional and rock elements through to choral singing and the pace of the musical passages that often take folk reels as their starting point. Elsewhere, an overzealous authenticity looked to medieval influences (such as Amazing Blondel, Gryphon or the more radical Univers Zéro), but Gentle Giant blended folk and medieval rhythms, fusing rock with hints of jazz and classical styles (as also found in French band Ange). Folk is only part of the band's palette, but its songs combine storytelling, personal narratives, meditations on nature and mythical beings.

On its first two albums, Gentle Giant marked out a trademark rapid alternation between time signatures, genres, instrumentation and different vocal styles. Pastoral is mostly fleeting, but it nevertheless arises in many songs via lyrics, acoustic guitars or a range of keyboards. The pastoral is often at one remove or something lost, as in 'Nothing At All' on *Gentle Giant* (1970). On this track a girl is introduced sitting by a river over picked notes on acoustic guitar, but the location becomes a melancholy site allowing reflection on a departed lover rather than filling the listener with cloying emotion. The pastoral becomes a creator of possibilities here, as it does in the shorter sections on other tracks from the first two albums. As Comus (but few other bands in folk rock) demonstrated, complex dissonance is also a route into the garden outside of modernity, or into stories and characters inspired by François Rabelais' sixteenth-century comic epic *Gargantua and Pantagruel*. Gentle Giant's *Octopus* (1972) has a more concentrated take on folk music, but the band's interest is in a pan-European folk culture that consists of literature, customs and musical styles, where baroque instrumental parts alternate with English folk sections.

In terms of classical music, Gentle Giant deployed a broader set of reference points than other 1970s bands that sought to incorporate or match classical style, stretching from late medieval through baroque to the Romanticism of properly classical music, and forward to Ralph Vaughan Williams. Instead of this being a display of the band's virtuosic musical knowledge, it is the recognition that classical music is actually a type of European folk music. Already on this album, Gentle Giant had become less utopian: the music is less complex, yet angrily discordant compared to the earlier albums. From the beginning, they were interested in psychological self-analysis; this is worked through in 'Knots' (derived from R. D. Laing's anti-psychiatry) as a return to dysfunctional mental states. This interest combines with an increasingly bitter attack on the culture industry on later releases, which, ironically or otherwise, are much more straightforward rock albums. In Gentle Giant, then, we see the garden being sought, only for it to be left behind or lost – an Eden that is too caught up in consumerist culture to be recaptured.

Notes

1. Cited at http://www.ukrockfestivals.com/hyde-pk-6-29-68.html.

2. Sheila Whiteley, *Women and Popular Music: Sexuality, Identity and Subjectivity* (London: Routledge, 2000), 27.

3. Robert Palmer, *Rock & Roll: An Unruly History* (New York: Harmony Books, 1995), 228.

4. See Joel Rosenman, *Young Men With Unlimited Capital: The Story of Woodstock* (New York: Harcourt Brace Jovanovich, 1974).

5. Brian Hinton, *Message to Love: The Isle of Wight Festivals, 1968–70* (London: Castle Communications, 1995), 19.

6. Ibid., 138–9.

7. See Rod Allen, *Isle of Wight 1970: The Last Great Festival* (London: Clipper Press, 1970).

8. Ian Middleton, 'Jethro Tull: "We're Really Human . . .", *Record Mirror* (12 October 1968): www.tullpress.com/rm12oct68.htm.

9. Andrew Blake, *The Land Without Music: Music, Culture and Society in Twentieth-Century Britain* (Manchester: Manchester University Press, 1997), 162.

10. Ronald D. Cohen, *Rainbow Quest: The Folk Music Revival and American Society, 1940–1970* (Amherst, MA: University of Massachusetts Press, 2002), 253.

11. For a heavily illustrated tour of the Laurel Canyon scene, see Harvey Kubernik, *Canyon of Dreams: The Magic and the Music of Laurel Canyon* (New York: Sterling, 2009), and Michael Walker, *Laurel Canyon: The Inside Story of Rock-and-Roll's Legendary Neighbourhood* (London: Faber and Faber, 2006). For the development of the San Francisco countercultural scene, see Charles Perry, *The Haight Ashbury* (New York: Warner Books, 2005).

12. See www.fairportconvention.com/the_liege_and_lief_story.php.

13. Jeanette Leech, *Seasons They Change: The Story of Acid and Psychedelic Folk* (London: Jawbone, 2010), 127. Leech notes the contrast between a 'verdant landscape of deceptive tranquility' on the inside of *First Utterance*'s gatefold sleeve and the 'emaciated, hideous creative' on the front cover 'ready to torment others while also shivering and suffering himself' (129). More broadly, the links between paganism, occultism and Satanism are exemplified in the early 1970s releases of Black Widow and Black Sabbath, but musically these bands veer away from progressive folk.

14. Leech, *Seasons They Change*, 31.

15. See *A Stereo Introduction to the Exciting World of Transatlantic* (Contour Records, 1972).

16. Tony Banks et al., *Genesis: Chapter & Verse*, ed. Philip Dodd (London: Weidenfeld & Nicolson, 2007), 71.

17. Although the cover of *Nursery Cryme* is designed to reflect the content of the album, the listener reorients this process, starting with the cover.

18. Quoted in Robin Platts, *Genesis: Behind the Lines: 1967–2007* (Burlington, Ontario: Collector's Guide Publishing, 2007), 20.

19. Blake, *The Land Without Music*, 148.

20. See the booklet accompanying the four-album *Mike Oldfield Boxed* (1976), which contains *Tubular Bells*, *Hergest Ridge*, *Ommadawn*, and a collection of new songs, *Collaborations*.

21. Mike Oldfield, *Changeling: The Autobiography* (London: Virgin Books, 2007), 61.

Chapter 4

The Concept Album

Through the 1970s, several high-profile albums made the 'concept album' synonymous with progressive rock. The concept album allowed scope for narrative, for genre mixing, for instrumental development that echoed jazz and sonata forms, and for lyrical complexity that was not possible in shorter form or even in single extended tracks. From the early to mid-1970s, during the high phase of progressive rock, virtuosity spread into group composition, sometimes at the cost of musical individualism. The full-blown concept album would expand on a theme over many tracks, and match this with musical and formal structures that advanced over the course of an album. The repetition of instrumental and lyrical conceits would offer an immediate coherence on first listen, only for other resonances to emerge on subsequent hearings. For example, *Sgt. Pepper* reprises the title track, but the sitar gradually works its way into the album, and on a lyrical level music-hall and circus references link together the otherwise diverse slices of life that make up the album. The concept album completes the move seen in mood-piece albums by Frank Sinatra, or in instrumental developments by composers Les Baxter, Martin Denny and Joe Meek in the 1950s and early 1960s. Duke Ellington had more or less arrived at the concept album by 1943 (see Chapter 1), but his thematic albums were always part of some greater multimedia project.

Can an instrumental release be a concept album? To some extent it can, but this needs limiting, or else anything with a suggestive title could be a concept album. Earlier we suggested that Ornette Coleman's *Free Jazz* (1961) is based upon a displaced concept: the concept is about its musical realization and cannot be located anywhere in its content. Similarly, we can also find a conceptual element in the social and political purpose of improvisation by the Association for the Advancement of Creative Musicians in Chicago. Joe Meek's *I Hear a New World* (recorded in 1960, released in full in 1991) is self-reflexive in a different way: it is about the idea of expanding sound while also expanding the sound-world through experimental instrumentation and recording techniques. Les Baxter's work is different in conception, particularly on orchestrated albums such as *Le sacre du sauvage* (*Ritual of the Savage*, 1952) with its exotic jungle theme and native South American masks on the album cover. *Ritual of the Savage* is a fully conceptualized mock anthropological piece, but is it so different from evocative classical compositions? Oddly, it would seem that actual concept albums, the locus of complexity, need a strong dose of literalism in order to move beyond suggestiveness and towards actualization.

For this reason, we might be tempted to include Sinatra's *Come Fly with Me* (1958) in the history of the concept album. This album is a collection of twelve tracks, each of which features travel. The concept of flying suggests the exoticism not only of the places visited but also of the method of getting there. Flying connotes wealth and freedom, and shows us Sinatra's commitment to the imagined romantic partner. Karen McNally notes that 'the highly stylized' cover represents 'Sinatra as a character within a scene, illustrating the album's mood and narrative as though a publicity poster for a film'.[1] The front cover depicts 'the jet-setting swinger' Frank beckoning his female listener (he loosely holds a woman's manicured hand) against a backdrop of two TWA aircraft. The back cover tells us about the moods of certain pieces in the form of a flight log; Sinatra is identified as our pilot and the orchestrators as co-pilots set against the background of a flight map and compass; the flight takes us from autumn in Manhattan to April in Paris, through Capri, Monterey and Brazil, before ending the journey with 'lazy Sinatra sound' in Blue Hawaii, emphasizing that this trip is about musical tourism. As obvious as all this seems, *Come Fly with Me* already performs the work of later concept albums in making everything of the album count towards the whole. The listener is transported into a world of ever-opening possibilities; we will be going to places of luxury, culture and romance, framed by the opening title track and the closing 'It's Nice to Go Trav'ling' (but 'so nice to come home', as if the listener were being told that a glimpse is all that is needed to make everyday life bearable). The album reflects Hollywood's love affair with international tourism in the 1950s and also foreshadows the late twentieth-century flattening of globalization. A strange homogeneity pervades the album; every track is more or less in the same easy listening style, and Sinatra's languid singing offers variety only at the level of individual lines. The exotic world of *Come Fly with Me* is like being taken to McDonald's (which opened its first US store three years earlier) in a range of different countries – reflecting a lack of musical progression on the album, which echoes the random sequence of travelling songs rather than forming a tightly plotted narrative.

A similar problem might be seen to afflict late 1960s albums that sought to impart profound lessons about the meaning of life but more effectively described the very local conditions of 1960s English society. The essential difference is that The Beatles, The Kinks, The Zombies and The Who used this contradiction as a tool for album composition. *Sgt. Pepper* and *Pet Sounds* mark the crossover point where an album has both coherence and development (this is not the case with *Come Fly with Me*), but the fame of these two albums has obscured the conceptual elements of The Moody Blues' and Pink Floyd's 1967 albums from the same year (see Chapter 2), and has hidden the shifts within psychedelic pop towards the structure of progressive rock in the shape of the concept album. In fact, if we are searching for what might define progressive rock as English, then it is to the everyday narratives of The Kinks and The Zombies that we should first look.

The year 1968 saw the release of three important staging posts in the story of the concept album: The Kinks' *Village Green Preservation Society*, The Zombies' *Odessey and Oracle* and The Pretty Things' *SF Sorrow*, which is the first unquestionably complete concept album. The first two albums developed The Moody Blues' expression of Everyman's sense of time in *Days of Future Passed* by including specific people, situations and locations. The Kinks' album looks at England in a way that combines fondness for and a critique of parochialism: the title song focuses on 'preserving the old ways' and suggests a warm nostalgia, but also signals the conservative nature of 1960s English bourgeois society. Nostalgia and melancholy permeate the album, whether it is in the character of old and boring 'Walter', who has signed his life away, or in the combination of pride, authenticity and solitude of 'Last of the Steam-Powered Trains'. On this track, the narrator praises that which has been sidelined as the trains become renegades in a misguided and ultimately conservative dash towards unheeding capitalist progress. The remainder of the album divides between character studies and rock pieces: in the case of 'All of My Friends Were There', it is actually about playing rock music, while pictures cover over the lack of real memory on 'Picture Book' and the closing track 'People Take Pictures of Each Other'. *Village Green Preservation Society* is an album about being uprooted and about knowledge of the past allowing a presence in the now; it manages to avoid clichés about freedom, other than on the track 'Sitting by the Riverside', where, strangely, the possibility of too much liberty prompts the narrator to ask, 'please keep me calm, keep me pacified'. The grounding of the temporal passage on both social and individual levels fleshes out The Moody Blues' attempts on *Days of Future Passed* to achieve an extended, cohesive meditation on temporal change.

The Zombies' *Odessey and Oracle* is more musically focused: the same rich sound-world fills every track and, unlike *Come Fly with Me*, the song structures alter considerably, even though there is no explicitly linear progression between tracks. Lyrically, the first side of the album is unrelentingly melancholic, while side two has two harsher stories to tell, and the remaining tracks on that side meander thematically. Side one places yearning and isolation at its core, particularly the Eleanor Rigby-like song 'A Rose for Emily' and the solitude and misery of 'Brief Candles'. When the mood lifts, it turns out to be a dream, soothing 'the worries of my troubled brain/mind' on 'Hung Up on a Dream'. This takes us back to the music itself, which features harmonic singing, rousing choruses and often gentle instrumentation (there are a surprising number of moments with no percussion): music is the soothing dream, the temporary release played out against everyday loss, failure and nostalgia. The second side looks outward; the opening track is a diatribe against a woman who used to be a hippie (or at least a 'free spirit') but now chooses fancy clothes and the high life. The fourth track, 'Butcher's Tale (Western Front, 1914)', concerns shellshock and the horror of World War I – which was much less the consensual view in 1968 than now. The final two tracks describe love, but from a distance. The penultimate 'Friends of Mine' praises happy couples, but the narrator has been cheated and disappointed, while 'Time of the Season' is an ostensibly hopeful love song disrupted by the line 'who's your daddy, is he rich like me', which troubles the whole song, making it surreptitiously bitter in a way that does not cast the narrator in a positive light. In fact, this question problematizes the entire album's narration. Is it a reliable expression of social observation, or is the listener to infer that it is narrated by an unreliable misanthrope who undermines all that at first seemed truthfully constructed? It is, in fact, more likely to be a sequence of different narrators to match the album's sequence of situations and characters.

How can we interpret the melancholic anger of these two albums? Does the sentiment mark a general mourning of the passing of earlier certainties and, despite their rhetoric, a bemoaning of the demise of British rigour? This is at least likely, but what is important is that both albums possess an awareness of the embeddedness of narrator, character and performer alike in postwar British society, rather than pretending to exist above it. We can also position *Village Green Preservation Society* and *Odessey and Oracle* as part of the British version of May 1968 – the revolt and reaction to old models of rebellion found outlets in popular music, which was circulated increasingly through unofficial channels such as pirate radio stations. We would go so far as to argue that these two albums are aware of the dangers of commodification in their peculiar take on failed radicality; the insistent rebelliousness continues, together with the endless and dispiriting persistence of moribund conservatism.

The Pretty Things' *SF Sorrow* is ostensibly very different, a parallel universe where we follow the life of one particular person: the annoyingly named SF Sorrow. The task of this name is to signal the otherworldliness that became a major part of 1970s concept albums (as discussed below), but in this other world the struggle between mundanity, creativity and futility plays out in a sequence of thirteen tableaux. The imagistic songs are connected by prose (on the liner notes) that supplies the intervening story. The story, made up of song and prose elements, presents the Sorrow family, who move from 'up north' to another industrial town, dominated by 'factories of misery'. Sebastian F. is born and brought into the world of factories, even though he dreams about the moon, which is presented as a symbol of freedom against the madness of mundane life and the insanity induced by this grim existence. As he goes to war and then emigrates to 'Amerik', waiting for his girlfriend to arrive on the

'Windenburg', we can see that this universe is part of a sequence of parallel worlds. Side one is dominated by oppressive factories, which are not just miserable industrial buildings but the place from where a miserable society emanates: the factories literally produce the misery that permeates all else. The war that is fought in 'Private Sorrow' (this is the only time punning really works on the album) closes with military drumming and a roll call of the missing and dead. The hope of 'Amerik' amid the lamenting of a futile war is dashed in 'Balloon Burning', where the girlfriend dies in the 'Windenburg' disaster. On one level, *SF Sorrow* seems to be an almost comical tale of woe, but the music and lyrical sections are much lighter; most of the tracks begin with a sole guitar riff or sequence that indicates both solitude and individuality. Only 'Private Sorrow' connotes sadness in a musically obvious way.

Side two of *SF Sorrow* is darker. The first half is dominated by the demonic Baron Saturday, who takes Sorrow on a journey into a hellish netherworld in a dream sequence that nevertheless indicates that Sorrow already leads such a beleaguered life. This is signalled musically by the return of the opening guitar figure of 'Private Sorrow', slightly altered but recognizable in the connections between the 'factories of misery' and an increasingly empty internal world. Worse than this, the place he is already in is actually himself, empty, destroyed and aimless. Following an interlude-style track ('Well of Destiny', with backwards and slowed-down tapes), the album leads into the last three tracks about ageing and mental isolation. As such, rather than concentrating on Sorrow's personal breakdown, the album focuses on social nihilism and a cruel society that cares nothing for individuals.[2]

SF Sorrow initiates a long tradition of concept albums based on alienation, from King Crimson's *In the Court of the Crimson King* (1969) through Pink Floyd's *The Wall* (1979) to Radiohead's *OK Computer* (1997) and beyond, both in terms of isolation from the sources of power and where the powers at work in society heighten personal alienation. Very few albums of the 1970s matched the caricature of escapist fantasy worlds to which the middle-class would-be alienated could retire while reading J. R. R. Tolkien's *The Lord of the Rings* (1954–5), despite the trilogy's allegorical references to industrialization, world war and the Bible. The concept album is rarely about absolute escapism, though, even if it offers the prospect of freedom. Instead, we need to think of it in terms of immersion, not the sensory overload of psychedelic music but an immersion that engages the intellect as well as the senses. Whether the concept album is straight social critique, or musing on the state of the world, humanity or nature, or simply strolling around alternative cosmology, the recording creates a complete system within which the possibility of sustained narrative alters how an album is listened to. The music itself becomes more complex, even if only to connect up the song-cycle, and the lyrical narrative often demands complementary images on the sleeve to keep the whole album in play: for example, Genesis's *The Lamb Lies Down on Broadway* retells the whole story over the inner part of the gatefold; The Who's *Quadrophenia*

(1973) contains a photo essay; and Jon Anderson's *Olias of Sunhillow* (1976) features a sequence of ultra-vivid illustrations to flesh out the lyrics. The concept album often stretched beyond the single album to take up four sides of vinyl, and its integral artwork became a way of signalling the musical direction of progressive groups. Jethro Tull produced a stream of concept albums in the 1970s on different themes, including a thematic musical study of the concept album itself on its 1972 release *Thick as a Brick*. Magma spent the decade creating a space mythology, while the Canadian bands Saga and Rush spread a concept over tracks on several albums: Saga's Chapters ran over many albums (1978–2003) and Rush released three songs of its Fear trilogy in reverse order on consecutive albums (1981–4), and then reprised it with part four, 'Freeze', on its 2002 album *Vapor Trails* (see Chapter 10). As such, the concept is both the apotheosis of the album and the pushing of its limits.

These forms of continuity can be signalled in the use of an artist with a signature style just as much as in the cover art itself. The classic example is Roger Dean's work with Yes, portraying a succession of fantastic worlds that somehow belong to the same universe. Oddly, the closest Yes come to a fully conceptualized release prior to its 1973 double album *Tales From Topographic Oceans* is on *Close to the Edge* (1972), which contains almost no art at all – other than Dean's Yes logo – as if Yes's concept were playing out across the plain, if gradated, green cover as figure to ground (if there is a concept, it is about the destruction and possible recovery of a world ecology, so the emptied green field can work in both dimensions). The gatefold sleeve signals the immersive intent of an album. Literally, the listener becomes a reader of images, particularly when the cover picture spreads over two, or even four, 12-inch surfaces. As the concept album exceeds the world of the rock album, so it becomes a contained whole in which the listener is a willing captive. Many listeners switch off and do not read lyrics or look at the cover art while listening, but the purpose of the artwork is to involve the listener in a separate, self-contained world signalled in the act of opening up the internal surfaces of the double cover. The extravagant album art invites in the listener/reader even before the listening act, and has the potential to keep playing once the record has been re-sleeved. *Sgt. Pepper* began this expansion of the album into materiality beyond the playing surface by including extra-musical features: multiple images of the costumed band, the cast of twentieth-century cultural figures on the front cover posing for a photograph, and full lyrics on the back sleeve. This would be more than matched in King Crimson's debut album, *In the Court of the Crimson King*.

The cover of *In the Court of the Crimson King* is a signal of the dystopia that lies in the music – a bright-red face screams and distends over the two outside panels of the cover. On the inside, a smiling moon-faced figure beckons, either in welcome or in demand. The outside face of *In the Court of the Crimson King* is taken to be the 'schizoid man' of the opening track and the inner face is the Crimson King, with whom the album closes: the

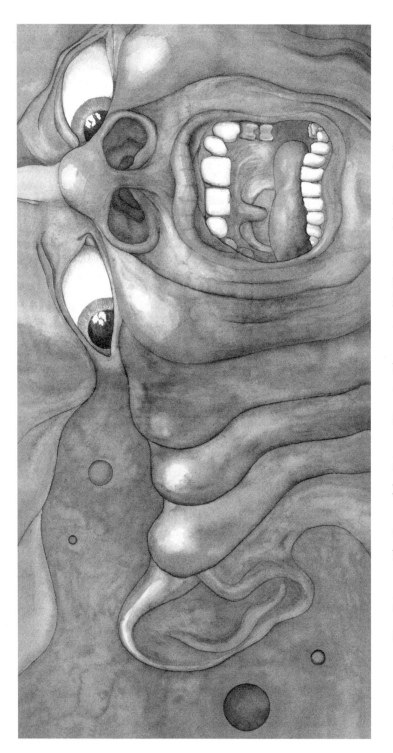

King Crimson, *The Court of the Crimson King: An Observation* (1969). Artwork by Barry Godber.

figure on the cover is presumed to be the alienated victim of the powerful figure inside.

The album opens with the sound of a declining but still throbbing machine, which gives way to the whole group blast of the defining riff of '21st Century Schizoid Man'.[3] This discordant, complex track maps out a world where power is on course to destroy all, and points directly to involvement in the Vietnam War:

> Blood rack barbed wire
> Politicians' funeral pyre
> Innocents raped with napalm fire
> Twenty first century schizoid man

The vocal is distorted, itself machine-like, emphasizing the infiltrating reach of power and the corruption of humanity. The second track, 'I Talk to the Wind', opens with flute and has a more organic feel. The gentle vocals and instrumentation suggest a pastoral interlude, an alternative to the schizoid world; but this track is just as bereft of hope, as 'my words are carried away' without issue.[4] 'Epitaph' follows with the vision of a decaying empire. All three tracks speak of confusion and question the direction humanity is taking. Side two opens with 'Moonchild', an even sweeter song on first listen, but the subtitle indicates that this is 'The Dream' – again, a false hope or mirage – or, at least, a deferred realization. And the final track, 'In the Court of the Crimson King', brings us directly to the source of power.

Bill Martin reads the album as an allegorical take on earth's fate, as seen in 1969, and as shown through a specific but fantastical science-fictional cosmology.[5] Martin is right to see the album's unity of purpose, but he overstates the literalness of the setting. If we return to the cover, and indeed to the name King Crimson, we need to take into account that 'King Crimson' is one of Beelzebub's, or the devil's, other names.[6] Is the inner figure really separate from the outer one on the cover? What if the 'crimson king' is both figures, a demonic presence within humanity, not outside of it? There is evidence that this king could be akin to John Milton's Satan in *Paradise Lost* (1667), as a dangerous but creative force; Robert Fripp even spoke of music coursing through the band and has suggested that the spirit of King Crimson is present at successful live concerts.[7]

There is no alternative world, as such, but a sequence of images that prompt the listener to reassess the contemporary world in the context of global, but mostly clandestine, warfare. This is demonstrated in the subtitles 'Mirror' for '21st Century Schizoid Man'; 'Dream' and 'Illusion' for 'Moonchild'; and the creaking power in both of the grandiose epics of 'Epitaph' and 'Court of the Crimson King'. These two tracks (closing each side) demonstrate how power has become rotten at the core, with buildings and tools cracking apart to reveal nothing within. The other three tracks, alternatively harsh and pastoral, illustrate the emptiness of all that lies outside power, while the lengthy instrumental section of 'Moonchild' presents a failed pastoral because nature no longer answers. As such, a set of specific connections link tracks, imagery, lyrics and music into a deconstruction of the late 1960s belief in the value of humanity, nature and society. Like the pastoral void on the track 'Stagnation' on Genesis's *Trespass*, King Crimson's musical critique can be heard in the failing pastorals surrounding 'Schizoid Man', and most explicitly in the beautifully portentous progression of 'Epitaph' and 'Court', the latter pausing, only to spring into diseased life with a final, harsh reprise of the main theme.

Like many concept albums in the early years of progressive rock, the concept is not absolutely present at every point in an explicitly connected musical progression, but the links on the album are deeply embedded, and the model of the concept album as a vehicle for alienation, dystopia, breakdown and critique is fully developed on *In the Court of the Crimson King*, with a harshness not present on *SF Sorrow*. From ELP's *Tarkus* (1971) to Pink Floyd's *Dark Side of the Moon* (1973), or from Marvin Gaye's *What's Going On* (1971) to The Who's *Quadrophenia*, the concept album would explore different ways of mining alienation, anomie and loss of autonomy. *Tarkus* takes part in a different trajectory – the separating of the conceptual world from the apparent real world – but, like King Crimson's first album, it deals with a world gone wrong. Technically, it is not even a complete concept album. The title track comprises a side-long piece; however, when the title track is such a substantial part of an album and the whole is unified by artwork based on the main track (as it is on *Tarkus*), it does not seem a stretch to regard it as such.[8] In this way, Yes's *Close to the Edge* and Rush's *2112* work as concept albums in a way that is not true of the 1972 Genesis album *Foxtrot*, even though it is dominated by the 24-minute 'Supper's Ready'.

Tarkus pictures an unfolding war where there is destruction and nothing else to show for it. The tank-armadillo hybrid Tarkus on the cover crushes all before it, until the hybrid manticore faces it down: 'like the creatures it destroys, Tarkus is cybernetic; it is as much machine as it is animal, and hence it is "unnatural"'. As Macan argues, 'Tarkus can be seen to symbolize a totalitarian society'.[9] The manticore is the counter to Tarkus, but it is no less threatening. There is no sign of anyone being either protected or freed, so we would argue that the story of *Tarkus* is one where machine and human have combined to create a nightmare existence of permanent and futile war. Could it be about the Vietnam War? Macan hesitates, clearly because the piece does not attempt to convey a story too directly or literally. ELP's vocalist Greg Lake has said that 'it's about the futility of conflict expressed in the context of soldiers and war'.[10] This is, of course, a profound subject, but it is so vast a topic that Lake has difficulty expressing it in his lyrics, which centre on foolishness, short-sightedness and futility. This is especially true of the 'Battlefield' section, where the narrator asks to 'clear the battlefield and let me see', but what is seen is nothing, just destruction. In fact, the most interesting element is the insistence on vision and being able to survey developments from the perspective of either a leader or a visitor from another planet. Is Lake's voice that visitor, bringing back the message that Earth will be doomed if we do not heed his words? Meanwhile, the music resolutely attempts to signify warfare through aggressive keyboard playing and military-style drumming – interspersed with calm, brooding sections, where the vocals mostly occur. Keith Emerson, in particular, was still feeling his way to conveying in rock format the scope of narrative development permitted in the classical music of the nineteenth and early twentieth centuries. *Tarkus* also signifies classical music, as does ELP's take on Modest Mussorgsky's *Pictures at an Exhibition* (1971), which, by virtue of being literally a transposition of classical pieces, connotes classical music even more strongly than just being it. This is what really riled critics of progressive rock: the literalness of ELP is a weaker statement of the band's classical music ambitions than Yes's attempts to match what an orchestra could do through ensemble composition.

The abstraction of war in *Tarkus* allows reflection on the part of the listener, even if the music is often didactic. As a counterpoint, Marvin Gaye dealt more directly with social breakdown and its relation to US involvement in Vietnam in his 1971 album *What's Going On*, which is closer in form to progressive concept albums than might be imagined. It is much more abstract than Gil Scott-Heron's socially critical albums of the same period, such as *Free Will* (1972) and *Winter in America* (1974). Gaye used precise formal strategies to unite the album, most obviously in the reprise of the musical theme of opening track 'What's Going On?' and in the closing track of side one, 'Mercy Mercy Me (The Ecology)'.[11] Where King Crimson's and ELP's albums cited above are 'post-Altamont' – part of the fading hippie idealism also heard in Van der Graaf Generator and Jethro Tull at the time – *What's Going On?* posits a parallel world, even with its realism: a critical alternative to domestic and foreign unrest and a vision of a resuscitated community. The album begins with a background voice murmuring 'damn good party' with funk and orchestral sounds and regular choral vocals, which all suggest a self-sufficient but open community. Gaye positions himself as part of an excluded community based on race: regular references to 'brothers' indicate this, and its reaching out marks a movement beyond individualism towards inclusiveness, partly based on the Civil Rights Movement's notion of the beloved community. He even sets up a community within himself as he divides into two voices, the second repeating the first voice's spoken words in song as a version of call and response on 'Save the Children'. At one level, Gaye's message seems dominated by the Christian God, but this is a minimalist god that signifies a fraternal love, which is replicated in 'all of us'. This album is about the application of that mercy or love in the form of active community, a theme that spreads through lyrical and musical reiterations. Unlike *Tarkus*, Gaye's *What's Going On?* maintains its lyrical focus on early

1970s America, but side two does not attempt the intertwining of form and content that makes side one effectively an essential part of progressive rock. Its cohesion as an album is emphasized in another reprise: the opening theme in the second track, 'Wholy Holy', which indicates the gradual growth of love over the course of the album. A circular return to the very beginning marks its overall conclusion.

Many concept albums envision another world lost elsewhere in time and space, or in topographies only marginally different from our own. Individual songs or entire albums are built on myths in a way that was not possible before the development of the extended rock form. Very often, the narratives would derive from already existing stories – sometimes literally, as in David Bedford's *Rime of the Ancient Mariner* (1975), Jeff Wayne's *War of the Worlds* (1978), and Rick Wakeman's use of historical figures on *The Myths and Legends of King Arthur and the Knights of the Round Table* (1975) or his *Journey to the Centre of Earth* (1974). Progressive rock, then, not only references and deploys different musical genres but also opens up cultural history as a resource. These sources are sometimes linked to an established genre such as the pastoral, or signal an ancient past through the contrasting use of instrumentation (as practised by the Belgium band Univers Zéro), or centre around the figure of a storyteller (as on Jethro Tull's *Songs from the Wood* or Ange's 1974 album *Au-delà de mon délire*). Sometimes the sources are stories that revolve around a fictional character, as in David Bowie's *Ziggy Stardust and the Spiders from Mars* (1972); Peter Hamill's *Nadir's Big Chance* (1975); Nilsson's cartoon-based *The Point!* (1971); and Gong's 'Radio Gnome Invisible' trilogy, featuring the 'Zero the Hero' character (1973–4).

The Greek band Aphrodite's Child refers to the Christian Book of Revelations, particularly its violent apocalypse, on its 1972 album *666*. This album possesses a fatalism completely at odds with the version of faith on *What's Going On?* It does not attempt to deal with the detail of the biblical story but assembles a world based upon it, with key symbols (the four horsemen, 'the Beast', 'the Lamb', seven of everything, the final trump) acting as shorthand for the Christian apocalypse playing out the final days of earth. On a very general level, the album is an allegory of war and destruction, but there is little attempt to connect to the world of 1972. This refusal to break the unity of the constructed world might be seen as an aesthetic strength, but it also means that to consider the concept album as an allegory is a speculative enterprise. Were we to think deterministically, we might imagine that Aphrodite's Child and its album *666* somehow reflected the turmoil in Greece at the time, but it is so deeply coded that the historical events are not even inscribed in lyrics or music. The double album veers from freak-outs to choral sections via narrative passages; moving through rock; stopping by funk; and then throwing this altogether in the near 20 minutes of 'All the Seats Were Occupied', which makes up the bulk of side four. 'Loud Loud Loud' establishes the telling of the story; the sole plaintive voice is pitched against a chorus, indicating the mass consequences of the apocalypse and the isolation of the individual in the face of the impending end. The key to the album is alternation between quieter, mournful sections and tracks and aggressive instrumental or vocal rock tracks. The progression of the apocalypse is marked, predictably enough, by increased cacophony towards the end of the third side, notably in the weird '∞', composed mainly of female vocal shrieking, growling, panting, shouting, whispering and intoning 'I am to come at once' – the most effective part of the band's narrative escalation, as orchestrated by Vangelis. 'All the Seats Were Occupied' meanders through rock and funk before breaking up at various points with reprises of sections of the previous three sides, which speed up and by the end collide. The wistful ballad 'Break' acts as a coda. Side four seems to be the aftermath of the end, with the chosen survivors in the occupied seats. Or perhaps the seats are within some other type of escape vessel, with the last people 'left behind'? The very last lines, with seemingly no narrative link to the rest of the album, end on a high (even if it is a melancholic high), as 'Fly/High/And then/You make it' is intoned as the final words.

The scope of 666 is impressive, even if the lyrics and narration heavily date the album. Unlike Keith Emerson, Vangelis tried to replicate the scale of an orchestra, rather than signifying a similarity to classical music through endlessly varying instrumentation, including traditional instruments, keyboards, rock, orchestral and jazz instruments, bells, objects, and a diverse range of singing styles. Aphrodite's Child also attempted to recreate the narrative drive of Wagnerian opera, mobilizing myths as formal structures. The same is true of concept albums based on the theme of music itself, such as Magma's nine-album sequence telling the tale of aliens who come to rescue Earth through music in ways that link jazz, modern opera, rock and traditional European sounds (the aliens are responsible for the entirety of Earth music). Jon Anderson's solo album *Olias of Sunhillow* never comes to Earth, but invents fantastic beings that travel the universe in search of music.

The two most famous concept albums were released within a year of each other – Genesis's *The Lamb Lies Down on Broadway*, in late 1974, and Yes's *Tales from Topographic Oceans*, in late 1973 – and each develops intricate narrations in structures that are both lyrical and instrumental. Each album establishes a parallel reality, with the former an uncanny but nearby world underneath New York City, and the latter a mystical conception of a world that lies beyond appearances. Other than this cosmological unveiling, and their reception as the final decadence of progressive rock, the pair have little in common: Genesis's album is dominated by Peter Gabriel's vocals, lyrics and accompanying version of the story inside the cover; *Tales from Topographic Oceans* features large sections of instrumental work, despite the volume of lyrics, and even when there are lyrics the music often dominates (and the musicality of the lyrics signifies more than their linguistic meaning).

The Lamb Lies Down on Broadway follows Rael, a New Yorker of Puerto

Rican origin, into a netherworld somewhere close to Manhattan. The narrative is dreamlike, held together by a double quest to escape the netherworld and for self-awareness. Rael encounters mystery, torture, physical events, monstrous creatures in the form of the sexually voracious Lamia and the Slippermen distorted by their desire, as well as a mass of near-faceless people caught in the machinations of this parallel city. The story is presented in three forms: the lyrics, an accompanying prose version (written by Gabriel), and a portmanteau of six pictures that nearly match scenes conveyed by the words. The pictures are being looked at by Rael, thereby positioning him both inside and outside of the story – both subjective and objective – as one of many doublings set up in *Lamb*. New York is doubled as reality and netherworld; Rael is doubled in the form of his brother John, who turns out to be a mirror of the protagonist; Rael himself is doubled by 'the real' – '*it* is Real, *it* is Rael' (on the final track, '*it*'); and this closing track doubles the album, acting as commentary on all that preceded it. Numerous moments are reprised: for example, the title track returns in 'The Light Dies Down on Broadway' (mixed in with a return of 'The Lamia'), while the structure and key of the third verse of the title track recurs as the opening to 'Carpet Crawlers'.[12] The first of these reprises links together sides one and four; the second connects sides one and two.

Peter Gabriel as the Slipperman, *The Lamb Lies Down on Broadway* tour, Copenhagen, Denmark (January 1975).

According to Kevin Holm-Hudson (and echoing Peter Gabriel), *Lamb* represents a significant change in Genesis's approach, consciously departing from its mining of English and classical myths, literature and the everyday of previous albums:

> with *The Lamb Lies Down on Broadway*, Genesis made a decisive break from their earlier image of myth and fantasy, nurtured by such albums as *Nursery Cryme* and *Foxtrot. Selling England by the Pound* had been a transitional step in that direction.[13]

This idea works when reflecting on the most explicit level of the album, and Holm-Hudson points to the simplified music as 'reflecting the album's streetwise protagonist'.[14] But *Lamb* has a more complex relationship to realism that extends the band's practice on earlier albums. For all its realism, the story unfolds in a contemporary parallel world, and the events cannot be read either as a stand-alone story or as a metaphor for New York street life. The further we move into the story, so Manhattan and its doubled self become increasingly intertwined. Like *Selling England by the Pound*, the mundane world of *Lamb* is saturated by myths, dreams, legends and fictions, and the 'real' is elevated to myth, just as myth takes on the status of reality. Genesis thereby offers the listener (and reader) a displaced social realism, comparable to the higher (and deeper) reality that the 1920s Surrealists set out to reveal.

For this to happen, Rael does not leave behind the real world: the two planes cross over and define each other, like the over and under of the Möbius strip rather than the above and below of a flat sheet. The status of the two worlds depends on the moment Rael first slips from one to another, when a thick cloud forms over the city and 'a wall of death is lowered in Times Square' ('Fly on a Windshield'). Holm-Hudson reads this as a moment when everyone dies, including Rael, but 'no-one seems to care/They carry on as if nothing was there' ('Fly on a Windshield').[15] In the immediate aftermath, all periods of Manhattan appear, studded with movie stars and cultural icons on 'Broadway Melody of 1974'. A crack opens between worlds and between different moments of history – only Rael can see this and is able to move through it. In this way, the truth of the world is revealed as the eternal return, everyone repeating every moment forever. Like Friedrich Nietzsche, Rael is now able to dwell in the eternal return rather than live it passively.[16] This dwelling is painful, though, lived in an ever-closing prison ('In the Cage'), which suddenly and arbitrarily dissolves.

Side two opens with 'Back in N.Y.C.', suggesting a flashback, but it is more an access to the past that is still present: a view of a past that is somewhere happening right now. The reality of New York gang life revisited in this track is also threatened by being a simulation; Gabriel describes this point in the story as one where 'our hero is moving into an almost perfect reconstruction of the streets of New York'.[17] As the album nears its conclusion, Rael walks along a gorge but is also somewhere in the Manhattan subway spraying graffiti. All hope of a real world free of myth, illusion, sex, fear and every-thing else (in other words, the mundane world with the veil back in place) disappears, not once but twice. First, in 'The Light Dies Down on Broadway', Rael wearily opines 'is this the way out from the endless scene?/Or just an entrance to another dream?' John drifts away in the rapids, and Rael returns to save him; the hope of the normal world fades forever at exactly the point where Rael realizes that John and he are one and the same: 'Hang on John! We're out of this at last/Something's changed, that's not your face/It's mine! It's mine'. The only possible real is a reflection with no original, like the figure of Rael that has stepped outside the sixth image on the cover to observe other images of himself. The 'it' then closes the album on the track 'it', the doubling of the track emphasized by Rael's double cry of 'It's mine!'. As well as com-menting on the album ('it is chicken, it is eggs/it is in between your legs'), 'it' acknowledges 'itself' in multiple ways as a progressive rock album; pre-empts criticisms about the album's conceptual pretention; and, finally, closes on the repeated line 'it's only knock and knowall, but I like it': a line that parodies The Rolling Stones' hit of summer 1974, 'It's Only Rock 'n' Roll (But I Like It)', and invents a new linguistic register to act as a warning to 'knowall' listeners who might invest too much meaning into Gabriel's lyrics. In this way, Lamb is a profound meditation on personal identity (either the Nietzschean eternal return or the then current explorations of 'personality disorders') and a sustained narrative joke, connecting the serious and whimsical faces of prog.

Lamb offers a picture of a hidden netherworld that is dark, monstrous and entwined with the real, as exemplified in New York City and based largely on Gabriel's lyrics. Turning to the 1973 Yes album Tales from Topographic Oceans, we see another world that has been hidden. Instead of darkness and travail, however, this is a higher world, an all-encompassing reality with which humanity has lost touch. This album charts the attempt to recover this animistic universe. Necessarily more abstract than Lamb, it flirts with what Bill Martin calls 'an apolitical New-Ageist otherworldliness'.[18] With little connection to history as lived by humans, Tales from Topographic Oceans risks not speaking to those listeners who were realizing their identities through the communal living suggested by the album. Martin is suspicious that 'without dealing with the real struggles that people must confront, including that of "our class", transcendence is hollow, and the "alternative view" is merely a mind-trip'.[19] This is precisely the problem that arises for many with regard to the avant-garde aspirations of progressive rock; given that Martin is a fervent supporter of Yes, it illustrates the suspicion of decadence that even fans of progressive rock can feel in the face of the mystical onslaught of Topographic. However, the album is not so simply ethereal, despite its basis on a superficial reference to Hindu mysticism. Its often dissonant and forceful monumental-ism makes it a subtle exploration of ecological identity and phenomenological Being-in-the-world. Though the lyrics are resolutely and mystically arcane, the structure of the songs and the inclusion of the lyrics indicate much more of a '*working through*, not a contemplative leap beyond'.[20] It is the structuring, rather than the explicit content, that creates the meditation proposed to the listener.

Topographic consists of four pieces, one per side of the album (a symmetrical arrangement ignored in the most recent CD reissue, which has sides one to three on the first CD). Each is introduced by a short summary of how the 'story' is expressed musically, on the lyric sheet on the inside of the gatefold cover. Each record forms a system within the whole, with sides one and two focusing on the search to rediscover the lost unity of the earth with humanity; sides three and four develop the interaction of human with 'what lies beyond', and the search for knowledge and respect for nature through ritual. This structure is established on record one by the reprises of elements of side one as side two nears its end, and on sides three and four by percussion and dissonance giving rise to resolution. All four sides end with repetition of a phrase ('For you and you and you'; 'Surely, surely'; 'Along without you/along without you'; 'Nous sommes du soleil' four times), showing not only the unity of all four parts but also that structure is unity. Each side has a resolution, even if 'Ritual', on side four, seems to offer more of a sense of completion. This indicates that the four sides do not make a linear narrative but parallel each other in lateral form, stretching (skywards from the sea) through reiterations. The album opens with 'The Revealing Science of God – Dance of the Dawn', and the opening section acts as an invocation, tracking humanity leaving the sea, leaving the light, and becoming earthbound. Like Yes's previous album, *Close to the Edge*, this project centres on a mystical general ecology where humans and all other life-forms live harmoniously together. The first record of *Topographic* deals with this terrestrial loss and also with an onward search – it is not lost forever, but a lostness that defines human existence as occurring in the shadow of the loss of something to be regained. We were not ejected from the sea but 'fled from the sea whole' and 'danced from the ocean'. If there is a utopia to be rediscovered, the loss and search are central to its discovery. The alternative of continuing to exist in the ocean would be an inauthentic existence; the distancing of identity from itself is what makes identity possible. In other words, to regain the ocean requires an apprenticeship in the world as we see it, the world of 'thrownness into Being', as Martin Heidegger would put it. This mode of existence will not be easy, as there will be war, the destruction of nature, and amnesia about our place in the world.

The return to the higher harmony of the ocean is hinted at by the music; 'what happened to this song we once knew so well' is a recurring motif of 'The Revealing Science of God', and the concept of 'the song' recurs on all four sides. Side one illustrates the quest to awaken an awareness of the lost ocean. The several melodies that constitute the song intertwine, as refrains from one section migrate to the next one, and two sections repeat as higher-level refrains. These ultimately mesh in the return at the end, signified in the line 'what happened to this song'. The quest is restless, though, as the connections unfold gradually over 22:22 minutes. The progress to awareness can be glimpsed in the slower section that begins at 14:55, in the sound of the acoustic guitar that segues into a gentle verse and self-consciously comments on the music ('and through the rhythm of moving slowly'), and then has a further minute and a half before the keyboards build up to a sequence of reiterated elements of earlier parts of the song. The invocation returns, which is not completion as such but rather the possibility of remembering and return.

The accompanying text to 'The Remembering – High the Memory' connects humanity to the entire history of earth. This is the moment to note that for all the mysticism of the album, its narrative more closely concerns evolution than it does creation, but an evolution that is permanent and spiritual as well as physical. Human life is mirrored in the life of the planet and vice-versa, and the restoration of our consciousness of this mirroring is 'the topographic ocean'. The ocean is not separate from or previous or secondary to human thought but a chora-like structure of possibility brought into being by the possibilities that could fill it. 'The Remembering' is the only place where the urban environment is explicitly mentioned; despite the loss that it represents, urban life is shown as a necessary experience through the section that pivots on the line 'out in the city running free' (5:40 to 7:44), together with a reprise by Rick Wakeman of the theme that follows the realization section of 'The Revealing Science of God'. The recognition of urbanism as only one of a huge set of possibilities appears in the next section, where 'other skylines' emerge and a 'relayer' moves us forward through them.[21] As the track nears its end, the 'remembering' takes the form of the return of elements from side one: the 'what happened' refrain returns (18:30 to 18:46), and, in the recall of the instrumental part that accompanies the 'we moved fast' line, our sense of the greater reality is heightened as the need for explanation (or lyrics) falls away.

'The Ancient – Giants under the Sun' opens with crashing percussion that recurs later in 'Ritual'. 'The Ancient' is the most dissonant part of the album, and the least song-like. It brings in many other civilizations, slightly mitigating the overly Christian elements of sides one and two and Jon Anderson and Steve Howe's quasi-Hindu take on spiritual truth. The multiplicity of beliefs indicates possible harmony, as evident at 4:15 by the line 'as one with the knowledge of the source/Attuned to the majesty of music/They marched as one with earth', which emerges from thudding drums. Dissonance permeates every aspect of the track until the closing section (acoustic guitar and vocals dominating) indicates that we are not in noble savage territory, as even the ancients who had a grasp of higher matters ended up fighting ('Where does reason stop and killing just take over?'). Once more, this loss of innocent unity seems to be inevitable: on one hand, if Jon Anderson were writing philosophy then we would question why reason is deemed to be a central part of essential knowledge, rather than as something that regiments humanity; on the other hand, the presence of reason as a given for humanity, even if it fails over time, indicates that *Topographic* does not need God, and nor is it about unthinking acceptance of the true nature of things. The track closes with a verse that suggests the insignificance of human thought ('Or does it all come out along without you'). The address to 'you' in the closing line connects it back to side one.

'Ritual' continues the emphasis on percussion (percussive playing of the bass, in particular) and concludes with a section dominated by vocals, reflecting the structure of 'The Ancient'. Internally, it begins and ends with 'nous sommes du soleil' ('we are of the sun'). This, in turn, returns us to the very beginning, to 'Dawn of light', the opening phrase of the album. Like 'The Ancient', the time of 'Ritual' is less about lyrics and more about musical process reflecting (or bringing) the universal process of being – in a way not dissimilar to Mike Oldfield's use of Hergest Ridge as a paradoxical place of temporal permanence and transition. Cyclical, lateral, and also developing over time, *Topographic* is about time, being in time, even if only tangentially in the local version of time known as history. For all its obscurantism, the album is still about time, rather than looking for timeless truth ('Change we must as surely time does'). Its aim is to present an all-encompassing mythology of individual and world in unity, to be achieved through human practice in the shape of 'Ritual'.

A long instrumental passage opens (vocals arrive at 5:25), and 'nous sommes du soleil' announces the altered existence now close to hand, crossing easily from the epic and universal to the mundanity of a life lived well. Within this, though, resolution is still not achieved ('Life seems like a/Fight, fight, fight'). The section ends with the prospect of harmony ('As clearer companions/Shall call to be near you'), as well as with the possible absence of meaning or an eradication of the voice of nature, which do not appear to matter 'at all' – this is repeated several times until the extended instrumental that begins at 11:09 and features all the band members playing lead, often at the same time (a defining part of the anarchistic community of Yes, where there is equality rather than class distinction between lead and rhythm). Finally, after a section where percussion dominates, Steve Howe's guitar chimes out alone, and the ritual nears completion. The return of the voice (17:38) completes a journey ('Going home'). The resolution occurs in the final 'nous sommes du soleil', where we both see the light of the sun and become that light, as we were in a beginning that emerges only after it has always already gone. The group gradually becomes louder through this section, and the song and album close with the band, without vocals, reaching into openness. This finale is not so much a coda as a part that could otherwise be the middle of a song, and, finally, Chris Squire's bass chimes the end and the rest fades around it.

In many ways the apogee of progressive rock's ambitions, *The Lamb Lies Down on Broadway* and *Tales from Topographic Oceans* also signal an endpoint, prompting the question: how could these albums be exceeded?

Mobilizing existing myths into new forms with complex structures, these albums were possibly too avant-garde to be accepted as popular rock music, despite selling extremely well. The twin individualism of punk rhetoric and a nascent neo-liberalism would be a call to order against such conceptual ambition, representing a demand for the listener to be in charge again (Yes played *Topographic* in full in live performances before it was released, as did Genesis with *Lamb*, albeit in the latter case because of a delay in its release date).[22] The concept album was far from finished, though, and nor were the engagement with myth, the extravagance of album covers, or progressive rock performance, as we will discuss in the following chapters.

Notes

1. Karen McNally, *When Frankie Went to Hollywood: Frank Sinatra and American Male Identity* (Urbana: University of Illinois Press, 2008), 103.

2. Even though parts of the Baron Saturday sequence on *SF Sorrow* might suggest a bad acid trip, this hallucinogenic experience exposes what is true in the world of the album.

3. Sid Smith, *In The Court of the Crimson King* (New York: Helter Skelter, 2007), 59.

4. Martin argues that 'I Talk to the Wind' 'can be heard both on the level of personal melancholy and as a herald that something in the world is seriously out of joint' (Martin, *Listening to the Future*, 158).

5. Martin, *Listening to the Future*, 160.

6. Smith, *In the Court of King Crimson*, 46.

7. Ibid., 78–9. In response to the King Crimson concert in Chicago on 7 August 2008 Robert Fripp said, 'I felt the presence of King Crimson entering into the music, and almost wept', www.dgmlive.com/archive.htm?show=1301.

8. For discussion of *Tarkus*, see Macan, *Rocking the Classics*, 87–95.

9. Ibid., 89.

10. Quoted by Bruce Pilato, *Tarkus* liner notes (2001 CD reissue).

11. However well CD covers represent the original vinyl issues, through facsimile covers or accompanying text, such moves are seriously compromised in unifying an album as one sequence, rather than as a set of two.

12. Kevin Holm-Hudson, *Genesis and* The Lamb Lies Down on Broadway (Aldershot: Ashgate, 2008), 57.

13. Ibid., 55.

14. Ibid., 60.

15. Ibid., 83.

16. After Nietzsche writes of the 'eternal return', where every moment coexists forever, he takes on its power. See Nietzsche, *The Will to Power* (New York: Vintage, 1968), especially §1067.

17. Taken from one of Gabriel's onstage narrations, quoted by Holm-Hudson, *Genesis and* The Lamb Lies Down on Broadway, 104.

18. Martin, *Music of Yes*, 156.

19. Ibid., 151.

20. Ibid., 147.

21. Martin argues that *Tales from Topographic Oceans* is completed by *Relayer*, the next

album, particularly in the harshest of Yes tracks, 'The Gates of Delirium', with its depiction of war and its accompanying brutalities (Martin, *Music of Yes*, 156).

22. Holm-Hudson argues that record companies grew tired of the expense of the recording and material cost of the integration of artwork into the album, and, far from being threatened by it, welcomed punk's simplicity as a way of increasing profit margins (Holm-Hudson, *Genesis and* The Lamb Lies Down on Broadway, 4, 19, 39–44).

Chapter 5

Myth and Modernity

In the previous two chapters we discussed the ways in which progressive rock bands in the early 1970s explored the relationship between nature and the technologies they used to create their soundscapes. Conceptual material helped to project alternative worlds, but musical arrangements were often self-referential in the creation of drama and resolution. This was rarely a directly associative relationship in which the instrument plays a character (as it does in Russian composer Sergei Prokofiev's 1936 children's musical story *Peter and the Wolf*) but more often one where words and music intersect on the levels of sound, meaning and emotion.[1] Although progressive bands usually worked together as an ensemble with complementary instrumentation, tension can be seen as a key ingredient of progressive music in terms of the narrative extension of songs and the complex musical systems that drive the stories. There are examples when the music overshadows the lyrics (*Tales from Topographic Oceans*), and others where the words propel the music (*The Lamb Lies Down on Broadway*), but arguably the most successful progressive rock albums are those where the two dimensions – the musical and linguistic, the formal and semantic – are held in creative tension. In Chapter 7, we examine these issues within the context of musical performance, but in this chapter we want to use this notion of tension to explore the ways in which progressive bands in the early to mid-1970s were drawn to myths and the retelling of familiar stories.

One of the central tensions in progressive rock is between nature and machines, harking back to modernist culture of the early twentieth century. For every romantic yearning for a more noble courtly age or a visionary future, there is usually an expression of lost innocence or of alienation in a world increasingly dominated by technology and governed by invidious forms of authority. The literary dimension of progressive rock from the late 1960s through the mid-1970s sometimes directly references modernist culture: T. S. Eliot's 'The Waste Land', for example, is used as a structuring device for Genesis's 'Supper's Ready' (1972) and is filtered through the figure of the mythical seer Tiresias and the 'young man carbuncular' sequence in 'The Cinema Show' (1973). Eliot is an interesting case of a modernist poet who was experimental in the aesthetic realm but conservative on the level of personal politics and in his literary attempts to preserve an endangered past in the face of modernity. The modernist trajectory of progressive rock is often more expansive than this, though, combining science fiction and fantasy motifs through a combination of old, reworked and original stories, which often rescue a lost past or project a hypothetical future that forewarns of wrong turns society might take and offers new possibilities for individual and collective activity. A number of topics discussed in Chapters 3 and 4 reflect these modernist tensions: music that is both within time and an escape from time; the complex relationship between subjectivity and objectivity; the fall from innocence into experience; war as an agent of renewal and destruction; and psychosis as both a threat to identity and an outlet for creativity. These ambivalences reveal an uncomfortable relationship to modernity, in which recognizable modernist topoi (alienation, exile, fantasy, escape) are combined with recycled traditional forms (myth, folktale, ballad, suite). These temporal and formal relationships offer a complex politics – in some respects radical, in others conservative – and also raise an interesting set of aesthetic questions about the relationship between words and music within the framework of collaborative composition.

One way of thinking about myth is to see it as an exploration of a mid-world (see Chapter 2) at the interface between everyday preoccupations and imaginative fantasy realms. The fulcrum between these two elemental dimensions is evident in The Beatles' juxtaposition of earthy themes in 'Strawberry Fields Forever' with flights of fancy such as 'Blue Jay Way', a track on which George Harrison's sitar aims to transport the listener into another time and place. Within this musical mid-world, progressive rock groups were able to explore aesthetic tensions rather than resorting to pure immediacy (the everyday, the near to hand, the prosaic) or transcendence (the visionary, the mystical, the theological). Myth can also be described as a discursive mid-world in its intersection of spatial and temporal planes and by exploring the relationship between higher truths (founding myths) and fabrication (fictive myths). More than those of any other popular musical form, progressive bands were drawn to myths as basic structuring devices and also as a temporally elastic tool for exploring creation stories, historical change, alternative identity positions and possible futures.

There are examples of epiphanic moments in progressive rock akin to those in Romantic verse, in which the poet/musician and listener experience a blinding flash of insight: for example, 12:27 into *Ommadawn*, when the main choral theme and tribal drumming breaks through Mike Oldfield's synthesizers, or during the instrumental section on Yes's 'Gates of Delirium' (*Relayer*, 1974). However, the extended dimension of concept albums and song-cycles use the layering of stories (sometimes drawn from Romantic poetry) most often to transport and trouble the listener. Rarely wholly utopian or dystopian in the stories they tell, extended progressive tracks often defy strict allegorical readings, usually providing skewed readings of classical, historical or contemporary myths. This view is consistent with Paul de Man's poststructuralist take on allegory (discussed in his 1979 book *Allegories of Reading*) in which a stable underlying story (the 'real' story behind the 'fictive' story) cannot be fully recouped in its recycled form.[2] The act of storytelling drew de Man to Walter Benjamin's 1923 essay 'The Task of the Translator', in which Benjamin argued that cultural translation is always a singular event.[3] The retelling of mythical stories within new musical contexts might be read as convenient material for early 1970s bands, providing a countercultural statement but without direct political engagement. However, following Benjamin, every re-reading of the past can be read as a singular act that transforms history into something new. This is true of musical translation, in which tonal change and interplay between music and voice create a new 'textual event' (in de Man's words) that accretes change rather than merely repeating a standardized pattern. It is particularly true of progressive rock in its reworking of myths into new arrangements that contain spoken, musical, written and pictorial elements, enacted through a combination of song, instrumentation, lyrics and artwork.[4]

This mode of retelling also connects to Benjamin's essay 'The Storyteller' (1936), in which he describes the storyteller as overburdened by modernity but whose bardic calling is to force the past into the present in order to better engage readers and listeners. In progressive rock, sometimes the invitation into an alternative world asks the listener to suspend his or her critical functions to delight in soundscapes, but prog lyrics rarely leave the listener without a signal that this world is problematic or out of reach. If we read progressive music through Benjamin, then we can see that the linguistic-musical continuum often reaches out to the past and the immediate present, setting off historical and contemporary resonances, but it also establishes an alternative world through an act of translation: what Benjamin described as a 'removal from one language into another through a continuum of transformations'.[5] Progressive rock not only transforms myths but also draws the reader into the alternative, hypothetical world of the album through suggestive imagery and cover art – both during and beyond the length of time it takes to play the disc or discs. The tension between immediate experience (the total immersion of psychedelic music) and critical distance (the critical deciphering of meanings and resonances) is often signalled in the album's artwork and on the songs themselves, particularly 'prelude' songs, which set the tone for a concept album or song-cycle, and 'signature' pieces, which amplify the central theme.

To illustrate this, we want to take two tracks from two albums released in 1977 that function both as preludes to the more substantial parts of the respective albums (even though one track opens side two) and as distinctive musical statements that link to the other tracks and the cover art. The year

1977 might have been the peak of punk – a year which, according to Edward Macan, marked the 'fragmentation of the genre' of prog – but it also saw the release of a number of interesting progressive albums that grappled with lyrical and musical complexities.[6] Suitably, then, a reading of Yes's *Going for the One* and Rush's *A Farewell to Kings* provides an entry point for thinking about the place of myth in progressive rock.

'Wonderous Stories', the first track on side two of Yes's *Going for the One*, appears on first hearing to be a straightforward song that entices us to listen to the enchanting tales of the singer. But the song is full of paradoxes: the singer awakes but seems to be within a dream throughout the song; as he drifts on the river of waking and sleeping, he is both active ('turned on upstream') and passive ('laid me down by the river'); sounds silence the singer just as the stories entrance him; the lands of which the storyteller speaks seem 'not far' away, but they are also mythical lands 'in his mind'; and he seems unable to see clearly yet 'sees deeply into the future'. Throughout the song, the lyrics are elusive and ambiguous: a phrase such as 'bound for my forgiver' (rather than the more meaningful 'bound by my forgiver') suggests a problematic interpersonal relationship that threatens to float free of grammatical sense ('bound' could mean the destination of a journey) but nevertheless resonates musically through the song. The singer also has a complex association with the stories of the song's title: he has to 'beg to leave' in the first verse 'to hear your wonderous stories'; in the second verse, the singer is at a gate where he can see simultaneously into the past and future, but suddenly he checks the time and has to leave to hear the wondrous stories; and in the extended third verse, the stories envelop the singer in the first few lines and lead to his spirit's soaring into the sky, before he requests that he is brought back to earth ('I bid it to return') to hear stories of this world rather than of other lands. The 'wonderous stories', then, offer the possibility of transcendence but root the singer and listener in a material world in which story, music, perception and understanding are intertwined. The song's lyrical qualities promise an innocent escape, but as the song progresses the syncopation becomes more complex and the cadences never quite transport the listener beyond the here and now. This reading locates the song within a mid-world, which corresponds with Jennifer Rycenga's interpretation of Jon Anderson's lyrics as producing an aura: 'a transient, shifting kaleidoscopic play of meanings, tinged with physical and dream affect, but concerned with vital meanings, creating flashes of understanding but nothing denotative enough to be static or permanent'.[7]

Similar thematic tensions can be found in the title track of Rush's *Farewell to Kings*, which functions similarly to 'Wonderous Stories' in self-consciously inviting the listener to enter an alternative world. Whereas the album cover of the Hipgnosis-designed *Going for the One* depicts a rear view of a naked man staring at the blank planes of skyscrapers (the skyscrapers meld with the back and inside covers of the triple-gatefold cover), the Canadian graphic artist

Hugh Syme uses more recognizably mythical imagery on the front cover of *A Farewell to Kings*, in which an industrial wasteland (depicted by a midrise apartment block and pylon in the background and a dilapidated building and debris in the foreground) is juxtaposed with the focal image of a marionette puppet dressed as a king, sitting on a burnished throne. A cape thrown over one side of the throne shields the figure from the wasteland, but he has lost his sovereignty: his body has fallen over to the left, his crown on the floor out of reach on the other side of the throne; his costume is awry and ragged; and the marionette strings are seemingly disused – an image reinforced on the reverse of the album cover, where we see red strings descending limply against a black field, without a puppeteer in sight. *Going for the One* juxtaposes the perceptual strain of staring at skyscrapers (represented by solid and broken coloured lines heading off in diverse directions) with the romantic twilight vista of a lake isle on the inside cover, an inset of the five band members photographed against a scene of Swiss lakes and mountains, and lyrics printed on a peach-coloured record slip embellished by perspective lines that echo those on the front cover. In contrast, *A Farewell to Kings* presents the image of the fallen king on the front cover and marionette strings as a virtual abstraction on the back.

Rush, *A Farewell to Kings* (1977). Design by Hugh Syme.

Both albums combine figurative and abstract art. *Going for the One* juxtaposes strong vertical and horizontal lines, but *A Farewell to Kings* takes this a step further, giving over the gatefold interior to the lyrics (black on a plain white background) and a single picture of the three band members in a stately house, where the darkness of the interior and the heaviness of the furniture contrasts with the bright light streaming through the half-open French window. Both album covers juxtapose the urban and the pastoral: Hipgnosis provides contrasting images on the exterior and interior of the Yes gatefold, whereas *A Farewell to Kings* depicts this juxtaposition on the front cover itself; the tensions embedded in the lyrics are subtly introduced through the lighting of the inside-cover band shot, where darkness and light meet at a strong vertical line that cuts downwards between the three band members.

The song 'A Farewell to Kings' (longer, at 5:53, than 'Wonderous Stories', at 3:45) is a prelude to the songs that follow, which will take us from Kubla Khan's 'Xanadu' and mythical blacksmiths and artists on 'Closer to the Heart' to the delusional 'Cinderella Man', the storybook 'Madrigal', and the science-fiction space voyage into a black hole on 'Cygnus X-1', with its own sci-fi prologue, its reference to Don Quixote's horse 'Rocinante' (the name of the spaceship), and its spiralling, unending descent into the black hole.[8] Rush later reprised the Cygnus voyage on its next album, *Hemispheres* (as indicated with the 'To be continued' line on the inside cover of *Farewell to Kings*), but the centrepiece of the album is the loss of mythical innocence, as evident in the cover illustration and the lyrics of the title track. The 'Farewell to Kings' track establishes a dual temporal plane, inviting the listener to 'turn the pages of history', not to view a mythical past of heroic kings but a moment when courtly heroism was crumbling; rather than grand castles, these kings preside over 'cities full of hatred/Fear and lies', where it is difficult to distinguish 'scheming demons/Dressed in kingly guise' from the kings themselves. The 'halls of Truth' are full of slander, and benediction has turned to bitterness. The appeal of the song, taking us back to the first line about history, is to rediscover a lost capacity to distinguish between right and wrong, and to bridge 'minds that make us strong' with a belief that thoughts and feelings can be severed only at a great cost.

The suggestive lyrics turn to a more didactic approach in the last four lines of the song, appealing to the listener to 'make a start' with a conviction that can lead us 'closer to the Heart', a line that Geddy Lee repeats and then reprises in the title and lyrics of the opening track on the second side. Neil Peart's lyrics are more coherent on 'Farewell to Kings' than those of Jon Anderson's on 'Wonderous Stories', and they have a much stronger narrative drive, using history (rather than a dreamscape) as the song's topos. Both tracks invite us to feel and think at the same time; they shift us onto new spatial and temporal planes as an entry point to the imaginative album world, but without entirely disorientating the listener. Compared to the all-enveloping experience of psychedelic bands or the perceptual disorganization of Syd Barrett's Pink

Floyd, these two tracks are both immersive and contemplative, weaving old and new stories, inviting listeners to open their senses (hearing, feeling and imagining), but also prompting them to think about the interrelationships between past and present and between their real worlds and the alternative cosmologies projected on the two albums.

The singer as a mid-world storyteller comes in different guises in progressive rock, but the persona often shuttles between the roles of narrator and participant, as evident in *The Lamb Lies Down on Broadway*, where Peter Gabriel switches from omniscient observer to playing the lost and bewildered character Rael. Sometimes the storytelling role is inflected by the musical medium itself, such as the medieval minstrel on Jethro Tull's *Minstrel in the Gallery* and, within a more contemporary frame, the figure of the old greaser Ray Lomas, who features on the cover of, and is the musical subject of, *Too Old to Rock 'n' Roll, Too Young to Die*. Ian Anderson's stage persona was often the unifying concept for a group of songs that drew from mythology, such as the 'Cold Wind to Valhalla' track on *Minstrel in the Gallery*. But the persona on *Too Old to Rock 'n' Roll* is comically presented in the cartoon-strip artwork and takes on a more challenging guise in the ambivalent song 'Pied Piper', which ironically reworks the Hans Christian Andersen myth for a middle-aged biker who hands out 'small cigars to the kids from school'. Experience and innocence are key themes on both albums, but Anderson was often playful and knowing in his mythical references. On *A Passion Play* (1973), for instance, he adopts a Christian narrative framework but starts the four-act story with a funeral and proceeds to parody the passion of Christ and to critique organized religion. *A Passion Play* does not relate a tale of redemption, but it tells a very English story of everyday endeavour and frustration, where the 'rush along the Fulham Road' tempers mythological references to 'icy Lucifer' and the 'son of man'. Time shifts forwards and backwards through allegory, odd juxtapositions and linguistic playfulness, in which the listener is invited to collude with a concept album that is at once meaningful and nonsensical, as implied by the whimsically absurdist bridging song 'The Story of the Hare Who Lost His Spectacles', which separates the two halves of the passion play narrative.

A number of progressive albums deal with the growth cycle and destiny of human beings through an explicitly mythological lens. Italian band Le Orme's 1973 concept album *Felona e Sorona*, for example, pushed the dramatic musical style of *Collage* (1971) in the direction of a story about the conflicting planets Felona, the planet of sadness and darkness, and Sorona, the planet of happiness and sunlight. Everything is in harmony until the mythical Creator turns his attention on trying to cure Felona of its sadness, only for Sorona to feel neglected, leading to a situation where planetary balance (on the track 'L'equillibrio') disintegrates into a destructive void on the final track ('Ritorno al nulla'). The planets metamorphose into human form on the Italian modernist artist and sculptor Frigeri Lanfranco's Surrealist cover image. In Lanfranco's painting, the psychodrama unfolds in a dark, moonlit space between a naked heterosexual couple and a third female onlooker, reinforcing Le Orme's dramatic musical suite and implying that this relationship is doomed to fail.

The theme of destiny is also investigated on Genesis guitarist Steve Hackett's largely instrumental 1975 album, *Voyage of the Acolyte*, which mixes tarot-card imagery (reflected on the album cover and in the song titles) with a quest into unknown spaces. This interest in the occult was embraced more fully by rock bands: Led Zeppelin's Jimmy Page was heavily influenced by the occultism of Aleister Crowley in the early 1970s (especially on *Led Zeppelin IV*), while British rock bands (Black Sabbath, Deep Purple, early Fleetwood Mac) engaged with darker myths that tempered the wistful lyricism of 'Stairway to Heaven', complete with ladies, songbirds and pipers. In the darker world of heavy rock, the journey into psychopathology is often a frightening one; death rarely promises a passage into a potentially higher state and more often lays a path into the realm of purgatory, destruction and the undead. An extended rock track such as Deep Purple's 1970 track 'Child in Time' (10:18) uses a progressive compositional pattern, extensive use of organ, and a slowly building crescendo to dramatize a child trapped temporally between a purgatorial vision of 'the blindman shooting at the world' and his fears that 'being bad' will lead to consequences ('the ricochet') that are potentially disastrous for his soul. These ricochets are dramatized by lead singer Ian Gillan's piercing scream at the two major climaxes of the song, as well as the confused shouting and cacophonous percussion at the end.

The mythical interest in leave-taking and return, and the need to counterbalance order and chaos (in terms of the interplay of instruments and the narrative trajectory of the songs), led progressive bands to see that the human life cycle could be broken by journeys into the unknown: the voyage of Hackett's acolyte, the journey of Rush's spaceship Rocinante in search of the black hole of Cygnus X-1, or the lost space explorers of Van der Graaf Generator's 'Pioneers Over C' on *H to He Who Am the Only One* (1970). The life cycle sometimes remains earthbound, as it does on the 1972 instrumental ensemble album *The Seven Ages of Man* on the Rediffusion label. Here the song-cycle draws heavily on a set of fifteenth- and sixteenth-century images depicted as vignettes on the cover (including illustrations from biblical images, Aesop's Fables and Holbein's *Dance of Death*) linked to different bodily parts of an early modern European man, presented as an anatomical object. The seven images depict stages of human growth and suggest that the cycle of maturation and ageing is a biological pattern common to all humans, particularly as 'Birth & Early Childhood' is highlighted in its link to the disembowelled central figure on the cover.[9] Running through progressive rock is the paradox of being both time-bound and potentially free of time by journeying to other places or discovering higher spiritual states; this is often conveyed through stories of natality (birth, rebirth, transformation

and water imagery) and existential meditation on life and death, combined
with a mixture of classical, biblical, modern, occult and esoteric mythology.

On Van der Graaf Generator's *Pawn Hearts* (1971), this complex layering
and interplay is clear from the album cover, on which mythical and real
figures from different periods and cultures hover in plastic pawn shapes above
a watery planet, wrapped in a floating curtain with patterned clouds. The
songs are very complex constructions, particularly the ten-part, 23-minute
'A Plague of Lighthouse Keepers', on the second side. All three tracks have
moments of extreme dissonance, crossing into free jazz combined with rock
instrumentation, and alternating with much calmer sections where Peter
Hammill's more direct singing stands apart from the instrumental drive of
the band. The opening track, 'Lemmings' (11:37), focuses on the decaying
aura of the powerful ('We have looked upon the High Kings/Found them less
than mortals'), soon to be replaced by cowards, who are as much lemmings
as the populations they would sacrifice in a world 'out of control, out of
control'. The more critical verses are almost barked by Hammill, as he outlines
the destructiveness of war machinery within a blast of saxophone, bass,
keyboards and drums (the band uses guitar very sparingly and resists solos).
When the song considers what is to be done, it is much more meditative, and
in the final lines Hammill's echoed voice shows that his is not a despairing
position but a critique that holds out the need for hope and change: 'What
choice is there left but to live/In the hope of saving/Our children's children's
little ones?' This is emphasized by the pastoral drift of the closing 2 minutes,
dominated by slow cymbals and gently mournful keyboards and reeds.
'Man-Erg' (10:20) expands an individual's fear of one's own hidden evil on a
mythical scale by attributing this to all humanity, where the world of political
warfare and power is filled with 'dictators, saviours [and] refugees'.

The lighthouse in 'A Plague of Lighthouse Keepers' represents human
aid and a beacon of truth, as well as isolation and the danger of extreme
weather. Within this turbulence, the lighthouse keeper becomes an exem-
plar of humanity: he is less an Everyman than an all-encompassing being,
who is nonetheless far from in charge of his destiny. The compositional
complexity parallels the difficult attempt to capture all human existence in
a single figure – or what a colossal task any such figure would have if he did
exist. The keeper finds that he is 'overcome' when ghosts and imagined perils
mount from the fourth section of the piece onwards, even as the lighthouse is
threatened in the real world by the lack of supplies and dangerous conditions.
Ultimately, self-awareness is overwhelming in a universe without meaning
but full of threat: 'I know no more ways, I am so afraid/Myself won't let me
be myself'. The piece soon lurches into messy jazz that spirals out of control,
first via percussive time changes and then with the full band playing against
each other in time and key. The seventh section, '(Custard's) Last Stand',
is a ballad-like return to awareness; but when Hammill's voice mounts, it
emphasizes a lack of realization. The next section reprises the narrator's loss

of identity; Hammill's treated voice sneeringly looks for help over a broken carnival ride, as the band veers out of control (keyboard tones are distorted and atonally distended, and drums play in a different metre). The last vocal part signifies collapse and a glimmer of something other than disaster: 'All things are apart/All things are a part'. This gives way to a guitar solo and, as the drums clatter, a choral, wordless voice builds and then tails away. Through these means, *Pawn Hearts* uses horizontal developmental complexity to create a layering of ideas, images and ideological positions that elevate the real world of politics and individual concerns to an archetypal level. In doing so, Van der Graaf Generator offers a worldview where complexity and difficulty are the keys to authentic, reflective, awkward existence and a bulwark against the abuses of political power.

More broadly in 1970s progressive rock, the layering of time often works across a whole album, where medieval and modern motifs and classical and contemporary references sometimes meld and at other times jar against one another. On *The Seven Ages of Man* and *Pawn Hearts*, this serves to build new narratives where the 'condition of man' can be explored in ways that take account of historical positioning. For progressive bands, this was an active form of mythmaking in the Benjaminian mode, but close to postmodern pastiche at times in its eclectic referencing of the past and its fusion of musical styles.

Mythology was sometimes brought in by reworking an identifiable literary source, perhaps arbitrary in particular cases but meaningful in others. Camel's album *Music Inspired by the Snow Goose* (1975), for example, follows the narrative arc of Paul Gallico's sentimental novella *The Snow Goose* (1941), but the album does not do much more than musically relate the intertwined stories of a disabled lighthouse keeper and a wounded snow goose that he nurses back to life at the time of the Dunkirk evacuation. Early in his story, Gallico stresses that *The Snow Goose* is a legend garnered from 'many sources and from many people' and retold through 'the form of fragments from men who looked upon strange and violent scenes'.[10] This is a reminder that stories and folktales do not 'easily and smoothly' fall 'into sequence', and that the reworking of myths is a creative act, particularly when translated into a different medium. In this regard, one of the best examples of myth-making is Rush's 11-minute centrepiece of *A Farewell to Kings*, 'Xanadu', in which Samuel Taylor Coleridge's dreamlike poetic fragment 'Kubla Khan' (1816) is reworked into a musical epic. In the Rush version, an explorer yearns to see Kubla Khan's mythical palace, but he is seduced by the promise of immortality and, by the end of the song, finds that he has nothing to do but 'walk the caves of ice' for eternity. The song relishes the splendour of Kubla Khan's palace, but it emphasizes the consequences of overreaching and the explorer's solitary endless quest in the fade-out at the end of the song.[11] An epic stature is lent through reference to the Mongolian dynasty, but more importantly through the extended length of the track and its musical virtuosity. Neil Peart uses wind chimes, glockenspiel and cowbells to dramatize the icy caves and the seductive splendour of the mogul's palace, while the song's shifting instrumental passages mark the journey of the marvelling visitor towards the wondrous building.

Rush was far from being the only band to mine myths, as the interest in fantasy and science fiction among young readers in the late 1960s and the 1970s gave many bands the opportunity to invest in mythical stories. This is most obviously the case with Tolkien's *The Lord of the Rings*, which became the source text of Swedish instrumentalist Bo Hansson's *Saman om ringen* (1970, released in the UK as *Music Inspired by The Lord of the Rings* in 1972), composed and recorded in near seclusion on a Swedish island. The back cover of the UK version reinforces the personal connection with Tolkien's trilogy, which is described as reaching deep into Hansson's 'remote and rather other-worldly nature'.[12] As an instrumental album, *Saman om ringen* relies on Hansson's use of song titles ('Leaving Shire', 'The Black Riders', 'The Ring Goes South') and the artwork to allude to Tolkien's quest narrative. The individual songs link closely to the cover art, which reflects turbulent episodes from Frodo's journey from Hobbiton to Mordor, set against a large hand in the foreground that cups the magic ring and points towards Mount Doom and scenes of battle. On the back cover, the hand is depicted once again; this time it is turned sideways towards the viewer, the ring on the fourth finger and the palm revealing a glimpse of a peaceful and arable land, perhaps lost in another time. Throughout the 1970s, progressive bands developed Tolkien mythology on isolated tracks, such as Barclay James Harvest on 'Galadriel' (1971), Rush on 'Rivendell' (1975) and Styx on 'Lords of the Ring' (1978), or on the White Riders suite on Camel's 1974 *Mirage* album. These examples most obviously represent the attempt to find common ground with listeners who would have been reading Tolkien in the early 1970s. But rather than pursuing a grand concept, these tracks link an episode or character to other musical moods and lyrical directions or to the iconography of the album cover.

Where bands did engage more deeply with their source texts, the results were often complex rearrangements of ideas, words and music, which often extended the mythical status of the original story. Led Zeppelin did this on its fourth album, through a series of songs that borrow widely from Tolkien mythology, particularly 'The Battle of Evermore' (1971), which blends Tolkien, Arthurian mythology and occultism with a musical hybrid of blues, rock and folk styles. The reworkings of classical music on ELP's *Pictures at an Exhibition* (1972) and Renaissance's *Scheherazade and Other Stories* (1975) layer new arrangements and imagery onto original suites by Russian composers Modest Mussorgsky (1874) and Nikolai Rimsky-Korsakov (1887–8). The mythology is sometimes difficult to interpret, such as on rock band Baker Gurvitz Army's 1975 album *Elysian Encounter*, in which neither the songs nor the fantasy/sci-fi cover art really give a clue to how the Greek Elysian Fields are being used, or on Atomic Rooster's *Death Walks Behind You* (1970), which borrows Romantic poet-artist William Blake's famous painting

'Nebuchadnezzar' (1795) for the cover but does little discernible with the concept on the album itself – Blake's poetry was also a source for ELP's *Brain Salad Surgery* (1973) and Tangerine Dream's *Tyger* (1987).

Wishbone Ash's *Argus* (1972) provides a more interesting case, in which the giant watchman Argus (shown from behind on the album cover) signifies martial lore on one of the band's most famous tracks, 'Warrior', and the potential redemption of the closing track, 'The King Will Come', with its Christian and Tolkienesque resonances. This pair of songs (usually performed together) lends grandeur to the intimate vulnerability of the second track, 'Sometime World', in which the singer worries that time will slip by without consequence. Across the song-cycle, *Argus* focuses (according to singer Martin Turner) on the problem of making purposeful choices in a meaningless world.[13] This concept is unified through the figure of Argus: he appears to be a watchman protecting the pastoral valley depicted in the distance below, but he might equally be a soldier returning from battle, forced into warfare to fend off the destruction of the valley or the subjugation of his people. *Argus* can be read as an anti-war album (given the currency of the Vietnam War and the lyric of 'Throw Down the Sword' when the battle is 'neither lost, neither won'), but the album is better read on a conceptual level as the need to preserve a communal (possibly agrarian) identity that may be at risk of invasion or extinction (the observation of a mythical guardian corresponding thematically with the opening track, 'Watcher of the Skies', on Genesis's 1972 *Foxtrot* album). More specifically, it helps Wishbone Ash to explore the relationship between history, mythology and personal concerns about making meaningful choices in the face of change.

The sense of a second coming or redemption for a fallen world often intrudes on the narrative framework of progressive tracks. 'Watcher of the Skies' – which takes its title from a Keats poem and its narrative arc from Arthur C. Clarke's 1954 Cold War novel *Childhood's End* – begins with a slow instrumental build-up played on the Mellotron, before offering a stable viewpoint of the figure of the watcher or 'Overlord' (a figure played by Gabriel with heavy eye-shadow and a bat-winged head-dress), who surveys all humanity and sees beyond the 'childhood games' that preoccupy human activity. Whereas Clarke's overlords have wrested powers and 'supreme decisions' from Earth's 'precarious sovereignty', Gabriel's watcher cannot offer human salvation, but he can see the fate of the world as it unfolds below him.[14] In contrast, the last track on *Foxtrot*, 'Supper's Ready' (22:48), an original composition with a number of mythical references, has a much less stable viewpoint. This corresponds to an anti-programmatic tendency in the early music of Genesis, in which, as Macan describes, 'the mythological imagery is not used as an allegory through which to address the problems of here and now'.[15] The story of a fall into a dreamlike netherworld where personal, family, national and mythical dramas fuse into one another is left open for listeners to actively make meaning, rather than having them identify a central message or a well-worn story to which 'Supper's Ready' covertly refers. This lack of stability is amplified by the playful titles of the song sequence, through the varied vocal styles that Gabriel adopts, and by the costumes in which he acted out episodes during live performances. 'Supper's Ready' is a good example of a conceptual mid-world in which boundaries between reality, dreams, myths and religion blur. Myopic and panoramic views are juxtaposed and surrealist lyrics are set beside meditations on battle (with both good and bad consequences) and the search to re-establish a divine or sovereign order.

'Supper's Ready' begins with the domestic scene of a couple sitting in a front room who switch off the television and listen to the sound of traffic. They have doubts about whether their love for each other is true, or if the beloved's 'guardian eyes so blue' can offer adequate protection from the unknown. These doubts are interrupted by six shrouded figures that materialize in the garden and presage a dreamlike world into which the storyteller falls into a series of visions. The first character he meets, 'The Guaranteed Eternal Sanctuary Man', is perhaps a more worldly personification of the 'Watcher of the Skies', but the mythical figure cannot distract the quester from scenes of war in which 'the children of the west' and a 'host of dark skinned warriors' wait for battle. This battle between civilization and savagery ends in jubilation, where dancing and rejoicing suggest a change of order, but it does not disguise the 'pile of human flesh' that the singer is compelled to slowly climb in order to achieve a higher perspective. The vision starts mournfully and builds slowly. Gabriel intones the loss of life as we imagine him climbing the pile of flesh, and he bemoans the enslavement of survivors who have been 'stamped human bacon by some butchery tool'.

Rather than an extended critique of the battle or a moral assessment of the loss of life, the middle part of 'Supper's Ready' suddenly switches into an absurdist section, 'Willow Farm', which is structured around swift transformation through wordplay ('the frog was a prince; the prince was a brick; the brick was an egg; the egg was a bird'), biological transfiguration ('feel your body melt'), and an eschatological sense of finitude 'end with a whistle, or end with a bang' (which parodies the last line of T. S. Eliot's 1925 poem 'The Hollow Men': 'This is the way the world ends/Not with a bang but a whimper').[16] There is no psychological breakthrough, though, only a mightier battle between the mythical giants Gog and Magog (a battle narrated musically through keyboard, flute and percussion), which fuses with a personal psychomachia where the forces of evil and good rage deep 'down inside your soul'. The coda blends this cosmological story with the more worldly one: we are reintroduced to the lover with 'the guardian eyes so blue' and the possibility of reunion. The confidence that things will work out 'fine' links closely to natural processes ('how the river joins the ocean') and where home is figured as a mythical entry for humanity: 'Lord of Lords, King of Kings, as he turns to lead his children home, to take them to the New Jerusalem'.

Although the watcher and guardian are replaced by an angelic figure at the end of 'Supper's Ready', there is no specific reference to Christ or a second coming, although the closing section of 'The Waste Land', in which Eliot searches for spiritual reunion among the fragments of modernity, might be a possible source. The final lyric, promising the 'New Jerusalem', suggests the possibility of redemption for a fallen world marked by absurdity and conflict, or the actualization of the New Jerusalem that Clement Attlee's Labour Party promoted in its campaign slogans of 1945, as it promised to rebuild Britain after the devastation of World War II. The triumphant ending of 'Supper's Ready' seems to suggest that the New Jerusalem can be reached, but this was an elusive possibility by 1972, with the counterculture lacking the direction of the late 1960s and the Conservative government struggling to keep a grip on the British economy and union militancy. Given the grim social reality of Britain in the early 1970s and the unrealized dreams of the postwar years, it was unsurprising that bands such as Genesis looked for redemption in and through music. Alternatively, perhaps, the New Jerusalem already exists, awaiting discovery at one remove from the mundane world. Such is the message of Tim Blake's highly optimistic 'New Jerusalem' on *Blake's New Jerusalem* (1978), a 16-minute electronic and utopian pastoral. This track taps into spiritual ley lines through washes and sonic pulses emitted from analogue synthesizers. If the 'New Jerusalem' on *Foxtrot* is a defiant response to contemporary society, then Blake suggests that even this might be to look in the wrong place, because modernity has covered over the path to utopia and blocked off most escape routes.

The Lord of the Rings, the Bible and classical mythology, adapted either singularly or in combination, were not the only touchstones for progressive bands. Sometimes the connections were through personal taste or collaboration, such as Jon Anderson's choice of David Fairbrother Roe as the cover artist for his solo album *Olias of Sunhillow*; Roe's artwork works through what Jennifer Rycenga calls Anderson's preoccupation with 'earth and nature' and 'time and sound' within his 'pantheistic neopagan immanent cosmology'.[17] The album cover illustrates Anderson's story of planetary rescue by the architect and aviator Olias on his glider the Moorglade Mover (the original story is also illustrated on the fold-out inner sleeve), and the imagery closely reflects the book covers of popular fantasy writer Anne McCaffrey's Dragonriders of Pern story cycle, which first appeared in the late 1960s, with cover illustrations by Roe. The connections with a literary source in this instance are pictorial rather than thematic, but it is worth looking more closely at two other examples that explore the relationship between popular writing and musical mythmaking: the links between British fantasy writer Michael Moorcock and the space-rock band Hawkwind, and the influence of émigré American science-fiction author and philosopher Ayn Rand on Rush's musical narratives of the mid-1970s.

Hawkwind developed a distinctive form of space music in the early 1970s, drawing on Moorcock's fantasy fiction from the band's early stages.

Moorcock's influence on Hawkwind culminated in *Warrior on the Edge of Time* (1975) – for which the author provided lyrics, occasional vocals and the overarching concept – and, later, the *Chronicles of the Black Sword* (1985), based on Moorcock's Elric saga, which began in 1963. The title of the earlier album borrows from Moorcock's trilogy *The Dancers at the End of Time* (1972–6), which depicts an amoral and irresponsible future society challenged by the Victorian morality of the time-traveller Mrs Amelia Underwood. The album does not explicitly reference this female protagonist, but instead extends the 'end of time' concept through the more masculine figure of the 'eternal champion' (another of Moorcock's concepts), who can see all dimensions of 'the multiverse' simultaneously. However, rather than conveying the omniscient perspective of an all-seeing figure, the brooding and spacey music suggests that the eternal champion has an uncertain role in a universe full of warriors and wizards whose motives are hard to gauge. The album does not tell a specific story but, like Hawkwind's use of Herman Hesse's mystical German novel *Steppenwolf* (1927) on its 1976 album *Astounding Sounds, Amazing Music*, it offers a series of intersecting themes and motifs that are, paradoxically, both caught within and free from time, which on *Warrior on the Edge of Time* is figured in the shape of a spiral on 'The Demented Man' and in the musical vortex on the instrumental 'Spiral Galaxy'.

Hawkwind, *Warrior on the Edge of Time* (1975). Art direction by Pierre D'Auvergne.

These themes of bewilderment and the immensity of time are reflected in the front-cover image of a small silhouetted rider and horse standing on a fantastically curved cliff, as the red sunset and heavy sky both threaten and entice. The cover opens out into a four-square portmanteau to reveal an almost life-sized shield emblazoned with the word 'CHAOS' on the inside (while the cliff on the front cover sinks into a bottomless yellow void in the expanded version), as if traditional weaponry were needed to counteract the mazy cosmos created by the front cover's crooked cliff-top path being echoed in an almost symmetrical image on the rear. The opened-out cover suggests two optical illusions: first, a disembodied malevolent watcher can be discerned with the red sun and bank of cloud forming the right eye that corresponds with a symmetrical left eye on the back cover; second, there is also the hint that the broad central shaft of yellow light is a phallic image, with the void hinting at a masculine potency not yet diminished in this bewildering cosmos. Importantly, though, the undecidability of Hawkwind's full-cover image reflects one of the central facets of progressive rock.

Rather than depicting a future community, as Moorcock does in his novel cycle, Hawkwind's *Warrior on the Edge of Time* emphasizes the embattled individual (Moorcock's 'eternal champion') standing alone in the face of destructive forces, but the narrative dimension of the album arguably rests too much on Moorcock's input to represent anything like new mythmaking. The tensions between the individual and collective are more expansively explored in an album released in the following year, *2112*, on which Rush develops Ayn Rand's objectivist philosophy in a story of a noble young man in a mythical future who rebels against a theocracy that has banned the relics of the past world. The opening, fast-tempo track of Rush's 1974 album *Fly by Night* takes its title from Rand's novel *Anthem* (first published in 1946, but not widely available in paperback until 1961). 'Anthem' translates a story of courageous truth-seeking in a technocratic future world (where individuals are known by code names such as 'Equality 7-2521') into a 4:36 track celebrating the union of heart and mind and promoting a simplified version of Rand's philosophy: 'Live for yourself, there's no one else/More worth living for'.

Following an instrumental 'Overture', which ends with 'the strangely Christian-overtoned' words 'and the meek shall inherit the earth', the 20-minute eponymous song suite (which encompasses the first side of *2112*) enters 'The Temple of Syrinx'.[18] Geddy Lee adopts the voice of the priestly ruling class, who assert a strict moral order on their planet, Megadon, which has seen fifty years of peace under the 'Red Star of the Solar Federation' (its iconography suggests a totalitarian regime). Sung at a high pitch and in a fast-paced, heavy-metal style, the collectivist philosophy of the morally untouchable priests (presented in first-person plural) leaves no room for resistance. A lyrical fragment on the back of the album cover (linking to narrative text that accompanies the lyrics on the song-sheet insert) describes Megadon as a world in which the citizen has a 'pretty good life here, just plugging into my machine for the day, then watching Templevision or read-ing a Temple Paper in the evening'. The futuristic world of Megadon reflects Rand's *Anthem*, where citizens are granted limited freedom as long as they do not 'speak of the times before the Great Rebirth' (an act punished by impris-onment); only the 'Old Ones' whisper about yesterday's 'Unmentionable Times', but they are incarcerated in the 'Home of the Useless'.[19] While '2112' is not a straight rendering of *Anthem*, the two texts share social and political features, illustrated by a naked young man on the album sleeve recoiling from the totalitarian symbol of the Red Star.

Following the assertion of the priests' assumed right to rule on 'The Temples of Syrinx', in the next section, 'Discovery', the unnamed young man (author of the written fragment on the album cover) experiences a moment of magical creativity when he stumbles upon a neglected guitar in a waterfall (this episode is described as an entry into an 'Unchartered Forest' in Rand's *Anthem*). The acoustic guitar that the young man starts strumming references the forgotten past ('it's got wires that vibrate and give music/What can this thing be that I've found') and represents a challenge to the priestly order, signalled through a stark contrast of musical styles from heavy guitar and percussion to unaccompanied acoustic guitar. When the young man presents the guitar to the priests (as he is beholden to do), they swiftly remove it from him. This suggests that the instrument is a trivial irrelevance, but they actu-ally fear that it has the power to evoke the past world and undermine their collectivist utopia (this track, 'Presentation', interweaves the musical styles of the last two pieces, contrasting the young man's new life-force with the priest's theocratic rule). The protagonist starts to protest, but he is quickly banished from the temple. Later that evening, an oracle appears to him in a dream and reveals images of a 'strange and wondrous land' by which he can glimpse a past world and 'the pure spirit of man', of which the guitar is a relic. The oracle opens up an epiphanic vista that makes the young man aware for the first time of the oppressive regime of Megadon. On the sixth track, 'Soliloquy', he wanders bewildered and frightened, as if some part of his identity has been torn from him with the destruction of the guitar, leading to his despairing suicide at the end of the track.

The listener's sympathy remains strongly with the young protagonist, who has no way to challenge the priests, and the song suite critiques their demotic rule through the amplified distortion of the lyric in the seventh track, 'Grand Finale', in which the priestly order is re-established: 'Attention all planets of the solar federation . . . We have assumed control', repeated twice in a 'disembodied and "multiple" voice'.[20] Read through the filter of Rand's philosophy, this story is a critique of a totalitarian, left-wing government in which noble Republican ideals are favourably contrasted, but where the music incorporates a paradox as its centrepiece: a tightly knit song played collectively by a three-piece band on electric guitar, bass and drums has as its symbol of freedom and creativity an acoustic guitar plucked gently by

Alex Lifeson during the 'Discovery' episode – as Durrell Bowman notes, the 'tentative and gentle' strumming is distinct from the 'forceful and determined' individualism that Ayn Rand would promote as an embodiment of her philosophy of libertarian rationalism.[21] The tensions between individualism and collectivism work on various levels, then, but the song suite's politics are not as clear as the Randian framework suggests.

Warrior on the Edge of Time and *2112* are each based around conflict: the former between a mythic protagonist and a hostile world, the latter between an innocent young man and a despotic regime. The Hawkwind album ends with an expression of freedom and mobility in 'Kings of Speed' (which follows the descend into a spiral galaxy), whereas '2112' concludes with a restoration of totalitarianism, leaving it for the second side to suggest that the variety of human experience (travel, dreams, emotions, thoughts) still survive. Rush played out these tensions in other ways, particularly on *Hemispheres*, in which the 'battle through the ages' between Dionysus and Apollo structures the second part of the 'Cygnus X-1' story, where the 'world is torn asunder' into hemispheres. This is both a mythical conflict and a self-referential one: the attempt to balance chaos with order is a signature style of progressive rock, as distinct from the Dionysian impulses that Simon Reynolds claims for the music of The Doors, The Stooges and heavy metal bands.[22] A similar story is related within a different topos on 'The Trees', on the second side of *Hemispheres*, where the oaks and the maples fight it out for dominance in an ancient mixed woodland. In each case, the bands try to say something profound about a generalized human condition (in the case of 'The Trees', the ideological problems of enforcing equality) but arguably at the expense of intimacy with a particular, feeling subject. Battles do not always lead to the resolution offered on the first side of *Hemispheres*, in which the new sensibility of the god of balance, Cygnus, creates a 'single, perfect sphere' from fractured parts, or on 'The Trees', in which a woodsman solves the squabble between the oaks and maples by keeping them equal with 'hatchet, ax and saw'. In Led Zeppelin's 'The Battle of Evermore', for example, the conflict between warring elements plays out eternally, while Genesis's 'The Battle of Epping Forest' tells a comic tale of class warfare without any resolution.

Specific allusions are sometimes hard to catch, myths are blurred and the provenance of sources is often hard to determine. This might be characterized as an early form of postmodern pastiche, or, as suggested earlier, a late modernist response to the irreconcilable tensions embedded in Western modernity – what German theorist Jürgen Habermas (following Max Weber) called the 'separation of the spheres', in which the realms of art, science and morality become disconnected from each other through processes of modernization and rationalization.[23] In this model, we can see progressive rock as a mode of musical re-enchantment, an attempt to reconnect these distinct spheres with each other, linking themes of art and technology with ethical considerations about future social models or exploring what has been lost through modernization. Potentially radical in projecting alternative futures, but also potentially conservative in recouping a lost past, the cultural politics of progressive bands are complex and sometimes undecidable. The interest in myths and mythology within an early to mid-1970s context reveal a more contested cultural politics – at times engaged politically, at others self-absorbed, escapist or esoteric – than the participatory leftist politics of late 1960s counterculture. But for most listeners of progressive rock, the act of retelling and rehearing stories within new musical arrangements was more important than any political messages that might be gleaned from the song-cycles.

Notes

1. For a discussion of the mimetic and emotional functions of music, see Philip Ball, *The Music Instinct* (London: Bodley Head, 2010), 267–71.

2. See Paul de Man, *Allegories of Reading: Figural Language in Rousseau, Nietzsche, Rilke and Proust* (New Haven: Yale University Press, 1979).

3. Walter Benjamin, 'The Task of the Translator', *Illuminations*, trans. Harry Zohn (New York: Random House, [1968] 2002), 69–82.

4. Paul de Man, 'Conclusions: On Walter Benjamin's "The Task of the Translator"' (1985), in *The Resistance to Theory* (Minneapolis: University of Minnesota Press, 1986), 73–105.

5. Walter Benjamin, 'On Language as Such and on the Language of Man' (1916), in *Reflections: Essays, Aphorisms, Autobiographical Writings*, ed. Peter Demetz, trans. Edmund Jephcott (New York: Harcourt Brace, 1978), 314–32.

6. Macan, *Rocking the Classics*, 179.

7. Jennifer Rycenga, 'Tales of Change within the Sound', in *Progressive Rock Reconsidered*, ed. Kevin Holm-Hudson (New York: Routledge, 2002), 146.

8. Durrell S. Bowman offers a detailed musicological reading of 'Cygnus X-1' in 'Let Them All Make Their Own Music: Individualism, Rush, and the Progressive/Hard Rock Alloy, 1976–77', *Progressive Rock Reconsidered*, ed. Holm-Hudson, 207–13.

9. The cover describes *The Seven Ages of Man* as an eclectic work: 'this story of man's life cycle, although conceived and performed in the idiom of the seventies, utilizes in its construction virtually everything we have assimilated in popular music over the years' (Michael Ferguson, *The Seven Ages of Man* liner notes [Rediffusion, 1972]).

10. Paul Gallico, *The Snow Goose and The Small Miracle* (London: Penguin, [1941] 1967), 9.

11. This fade-out is noted by Richard Middleton, *Studying Popular Music* (Buckingham: Open University Press, 1990), 232, and Durrell Bowman, 'Let Them All Make Their Music', in *Progressive Rock Reconsidered*, 202.

12. Bo Hansson, *Music Inspired by Lord of the Rings* (Charisma, 1972).

13. Gary Carter and Mark Chatterton, *Blowin' Free: Thirty Years of Wishbone Ash* (London: Firefly, 2001), 41–2.

14. Arthur C. Clarke, *Childhood's End* (London: Tor, [1954] 2010), 12.

15. Macan, *Rocking the Classics*, 109.

16. T. S. Eliot, 'The Hollow Men', *Collected Poems 1909–1962* (London: Faber, 1963), 92.

17. Holm-Hudson, ed., *Progressive Rock Reconsidered*, 145.

18. Bowman, 'Let Them All Make Their Own Music', in *Progressive Rock Reconsidered*, ed. Holm-Hudson, 194.

19. Ayn Rand, *Anthem* (London: Signet, [1946] 1995), 19.

20. Holm-Hudson, ed., *Progressive Rock Reconsidered*, 198–9.

21. Ibid., 195.

22. Simon Reynolds, 'Ecstasy is a Science: Techno-Romanticism', in *Stars Don't Stand Still in the Sky: Music and Myth*, ed. Karen Kelly and Evelyn McDonnell (New York: New York University Press, 1999), 200–1.

23. See Jürgen Habermas, 'Modernity – An Incomplete Project', in *Postmodern Culture*, ed. Hal Foster (London: Pluto, [1983] 1987), 3–15.

Chapter 6

Progressive Fusion

The late 1960s witnessed a rich interplay between rock and jazz that would come to be known as fusion. Miles Davis, Tony Williams and John McLaughlin are the founding figures in the move to the genuinely hybrid musical forms of jazz rock, but fusions had already been occurring in the incorporation of ethnic elements in rock and, more pertinently, in the shape of the British blues revival, which not only combined folk and blues from the United States, Britain and Ireland but also incorporated jazz in, for example, the Graham Bond Organisation, the numerous line-ups of Alexis Korner's bands, and the playing strategies of guitarists (in such bands as The Yardbirds) who owed much to the iterations and improvised flights of musicians playing live in jazz groups. For Robert Wyatt, jazz was a place for experimentation rather than conceptual or narrative-based compositions: 'as far as we were concerned, there was already something called progressive rock – which was jazz'.[1] Before his solo career, Wyatt was a central part of the Canterbury scene, playing in Soft Machine, Matching Mole and, as far back as 1963, a hybrid experimental-rock band with Daevid Allen. All these English bands blended jazz elements to a high level, often at the wilful expense of conceptual coherence.

For progressive rock bands, the direction of interaction is from jazz towards rock, but late 1960s fusion was built on bringing rock to jazz. Miles Davis increasingly used electric instruments and microphones, while playing more as a rock ensemble with far less turn-taking in solos, and Davis and McLaughlin (along with many rock instrumentalists) wanted to reseed jazz with the recombinant blues of Jimi Hendrix. Through fusion, 'the rock age (or at least the best elements of it) flowed into the new jazz'.[2] By the mid-1970s, the direction changed, especially in Britain, where an autonomous fusion genre and a parallel jazz-rock variant of progressive rock emerged, which, in some of its forms, seemed to be on the path to decadence or a virtuosity gone to seed. But before assessing this trend, we need to return to the beginnings of fusion, with a discussion of Miles Davis. This chapter then considers the development of jazz-tinged rock in Britain, with a focus on Soft Machine and the Canterbury scene, before moving on to discuss Sun Ra's Afrofuturist mythology, which fed into the visionary space-worlds of Magma and the acid visions of Gong.

Miles Davis provides two essential moments in fusion with *In a Silent Way* (1969) and *Bitches Brew* (1970), not least in the composition of his bands, whose members went on to form their own fusion groups: The Mahavishnu Orchestra, Weather Report and Return to Forever. Davis's influence on progressive rock began much earlier, with the albums he made with Gil Evans – most notably *Sketches of Spain* (1960), which makes the classical music of Rodrigo's *Guitar Concerto* the centrepiece of what Berendt calls the 'opening up of jazz to world music' as it works through Spanish music styles.[3] There is a clear connection to later incorporations of classical music in rock. Keith Emerson, whose albums with The Nice and ELP arguably went furthest in incorporating classical forms (as opposed to replicating the drive and purpose of the sonata in rock form), noted that his early interests 'revolved around listening to a lot of Blue Note recordings, Miles Davis'.[4] The channelling of a classical style through Miles Davis can also be heard in King Crimson's 'Bolero' on *Lizard* (1970). Like Emerson, many members of early King Crimson were keen followers of Davis, although Robert Fripp was not one of them.[5] This interest derived from the creation of mood through tone, and the sense that this mood could be sustained in groups other than orchestras (even though Davis's albums with Gil Evans feature orchestras). In the long run, the Davis influence appeared in sections on prog albums rather than structuring the whole album, but, despite Fripp's misgivings, *Islands* (1971) is very much dominated by a stately mood development, particularly 'Formentera Lady' and 'Islands'. The former, argues Sid Smith, is redolent of the 'modal explorations of Miles Davis's 'Shhh/Peaceful' on *In a Silent Way*.[6]

Like, but before, early progressive rock artists, Davis exploited the opportunities offered by the long-playing record; as jazz began stretching out (on *Kind of Blue* and the Gil Evans collaborations), it moved away from sequences of solos framed by statement and restatement of theme and towards a more holistic structure. Paradoxically, in Davis's case, this meant a 'reduction of incident' in favour of mood.[7] This would have its more obvious impact on American minimalism and on the ambient music pioneered by Brian Eno, but, in the late 1950s and early 1960s, Davis foreshadowed the move away from rhythm and blues that progressive rock bands enacted a few years later; the title, *Kind of Blue*, hints at emotional mood by referring not to 'the blues' but to blue itself.[8] Both *Kind of Blue* and *Sketches of Spain* open up jazz to self-reflection: reflections on the genre itself and where it meets other musical forms. If the content of Davis's albums from this period does not feed directly into progressive rock, then the attention to form does. Paradoxically, jazz fusion leads to an emphasis on virtuosity and jazziness that ultimately contradicts the utopian merging of genre signalled by Davis. When it finally emerges as a distinct form in Davis's music, fusion aims to bring jazz, rock, classical and Indian elements together, with funk never far away.

On *In a Silent Way*, Davis stretched the jazz mood to its fullest extent, albeit smoothly. This album withholds resolution, achieving its harmoniousness not through the realization of a narrative but by occupying time. The percussion is very simple throughout, other than 40 or so seconds two-thirds of the way through side two ('In a Silent Way/It's About That Time'), where the drums are actually hit as a whole instrument, rather than touched in part. 'Shhh/Peaceful', on side one, sees individual instruments step out from the background of light hi-hat and group ambience as McLaughlin's guitar becomes the glue around which the piece coheres. The solos are short and cumulative, and, for all the lack of forward motion, they contribute to the whole mood through their individual acceptance of the shared setting. This is jazz with a strong electric and electronic involvement: instead of being a return to a source, it is a knowingly avant-garde ambience, an electric pastoral, as we also hear in the Canterbury scene or on Mike Oldfield's *Tubular Bells*.

Bitches Brew offers a more funk-oriented counterpoint to *In a Silent Way*. Here the compositions begin to spread vertically again, with more of the group driving on the piece at the same moment, as they do on the later work of Davis's band members: for example, Herbie Hancock's *Headhunters* (1973), McLaughlin's Mahavishnu Orchestra's album *The Inner Mounting Flame* (1971), and Chick Corea's jazz-fusion group Return to Forever, with progressive rock elements particularly prominent on *Hymn of the Seventh Galaxy* (1973) and *Where Have I Known You Before* (1974). On *Bitches Brew*, Davis also mirrors the exploration of form in progressive rock, even as he pushes the group towards funk. The album is free of identifiable narrative elements, but the group tries to establish a sound-world based on completion: hence the band's united playing and syncopation. This unity is held together in the striking gatefold sleeve, illustrating in attenuated form a range of emblematic figures of African life and the transportation and displacement of that heritage: the front cover shows a flower bursting into flame, the head of one of the figures flying out, tornado-like, to join a storm above, while a much larger-scale face looks on impassively, beaded with sweat. Equally impassive is the white face that backs on, Janus-like, to the first black face, only this one is dripping blood. Nonetheless, their fingers entwine. There is little by way of dissonance on the two records, but the four sides could be read to represent a sense of epochal time; hints of dissonance provide the thread to the time that builds to fusion and ultimate harmony. The cultural message of the record seems to be that difference (racial and sonic) must be recognized, not annulled, for fusion to occur.

The scale of this album is nearly matched by The Tony Williams Lifetime's album *Emergency*, also from 1969. This two-album set is closer in intent to the rock side of progressive music, at the same time as Davis was fashioning a form of progressive jazz. Williams' band, featuring John McLaughlin, adds psychedelic elements to the meeting of jazz and rock, notably in 'Vashkar' and especially in 'Via the Spectrum Road', where Williams' vocals approach the non-rock, non-jazz softness of Robert Wyatt. *Emergency* offers reprises, crescendos, an oscillation between the simpler time signatures of rock and the more progressive metres of jazz, and a number of extended songs or instrumentals as opposed to choruses interspersed with jamming (the two longest tracks are 12 and 13 minutes, and only two tracks are under 6 minutes). This album and *Bitches Brew* drive forward the idea of an extremely expanded studio recording rather than the documentation of a live performance. Fusion groups in the 1970s complicated studio recordings: for example, Santana's double album *Moonflower* (1977) alternates between live and studio recordings, and side two of Weather Report's *I Sing the Body Electric* (1972) was recorded live.

Weather Report sought to develop Davis's experiments, essentially on an instrumental level, and create a fusion of jazz styles (albeit with some input from Latin American music) rather than a complete merging of rock and jazz. What it took from rock was almost the complete opposite of progressive rock; it reintroduced the tighter instrumental song format that Davis, McLaughlin and progressive rock attempted to leave behind. There is, then, a rock dynamic to Weather Report's early albums, and an attempt to construct choruses as epiphanies, expanding the epiphanic moment by reducing its occurrence and increasing anticipation so that it functions more as a completion of the whole track, akin to the drive of progressive rock of the same period. This is particularly clear on the studio side of its second album, *I Sing the Body Electric*. Unlike the progressive bands of the early 1970s, Weather Report seems to hark back to a musical style before the intrusion of free jazz, and the occasional dissonance of that album gives way to a smoothness that combines synthesizers with elements from the history of jazz, and blends them into a new style. Unlike the modernist impulse of free jazz, some fusion and progressive rock, Weather Report is postmodern, in the way Fredric Jameson imagined this term to include the flattening out of styles.[9] This music does not break free of the music of the time, but it affirms the democracy of the freeway and communal mobility.[10] Weather Report, in its early days, approached rock form as a reassuring structure, and the resultant merging of forms seems to detract from both sides, becoming a mood that is 'mood', a conscious re-creation of something absent. This self-conscious mood heightened in the 1970s (as it did with English jazz-inflected rock), such as on the band's seventh album, *Heavy Weather* (1977), which conveys the memory of jazz, like a homeopathic tincture's memory of the elements it has removed.

In regard to this book, two bands McLaughlin was involved in – his own Mahavishnu Orchestra and The Tony Williams Lifetime – are more significant, and are not simply precursors to avant-garde rock or inspired by it. These two groups represent an authentic fusion that should be heard as a form of, not just a tributary to, progressive rock. The fusion at work in Lifetime's *Emergency* or Mahavishnu's *Inner Mounting Flame* is not about the blending of forms. The latter album shows rock and jazz colliding, with both parts influenced by free jazz. Rock and jazz elements deconstruct one another, raising form as a question rather than repletion in a newly homogenized style. How it does this is often simple – for example, it alternates crunching band riffs with complex passages of upward motion (echoing the spirituality of track and album titles), dissonance with unified tonality. The opening track, 'Meeting of the Spirits', foreshadows King Crimson's mid-1970s style, and also '21st Century Schizoid Man' on *In the Court of the Crimson King*, but this time the acidic chords set the terms for a reunion (conveyed in form), a reunion couched in terms not of fusion but of differences coming together. Opening with a sequence of crescendos, 'Meeting of the Spirits' gives us Pharoah Sanders, John Coltrane and the corrupted overtures to be found elsewhere in progressive rock. In this, it even looks forward to the vastly expanded tracks of twenty-first-century bands such as Transatlantic, Dream Theater and The Flower Kings. Between the group's crescendo moments are ecstatic restatements of the key theme by individual musicians or parts of the group. This is a version of community ('the meeting') that allows for individuality, on the understanding that the moulding into combination maintains dissonant views – an extension of Duke Ellington's view on the democratic nature of the jazz group (see Chapter 1). This key element of free jazz permeates early 1970s progressive rock: all individual band members can express themselves, often concurrently, unlike, say, in the blues rock of Cream. The band members do not move off into solos but create spaces for group composition or improvisation, as exemplified by Yes and King Crimson respectively. McLaughlin's guitar sometimes appears to dominate Mahavishnu, but on *Inner Mounting Flame* and the second album, *Birds of Fire*, solos are often tracked in parallel (or staggered) by more than one instrument, and the high-speed syncopation strips away polite fusion, only to reunify the group: this is present throughout *Inner Mounting Flame* but comes to the fore in 'The Noonward Race'. These strategies were well established by avant-garde jazz groups in the 1960s. A few years later, progressive bands, including Mahavishnu, adopted this position in order to dismantle a fixed hierarchy in rock composition that was a hangover from rhythm and blues, where the rhythm section provided the base for the vocals and solo work of the group leader's instrument.

'Vital Transformation' and 'The Dance of Maya' are microcosms of the metallic jazz of King Crimson on three albums: *Larks' Tongues in Aspic* (1973), *Starless and Bible Black* (1974) and *Red* (1975). On these three albums, with a core of Robert Fripp, Bill Bruford and John Wetton (abetted by David Cross and Jamie Muir), the band worked with riffs and repetition, but the internal complexity of the short themes led to a narrative dissonance, unlike the somewhat settling effect of The Velvet Underground's interest in musical repetition. Whereas King Crimson's 1970s albums reveal modernist alienation, Mahavishnu's *The Inner Mounting Flame* aspires to spirituality. The appearance of a sardonic blues section midway through 'The Dance of Maya', though, hints at the alienation of contemporary life, as the tunefulness is shown to be the error, the veil of Maya, to be lifted through conscious atonality (echoing Coltrane's later recordings and concerts). The penultimate track, 'You Know You Know', works through the same idea, but inversely, with an atmospheric track dominated by Jan Hammer's electric keyboard broken by sporadic and very short guitar bursts, which could be interpreted as anti-solos. The closing track, 'Awakening', opens with a group crescendo but thereafter deadens the conflicts on the rest of the album in a display of fast playing and turn-taking short solos. If anything, this track should be read as a coda about the band's realizing the spiritual ideas explored earlier on the album.

Spirituality offered a metanarrative for fusion albums (as well as the music of Yes), where the coming together of many types of music was respectful of the mystical creation of the world, and also an attempt to recoup the supposed primordial unity of all things. Music is a privileged conveyor of this mysticism, connecting musician to cosmos. Carlos Santana followed the lead of McLaughlin to the guru Sri Chinmoy, and from 1972 onwards Santana's music was dominated by a spiritual framing, alternating between questing, meditation, discovery, harmony, overcoming, and the embracing of dissonance. Alternatively, it could be that by suggesting something 'spiritual' on its album covers, Santana could direct the listener to find and to experience spirituality within its music.

For English bands, when progressive rock approached fusion it tended to eschew spirituality in favour of eccentric radicalism, typified not only by non-conformist political thinkers but also by visual surrealism from the likes of Peter Blake and George Melly. Robert Wyatt lists Heath Robinson, Edward Lear and Tony Williams as inspirations for his drumming and singing in Soft Machine.[11] The band's version of fusion takes off from and shares the lyrical interests of psychedelia, refusing virtuosity in favour of complex musicality. Soft Machine paralleled Pink Floyd's musical development in this respect, travelling from unpredictable experimentalism to jazz atmospherics, even before Wyatt left in 1971, following the fourth album. On its debut 1968 album, *The Soft Machine* (the band's original name an exact copy of the 1961 William Burroughs novel), Wyatt, Kevin Ayers and Mike Ratledge constituted a guitar-free psychedelic-rock band. The model of the jazz group, where even if there are solos they are shared around, is an essential component of progressive rock; so too is the refusal to adhere to a predictable song structure facilitated by a group with lead vocals and guitar – the guitar is often minimized or even absent in progressive rock, in a refusal of pop or rock music dominated by a single voice.[12] Soft Machine rarely reverted to song-chorus development ('We Did It Again' repeats its one line over and over), and other tracks break down into sections, altering direction entirely. Even the more

Soft Machine outside the Albert Hall in London (12 August 1970).

obvious rock tracks are distorted by no-key organ playing, percussion that refuses to adhere to a guiding rhythm, or Wyatt's voice roaming widely across keys. Paul Stump's view of 'We Did It Again' applies to much of this first album, where 'parodic pop is brought to bear on jazz-rock tempi'.[13]

Not quite holding this all together is Wyatt's challenging vocal style, with its aggressive 'weakness' (in the sense noted by Gianni Vattimo) an explicit refusal of mastery.[14] From the opening moments of 'Hope for Happiness', Wyatt's fitful croon is both a structuring and destructuring instrument, refusing to settle on a central tone. The occasional choruses are made to feel like intrusions on the stream of consciousness and drift of melody (on 'Save Yourself' and 'Lullaby Letter'). Ayers' vocals on the song 'Why Are We Sleeping' are not only a call to order before the anti-conclusion of the 49-second 'Box 25/4 Lid' but also a way of emphasizing the unruliness of Wyatt's musings. After Ayers' departure, *Soft Machine Volume Two* offered an almost parodic level of ordering, its excess proving the illusoriness of its control. Side one, 'Rivmic Melodies', consists of ten tracks, including two parts of 'Pataphysical Introduction' and two of 'A Concise British Alphabet' (one of which is the alphabet forwards, the other backwards).[15] The intent to frame the music as anti-art is present not only in the reference to Alfred Jarry's theory of pataphysics but also in the title of the sixth track, 'Dada Was Here', and on the following track, 'Have You Ever Bean Green', where Wyatt thanks Noel, Mitch and Jim – The Jimi Hendrix Experience – rather than, say, Arnold

Schoenberg, composer of the piece they thank in the preceding 'Thank You Pierrot Lunaire'. Musically, this part of the album is in the vein of jazz, or even funk, in the first 2:49 of the third track, 'Hibou, Anemone and Bear'. Caravan also often adopted the jazz-funk instrumental passage based on organ and driven in a non-standard tempo for its rock compositions, but Soft Machine alternated such moments with dissonance and perverse breakdowns: at 2:49, 'Hibou, Anemone and Bear' stops, to be replaced by reverberating vocals with very bare and subdued instrumentation.

In addition to subverting musical and narrative order, Wyatt often refers to singing, to the song that he is actually in, or to the playing of music – equally on early Soft Machine albums, his recordings with Matching Mole, and his solo work. Through this preoccupation with singing, Wyatt is not only reflexive; he indicates or connotes reflexivity. In later years, he became openly political, directly presenting his left-wing perspective (most explicitly in the 1980s), but the Dadaist strategies, titles, 'weak' vocals, and the position-taking on the music are part of a formalist radical politics, the suggestiveness of which, in the context of the late 1960s and early 1970s, are enough to confirm Soft Machine's authentic political involvement in its cultural moment. Such involvement would later be a benchmark for the generation of British music critics writing in or after the arrival of punk, particularly the establishment of a hierarchy of acceptable groups such as Henry Cow, Soft Machine and free festival bands at the top; a middle ground of those who are deemed acceptable if not directly political (Krautrock groups, King Crimson, Van der Graaf Generator); and at the bottom those who ventured into more fantastical realms.[16]

By the time of its third release, *Third*, in 1970, it is hard to recognize the messy Dada fusion of the 1967–9 version of Soft Machine. Three of the four side-long tracks follow the same path as Pink Floyd into extended atmospheric pieces – 'pieces' as opposed to porous disorganizations. On *Third*, parodic order becomes the forced freedom of 18 to 19 minutes each to 'explore' on their own track. Only Wyatt's 'Moon in June' (19:08), on side three, forces an anti-art aesthetic into an attenuated version of Soft Machine. The first half of the track is made up of song fragments, and while the voice meanders across lyrical ideas, keys and metres, the drumming is often oddly 'rock standard', as if Wyatt has become his own unwilling session drummer. This tension breaks into an epiphanic change not dissimilar to mid-1970s Genesis (on *Selling England by the Pound*, for example), and then into a relatively free jazz instrumental, closed off by a finale that is more pots and pans than drum-kit virtuosity. It is maybe too easy to read into this rough style Wyatt's displeasure with the increasingly tuneful, tonal, atmospheric jazz that the other members of Soft Machine wanted to pursue, but where the first two albums offered group disorder, Wyatt represents disorder to the order and near stasis of the rest of the band.

While Caravan drifted into a more rock-based sound, Dave Stewart's part in the Canterbury scene moved towards fusing 'Canterbury' styles by switching his allegiance to Hatfield and the North (named after the signpost that marked the beginning of the northbound side of the M1 motorway from London) to release the band's eponymous debut album in 1974. Stewart had previously been in the abrasive band Egg, which had combined a hankering for classical sonata form with jazz metres, awkwardly phrased psychedelic excursions and crunching organs. Hatfield and the North included one of Caravan's two singers and principal writers, Richard Sinclair, on bass, and also featured Robert Wyatt on its first album. Caravan reached a point of whimsical no-return on *In the Land of Grey and Pink* (1971), heavily dominated by Sinclair. Hatfield and the North's eponymous debut reins in Sinclair, though, by juxtaposing his songs with an array of instrumental tracks and sections that cross between jazz, pastoral, metal fusion and constantly changing time signatures.[17] Conversely, Stewart's keyboards give us a tempered harshness compared to Egg on *The Polite Force* (1970) or the belatedly released *The Civil Surface* (1974).

The cover of *Hatfield and the North* shows what we presume to be Hatfield at twilight, with suburban houses in the forefront and the bulk of the landscape portrayed as a waste ground or in the early stages of a building project. The top half of the front of the gatefold shows a painting of hell emerging from the clouds. Superficially, this would seem to be about the misery of commuting from a dormitory town, or perhaps the dark underbelly of suburbia. But the cover is also deeply nostalgic, emphasizing how the music pursues its elegiac vision of the melancholy of everyday lives as it attempts to refashion a community (the lyrics about listening are less an affirmation than a recognition of failure and awkwardness). Like Soft Machine's second release, *Volume Two*, this album is a disrupted whole, framed by a short instrumental track that repeats with slightly more obvious guitar to close the album, but fades in its return to the beginning, disappearing in a manner that parallels its earlier arrival. Numerous short tracks suggest disruption, and there are many mood shifts that flow together rather than mapping onto individual tracks.

In its song titles, Hatfield and the North may seem to overdo comedy on nearly every other one of the fifteen tracks – such as the titles of 'Big Jobs (Poo Poo Extract)' and 'Lobster in Cleavage Probe' – and it would be true to say that the influence of The Bonzo Dog Band filtered through much English progressive rock. Even the most serious of bands, such as ELP, Genesis and Jethro Tull, included comedy tracks ('Jeremy Bender' on *Tarkus*, 'Harold the Barrel' on *Nursery Cryme*, 'The Story of the Hare Who Lost His Spectacles' on *A Passion Play*), and few could resist excessive punning. Here, though, there is an almost total mismatch between title and song: a disjunction to mirror that between structure and apparent disorder. The opening track of side two, 'Fol de Rol', is one of the most straightforward titles (signalling traditional English folk music and minstrelsy), but it also signifies nonsense and is, therefore, deceptively deconstructive. One of several tracks that features scat-style singing, it is given emotional depth by the mournful keyboard, vocals and bass section. More pathos is provided by the closing vocal's sounding like a recording heard on a telephone. This can be imagined as the moment where the album's vision of a disappearing society comes to fruition (it is also hinted at in the first few seconds of 'Licks for the Ladies', where running steps and closing doors frame fragments of other songs). As the album moves towards its close, Sinclair returns to sing about singing – by this stage what could have been a conservative vision of English life in the 'good old days' is shown to be a closed circuit; on 'Licks for the Ladies', Sinclair opens up reflection with his line 'try to sing a sober song after all that din'. This return to home moves through another song about singing and about the album itself: 'we have to leave here tonight'. Ostensibly, our 'troubles all melt away', but the melancholy of the three-piece choir prevents the listener from feeling comforted.

Following the disbanding of Hatfield and the North in 1975, the late 1970s saw its core members form National Health with Henry Cow's John Greaves, representing a move back to a progressive take on 'free music' that emerged from free jazz. Henry Cow occupied a similar position, if even more discordantly, but much of the British fusion dimension of progressive rock retreated from the radical implications of developing 1960s jazz styles, mirroring the move in American fusion to tune-based tonal jazz rock, with Soft Machine at the forefront. Newer groups such as Brand X and Gilgamesh, for all their complexity, represented a retreat into virtuosity and atmospherics. Outside Britain, the Italian band Goblin followed a similar path, with a radical brand of prog funk descending into derivative synth funk, on the soundtrack album *Dawn of the Dead* (1978), while, in France, Magma lost the drift of its Sun Ra-inspired cosmic choral jazz in favour of late 1970s jazz-funk clichés.

Despite not being part of progressive rock, there are elements in Sun Ra's music, mythology and albums that connect him to progressive narratives. Sun Ra claimed to be from Saturn, and, prefiguring Magma and Jon Anderson's *Olias of Sunhillow*, he was to bring the message of peace to Earth, apparently through an endless amount of unpredictable, often free music. Sun Ra brought together the nascent space mythology of the 1960s with a Gnostic take on the universe as a living force. On *The Heliocentric Worlds of Sun Ra II* (1966), a beautifully detailed map and illustrations of the solar system are accompanied by a set of human greats: Leonardo da Vinci, Copernicus, Pythagoras, Galileo Galilei, Tycho Brahe and Sun Ra himself. In positing himself as an alien, he makes 'otherness' into something positive and creative: a hyperbolic version of negritude. In identifying with scientific discoverers, he asserts both his genius and their otherness. Already at this point he introduces a range of non-jazz instruments into a free jazz band that is not quite as free as we hear in John Coltrane at the time. Sun Ra was a very early adopter of electronic keyboards, which can be heard at some length in one release, *Concert for the Comet Kohoutek* (1974), which does seem to approximate progressive rock. *Concert for the Comet Kohoutek* is the document of a concert at Town Hall,

New York City on 22 December 1973, to mark the arrival of this particular comet. Sun Ra brought his worldview into contact with a material, factual space event. Not only that, but as 'Astro Black' outlines, shortly after the beginning of the concert, this is all about 'Astro Black Mythology': in other words, black consciousness should use space imagery and the refusal of earthly limitations to structure a radical and assertive identity not determined by the history of colonialism and slavery. Here, African culture goes straight to the stars, as it was also doing at this time with George Clinton's bands Funkadelic and Parliament, which also used studio technology, extended jams and effects to create a cosmic identity. *Concert for the Comet Kohoutek* continues through some tuneful jazz passages that gradually give way to fevered and almost random prodding at electronic and analogue keyboards, especially 'Discipline' and 'Outer Space E.M. (Emergency)', towards the end of the concert. 'Space is the Place' ends funkily and connects straight back into the mainline of Afrofuturism.

Magma created a similar worldview but presented it as fiction, opening up the universe of 'Kobaïa' and the language of kobaïen that came from that planet, first on the album *Magma* (1970, later retitled *Kobaïa*) and then on a seemingly endless array of albums and further tracks that were initially played only live. The story of that first album revolves around aliens arriving on earth and discovering the planet's alienation from the wonder of the universe to which the kobaïens have access. A few humans travel back with them and witness the wonder of harmonious living. Kobaïens return to earth at the end to find nothing has changed, but they offer the chance for everyone to leave. This offer is met with defensiveness and the fear of attack, so the humans are pre-emptively dealt with and Earth's 'clamour is stilled' on 'Müh'.[18] The music continually shifts between jazz and rock overlain with vocals that cross the range from chant to scream. Like an opera or Prokofiev's *Peter and the Wolf*, the music enacts the story as narrated in the written notes; 'Müh' moves from gentle passages where the flute features heavily, along with a somnolent vocal mumble and more strident elements, to over 2 minutes of cacophony, before ending in a final chant that emphasizes the ultimate power of the alien visitors. If the message is about humanity's not hearing the natural universe, then the language of kobaïen gives material form to this lack of comprehension: the language signifies a universal harmony that cannot be heard by humans. Humans reject the possibility of utopia (this recurs throughout the sequence of albums) and fall into discord. The message is that this utopia can be resolved only by a better kind of dissonance – a view that corresponds broadly with Nietzsche's idea of an active nihilism in opposition to the passive nihilism of those who believe in objective truth.

Perhaps the highpoint of the realization of this vision of an avenging utopian world is Magma's 1973 album *Mëkanïk Dëstruktïw Kömmandöh*, where this time the alien language of the songs is given a gloss in French. Here, we discover that the prophet Nebëhr Gudahtt (a human) has communicated his message to band leader Christian Vander, wherein all humans must die to atone for their loss of connection to the truth of the cosmos and their failure to be interested in self-realization. This, in turn, has been transmitted from a god with a kobaïen name: Kreühn Köhrmahn. The prophet eventually convinces humanity of the truth of its existential lostness, and humanity dissolves into the universe, finally attaining a form of enlightenment (liner notes, 15–19). Vander adds that, for him, 'with *Mëkanïk Kömmandöh* [*sic*], Magma was born'.[19] The music is much more complex and unified, albeit fractally. The band is augmented by a choir, and the album is essentially one long piece where 'the melodies build infinitely, each more intense than the last'.[20] Vander often cites John Coltrane and describes this album as his 'My Favourite Things'.[21] Presumably, he means this in the way 'My Favourite Things' was performed in Coltrane's late concerts (*The Olatunji Concert: The Last Live Recording*, recorded in 1967), as *Mëkanïk Dëstruktïw Kömmandöh* is more like a non-improvised take on Coltrane's *Ascension*, and is also reminiscent of 'The Creator Has a Masterplan' on Pharoah Sanders' *Karma* (1969). This is a difficult path to spiritual realization, undergoing the judgement outlined in the liner notes and a punishing series of crescendos. If this is fusion, then it is in the service of a new form: a fusion of a different kind, where fusion itself signals spiritual awareness through atonal harmony, presumably indicating the continuity between bad discord and positive dissonance.

Like Magma, Gong also developed a space mythology, although as it is gnome-based it is slightly less portentous. Gong's acid quirkiness is tempered by the sprawl of the Radio Gnome Invisible trilogy, comprising *Flying Teapot*, *Angel's Egg* (both 1973) and *You* (1974). Like Magma, there is a change of stylistic emphasis as the musical narration progresses. The albums take off from Sun Ra's mythology (based on his origins in space), shifting the space mythology into a reported narrative. Gong had clear connections to French jazz, alongside its participation in the hippie festival world and its kinship with the space band Hawkwind. Whereas Hawkwind imports Michael Moorcock's science-fiction cosmologies (as discussed in Chapter 5), Gong's trilogy ambles around in a mythology, as Zero the Hero goes on trips, running into Pot Head Pixie and others of his ilk. The music is not so much fusion as non-fusion, indicating a utopia that is not about unanimity but about individual lifestyles co-existing with each other and combining when it feels right (on the bass-driven longer tracks on each album, for example). From jazz to funk to ambient analogue synth tracks and even space shanties, the music offers the same kind of non-progression as the narratives. But the trilogy is a narrative in itself: just as modernist film and literature still contain fragments of narrative, the album cycle imagines a world that is better for being disjointed and free-flowing. Jon Mills observes that Daevid Allen's vision has ideological weight beyond this cyclical coherence on two levels. First, Mills suggests that Allen's 'deliberately silly story about pothead pixies, flying teapots and octave doctors was in fact an ideal way to open up people's minds to his philosophy' and, second, highlights 'a more serious "floating anarchy" ideology – Planet Gong was Daevid's imagined version of what Earth would become [. . .] Daevid extolled the plight of capitalism, governments and central structure'.[22]

Pirate radio (received and retransmitted by Gong) not only alerted listeners to perils ahead but also served as an operational model for an alternative society, as well as signalling that Gong could be seen as an avant-garde community (in terms of gender balance, at least – women feature substantially on these albums). *Angel's Egg* shows this community developing through the division into yin and yang, masculine and feminine sides (the latter being the more coherent and flowing side two of the original album), suggesting a new balance not just amid, but precisely created by, the album's chaotic structure. For all the appearance of a protean version of industrial music's take on William Burroughs, Gong's complexity is fuzzy rather than dissonant, a community to be attained through consensus amid fusion. This is certainly the outcome on *You*, musically the most harmonious of the trilogy, as Allen's oddness is caught within Tim Blake's all-embracing synth warmth and the proto-trance of Steve Hillage's development of Allen's guitar glissandos. Oddly, Gong's prescience about alternative post-hippie or anti-hippie communities puts them out of time, as the music is outside of a recognizable sequential progression. Its closest relatives are Hawkwind and Funkadelic, but for all Gong's visions, these two bands, in different ways, aim for a progressive listenership through harshness or ultra-repetition, while Allen and his band attempted to befriend listeners by reaching out to them from the outset.

Gong and Magma offer world visions, as did even Miles Davis in the shape of enveloping ambience and the idea of fusion. Others created unified albums that suggest autonomous worlds. Where these fusions with jazz rootedness recombine with other streams of progressive rock is in the staging of the music. Whereas Gong pursued this in the late 1960s by expanding into the 1970s free festival scene, Magma's live shows became spectacular and offered new parts of the kobaïen mythology. The jazz rock that arose in the mid-1970s, in a viralizing of American jazz fusion, eschewed such visceral realities. In Britain, jazz rock, like free jazz or 'free music', looked for a call to order, where simply playing would be everything, representing a weird prefiguring of punk.

Notes

1. Robert Wyatt, cited in Stump, *The Music's All That Matters*, 23.
2. Joachim E. Berendt, *The Jazz Book: From Ragtime to Fusion and Beyond* (6th edn, revised by Günther Huesmann) (New York: Lawrence Hill, 1989), 38.
3. Ibid., 101.
4. Cited in Macan, *Rocking the Classics*, 148.
5. See Smith, *In the Court of the Crimson King*, 129, 145.
6. Ibid., 136.

7. Richard Williams, *The Blue Moment: Miles Davis's* Kind of Blue *and the Remaking of Modern Music* (London: Faber and Faber, 2009), 19.

8. Ibid., 36–7.

9. Jameson, *Postmodernism, or the Cultural Logic of Late Capitalism*, 16–20.

10. This is not to be confused with the freedoms of Kraftwerk's *Autobahn*, where the pristine clarity of movement is compromised by the Hitlerian origin of the means to freedom, and at the same time suggests Paul Virilio's speed pathology in *Speed and Politics: An Essay on Dromology* (New York: Semiotext(e), [1977] 1986).

11. Wyatt, cited in Stump, *The Music's All That Matters*, 124.

12. Soft Machine's original guitarist, Daevid Allen, was a major influence on the whole Canterbury scene.

13. Ibid., 33.

14. See Gianni Vattimo, *The End of Modernity* (Baltimore: Johns Hopkins University Press, 1991), 11, 86 and *passim*.

15. Side two of *Soft Machine Volume Two* is mostly the track 'Esther's Nose Job' (the entire side is presented under this title), and, similarly, offers the prospect of order so as to withhold it. The extravagant subtitles are a response to the record company's demands that tracks be broken into sections. See Graham Bennett, *Soft Machine: Out-Bloody-Rageous* (London: SAF, 2005), 162.

16. Paul Stump is guilty of this to some extent: he is dismissive of Caravan's whimsy (Stump, *The Music's All that Matters*, 126) and somewhat wary of a moment when progressive rock apparently loses its politically progressive character.

17. Richard Sinclair is similar to Robert Wyatt in often providing lyrics about singing or that comment on a particular point in the album.

18. See the liner narration notes on Magma, *Magma* (1970).

19. Vander, *Mëkanïk Dëstruktïw Kömmandöh*, liner notes, 11. Translations from French by Paul Hegarty.

20. Ibid., 10.

21. Ibid.

22. Jon 'Jojo' Mills, liner notes, *Flying Teapot*, 4.

Chapter 7

Performance and Visuality

A fusion of mythology and sonic innovation came together in the performance of 1970s progressive rock, echoing multimedia art forms of the late 1960s and highlighting an ongoing interest in theatricality and visuality. The shift away from the total immersion of psychedelia and happenings to a shared space where engagement and contemplation were equally possible meant that progressive bands could test out the fourth wall of musical performance and, in doing so, their relationship with the audience. Smaller university venues in the early days of prog rock made only a limited level of theatricality possible, but more spectacular events were common through the 1970s, as venues became larger and bands needed to create special effects and dramatic stage-sets to connect with a more physically distant audience. Such theatricality was not without its risks, though. When Emerson, Lake and Palmer used three gigantic tour trucks (each one emblazoned with a band member's name), a fifty-nine-member orchestra, six-member choir, a portable stage with a roof and hydraulic lift, and a road crew of 120 for its 1977 *Works* tour, it seemed as if musical performance (in its broadest sense) had blurred with the grandiosity that punk bands would exploit to condemn progressive rock wholesale.[1] Examples are easy to find: Keith Emerson suspended in the air to play the grand piano at ELP's April 1974 California Jam appearance, or Rick Wakeman's lavish performances of *The Myths and Legends of King Arthur and the Knights of the Round Table* at Wembley Arena in 1975, with Arthurian ice-skating characters and a full orchestra.[2] It is easy to dismiss the indulgences of mid-1970s rock groups as indicative of a decadent music industry, but the preoccupation of progressive bands with visual media – performance, ritual, theatre, masks, costume, lighting, film, video, typography and artwork – reveals a variegated aesthetic, often treated with a high seriousness but sometimes marked by humour, whimsy and glimmers of self-parody.

A useful starting point for thinking about prog performance is British theatre director Peter Brook's widely read book *The Empty Space*. Published in 1968, just as progressive rock emerged on both sides of the Atlantic, Brook's book offered a typology of theatrical modes. Brook's interest was in the 'bare stage', which becomes theatrical as soon as 'a man walks across this empty space whilst someone else is watching him'.[3] Brook wanted to rescue the spirit of theatre from the paraphernalia – the 'red curtains, spotlights, blank verse, laughter, darkness' – often associated with the kind of commercial theatre that, to his mind, had ossified into a 'deadly theatre' based on 'old formulae, old methods, old jokes, old effects, stock beginnings to scenes' designed to make drama reassuringly familiar for bourgeois audiences, evoking senti- ment but often at the expense of craft or meaningful social engagement.[4] Rather than celebrating a seamless or unified theatre, Brook contends that it is made up of numerous pieces, some of which 'jar', particularly in the 'shifting, chaotic world' of 1968; theatre, for Brook, has two possibilities: 'a spurious "yes" or a provocation so strong that it splinters its audience into fragments of vivid "nos"'.[5] The opposition between a theatre of spurious affirmation and nihilistic denial is not straightforward, though. Brook goes on to detail two other types – holy theatre and rough theatre – that complicate this dichotomy and look beyond commercial imperatives. Holy theatre is an attempt to find a suitable language for invisible forms through the restaging of ritual; rough theatre recalls the 'low' performance of vaudeville, comedy and a theatre of noise: 'if the holy makes a world in which prayer is more real than a belch, in the rough theatre it is the other way round'.[6] Whereas holy theatre deals with the 'hidden impulses of man' that move beyond corporeality, rough theatre deals with earthy realities and bodily pleasures.

We would argue that progressive rock of the 1970s combined versions of holy and rough theatre, fusing them in different ways and with divergent aesthetic and, at times, political ends. Mystical, religious and social elements often crossed over, such as the 'New Jerusalem' lyric as the coda of Genesis's 'Supper's Ready', or on the 10-minute track 'Lord of the Ages' (1973) by the English progressive folk band Magna Carta, in which a spoken prologue (telling of a messianic birth that promises to dispel bewitchment and destruc- tion) segues into an electric guitar-led progressive section (in which 'death and destruction' are set against the diurnal forces of the harvest) and ends with potential emancipation and the choral reprise of 'Lord of the Ages/ Nobody knows/Wither he goes/Nobody knows'. Romanticism was the favoured aesthetic mode for projecting alternative cosmologies (sometimes idealistic, sometimes dystopian) and to excavate the space between self- examination (on Wishbone Ash's soul-searching track 'Sometime World' on *Argus*, for example) and epic historical dramas (on 'Warrior' and 'The King Will Come', from the same album), but this was often inflected with a modernist interest in revisiting myths through psychological investigation. This Romantic-modernist mode was not exclusive to prog rock: it infused, for example, the literary experiments of William Burroughs, the avant-garde filmmaking of Kenneth Anger, Jim Morrison's interest in shamanism and the hypnotic power of live performance, and The Who's fusion of the 1960s synth experimentation of American composer Terry Riley and the mystical thought of Indian guru Meher Baba on its quasi-prog track 'Baba O'Riley' (1971). Rough theatre might be most closely associated with a certain strain of progressive folk such as The Incredible String Band or the acid folk of Comus at the turn of the 1970s, with their alternately earthy and other-worldly vocals and strange musical arrangements. But it also punctured the transcendent themes that linked back to the late 1960s counterculture and propelled progressive rock beyond the immersive psychedelic experience into a performance mode where participation and contemplation could co-exist. Writing more generally about musical theatre, Brook describes this trend as a reminder that theatre is about 'colours and sounds, of music and movement', offering an escape route from daily life and a reminder that human discord and hope are often entwined.[7] Stories from a lost past were attractive to progressive bands (as discussed in Chapter 3), but they were often performed in a musical-theatrical mode that could drag the past into the present through ritual or ceremony.

Brook's call was to develop a new language: 'a language of word-as-part-of-movement, of word-as-lie, word-as-parody, of word-as-rubbish, or word-as-contradiction, of word-shock or word-cry'.[8] We would argue that progressive rock at its most creative attempted to develop such a language in the 1970s, albeit unevenly and with some failures. Prog rock was certainly not something that Brook would have had in mind had he published *The Empty Space* five years later, but he did acknowledge that music deals 'with a fabric that is as near as man can get to the expression of the invisible', and when music is linked to dramatic visual forms (what Brook calls the 'flesh and blood' of performance) it combines the holy and the rough.[9] This did not prevent progressive performance from being pretentious or empty at times, but in its eclecticism and exploration of an aesthetic mid-world between conceptual levels, musical styles and expressive modes, prog rock gave rise to some interesting versions of what Brook found missing in much mainstream 1960s drama. Arguably, progressive performance inclined towards the holy – take Rick Wakeman's fondness for the church organ as keyboardist of Yes or his solo work such as *The Gospels* project in the mid-1980s, which involved a tenor vocalist and the Eton College Chapel Choir; or take the interest in protagonists with special or quasi-divine talents, such as the 'deaf, dumb and blind boy' in The Who's rock opera *Tommy* (1969), which mixes holy and rough theatre (to use Brook's terminology) by juxtaposing existential themes relating to sensory deprivation, trauma and second-sight with musical-hall elements and a seaside holiday-camp setting, or Nektar's concept album *Remember the Future* (1973), in which a blind boy attempts to communicate with an alien. More recently is the albino protagonist of Spock Beard's 2002 album *Snow*, who has the gift of seeing into others' lives, a sequence of albums by Spock Beard's ex–lead singer Neal Morse exploring

Christian Enlightenment, and the prominence of Martin Luther on Morse's *Sola Scriptura* (2007). Despite the grand gestures and profound themes of progressive rock in the 1970s, albums and gigs often combined low musical elements or included comic sections that kept the performance grounded or fractured theatrical illusion.

Another element to consider is the mediatization that linked to musical performance, well before the advent of MTV in 1980 or the use of video monitors at rock concerts later in the 1980s, which gave mass audiences the chance to see bands close up. Philip Auslander traces musical mediatization back to electric amplification, experimentation with reverb and echo, the use of the Mellotron for creating layered music, and designer instruments such as Emerson's modular Moog (which he plays with his buttocks in ELP's December 1970 Lyceum Ballroom performance, released as *Pictures at an Exhibition* in 1972). Such musical mediatization was heightened in the late 1960s and 1970s, when the visual dimension of performance began to be taken seriously.[10] Experiments with still and moving images and with special effects such as solarization (used liberally in the *Pictures at an Exhibition* film) were linked closely to the potential for incorporating theatrical costumes, graphics and performance art that went well beyond the psychedelic swirl of lights, imagery and costumes of the late 1960s.[11] These experiments worked on different levels. Some bands, such as Hawkwind, used projected slide tape in their performances, to refine the disorientating effects of liquid light-shows favoured by psychedelic rock bands such as The Grateful Dead. This trend was at its peak on Hawkwind's 1973 *Space Ritual* tour, which included performance art and a DJ playing records backwards, and was also part of the band's 1974 tour, in which space-scape slides created by science-fiction artist David Harvey combined with more abstract images as a way of fusing vision, sound and narrative. In a more conventional theatrical mode, Peter Gabriel's use of grease paint from 1970 onwards (during and beyond his time as lead singer of Genesis) to create an odd cast of characters was linked to a fondness for bizarre costumes set against abstract stage sets, through which Gabriel became a character in the song or morphed into a mythical figure such as the Watcher of the Skies, as performed at De Montfort Hall, Leicester, and as recorded on the *Genesis Live* album (1973).

This interest in costumes and masks was not the exclusive domain of progressive rock. The use of theatrical stage sets can be linked to musicals and opera, and also at a more carnivalesque level to The Rolling Stones' Rock and Roll Circus of December 1968, in which a replica of a big top and Mick Jagger's role as circus-master set the stage for a series of rough performances from The Rolling Stones, Jethro Tull, The Who, Lennon and McCartney, and Taj Mahal. Dressing up was most obviously associated with glam rock in the early 1970s, but also with the genre-bending music of David Bowie and early Roxy Music, and the use of grease paint and death masks by Arthur Brown in the late 1960s or by Alice Cooper and Kiss in the mid-1970s. Although there are discernible crossovers between glam rock and progressive rock in the use of theatrics (as Kevin Holm-Hudson has argued),[12] what differentiates their respective use of costumes is glam rock's intense focus on the individual performer (for Bowie) or the outlandish costumes of Brian Eno, Marc Bolan and Alice Cooper, which 'exaggerated [their] physical presence on stage'.[13] The androgyny and gender-mixing of glam rock crossed over into prog rock to a degree, but singers in progressive bands were arguably more enigmatic, equally 'familiar and foreign' and suggestive of both 'surface and depth', as Richard Leppert has described the performed body.[14] Flamboyant glam costumes were largely about external show (perhaps apart from Bowie's) and did not have the same narrative function as Gabriel's dressing as a rural mower in 'I Know What I Like (in Your Wardrobe)' in 1974 (a tour in which Gabriel used narrative segments to link songs while the other band members tuned their instruments), or as his turn as the deformed, bulbous Slipperman in 'In the Colony of Slipper Men' for the 1975 *The Lamb Lies Down on Broadway* tour (see the image in Chapter 4). The integration of costume and narrative is part of what Macan calls the organicist trajectory of 1970s progressive rock, 'fusing its disparate stylistic sources together into a single alloy', rather than relying on pastiche or high camp to project a strong image of the musical performer.[15]

Indeed, the experiments in prog rock went much further than those in glam rock, which quickly settled into being a style. By 1975, on the *Lamb* tour, for example, Genesis combined theatricality and experimentation with projected images, using seven slide carousels and fifteen hundred images to provide a backdrop to Gabriel's theatrics and to illustrate the surreal imagery of the album: 'a greatly magnified and grotesque insect against a stolid fifties Ford' or a 'snowy white feathered heart nestled in crimson satin drapery' shaved by 'a rubber-gloved hand . . . with cruel precision'.[16] Without sophisticated visual technology, a spotlight on the costumed singer in the centre of a concert stage arguably lacked the drama of a cinematic close-up, but the use of image projections to tell stories and to echo cover art, the deployment of props, or even the distribution of merchandise such as T-shirts emblazoned with reproductions of album covers and band iconography functioned as proxies for the close-up and helped to mythologize bands in the process. Examples of these techniques can be found variously in the red-dressed fox on *Foxtrot* (another of Gabriel's iconic stage costumes); the fifty-foot inflatable octopus on dry ice in Pink Floyd's 1971 Crystal Palace concert, or the airborne inflatable pig on its live set of 1977, based on the cover of *Animals*; and Led Zeppelin's four occult symbols, which featured in the band's merchandise as well as its stage set. The emphasis on mesmerizing graphics as an element of a band's performance in the broader sense is exemplified by the graphics agency Hipgnosis, which was widely used by the likes of Pink Floyd and Led Zeppelin in the 1970s and based its craft on the concept of visual hypnosis, combining the hip ('new and groovy') with Gnostic learning:

'the old and the new, cohabiting a world that implied bewitchment', as Storm Thorgerson described it.[17]

Auslander roots what he calls 'the incursion of mediatization into the live setting' in avant-garde performance going back to pre–World War I experiments, such as Hugo Ball performing with a box on his head to fellow Dadaists in Zurich, or the proto-happenings of the Surrealists in Paris in the late 1910s and 1920s.[18] While avant-garde performance sometimes focused on an individual performer, it more often involved a performance group in which staged and improvised roles intersected in surprising ways, combining band members' taking turns to showcase their own instruments and blending musical sounds within the ensemble. The international Fluxus movement and the Living Theatre in the 1960s are two examples of the ways in which everyday life and heightened aesthetic states melded and fused – with deliberate political intent in the case of the Living Theatre (in 1968, the group performed for the Students for Democratic Society and its members promoted anarchic revolution at public venues).[19] Arguably, outside of Henry Cow and the later Rock in Opposition (RIO) groups, progressive rock had a different avant-garde agenda and was more formalist in its song composition than these earlier art groupings. Sometimes characters were represented on stage via costumes, voice or gesture; and for groups that did not use costume to illustrate characters, flowing costumes (flares, stack heels, robes, capes, tunics, lamé suits, long hair) favoured by bands in the early to mid-1970s were important performance elements, bridging avant-gardism, contemporary fashion and the mass-mediatized performance of the 1980s and 1990s.

This emphasis on live performance is arguably in tension with what many critics see as the source text of popular music: the single or LP. Auslander points to Theodore Gracyk's argument that 'rock music is not essentially a performing art' but a recorded one, but Auslander contends that live performance is also an essential ingredient in meeting the demands of fans as well as in increasing a band's revenue.[20] Nonetheless, performance and recordings had a symbiotic relation, particularly in prog, we would argue, in that fans wanted to see and hear the fullness of album tracks away from a studio setting. Studio virtuosity put pressure on performers to develop the skill to reinvent, replicate or expand what they had recorded. Equally, progressive bands often challenged their audiences by playing previously unheard and complex material – as a mode of avant-garde music – or by building new material from improvisations (as mid-1970s King Crimson did, notably on *Starless and Bible Black*). At a more practical level, 1980s neo-progressive bands had often been touring for some time before they released any recordings (see Chapter 9).

Sometimes a band could project an image not based on live performance: take, for example, the psychedelic personae of The Beatles in the late 1960s – well after they had ceased to perform live – but they were in the eye of the media and had other channels for promoting their interest in psychedelia and mysticism. Moreover, Auslander argues (following Simon Frith) that performance is essential for establishing musical credibility – whether through a band's ability to perform complex arrangements live on stage or by reaffirming 'extra-musical knowledge and beliefs' such as a group's image, its use of cover art and iconography, and the mythology of 'the band', which grew in the early to mid-1970s through the mystique of 'supergroups' and when the excessive behaviour of touring bands contributed to the myth of rock stardom.[21] The touring excesses of Led Zeppelin or ELP overshadowed more restrained behaviour of other tourists: Peter Gabriel, for example, was flamboyant on stage but otherwise introverted and not tempted by an excessive rock lifestyle, as was the case for Justin Hayward, Mike Oldfield and Rush.

It is worth examining two filmed examples in some depth to illustrate these points and to explore the ceremonial and ritualistic elements of performance that Peter Brook discusses in *The Empty Space*. Both examples are embodied in audio-visual recordings – Pink Floyd's *Live at Pompeii* (1972) and Led Zeppelin's *The Song Remains the Same* (1976) – and mix meticulously rehearsed material with an interest in improvisation. The two performances fuse live concert footage (partially staged, as explained below) with process shots and, in the case of a second cut of *Live at Pompeii*, a studio recording that emphasizes both traditional virtuosity (piano, guitar) and experiments with technology (Mellotron, echo machine).

Brook's interest in ritual was taken up by Pink Floyd's film *Live at Pompeii*, directed by Adrian Maben. It combines a live performance of tracks from *A Saucerful of Secrets* and *Meddle*, filmed in October 1971, with a studio session including tracks from *The Dark Side of the Moon*, recorded at Abbey Road Studios in 1972. Moving away from the totally immersive experience of Syd Barrett–era Pink Floyd, the surreality of the promotional video for the band's debut single, 'Arnold Layne' (1967), and the rough cover art of *A Nice Pair* (the 1973 re-release of the first two albums), the empty Roman amphitheatre of Pompeii provides a dramatic setting for a set of six songs that resonate eerily with the empty landscape. Conceived as a kind of 'anti-Woodstock' recording without an audience, the amphitheatre sonically represents the theme of the long track 'Echoes'. There is, however, as Nicholas Schaffner comments, a surrogate audience: the ghostly 'two-millennia-old faces on the ancient amphitheatre's frescoes and statues', an 'echo of a distant time' buried undetected for fifteen hundred years.[22] The director's cut of *Live at Pompeii* (2003) emphasizes the musical ambition to capture the infinite realms of space, prefacing the performance with a rocket launch and a planetary montage, the camera slowly moving towards the earth before dissolving into an establishing shot of the amphitheatre, volcanic ruins and damaged classical statuary (the initial release focuses on the ruins of Pompeii before offering the same vista of the empty amphitheatre). The band is dwarfed by the bare circle and a dark bank of amplifiers, before slowly coming into view as a tightly knit four-piece. This is the plainest example in progressive rock of

Peter Brook's empty space; 'Echoes' forms a prelude to the whole performance and is a version of holy theatre in its own right, with its sustained chords and lyrical lead guitar and vocal textures. The theatricality derives from the panning shots of the empty amphitheatre (itself a ritualistic space), the atmospheric lighting (filmed variously in daylight, at sunset and at night), close-ups of the musicians playing, shots of the band visiting the smouldering Vesuvius, and (in the director's cut) a volcanic montage that emphasizes the earth's being a living and violent organism.

The sequence of shots in Abbey Road Studios is part of the filmed performance, as Roger Waters plays with reverb, echo and distortion at the mixing desk and debates with guitarist David Gilmour the possibilities of pure musical experimentation versus the mastery of new 'electronic goodies' that can extend the sonic range – a musical version of the 'new language' that Brook recommended. After shots of the band members eating together in the Abbey Road canteen (perhaps a version of rough theatre), the footage switches back to a night performance of the sinister 'Careful with That Axe, Eugene' (actually shot in Paris), which grew out of instrumental experimentation in 1967–8, when Syd Barrett was still in the band. In this performance, the band is positioned closer together in a more conventional stage shot, emitting a quasi-psychedelic, quasi-ambient sound based on a single sustained chord over which the group creates 'textures and moods', as Gilmour described it.[23] Waters intones virtually incomprehensible lyrics, suggesting a form of musical possession, interspersed with whispers, heavy breathing and a scream in the middle of the song (which the band accompanied in other live performances with actual explosions) as his voice becomes a fifth instrument with the sonic power to wake the dead. Whereas 'Echoes' evokes a version of holy theatre, 'Careful with That Axe, Eugene' is the obverse, emphasizing menacing, demonic elements that give musical expression to the volcano that once destroyed a whole city and has the power to do so again. Such demonic elements often complicate – or even subvert – the holy dimension to progressive performance, such as the parody of Psalm 23 on 'Dogs', intoned through a vocoder by Nick Mason during Pink Floyd's 1977 concerts, or the citation of religious verse in Marillion's 'Forgotten Sons', which is shot through with political violence and formed a dramatic finale to the band's early 1980s concerts.

Such experimentation was not confined to the musical realm. Stemming from its early interest in multimedia performances, Pink Floyd was drawn to the filmed image in its earlier scores for the British film *The Committee* (1968) and the French films *More* (1969) and *La Vallée* (released by Pink Floyd in 1972 as *Obscured by Clouds* – another album influenced by Arthur C. Clarke's *Childhood's End*), and the band came close to writing a soundtrack for Michelangelo Antonioni's 1970 countercultural movie *Zabriskie Point*. *Live at Pompeii* emphasizes the control of technology, finding a slightly simpler, organized format to suit the band's ancient surroundings. While the performance is tight, all is not controlled ritual, particularly the dissonant and cacophonous jam that leads into 'A Saucerful of Secrets', during which Gilmour uses the guitar as an electronic keyboard while Waters crashes cymbals and a huge gong with a circular case around it like a penumbra. The camera cuts away to another shot of the gong and Waters in silhouette before fusing with another circle (in the director's cut): a visual fusion of the burning sun and molten lava bubbling in the volcanic crater. The totemic gong had previously been seen as the first instrument carried into the empty amphitheatre; it appears behind Nick Mason's drum-kit during another night track, 'One of These Days', and is the centrepiece (played softly in a hypnotic rhythm by Waters) of the quasi-mystical, ritualistic track 'Set the Controls for the Heart of the Sun'. For this song, the camera swirls hypnotically in a tight circular motion around the four musicians and picks out a series of geometric circles surrounding the band – the concentric rings of the gong and its outer case, a ring of spotlights, drums, cymbals, and another close-up of the burning sun – interspersed with images of Pompeii's ancient frescoes, with one haunting shot of Richard Wright playing his keyboard in virtual silhouette against a projection of images depicting petrified bodies in the wake of the Mount Vesuvius eruption.

Led Zeppelin's audio-visual record of its Madison Square Garden concert in July 1973 is in stark contrast to Pink Floyd's *Live at Pompeii* but offers some interesting insights into progressive rock performance. As a blues-rock

Pink Floyd: Live at Pompeii (1972).

band (although they combined folk and progressive elements), Led Zeppelin performed with characteristic flamboyant posturing and kinetic stage movements more closely associated with heavy rock than the studious stage poses of Pink Floyd and Yes. However, in the only authorized audio-visual release during the life of the band, the mythical iconography of *The Song Remains the Same* has strong progressive resonances. Rock journalist Mick Wall points out that the film was actually a hotchpotch of filmed material from 1973; offstage footage from the concert; fantasy sequences involving each of the four band members and their manager; and a restaged performance from 1975, added when the band realized that the quality of the earlier footage was patchy. Wall likens the film to The Beatles' *A Hard Day's Night* (1964) and to T. Rex's *Born to Boogie* (1972, directed by Ringo Starr), for which Marc Bolan took inspiration from Italian filmmaker Federico Fellini.[24] Including a series of pastoral shots of the band in the English countryside, *The Song Remains the Same* profiles each band member in a mythologized role: Robert Plant as an Arthurian knight, John Paul Jones a highwayman, John Bonham a yeoman farmer and racing-car driver, and Jimmy Page encountering a spectral hermit who resembles the iconography of The Hermit tarot card but also mirrors the stooped hermit on the cover of the fourth Led Zeppelin album. Filmed near Page's property Boleskine House on the shores of Loch Ness – a previous owner of which was the occultist Aleister Crowley – this segment features Page climbing a rock face in the dead of night towards the looming figure of a hermit. As he approaches the hermit's lantern, we are drawn into the ancient figure's visage through a series of facial metamorphoses that take us backwards in time through Page's life, back to his childhood and, before that, as a foetus, before accelerating forward again to fuse with the old hermit's ancient features, which imply both occult recognition and the blending of past, present and future. As Wall points out, this sequence melds with the live performance by cutting to Page's use of the violin bow to play his guitar during the extended riff of 'Dazed and Confused'. Here the bow is both a magical wand and a symbol of musical virtuosity:

> the bow melding into one clearly occult image as the Hermit/Magus waves his bow/ wand and in a slow arc through the air, left to right, its colours showing eleven . . . it's as if the 'Barrington Coleby' painting from the inner sleeve of the fourth Led Zeppelin album has been brought to life, its visual metaphor obvious: the journey to occult enlightenment.[25]

Although the film was dismissed by the musical press of 1976–7 as pretentious, this hermit sequence successfully fuses media – music, imagery, action, mythology and costume in the fantasy sequences, as well as the flamboyant costumes adorned with dragons, moons and stars that Page started to wear for concerts from 1973 – on a level that was in tune with, but also extends far beyond, the band's Madison Square Garden live performance. Indeed, as

Hermit sequence from *The Song Remains the Same* (1976).

Susan Fast argues, the violin bow was part of the theatre of Led Zeppelin: it is 'a powerful symbol borrowed from the tradition of "classical" Western music' that connected Page 'not only with progressive rock but also with the avant-garde', particularly as the bow was often used in connection with a theremin (which Page began to use for concerts in 1969) to create new electronic sounds in extended versions of 'Dazed and Confused', a blues track that stretched out to 40 minutes in some performances.[26]

This performance mode was echoed in an essay that William Burroughs wrote for *Crawdaddy* in June 1975, based on an interview with Jimmy Page that included a discussion of Aleister Crowley, Page's soundtrack for Kenneth Anger's 1973 avant-garde film *Lucifer Rising*, and the relationship between ancient ceremonies and rock music played to a mass audience. Reflecting on the 'musical exhilaration' of his first Led Zeppelin concert, Burroughs focuses on the control of the band and the special effects (laser beams, dry ice, smoke), mixed with a 'palpable interchange of energy between the performers and the audience which was never frantic or jagged'.[27] Linking to the 1960s interest in the synaesthesia or the cross-cueing of senses that can be stimulated by psychedelic drugs and enhanced by circular-like song structures and 'layered mixes' of 'reverb, echoes and tape delays that can give a sense of space', Burroughs focused on the 'magic' of the performance based on repetition and energy.[28] This energy can be dangerous, but when controlled it is an effective conduit between performers and audience. While discussing the magical power of musical performance, Page admitted that he was not seeking to release uncontrollable energy or to induce a hypnotic trance in the audience that could cause psychological harm – topics that also interested Jim Morrison, as embodied in the shamanistic dance he performed when The Doors played live at the Hollywood Bowl in 1968. Burroughs and Page discussed the potentially harmful effects of ultrasound, but they also reflected on the pleasant effects of 'vibrations in the body' stimulated by music played at a 'safe range' and linking the power of a mass event to ancient sonic and ceremonial energies.[29] A release of sexual energy is not required for the effects of 'sonic necromancy' to take place; progressive rock was often a more subtle assault on the senses, as one might describe Brian Eno's synth contributions to two Genesis tracks on *Lamb* – the disturbingly surreal 'The Grand Parade of Lifeless Packaging' and the eerily beautiful 'Silent Sorrow in Empty Boats'.[30]

Led Zeppelin's music is arguably too visceral and its lyrics often too direct (dealing with love and lust) to fit within progressive rock, which tended to sublimate sexual energy rather than putting it on display.[31] Perhaps progressive rock adopts a more subtle and complex sexualization of music, where it is not so literal, and certainly less stereotypically masculine. Led Zeppelin's combination of acoustic and electric instrumentation (including a folk-based interlude in many of its 1970s concerts and its folk performance at the 1970 Bath Music Festival), together with Page's interest in combining light and shade as contrasting moods in his song writing, pushes the band towards progressive rock on a compositional level. This similarity can be best detected on long tracks such as 'No Quarter' (1973) or 'Kashmir' (1975), which combine different mood segments within a quasi-narrative structure, but also in what Susan Fast describes as the 'sonic journey' of its performances, in which the band and audience 'experience an openness to musical form and timbre' through a blending of musical styles and a combination of tightly performed pieces and improvisation.[32] The 1973 Madison Square Garden performance moves through a variety of musical styles, while the acoustic segments in the band's sets (as evident in its Earls Court performance of 1975) are close to progressive folk.[33]

The emphasis on the musicianship of the band members is arguably more pronounced in Led Zeppelin than in progressive bands that valued the ensemble above any band member or instrument. However, the liking for long drum solos as a virtuoso centrepiece of concerts crossed rock genres from John Bonham to Keith Moon to Carl Palmer. Two other virtuoso drummers, Neil Peart and Phil Collins, variously elongated and shortened drum solos or embedded them in songs and medleys to suit different phases in the lengthy careers of Rush and Genesis respectively. We have seen in the last chapter that musical turn-taking on stage was common to both rock and jazz, but this rarely undermined the effect of the whole group – a truism for many progressive bands, in which the rhythm section or keyboardist often (although it was rarely the case for Led Zeppelin) prevented the lead guitar or singer from dominating the performance.

The medium of film fascinated progressive bands. One of the reasons that Peter Gabriel left Genesis in 1975 was to start work on a film project, and he and Mexican filmmaker Alejandro Jodorowsky tried to turn *The Lamb Lies Down on Broadway* into a screenplay between 1979 and 1981. Although the film was never made, the project stimulated Gabriel's interest in film-making and computerized imagery, as evident in his music videos from the mid-1980s and 1990s. In 1978, the Italian group Goblin produced what has been described as a soundtrack to an imaginary film, *Il fantastico viaggio del "bagarozzo" Mark* ('The Fantastic Journey of "Beetle" Mark'). Released the same year as George Romero's horror film *Dawn of the Dead*, for which Goblin wrote the soundtrack, *Il fantastico viaggio* was described by music producer Claudio Fuiano as a depiction of a 'wild and wondrous world of a thousand different colours' that represent the fantastical side to the haunting music used in Romero's film and on the band's soundtrack for Dario Argento's film *Profondo Rosso* (1975).[34] Although not originally written for film, the opening theme in Mike Oldfield's *Tubular Bells* was used on *The Exorcist* (1973), another horror film about demonic possession; 'Tubular Bells' became a successful single helped by the movie's success. Even more oddly, Pierre Bachelet borrowed King Crimson's 'Larks' Tongues in Aspic (Part II)' for the soundtrack of *Emmanuelle* (1974). As well as *Tubular Bells*, the Virgin label from 1973 was home to the electronic German trio Tangerine Dream, a band that worked extensively on film soundtracks in the 1980s but whose live performance style in the 1970s varied from minimalist lighting to the use of dramatic lights and lasers later in the decade, reflecting the trend among performers such as Jean-Michel Jarre, who used strobes, projected images and fireworks during live performances of *Oxygene* (1976) and *Equinoxe* (1978), and ELP's use of over 300 spotlights and 60 dimmer controls on its 1977 *Works* tour.[35]

Paul Stump argues that the music industry's attraction towards super-groups, expensive tours and spectacular shows was a significant factor in the perceived demise of progressive rock in the mid-1970s, and there was certainly evidence, as DJ Bob Harris notes on the BBC documentary *Prog Britannia*, that in 1976 showbiz started to take over from serious composition and performance (Harris cites the example of Queen).[36] Nevertheless, the broad range of musical expression mixing sonic, theatrical and cinematic elements discussed here and in the previous two chapters serves to illustrate that late 1970s prog rock cannot be conceptually reduced so easily.

Arguably the two most complete fusions of music, narrative, performance and visuality are Jeff Wayne's *Musical Version of The War of the Worlds* (1978) and Pink Floyd's *The Wall* (1979), the latter of which gave rise to the 1982 Alan Parker film incorporating animated sequences by Gerald Scarfe that had been used in live performances of the album. The two projects straddled artistic virtuosity and commercial success in terms of album sales and radio exposure of the lead singles, 'Forever Autumn' and 'Another Brick in the Wall (Part II)'. Both albums have strong progressive elements: seamless transition between songs and moods; orchestral and conceptual ambition; organic integration of musical and performance elements; experimentation with the spoken word and sampling; the thematic fusion of war, captivity, isolation and psychosis; and narratives of invasion (whether by tripods from Mars or memories from childhood) and rescue (the world saved or moving outside the wall).

Beyond these elements, the histories of the two projects and their musical-theatrical dimensions diverged considerably. Jeff Wayne's *The War of the Worlds* was not performed on stage with a full orchestra until 2006, nearly thirty years after its original release, partly for technical reasons. The 2006 Royal Albert Hall concerts included composer Jeff Wayne as conductor; some of the original singers performing the songs (including Justin Hayward); an animated prologue; an actual fighting machine; and a giant disembodied head of the narrator, Richard Burton (who died in 1984), projected on stage and lip-synching to the narrative voice. The oral performance mode of the original album combined Burton as a narrator-journalist who both experiences and records the story of a Martian invasion, along with spoken dialogue and musical elements that convey drama and menace, and threatening electronic sounds that represent the tripods and the red weed that envelops the country. The aural performance of the double album references Orson Welles's 1938 CBS radio production of H. G. Wells's 1898 novel *The War of the Worlds*, which, when broadcast on the radio without a framing introduction, stimulated panic among 'frightened citizens' across America.[37] But after opening with Burton's spoken narration, Wayne's version moves into a musical-dramatic mode that loosely follows the two phases of Wells's late nineteenth-century story – 'The Coming of the Martians' and 'The Earth under the Martians' – offering a two-part structure that allows Wayne to zoom out to the epic proportions of the alien invasion and zoom in towards the stories of fearful and panicking individuals under attack. Although the first side of the album is better known for its 'Eve of War' theme, the drama of Wayne's version rests as much on the attempt to rebuild civilization following the alien invasion; in their efforts to survive, characters enter a subterranean world (purgatory and underground resistance) that only a humanist faith can restore. At a high point for anti-humanism in philosophical and cultural thought, and with Vietnam fresh in mind (Wayne began the project before the fall of Saigon), this humanist faith strikes a chord with other progressive albums of the 1970s and characterizes the project as a version of Peter Brook's holy theatre, giving a new language to old themes. In the end, the alien invaders die off as they fail to adapt to the otherwise benign bacteria within earth's atmosphere, but the survival of civilization rests on the rejection of regressive forces that veer towards religious superstition or materialist tyranny as blind turns for humanity.

Humanist comforts are harder to find in Pink Floyd's *The Wall*, which recounts the descent of the rock star Pink into psychosis, locked into the memory of his father's death in World War II, the authoritarian tyranny he experienced at school, and his uncomfortable psychosexual relationship with his mother that poisons his later relationships. The dual drama of war and psychosis is again on display, complicated as Pink toys with fascist dictatorship as an alternative (but ultimately false) route to personal redemption. Melodrama is the dominant aesthetic mode of the album and live performance, where an orchestra (on 'Bring the Boys Back Home') and choir (on 'In the Flesh') compete for attention with sound effects, 'from bomber planes and helicopters to babies' cries and schoolyard voices, ringing telephones and dial tones, and subliminal snatches of dialogue'.[38] Performances were also accompanied by Gerald Scarfe's animated projections and giant puppets of the frightening schoolmaster and possessive mother. The album's theme was stimulated by a contretemps between the band and the audience at a 1977 Montreal concert and by the huge, dehumanizing venues they played during the *In the Flesh* tour. The (by that time) band leader Roger Waters' theatrical notion of building a wall across the stage dramatized the central conceit as the ultimate alienation device (a highly theatrical version of Brecht's V-effect) during Pink Floyd's 1980–1 performances.[39] Depicted on the album cover as a blank white wall, the forty-foot wall was built brick by brick by the road crew during the early performances, completely separating the band from the audience by the intermission and coinciding with Pink's attempted suicide on 'Goodbye Cruel World'. The band performed the second half of the album behind the wall (with occasional appearances by Waters through a trapdoor and Gilmour via a hydraulic lift), before the structure is finally demolished after Pink is put on trial for his flirtation with fascism and then regresses into a childlike figure in the closing track, 'Outside the Wall', dramatically conveyed in Scarfe's final animated sequence in the 1982 film version, in which Pink is played by the punk-respectable singer Bob Geldof.[40]

It is harder to read *The Wall* album thematically as an example of either holy or rough theatre, but its live performances bring these two theatrical modes closely together. The physical immensity of the wall, the spotlight on Gilmour's lyrical guitar solos in the second half and the symbolic magnitude of the Nazi-like hammers are contrasted with rougher elements: the faint 1940s organ that starts *The Wall*, Waters' declamatory singing voice, the groupies in 'Young Lust', the yearning nostalgia and quasi-nationalistic 'bring the boys back home' in 'Vera', the children's chants in 'Another Brick in the Wall' and fascist chanting in 'Waiting for the Worms', the caricatures of headmaster and matriarch, the sampling of everyday noises, and Scarfe's animation and puppetry.

Whereas *Live at Pompeii* offers a purer example of Peter Brook's empty space, Pink Floyd's audience at its 1980–1 concerts experienced a different kind of empty space when confronted by the forty-foot wall during the second half of the concert. Waters exploited the 'empty' concept of the wall a decade later, when the fall of the Berlin Wall offered him a new historical resonance; he performed the album in July 1990 with guest musicians and singers in what had previously been no man's land between West and East Berlin, released as *The Wall – Live in Berlin*. This is not to say that *The Wall* is the apotheosis of progressive rock, even though it has come to define the Roger Waters's version of the band (just as *Piper at the Gates of Dawn* defined Syd Barrett's Pink Floyd), as demonstrated in the 2010–11 transatlantic tour of *The Wall*.[41] Although *The Wall* exists in multiple formats (album, film, and concerts over a thirty-year stretch), each can be criticized for being over-theatrical and lacking the subtlety of Pink Floyd's earlier work. Whereas ambiguous and undecidable imagery marks progressive rock earlier in the 1970s, both Jeff Wayne's *War of the Worlds* and *The Wall* sacrifice progressive nuances for more dramatically complete but conceptually straightforward projects.

Notes

1. For a discussion of ELP's 1977 *Works* tour, see Edward Macan, *Endless Enigma: A Musical Biography of Emerson, Lake and Palmer* (New York: Open Court, 2006), 395–405.
2. Macan, *Endless Enigma*, 24–5, 330. See also Akitsugu Kawamoto, "'Can You Still Keep Your Balance?" Keith Emerson's Anxiety of Influence, Style Change, and the Road to Prog Superstardom', *Popular Music*, 24(2) (2005), 223–44.
3. Peter Brook, *The Empty Space* (London: Penguin, [1968] 1998), 11.
4. Ibid., 44.
5. Ibid., 44.
6. Ibid., 80.
7. Ibid., 48.
8. Ibid., 55.
9. Ibid., 80.
10. Philip Auslander, *Liveness* (London: Routledge, 1999), 24.
11. *Pictures at an Exhibition* (Nicholas Ferguson, 1972) was released in the US as *Rock and Roll Your Eyes* in 1973. For further discussion, see Macan, *Endless Enigma*, 136–9.
12. Holm-Hudson, *Genesis and* The Lamb Lies Down on Broadway, 29–30.
13. David Sheppard, *On Some Faraway Beach: The Life and Times of Brian Eno* (London: Orion, 2008), 93.
14. Richard Leppert, *The Sight of Sound: Music, Representation, and the History of the Body* (Berkeley: University of California Press, 1993), xix.
15. Macan, *Endless Enigma*, xxiv.
16. Holm-Hudson, *Genesis and* The Lamb Lies Down on Broadway, 106–7 (the quotation is from a review of a 1975 *Lamb* performance by Ron Ross, cited in Holm-Hudson).
17. Storm Thorgerson (1978), cited in Schaffner, *Saucerful of Secrets*, 143.
18. Ibid., 28.
19. See John Tytell, *The Living Theatre: Art, Exile and Outrage* (London: Methuen, [1995] 1997), 245–52.

20. Gracyk cited in Auslander, *Liveness*, 64–5.

21. Ibid., 66.

22. Schaffner, *Saucerful of Secrets*, 173. See the interview with director Adrian Maben, *Pink Floyd Live at Pompeii*, director's cut DVD (2003).

23. Bruno MacDonald, *Pink Floyd: Through the Eyes of the Band, Its Fans, Friends and Foes* (London: Sidgwick and Jackson, 1996), 196.

24. Mick Wall, *Led Zeppelin: When Giants Walked the Earth* (London: Orion, 2008), 324.

25. Ibid., 325–6.

26. Susan Fast, *In the Houses of the Holy: Led Zeppelin and the Power of Rock Music* (Oxford: Oxford University Press, 2001), 28.

27. William Burroughs, 'Led Zeppelin Meets Naked Lunch', in *Very Seventies*, ed. Peter Knobler and Greg Mitchell (New York: Fireside, 1995), 121.

28. Jim Derogatis, *Kaleidoscope Eyes*, 10.

29. Burroughs, 'Led Zeppelin Meets Naked Lunch', 126.

30. Sheppard, *On Some Faraway Beach*, 174–5.

31. See Robin Sylvan, *Traces of the Spirit: The Religious Dimensions of Popular Music* (New York: New York University Press, 2002), 155–6.

32. Fast, *In the Houses of the Holy*, 47.

33. For the Madison Square Garden and Earls Court performances, see *Led Zeppelin: DVD* (2003).

34. Claudio Fuiano, 'Music to a Film that Doesn't Exist', CD insert of *Il fantastic viaggio del "bagarozzo" Mark* reissue, Gruppo Editoriale Bixio Cinevox Record, 2007.

35. Macan, *Endless Enigma*, 396.

36. Stump, *The Music's All That Matters*, 205–6. Bob Harris interviewed on *Prog Britannia* (BBC, 2008).

37. Edward Miller, *Emergency Broadcasting and 1930s American Radio* (Philadelphia: Temple University Press, 2003), 107.

38. Schaffner, *Saucerful of Secrets*, 231.

39. Pink Floyd audiences were much more tolerant of this device than those who saw John Lydon's Public Image Limited play behind a screen; one New York concert (The Ritz, May 1981) ended up in a full-scale riot. *The Wall* is a clear case of the Brechtian V-effect, in which alienation is encouraged in the audience to push them to become critics of social oppression.

40. Waters expresses his thrill with 'the theatricality' of the wall in 'Spotlight on Pink Floyd', Brisbane Radio, 2 February 1988, quoted by Schaffner, *Saucerful of Secrets*, 227. For Gerald Scarfe's collaborations with Pink Floyd and Roger Waters, see Gerald Scarfe, *The Making of Pink Floyd: The Wall* (New York: Da Capo, 2010).

41. For Roger Waters' 2010–11 tour of *The Wall*, see Jerry Ewing, 'The Hero's Return', *Classic Rock Presents Prog*, 17 (September 2010), 36–41. For the history of Gerald Scarfe's collaborations with Pink Floyd and Roger Waters, see Scarfe, *The Making of Pink Floyd: The Wall*.

PART 2

Beyond

Chapter 8

Social Critique

As we have discussed in the first section of this book, abstraction, complexity, experimentation and virtuosity characterized a large quantity of 1970s rock music. Despite the growing popularity of progressive rock in Europe and North America, prog bands increasingly saw themselves at a remove from popular music as represented in sales charts. In the second half of the 1970s and into the 1980s, this development was critically decried as progressive rock losing touch with the real roots of rock. Bands increasingly distanced themselves from the 'progressive 1960s' from which they had emerged, particularly in terms of lyrics. Their lyrical and musical ambitions became ends rather than means, and contributed to a gradual disconnection between socially progressive lyrics and music conceived as a model for social change. For example, King Crimson's music mutated into increasingly dense musical improvisational forms, but, from *In the Wake of Poseidon* (1970) onwards, the band's lyrics formed a sequence of often embarrassing macho rock clichés about women, alternating with vacuous utopias. *Islands* (1971) is the lyrical nadir of both these trends.

We can see this mirrored throughout progressive rock. Just as the dystopian vision of *In the Court of the Crimson King* swiftly vanished, so Emerson, Lake and Palmer never returned to the dark fear of machinery of *Tarkus*; Renaissance rarely touched directly on the ills of contemporary society; and Gentle Giant paused to consider social problems only on the excellent *In a Glass House* (1973, but withdrawn from sale), as they veered between highly individualized stories of angst and complaints about the rock industry. Paradoxically, in prog terms, Gentle Giant's most lyrically focused (and final) album, *Civilian* (1980), while insistently scathing about the consumerist culture industry, comprises very simple music. Jethro Tull retreated into moaning cynicism on *Too Old to Rock 'n' Roll: Too Young to Die*; Caravan lost track of all but the most whimsical elements of their early albums; and Robert Wyatt stepped back from social critique, even as his albums from *Rock Bottom* (1974) onwards reveal a highly personalized experimentalism that crosses from lyrics to music and back, paralleling the hyper-whimsy of Brian Eno's *Here Come the Warm Jets* (1974). These lyrical shifts coincided with the move to centre stage of electronic music and largely instrumental improvisation in progressive and other experimental rock forms.

It is clear that the dominant drive through the 1970s was to move away from social narrative. In this chapter, though, we want to review the wide range of social critique that persisted despite the apparent decline of prog rock as a progressive force – a trajectory we examine by discussing the social engagement of a number of progressive bands. Before we can look beyond the 'high point' or 'classic phase' of progressive rock, as we do in the second half of this book, it is important to see how social critique developed through the 1970s. From 1972 onwards, both Genesis and Yes heightened their sense of social commentary, while other groups such as Pink Floyd (as discussed in the previous chapter) used the alienation of consumer society as the basis for its music, lyrics and shows. Some groups adapted explicitly left-wing positions, even to the point of hinting at support for the armed revolutionary groups such as the Red Army Faction (RAF), as typified in the Baader Meinhof Gang in Germany, the Red Brigades in Italy, and groups in support of Palestine. Just being a rock group beyond Western Europe was often inherently subversive in situations where the formation of a progressive rock band could be a radical act from the outset.

Starting the discussion with Genesis and Yes provides a means for tracing social critique from the early 1970s, at a time when direct references to contemporary issues were most often disguised in allegory, explored in terms of a mythical past or projected onto a hypothetical future. For all their mythical quality and citation, Peter Gabriel's lyrics moved the narrative of Genesis's songs to a point where established myths and literary works collide with everyday 1970s Britain at its most mundane. As we discussed in Chapter 5, 'Supper's Ready' (1972) is precisely a coming together of these different genres, as (presumably suburban) domestic living meshes with news of war, historical figures, fragments of a Lewis Carroll world, and poetic legend.[1] The song-cycle nears an end with a long, mounting triumphant section, in which the figure in the opening of the song returns with the line 'and baby it's going to work out fine'. In the final part, this return is more of an apotheosis on a personal level ('our souls ignite') and on that of a social utopia, as ultimately they (and we) are taken home 'to the new Jerusalem'. Paul Stump points out that after all this grandeur, the track fades away, as if it is diminishing and questioning its own extravagance.[2] This echoes the disappearance of the dream-like vision when the song is brought back to earth with the return to the sitting room, which occurs after 20:30 of the track.

Gabriel continued to explore the quirks of contemporary English life in *Selling England by the Pound*, reiterating his almost hermetically personal fusion of a panoramic take on the nation with the tradition of English radicalism (much of which is to be found in the English poetic tradition). Written

GENESIS

SELLING ENGLAND BY THE POUND

Genesis, *Selling England by the Pound* (1973). Painting by Betty Swanwick.

against decimalization and the loss of the imperial British pound in 1971, and the UK's tentative entry into European Community in 1973 (a list of largely English food products and discounted prices is intoned at the end of the final track 'Aisle of Plenty'), Gabriel's apparently overblown poeticism emphasizes that what is at stake is a critique of Englishness rather than self-indulgent literary play, largely because it shows that the subject is to be taken seriously enough to be brought into contact with poetry and myth.[3] The opening track, 'Dancing with the Moonlit Knight', suggests heroic and playful adventure. This is reinforced in the second part but prefaced by a section about loss and the consumer destruction of a mythical past:

> Citizens of Hope and Glory
> Time goes by – it's 'the time of your life'
> Easy now, sit you down
> Chewing through your Wimpy dreams
> They eat without a sound
> Digesting England by the pound

Glorious vision is shown to be a sham; the experience of 'hope and glory' is the feeble dream of food (Wimpy was a relatively new British fast-food chain at the time, first introduced in the 1950s). In four lines, citizens become masses caught within a consumerist society, mindlessly replicating the greed of the banking economy. This 'selling England' section is reprised at the end, together with bad puns on supermarket names, as society moves towards becoming one giant shop. Alienation continues in the second track, 'I Know What I Like (in Your Wardrobe)', which continues to despair of the limited vision of the working classes, but emphasizes that this situation has been created by the twin problems of economic constraint and socialization into class roles within the English school system. It also stresses that compliance cannot be relied on: 'me I'm just a lawnmower – you can tell me by the way I walk' (the closing line) loses the easy assimilation of role, machine and person through surreal dramatization. 'Firth of Fifth' appears to be a mythical journey of discovery, centring on a slowly building instrumental passage and bounded by the observation that 'and so with gods and men/The sheep remain inside their pen'. This, too, is countered by the closing lines, where 'the sands of time were eroded by/The river of constant change', which look back to Buddhism and Heraclitus as well as to the eternal return as a way out of being 'sheep in a pen' – a theme captured more fully on Genesis's *The Lamb Lies Down on Broadway* and Pink Floyd's *Animals*.

Side two is dominated by the twin epics of 'The Battle of Epping Forest' and 'The Cinema Show'. The first of these tells of the fight between various nicknamed villains in a turf war of protection money; these are true figures of a fictional 1970s mythology at a time when criminal gangs from London's East End were heavily romanticized. In the 'Reverend' section a gangster speaks, telling of his absorption and power in this world and closing with the lines: 'He employed me as a karma mechanic [karmacanic on the lyric sheet], with overall charms/His hands were then fit to receive, receive alms'. Church and gangs merge seamlessly, their hands in other people's pockets. 'The Cinema Show' follows the mock-heroic mode of T. S. Eliot's 'The Waste Land' (see Chapter 5) and cannot quite decide between mocking its two protagonists going on a date ('can he fail, armed with his chocolate surprise?') and making them heroic, with choruses connecting them to gods, nature and the universe as a whole ('once a man, like the sea I raged/Once a woman, like the earth I gave'). The ensuing instrumental passage, with its choir-like crescendos, high tempo and soft drumming, suggests a journey that comes to a neat and melodiously virile conclusion. However, following a key change the song dissipates and an acoustic guitar arrives in 'Aisle of Plenty', announcing the return of the 'selling England' section from the album's opening track. Various special discounts are declaimed in different voices by Gabriel, and potential harmony becomes lost in the cacophony of consumer choice and customer care.

Given this reading of the album, why is it that *Selling England by the Pound* is not regarded as a significant work of social analysis? The problem is that the music is entirely melodious and harmonious (other than occasional vocal departures), particularly the contribution of Tony Banks' keyboard on the first and last tracks. Instrumental passages reach satisfying conclusions, and arguably the downtrodden are kept in their place by being praised for their existence. Genesis had by this point attained a very standardized sound (to later ears at least), and it is all too easy for the listener (past and present) to fall into the 'cleverness' of the lyrics at the expense of their purpose. Between these two problems, the critical element is subdued, and the whole can feel like a display of technique.

Yes presents a different case, as its increasingly abstract, even hermetic, lyrics head away from contemporary concerns. One tendency for Yes in the 1970s was the rejection of society by positing alternative worlds and ethical systems, but the band did not avoid the world around it, maintaining a strong anti-war focus in the 1971 anti-Vietnam War track 'Yours Is No Disgrace', on *The Yes Album*, which also largely absolves the soldiers themselves for that war, or in the complex 'Gates of Delirium', on *Relayer* (1975), based loosely on Tolstoy's *War and Peace* (1869) mixed with contemporary warfare.[4] Often the band posited alternative, spiritual ways of living, with varying degrees of lyrical success, and they were also ecologically aware, as witnessed in the direct plea on their 1978 track 'Don't Kill the Whale' on *Tormato* and, more interestingly, on *Close to the Edge* (1972), which both Edward Macan and Bill Martin see as exemplifying Yes's utopian critique of existing society.

Martin (somewhat selectively) takes the view from Theodor Adorno that a critical avant-garde art cannot be overtly outside or completely against the society it wishes to critique but instead must seek autonomy through the positing of other worlds.[5] Macan's position is similar, arguing for a spiritual utopianism as a form of critique.[6] As we have noted before, prog rock is precisely progressive in its worldview, an 'expression of this utopian, radical and transformative spirit', as Martin puts it.[7] But even for ardent fans of progressive rock, and of Yes in particular, this still seems a bit ethereal and abstract. Abstraction is a key move for Yes in terms of subject matter, but, as we have argued earlier in relation to the undecidability of progressive rock lyrics, this does not diminish its chances of supplying social critique, even if it cannot be identified with a clear ideological position. That Yes and many other progressive rock bands are not Marxist should not surprise us, as prog emerges from the same roots as May 1968 and the Civil Rights Movement – a rejection of traditional models of resistance that is just as strong as the rejection of the conservative values of mainstream society. Yes could even be said to be very close to one of those post-1968 political positions: that of the ecological movement.

The rear panel of Roger Dean's artwork for the *Fragile* cover (1971) shows the earth fracturing, and the group compositions on that album build a model of alienation, countered by hopeful striving towards greater awareness and renewed community. The album cover of *Close to the Edge* is simply green, with the title and Yes logo at the top and the colour shading from dark to light as it descends the front panel. The inside of the gatefold shows a raised plateau of a world made mostly of water, with outcrops of islands. Fog surrounds the edges of this plateau, and what looks like a road bridge connects the plateau to a rocky pass in the bottom right of the double-panelled picture. It is hard to see whether this image represents a post-apocalyptic world or a paradisiacal one. What is clear is that the snaking road disappears abruptly into the sea of the plateau. Macan conceives of this album and title track as representing a spiritual quest. 'Close to the Edge' would then be a four-part journey of 'the call', 'adversity and triumph', 'self-examination and assimilation', and 'attainment'.[8] This track then becomes paradigmatic of the whole countercultural search for identity at a remove from the problems, oppression and limits of urban consumer society.[9] Martin takes a broader view. Although he thinks that this track is about spiritual awareness, he considers it part of 'a hermetic view that does not separate spirit from matter; human fallenness and disgrace is primarily an ethical-political question, only secondarily a metaphysical or ontological question'.[10] For him, the album deals with ecological concerns, questions of gender and community, and a merging of religious ideas from different cultures in the spirit of respect for difference.[11]

These elements represent socially critical positions, but neither writer quite pinpoints what holds 'Close to the Edge' together. This interconnectivity is something akin to the Gaia hypothesis, which the British scientist and environmentalist James Lovelock had been researching in the 1960s while working for NASA.[12] The track begins to make sense only as either quest or social critique if we question who the 'I', 'you' and 'we' are in the lyrics; although the song is not a puzzle to be so easily resolved, for the most part the 'I' can be taken to be the planet earth itself, 'you' to be humanity, and 'we' to be the coming community that will not be socially or ecologically alienated. There are reversals, where the 'I' could certainly be humanity, and others that could go either way: for example, the lyric 'how old will I be before I come of age/For you'.

The album signals its ecological vision through the use of birdsong and the sound of water in the instrumental introduction, and if we look at the opening line of 'Close to the Edge' it seems to refer to humanity's folly against an Earth personified as female: 'A seasoned witch could call you from the depths of your disgrace' and go on to heal 'you' (the disgrace refers back to the 'disgrace' of war in 'Yours Is No Disgrace'). In the third section of the song, the relation between the earth and humanity is more complex, as sad Mother Earth (not named as such) accepts the damage done to her: 'the lady sadly looking saying she'd take the blame/For the crucifiction/Of her domain'. In other words, even humanity's worst behaviour is connected to its ontological nature and to how it was formed.[13] On occasion, the 'I' slips between being an individual on a spiritual quest and an 'I' that is the *chora* of the quest: that is, the space within which the quest occurs and that is brought into being by the quest. On this reading, the Earth needs observers to retain its purpose, and it is as if that purpose has always been there; this is the 'total mass retain' of part two, which starts with the line 'my eyes convinced eclipsed with the younger moon attained with love'.

Each of the first two parts of the song ends with a chorus centring on being 'close to the edge' by the river, corner or end. Sections two, three and four all end with the lyric 'I get up, I get down', repeated several times at the conclusion of parts three and four. Just like the ambiguous terrain on the inside of the sleeve, this 'edge' is both an approach to enlightenment and the proximity of disaster, reiterated in 'I get up, I get down'. Unthinking belief in progress is targeted by both possibilities, such that (as Martin describes) 'the true progress of humanity involves both the getting up and the getting down. It involves not a "pure time" which unfolds mechanically, but instead a human time, developed through "song and chance".[14] Like *Tales from Topographic Oceans*, time is not just restricted to a human perspective but extends to a universal, or at least a planetary, scale. It is also cyclical: the resolution of the song is carried by the pause before the return of the phrase 'seasons will pass you by', which announces the final return of the refrain 'I get up, I get down'. This shows both individual awareness and social enlightenment, which will occur when the earth is permitted to return to its natural chronology.

'I get up, I get down' is interpreted by Martin as a recognition of the problems of positivist, resource-hungry rationalism that places the short-term interests of humanity at the top of a hierarchy of priorities. Macan reads the track as being about personal doubt on the road to spiritual enlightenment, attended by the knowledge of emotional ups and downs.[15] Martin's view of social critique is useful here, whereas Macan seems to be forcing the question somewhat. This is where it is useful to reintroduce Lovelock's Gaia hypothesis, which has been misunderstood in the same way as Yes's music: both can simply be seen to argue for a harmonious ecology where we can all get along together. Both are in fact much harsher, partaking of a 'deep ecology' where if humanity does not take care of its use of resources it will disappear and the planet will persist. Lovelock's argument is that the Earth represents a self-regulating system. This does not mean that everything will be all right; it means that there are feedback systems between organisms and the planet that create a cycle that continues to encourage life. In short, Gaia is not about harmony and planetary sentience but about the priority of the feedback system above all else. It would be hard to find a better equivalent for 'I get up, I get down', which, having concluded the final song part of 'Close to the Edge', gives way to the opening sounds of the album. All is cyclical, and humans can either discover this and their true place or cause disaster for the rest of humanity. This can be taken as an example of New Age thinking where spirituality, ecology and fear of scientific progress create a 'non-thought' to cradle the stupid. But the complexity of the ecological interaction outlined in 'Close to the Edge' does not permit this, because it is full with the potential for disaster and for failure. It is a properly ecological critique of consumer

Yes recording *Fragile* at Advision Studios in London (September 1971).

society that connects with what is now used widely for scientific modelling of ecologies and environments. Its deep and multiple ambiguities (another example of the progressive rock interest in undecidability) mean it cannot be co-opted for an easy message, even if Jon Anderson and Steve Howe seem to have wanted an environmentalist one.

'Close to the Edge' is not musically consoling, but it is a tightly composed group composition with only one moment that could conceivably be thought of as a solo. We have mentioned earlier how Yes functioned as a dissonant democracy, with all the group members contributing to writing and arranging, and the instrumentation seeming sometimes to involve the entire group effectively playing lead at the same time. Martin identifies this as realized by the time of *Fragile*, and it certainly applies to *Close to the Edge*. In this way, the band's musical practice serves as a model for content meeting form, and is therefore properly political in an avant-garde way. So we need to ask: why was such fusion of form and content not read this way, or why was it so easily dismissed? Rock criticism, even in the heyday of progressive rock, was not particularly interested in ecological politics (which was only in a fledgling state in the early 1970s, despite musical promoters such as Joni Mitchell and Crosby, Stills and Nash). By the late 1970s, ecology seemed not only of little relevance to young Europeans and Americans but also like too big a story to contemplate, coinciding with Jean-François Lyotard's description in 1979 of 'the decline of metanarratives'.[16] Within this framework, the philosophical interest of Yes, which contains social critique and possibilities for new patterns of behaviour to correct the problems identified, just does not seem practical or focused.

As we discussed in Chapter 5 in relation to lyricist Neil Peart's interest in mythology, Rush also bemoaned the alienation brought about by mass society, filtered in the mid-1970s through the lens of Ayn Rand's extreme individualism, particularly on *2112*. Rand was vehemently against all ideas that start with society and social responsibility; in her fiction and philosophical writings she established models where the individual can reach their full potential, often at the expense of others. Rand's novel *Anthem* depicts a future world where a caricature of communism has removed all individuality and where all must share the same ideas and give up any sense of attainment. As a result, we gradually discover that even technological progress has been rejected and is no longer possible, but the main protagonist eventually breaks free and rediscovers electrical devices. On attempting to convince the rulers of the worth and potential of this long-lost power, he is expelled: a scene mirrored directly in the fourth section of *2112*.[17] Rand's book ends with the prospect of a new society founded on the heterosexual couple, where man praises the word 'EGO' (the last word in *Anthem*) and with the traditional power differential between men and women restored.

Despite Peart's admiration of Rand, Rush did not share her full vision, balking at the aggressively potent masculine version of individualism Rand posits. The band accepted the critique made by Rand of socialism but not the solution she proposes. Instead, Rush imagines a world where the individual must act but in so doing will benefit all. Praise of the individual struggling against society is a commonplace in rock music, but Rush offers a programmatic individualism redolent of Henry David Thoreau or Benjamin Tucker that does not ride roughshod over others; rather, it endorses an inspirational and responsible individualism that will bring about a better society. That this is a centrist liberal outlook in no way diminishes its status as a genuine political position, one that Chris McDonald identifies as 'an optimistic, uplifting enthusiasm for ideas deeply rooted in middle-class history, such as individualism, personal autonomy, rationalism, technological progress, capitalist free enterprise, and a respect for high culture'.[18] The middle-class models to which he and Rush refer are those of the North American middle class: a much wider and less elitist group than the middle class in a European context, but still distinct from the working class.

For Rush, the individual has to take responsibility for self-development and for the situation he or she finds themselves in. The closing track of *2112*, 'Something for Nothing', rails against people passively waiting for change, and this call for active involvement permeates Rush's lyrics as they introduce ideological themes situated historically, alongside the more mythical renderings of their worldview. This line of thinking offers a structure for social renewal, even if at first it seems highly traditional. To see this social vision develop we can take two tracks: 'Closer to the Heart' from *A*

Farewell to Kings (1977) and 'Freewill' from *Permanent Waves* (1980). From this model emerges the 1980s version of Rush, much keener to explore the specificity of suburban mass-living as a source of alienation, as on the opening track of *Signals* (1982), which locates contemporary angst in the anonymity of sprawling subdivisions. Five years earlier, 'Closer to the Heart' proposed a model of social integration based on everyone accepting their roles and developing them according to their own strengths: 'Philosophers and ploughmen/Each must know his part'. The almost feudal imagery seems very conservative (blacksmith and artist are the other roles identified), but the key is the creativity in every part of society, 'to sow a new mentality' by balancing heart and mind. There is a sense of restoration and a reattainment of a holistic society, where the individuals are specifically not alienated from their labour (an unexpected and unconsciously Marxist angle) and where labour is the essence of social and individual development. 'Freewill' returns to the theme of 'Something for Nothing' but is more precisely delineated. Instead of fatalism or blind belief in a superior power, secular or religious, we have free will, which should urge us to act:

> You can choose a ready guide
> In some celestial voice
> If you still choose not to decide
> You still have made a choice
> ('You cannot have made a choice' on the liner notes)

In fact, the very exercise of free will is subject to choice in the song ('I will choose free will'), even though it is presented as an inherent capacity. Rush's fear of over-insistence on the collective to the detriment of the individual gradually metamorphosed in the band's music towards a diagnosis of the late twentieth-century individual. The first responsibility is to act and to be aware of the situation in which one acts, not unlike the existentialist responsibility identified by Jean-Paul Sartre and Simone de Beauvoir as the route to authentic existence.

According to McDonald, Rush presents its social outlook in live performances, with Neil Peart, Geddy Lee and Alex Lifeson's individual virtuosity combining in a disciplined group display of skill and meticulous reproduction of the recorded releases.[19] Skill is used as a representation of middle-class values, and the band's tightly rehearsed virtuosity as a marker of authenticity.[20] Skill, in fact, crosses the class divide; it harks back to pre-capitalist artisan production and can be appreciated as an attribute that derives from disciplined training rather than from privilege or chance. Rush is far from being simply nostalgic and is strongly in favour of technology, with McDonald even describing the band as 'technocratic'.[21] The band insists on progress as both a driver and product of individualism, as illustrated explicitly in the opening track of *Permanent Waves*, 'The Spirit of Radio': 'All this machinery/

Rush recording *Permanent Waves* in Le Studio, Quebec (October 1979).

Making modern music/Can still be open-hearted'. In the face of massification, individuals cannot give in and should instead embrace the idea that they can take charge of themselves; the lyric 'open-hearted' suggests that this might be even more likely in a highly technologized era.

Social alienation is addressed in other ways, most obviously in the 1960s idea of the alternative community, which often takes the form of the commune but also of the free festival in Britain from 1972 onwards. The oppressed individual could discover a new elective community in the free festival, and in this regard bands such as Hawkwind and Gong led the way. Like much progressive rock, the individual's creativity needs to be released in ways that are not exploitative or harmful to others. No doubt the reality of free festivals was somewhat different, but this was the model that flourished across Europe. The rock festival did not take long to become corporate, so the free festival was already able to posit the rock festival as a compromised arm of the culture industry: this was the forerunner of stadium rock, which started to take off in the US in the early 1970s with groups such as ELP at the forefront. The free festival was the first of a series of socially critical developments that bridged the pre-punk and post-punk music worlds – anarcho-punk band Crass not only established a commune and a band composed of commune members but was also involved in setting up the Stonehenge Festival in 1974. Leaving society behind was a step further than most progressive bands were prepared to take, given that even the less obviously commercial groups were still likely to acquire record contracts, perhaps with new independent labels such as Virgin, which soon established a strong avant-garde dimension after its formation in 1972.

One of the central festival groups, Hawkwind, played for free several times outside of the 1970 Isle of Wight Festival (see Chapter 3) and provides a good example of a radical practical agenda with lyrical social critique. Hawkwind made a concerted effort to promote an alternative social model, linked to its ongoing interest in utopian and dystopian stories of other worlds, times and realities (this can also be heard in Arthur Brown's 1970s band Kingdom Come). The science fiction that interested Hawkwind, particularly lead singer Robert Calvert, went beyond Michael Moorcock's fantasy novels (see Chapter 5) and towards the new wave of science fiction given shape by Moorcock's *New Worlds* periodical (1946–71; Moorcock edited the magazine from 1964). Philip K. Dick was the initial inspiration, as well as William Burroughs and numerous British and American writers who formed the first wave to write literary science fiction that focused explicitly on contemporary society, including Moorcock, J. G. Ballard, Thomas Disch and Norman Spinrad. What united these writers was not just the idea that speculative fiction could be a properly artistic form, but also one that could chart the paranoia, fears and hopes of the 1960s. The Cold War and the endless threat of nuclear warfare, the Vietnam War, the rising of the US as a dominant and explicitly military power even outside of officially declared war, and the sense that society would not actually be able to adjust to the utopian practices of the 1960s are all central elements here, musically transposed by Hawkwind.

It would be wrong to see Hawkwind as a group whose only social model was a drug-based parallel world. In both practice (free festivals and communal living outside of 'straight' norms) and music (space, other worlds, musings on mental states), it represented a vanguard that brought marginal practices and creative, speculative ways of thinking to the masses. This entailed a merging of different styles and subject matter, as heard on *Space Ritual*, the recording of the 1972 tour of the same name. Here stories of space travel and journeys on the inside of the mind alternate with more poetic tracks in which the spectacle of consumer society veers towards decline and destruction. 'Sonic Attack' identifies the selfishness that drives Western society ('you must help no-one else'); '10 Seconds of Forever' surveys the debris of a mass-manufactured society; and the closing track on *Space Ritual*, 'Welcome to the Future', makes it clear that all the spaceship mythology has really been about escaping before it is too late:

> Welcome to the dehydrated land
> Welcome to the self-police parade
> Welcome to the neo-golden age
> Welcome to the day you've made

Even the songs about space travel turn out to be less a paean to the possibility of freedom than about the necessity of leaving in order to secure survival. It is clear that this mode of space travel is not going to be exclusively utopian: 'Space Is Deep' is about philosophical and spatial isolation, while 'The Black Corridor' probes space as a way of connecting inner and exterior emptiness in a full-blown nihilistic conception of the universe.[22]

Relentless riffing, hedonistic utopianism and anti-authoritarian posturing meant that Hawkwind had a much easier transition than many bands once punk came along. Hawkwind, in fact, did not really change at all, as evident in its single 'Urban Guerilla', the release and BBC's banning of which coincided with IRA activity in London in the summer of 1973. As well as the line 'I'm an urban guerrilla, I make bombs in my cellar', there was also a sense for Calvert of moving away from the simplistic hippie ideas of how society would change: 'Let's not talk of love and flowers/And things that don't explode'. Hawkwind's provocation was not intended as a manifesto, but other bands did present a more explicitly leftist worldview, where practice and theory would need to combine in praxis.

The role of Marxism in music, or the kind of cultural resistance developed against social norms, very much depends on location. It is clear that progressive rock emerged in countries such as Italy without having passed through the stages of blues, psychedelia or proto-punk seen in Britain and America. In the history of progressive rock, overtly espoused left-wing ideology was much more common in continental Europe than in 1970s Britain. The communal living model might have been present in pockets of Britain such as Notting Hill or in rural locations in Devon and East Anglia, but squatting and communes were significantly more important in Holland (and connected to the freakbeat scene) and Germany (where it fed into *kosmische* or Krautrock). Late 1960s protests in France were as much about the proffered alternative of party-sponsored communism as they were about state and national conservatism; Germany gave rise to the first generation more affected by reflection on the 1939–45 war than by the war itself, and, similarly to France, the liberal West German model of economic success would be as open to critique as the actions of Hitler's 1933–45 regime; and Italian communism itself was radicalizing the official party with the idea of 'Eurocommunism', which would not be beholden to the Soviet line. This meant that official communism (and groups beyond it) and progressive rock worked together, either in the shape of Italian bands such as Area and Stormy Six or in invitations to and sponsorship of Henry Cow or Van der Graaf Generator. In Italy, progressive bands played at huge festivals throughout the mid-1970s, largely under the auspices of the Italian Communist Party (PCI) or the more libertarian Partito Radicale. In Eastern Europe, rock was subject to extreme state control because of the possibility of capitalist subversion. In the former Czechoslovakia, for example, the experimental rock group The Plastic People of the Universe was perpetually harassed by state police and some members even served time in jail for their 'subversion', while in Hungary the best-known group of the 1970s, Omega, also had to play underground for the first few years of its existence, as did Aquarium in Russia.

These are just the most high-profile cases, and all would be rehabilitated in the glasnost of the mid- to late 1980s. In Eastern Europe, progressive or psychedelic music was not intended as an ideological argument against so-called Marxist regimes but was adopted to expand the possibilities of rock music. Inadvertently, perhaps, the social critique was there in these bands' very existence. Latin America also saw isolated cases of progressive rock, such as Cuba's Sintesis and Guatemala's Alux Nahual, both formed in the late 1970s, emerging in periods of reduced social control. Alux Nahual's existence was political in many respects; its name was in the indigenous Quiché language and its lyrics were in Spanish (as opposed to English, the dominant language for rock in 1970s Central and Latin America). In the midst of cycles of civil war and state suppression, Alux Nahual would often focus on a message whose neutrality (essentially 'stop the fighting') was its radicalism. The lyrics of the 1981 track 'Hombres de maíz' ('Men of Maize') states, 'I don't care for the government/or for the revolutionaries', while in 1987, on 'Alto al fuego' ('Cease Fire'), the group demands, 'Stop the fire, cease fire/On all Central American ground'.[23] The development of a progressive rock style was also a resistance to both Americanized culture and the Romanticism of 'authentic' local culture. Paolo Alvarado writes that Alux Nahual specifically refused to write or perform 'rhythmical' music, 'rock latino . . . salsa-rock dance tracks'. They were wary of overusing instruments that could be seen as providing local colour and instead were keen to combine acoustic and electric elements.[24] Alux Nahual exemplified a specifically middle-class rebellion that did not mirror the disaffected middle class of 1960s and 1970s Europe but reflected a dispossessed class in search of identity and representation akin to the 'third estate' of revolutionary France of 1789.[25]

German experimental music of the late 1960s and 1970s is often not seen as a version of progressive rock, partly because of retrospective critical judgements that separated them from the commercially successful English prog bands and also because of the general absence of narrative in the recordings of the *kosmische* bands. Recent thought about Krautrock is heavily indebted to Julian Cope's 1995 book *Krautrocksampler*, which links Can, Amon Düül II, Neu!, Faust and others into a heritage of garage rock and psychedelia, specifically separated from much of progressive rock.[26] Cope stresses the practice of the bands he details as emerging from and then driving a militant counterculture. The 'ultra-left-wing psychedelic freakout' band Psy Free, for example, totally refused commercialization of its music and was 'vehemently opposed to all capitalism – playing for hours for free', while Amon Düül II sprang from a commune in the late 1960s and Ton Steine Scherben openly supported the Red Army Faction and was in favour of dropping out of society.[27] Europe in the 1970s saw many examples of communal living, alternative lifestyles and a repudiation of mainstream values, accompanied by music that was very often experimental. Cope's point is, implicitly, that whatever the virtues of other types of rock, this was music that put into action its view of society through lifestyle choices, rather than simply being part of an industry. It is true that this is where explicitly countercultural or leftist groups differ from the likes of Yes and ELP, but we take this trend as an extension of the critique present in mainstream progressive rock. Cope insists too much on the authenticity of the commune-based bands, in the naive belief that this actually makes the music more authentically progressive.

Cope is wary of Kraftwerk once the group adopts its machinic pose; therefore he has little to say about *Autobahn* (1974), but this album is a strong yet ambiguous critique of 1970s Germany. The most obvious point is that the 'economic miracle' was entwined so closely with Hitler's road programme and the car he ordered, the Volkswagen Beetle, is one of the two cars shown on the cover illustration. As Biba Kopf notes, this is a road that stretches forever and seems to provide the source and fuel for the 'motorik' beat of Krautrock (perfected by Klaus Dinger, first in Kraftwerk, then in Neu!).[28] The repetitiveness of the 22:42 title track is both about conformism and an escape from it: the two locked together with no obvious escape. Kraftwerk's instrumentation, originally very organic on its first three albums, is much more synthetic on *Autobahn*; the industrial being of *The Man Machine* (1978) is already here, as is the restless mobility of the contemporary world of *Trans-Europe Express* (1977).[29] This shiny, mechanical world is the same as that extracted by Hawkwind's Robert Calvert from J. G. Ballard's fiction – a place where fascination seems to mix the opposed worlds of conformism and critique – but this is a world Kraftwerk addresses even when being wilfully complicit with it. Whereas Hawkwind stands in the glare of that world, Kraftwerk attempts to inhabit it. Every few minutes the short vocal section comes back to show that people live in this landscape, moving from the opening vocoder that intones the word 'autobahn'. The human presence is highlighted by the section where the song merges with a radio within the song (14:14 to 14:44) before re-emerging in the repetition of 'wir fahren fahren fahren auf der autobahn'. The machine sounds are warm and tonal, while sweeps of sound represent cars passing and the intermittent return of the vocoder chant 'autobahn' shows human and machine cohabiting in symbiosis. The ambiguity of Kraftwerk's position is striking and an essential part of the critique of 'Autobahn' because it enacts the complicity that would normally be repressed: notions of a machinic society resonate with the military machine of the 1930s and 1940s, and the endlessness of the autobahn life is redolent of the one thousand-year Reich. 'Autobahn' suggests an accommodation with the past that does not forget its legacy, much as the German artist Anselm Kiefer was doing in the late 1970s.

For all the critique offered by either the practice of alternative social models of living or critiques of contemporary society in album content, there has been little sight in this chapter of a praxis that combines both trends through a genuine engagement with historical materialism. Ton Steine Scherben is possibly the most overt proponent of the left-wing struggle in 1970s German music, but it is perhaps too obviously progressive for Cope. Its 1972 album *Keine Macht für Niemand* ('No Power for Anyone') mixes together praise for armed resistance and criticism of the acceptance of mundane life with a direct critique of capitalism and a consideration of how alienation affects interpersonal relations. The sound of the album is a collision between punk (especially in the shouted choruses) and prog fusion, with moments where dissonant free jazz meets rock (side three in particular). Even the packaging is a radical statement; the album came in a cardboard box instead of the now-obligatory gatefold art of other double albums.

In Italy, Stormy Six adopted progressive rock to match its politics, while Area emerged as a fully formed model of praxis in which their art would be matched by their everyday social practice (as did Ton Steine Scherben).[30] The same can be said of Henry Cow, a group that emerged from a background informed by the Marxism (even Maoism) of the British avant-garde composer Cornelius Cardew and his ideas of the orchestra as a space for social experimentation, as well as by the burgeoning free music scene in London which worked on a strong DIY ethic. Henry Cow, like Soft Machine, was much more in demand in mainland Europe than in Britain, which is not to say that other English prog was not equally in demand – many groups, such as Genesis, toured Europe extensively and featured at length on German and Italian television. As well as the more ideologically politicized state of Italy at the time, it was the activism of Italian prog groups that made the connection between ostensibly difficult music and mass musical events possible. Henry Cow developed an explicit way of expressing a leftist perspective that maintained the Marxist-inflected formal approach. As Stump points out, its 'collectivized dynamic' marks the core of its Marxist critique, and perhaps this is why the band's first two albums are only sporadically leftist in an overt way.[31] What counted for Henry Cow was the practice of playing live and of exposing the materiality of its work as a combination of collective improvisation and composition. This openness of form combined with collective action to represent more than individual creativity. The aggressive punctuations of the band's instrumental tracks in a range of often ridiculously complex and multilayered time signatures could represent both the turmoil of capitalist society and the need for dissonance to replace discord.

There is only one piece on *Leg End* (1973), Henry Cow's first album, that lyrically addresses the problem of contemporary society: 'Citizen King'. Its writer, Tim Hodgkinson, minimizes the critical thrust of this track and, somewhat disingenuously, the way in which the band's approach to playing functioned as a critical take on 'the spectacle' of consumer society.[32] The lyrics are clear, deriving from Marx's critique of the commodity and Guy Debord's idea of the then new phase of capitalism as that of the spectacle:

Down beneath the spectacle of free
No one ever let you see
The citizen king
Ruling the fantastic
Architecture of the burning cities
Where we buy and sell

Later on, we are reminded that we labour only to be further exploited through consumption and that consumption itself will destroy all. The alienation exposed by Henry Cow is always double: it is the material alienation that results from separating the workers from the means of production to become exploited drones, and it is also the alienation that is aware of the exploitative and largely futile nature of capitalism. The position of this track at the end of the album, after several tracks of essentially free rock interspersed with snatches of fleeting melodies, highlights the critical intent of the music (improvised music is not inherently left wing, even if its practice seems highly democratic from inside the performing group and its inner circle of fans). This working through, this counter-labour designed to gnaw at the inside of capitalist music, is fully realized in the highly narrative 1975 album *In Praise of Learning*, made with Slapp Happy, most notably on 'Living in the Heart of the Beast', which parallels the structure of the Yes track 'Gates of Delirium' from the same year.

In Praise of Learning is the third Henry Cow album ornamented by a cover of a painted sock by Ray Smith. *Leg End* has a sock with red and blue strands interweaved on a flat background; the sock on *Unrest* (1974) has shades of grey and is in a somewhat frayed condition, on a more painterly dark background with scratches and cuts; *In Praise of Learning* is red on red, the sock more clearly mounted on a shaping card than on the other covers. This cover is designed to be an antidote to the commercialization of other prog bands' narrative ambitions as realized in the gatefold and its typically extravagant artwork, which is often of other invented realms or heavily mythologized versions of this world. After the defusing of portentous narrative ambition acted out by the sock, we can see it as a signifier of craft, of labour as creativity; not only that, it also symbolizes organized labour through working people's clothing (these are aggressively sturdy socks, if not particularly comfortable) and as representative of the transition to mass labour. Textiles led the industrial revolution and a change in the conditions of exploitation, and not only the cover but also the titles and lyrics of this album reflect the growing awareness of exploitation as it develops through action: the title comes from Bertolt Brecht's modernist play *The Mother* (1932); other titles refer to Mao Zedong's mobilization of China's Communist Party after retreat ('Beginning: The Long March') or to the British communist paper the *Morning Star* in the track of that name; 'Beautiful as the Moon: Terrible as an Army with Banners' uses a line from the

Bible's Song of Solomon as a base for an imagined and re-mythologized insurrection.

'In the Heart of the Beast' maps the dereliction of revolt, where revolt is seen as the marker of individuality and freedom. Each of the first four verses charts the downward slide from rebellion to helpless loathing. The next two verses wallow in the hopelessness of capitalist society, which is exacerbated by the untrustworthiness of signs, media and language, which conspire to maintain the illusory freedom of consumer society:

> We were born to serve you all our bloody lives
> Labouring tongues we give rise to soft lies
> Disguised metaphors that keep us in a vast inverted stillness
> Twice edged with fear

The first part of the 15:30 track (up to 7:17) is composed of a bewildering sequence of microscopic songs, riffs and instrumental passages. Again, discord gives rise to creative impulse, even if it is hard to marshal. Given that the formalist part of Henry Cow and Slapp Happy's desired utopia revolves around tension and multiple points from which to count time, keys and words, we cannot read the jarring sections of this track as representing inherent capitalist problems – these are the responses that the system has brought upon itself, and from a Marxist perspective there would be no out-side position from which to resist capitalism. The self-aware dissonance of the music opposes the power that hides behind the spurious harmony of liberal democracy. The variation in instrumental passages is purposeful, illustrating the dormant hope of devising ways towards a new society. It moves from reflective and increasingly longer and atonal interruptions, themselves inter-rupted by short group crescendo moments, to the long developmental section (7:17 to 12:20). This part acts as a testing ground of future potential, before moving to the closing section of four verses and the ensuing instrumental, which maintains the momentum of the vocal section. These verses clearly identify the problem: labour and consumption alienate, and once we have established a discordant practice to unveil this fact then we should turn to a more steady group practice in order to overturn the existing order. Although there is always group improvisation at work in Henry Cow, the last section (12:21 to 16:07) uses unity of purpose to illustrate that a desired outcome must be established instead of deferred.[33]

This drive to revolution permeates the other long track on the album, 'Beautiful as the Moon' (7:02), which closes with these lines: 'Time solves deeds/Arise work men and seize/The future. Let ends begin'. Always, though, the emphasis is one of process that leads to revolution, otherwise it would be just a case of populist demagoguery. On this level, the oppressed must come to see what is wrong with the society that binds them. Dagmar Krause's note-shifting vocals complete the Brechtian didactic model at work here (she would later go on to record Brecht, Kurt Weill and Hanns Eisler songs), where disorientation or defamiliarization heightens the message that would otherwise be too easily dismissed by those in thrall to the capitalist version of freedom.

This language was somewhat alien, to say the least, to most listeners in Britain. Elsewhere, the language of revolution could immediately relate to social discontent that connected with leftist ideological outlooks. Italy was at the centre of this movement. Although the late 1970s would see Henry Cow, Stormy Six, Belgium's Univers Zéro and Sweden's Samla Mammas Manna unite in the Rock in Opposition movement (RIO), it was in Italy that internationalist politics could combine with the more politically radical elements of progressive rock. In Québec and the Basque country in Spain, progressive rock could act as a vehicle for nationalist demands against what they deemed a colonizing power (Harmonium and Errobi respectively). In these situations, folk blended into progressive rock to reassert the renewable powers of tradition and to act as a revolutionary tool. Stormy Six went further and moved to embrace a progressive quasi-folk sound, after being established as a folk protest band for many years. The turning point is the album *Un biglietto del tram* (1975), which concentrates on partisans and resistance in World War II through a series of vignettes that are linked only obscurely to 1970s Italian society until the closing track. Stormy Six praised the political revolutionary strike ('La fabricca') and included tracks about specific martyred Italian partisans and an attack on American neocolonialism, identified as beginning in 1944 ('Arrivano gli Americani') and centring on the dubiousness of American aid. The style is a progressive version of folk, with complex time-signature changes but entirely acoustic instrumentation. The release of *L'Apprendista* in 1977 developed the formal side of Stormy Six's music as a means of expressing its radical content.

L'Apprendista focuses on work and the situation of the worker under capitalism, and it plays this out amid a much more dissonant sound-world verging on atonality. As well as revealing similarities to Henry Cow, there is a clear (and stated) reference to the way Gentle Giant brought together popular, classical and folk singing and playing styles.[34] The tracks stretch and develop though a series of sections, mirroring the idea of learning through work and the importance of apprenticeship. To further emphasize the didactic purpose of the album, there are notes to each track outlining the meaning, purpose and the source of ideas of the formal musical structures. The title track has five footnoted points, the first three of which refer to the line that ends verses one to three – 'Non l'Uomo, l'apprendista' ('Not Man, Apprentice') – and how the sense of that line develops from verse to verse. The apprentice is not the complete man; he is the alienated young man who is indoctrinated into the system, and yet he can be 'the man who transforms, who learns, who struggles' and holds the potential for a new society (footnotes accompany both points).[35] In the final footnote, we learn that the story is told in an 'epic-grotesque manner' and that the instrumental part 'pretends to announce a positive development in the crescendo and instead concludes on the final verse'.

It is important to note the complexity of the Left in Italy in the 1970s and the key divide between established communism in the form of the PCI (Italian Communist Party), which organized many festivals of experimental music in the 1970s, at one end of the spectrum, and, at the other end, saw the violent insurrection of the Red Brigades (particularly in 1978) and other armed groups. Stormy Six and those who would go on to form RIO were mostly involved in the mainstream communist movement's artistic work, but occasionally there are glimpses of sympathy for the armed revolution-ary approach, most notably in the work of Area. Styling themselves Area (International Popular Group), the band refers to their group composition, which at the outset included Greek-Egyptian, Belgian, French and Italian members, as well as the internationalism of communism and leftism and the diffusion of pop music as an emergent global phenomenon. Their first album, *Arbeit macht frei* (1973), is militantly anti-capitalist and notionally anti-violence. The title derives from the slogan on the gates of the Nazi concentration camps, but we need to remember that originally the German labour camps were a place where Nazi party members would work to 'free' Germany. Labour itself is a target for Area, in common with the attempts of post-1968 leftist groups to move away from a hegemonic form of social change (official communism) as much as they rejected the values of capitalist liberal democracies.

The album begins with the track 'Luglio, agosto, settembre (nero)' ('(Black) July, August, September'), referring in its title to the recent killing at the 1972 Munich Olympics of eleven Israeli athletes by the Palestinian organization Black September. It opens with a woman's voice reciting a poem in Arabic that yearns for peace, and then moves into a vocal and keyboard section about the world's falling into ruin, brought to a close as the group bursts in over a keyboard theme adrift somewhere between Arabic, Turkish, Greek or even Israeli music. As the song progresses and the band builds, the lyrics turn to a critique of how the workings of contemporary society have led to further violence:

> It is not my fault
> If your reality
> Forces me to wage war against the conspiracy of silence
> Perhaps then we will know
> What it means to drown the whole of humankind in blood

The 'reality' in the second line 'forces me to wage/*war on humankind*'. As such, the song charts the demise of the wish for peace in the face of relentless and surreptitious violence. The bleak events of Black September are simply the consequence of black July, August and any other month. It would seem that the means to prevent violence is by propagating violence. It can be seen as the anarchist idea of 'propaganda by the deed', which reveals the workings of the whole system (as in the German RAF and the Red Brigades). It can also be taken as a legitimized reaction to what is perceived as the violence of the state – or, more simply, as a statement about violence begetting violence. This is, to say the least, ambiguous, as the peacefulness wished for at the outset is lost in bloodshed, just as the growing complexity of the music works in tandem with the acceptance of the need for violence in the lyrics to suggest that the escalation is inevitable. Following the lyrics is a chaotic section that acts out violence. The main theme returns ever faster before cutting out. It is clear that Area does not condemn violence; rather, it points out that the world system of capitalism has created the conditions for violence. As such, the band's own ambiguous position is itself a provocative act, as the album title of *Arbeit macht frei* suggests.

Area declared its leftist position by releasing 'L'Internationale' as a single in 1974, and the calls to 'seize power' or question work in *Arbeit macht frei* echo throughout the band's releases. *Crac!* (1975) exhorts a young man on the run to keep going on 'L'Elefante Bianco' ('The White Elephant'), because his actions (possibly theft or arson) are justified in the face of the never-changing powers that control everything around him, while 'Gioia e revoluzione' ('Joy and Revolution') is another call to arms ('A battle is fought [. . .] the double bass is my machine gun'). This career-long message of the right of the oppressed to defend itself by any means necessary is conducted within a jazz-driven progressive style reminiscent of Soft Machine, with a more direct rock narrative building to conclusions in line with Area's advocacy of direct action. Long instrumental sections surround the verses because Area did not believe that stripping away possibilities would in any way clarify its intent – an intent that pervades all elements of what it conceived as a revolutionary music.

As we have demonstrated in this chapter, progressive rock offered many visions of social critique in the 1970s, but numerous groups combined content and form that reflected each other and, in the most engaged cases, went further to comment on and critique social disharmony. As we discuss in the following chapter, from 1976 onwards progressive rock would have to contend with music that mashed content and form into a monadic attack on society, together with an assault on the 'dinosaurs' of 1970s rock.

Notes

1. Curiously, this multiple narrative is carefully separated out in two neo-prog moments: Marillion's 'Grendel' (1982), reinscribed 'Supper's Ready' as a purely Anglo-Saxon reverie (see Chapter 10), and It Bites' 'Once Round the World' (1988), which used a newspaper's recounting of mundane events for narrative connection.

2. Stump, *The Music's All That Matters*, 176.

3. For the European context of Britain in 1972, see Sandbrook, *State of Emergency*, 134–75.

4. On the first of these songs, see Bill Martin, *Music of Yes*, 61, 67–8. On 'Gates of Delirium' Martin notes that 'war can be ethically and politically necessary and yet ethically ambiguous is perhaps the central message of this work' (ibid., 165).

5. Martin, *Music of Yes*, xxi.

6. See Macan's reading of *Close to the Edge* in *Rocking the Classics*, 95–105.

7. Martin, *Listening to the Future*, 9.

8. Macan, *Rocking the Classics*, 98.

9. Ibid., 96.

10. Martin, *Music of Yes*, 140.

11. Ibid., 129.

12. See James Lovelock, *Gaia: A New Look at Life on Earth*, 3rd edn (Oxford: Oxford University Press, [1979] 2000).

13. The use of the spelling 'crucifiction' should be interesting, but we have to note that the lyric sheet is riddled with errors and misrenderings.

14. Martin, *Music of Yes*, 144.

15. Macan, *Rocking the Classics*, 97–8.

16. Jean-François Lyotard, *The Postmodern Condition: A Report on Knowledge*, trans. Geoffrey Bennington and Brian Massumi (Manchester: Manchester University Press, [1979] 1984), xxiv.

17. See Rand, *Anthem*, 69–77 and Rush, '2112: IV: Presentation'.

18. Chris McDonald, *Rush, Rock Music and the Middle Class: Dreaming in Middletown* (Bloomington and Indianapolis: Indiana University Press, 2009), 6 and *passim*.

19. Ibid., 144–6.

20. Ibid., 104.

21. Ibid., 11.

22. Arthur Brown explored the conceptual possibilties of space travel with his band Kingdom Come, supplementing his dramatic performances with an increasing interest in the possibilities of new technology, notably with the relentless use of the drum machine on Kingdom Come's final album, *Journey* (1973).

23. Paulo Alvarado, 'Guatemala's Alux Nahual: A Non-"Latin American" Latin American Rock Group', in *Rockin' Las Americas: The Global Politics of Rock in Latin/o America*, eds Deborah Pacini Hernandez, Héctor Fernández L'Hoeste and Eric Zolov (Pittsburgh, PA: University of Pittsburgh Press, 2004), 220–40. The lyrics are translated by Alvarado, a founding member of the band: 229 and 231 respectively.

24. Ibid., 237.

25. In summary, Alvarado comments that 'the band did, however, successfully reflect the wishful feelings of the urban middle class we came from and it idiosyncratically voiced the rejection that a very large number of people felt for the stupidity of war' (ibid., 232).

26. Julian Cope, *Krautrocksampler*, 2nd edn (Yatesbury: Head Heritage, [1995] 1996). See, for example, this comment on Amon Düül II: 'progressive rock like Van der Graaf Generator is progressive [. . .] beyond the mere intellectualism of shit like Genesis or Yes' (ibid., 65), and on the critically unreviled Henry Cow, he complains that Virgin chose 'a lame bunch such as Henry Cow' to support Faust (ibid., 25).

27. Ibid., 33, 10, 59–60.

28. Biba Kopf, 'The Autobahn Goes on Forever. Kings of the Road: The Motorik Pulse of Kraftwerk and Neu!', in *Undercurrents: The Hidden Wiring of Modern Music*, ed. Rob Young (New York: Continuum), 141–52.

29. Note also that *Trans-Europ-Express* is an extremely violent 1966 film directed by French writer Alain Robbe-Grillet.

30. Archie Patterson, *Eurock: European Rock and the Second Culture* (Portland, OR: Eurock, 2002), 202. For a clear outline of Ton Steine Scherben's political position, see 85–8.

31. Stump, *The Music's All That Matters*, 224.

32. See Hodgkinson, in *Henry Cow: The Road Volume I*, liner notes, 6.

33. At the level of overall structure, the piece recalls 'The Gates of Delirium', which has a long opening section of abrasive music and vocals detailing the horrors of war, the arbitrariness of massacre, and the futility of revenge. This is followed by an even more dissonant instrumental section where the individuals surge in and out of focus amid a percussive barrage set up by the group playing as a whole. After a long-withheld crescendo, we slide down to the tranquility of a hopeful future amid the rubble, in the only harmonious section of the 21:56 track. Another comparison with Yes (this time 'Close to the Edge') occurs in the opening track, 'War', as Dagmar Krause declaims the presence of war as a product of an unnamed female deity, the creator of war. As this reaches a close (as human history spreads war), the war deity announces ambiguously that 'war does what she has to/People get what they deserve'. War then becomes the struggle for existence against oppression, and a necessity against the pretence of social unity in existing societies.

34. See also Augusto Croce, *Italian Prog: The Comprehensive Guide to Italian Progressive Music, 1967–1979* (Milan: AMS, 2008), 490.

35. All references to 'L'Apprendista' from *L'Apprendista* liner notes, 5. All translations by Laura Rascaroli, to whom go our appreciation and thanks.

Chapter 9

Responses to Punk

For all the attempts of 1970s progressive rock to interpret social problems in the form of music played by an ensemble band alive to the power of visuals and performance, an explosion was coming that would seem to make it all irrelevant. In 1976–7 punk blew up in England, and although it would implode into caricature even faster than progressive rock, it had a huge impact, particularly in the popular press and in the emerging genre of music criticism, causing a wholesale rethinking of the purpose of prog. This rethinking took many musical forms, some more experimental still and others more commercially oriented.

The arrival of punk is often compared to the much more subterranean outburst of Dadaism during the 1910s, and the even more obscure Lettrist/Situationist movement of the 1950s and 1960s (notably by Greil Marcus, punk fanzine editor Mark Perry, and Sex Pistols manager Malcolm McLaren). The relevance of this connection is often decried, most eloquently by Stewart Home.[1] In one way, the connection makes more sense if positioned in relation to progressive rock. In the early 1900s, avant-garde arts were flourishing, with movements such as Cubism looking to revolutionize painting from the inside. By way of contrast, Dada asserted that all this had to be swept away: society was rotten and its art was just a method of pacifying the masses, even if it appeared to be avant-garde on the surface.

When punk took off in England, it was against a backdrop of social unrest, a disastrous economic situation, and the failure of the Left to do anything but shut down industry or, at the extremes, debate the role of the vanguard party in the always postponed Marxist revolution. Even if the idea of prog-rock decadence is overstated, for many its social relevance was in decline by 1976. What had previously been heard as a driving force of creative and inspirational individualism positioned within the collective composition or improvisation of the group now felt dislocated from the people. Captain Sensible of The Damned put it this way: 'all that overblown dinosaur stadium rock with those appalling coke fuelled rock stars singing songs about Merlin and Pixies and Henry the 8th's wives and the like – what did THAT have to do with a bloke on the dole in Croydon? Bugger all!'.[2] Steve Jones, guitarist with the Sex Pistols, puts it even more succinctly, in Julian Temple's film *The Filth and the Fury* (2000), calling prog 'fucking boring'. Ironically, this widespread view coincided precisely with the period of most commercial success for progressive groups, as performances and albums released in the period 1977–9 reached consistently vast audiences (as discussed in Chapters 5 and 7). But however experimental progressive rock may or may not have been by 1976–7, the moaning of millionaires about ruinous tax rates and the pain of being a tax exile did not win much favour with alienated British youth.[3]

The impact of punk on the fortunes of progressive rock was closely linked to the identity of punk, at least with the advantage of hindsight; as Home points out, what punk is has shifted over time: 'the genesis of PUNK itself [is] best understood as a dialectical interplay between the notions of novelty and genre which are projected further and further backwards'.[4] From its inception, punk embodied a revolutionary para-discourse, fuelled by the outrage of the popular press over the stunts that Malcolm McLaren and others organised. As with all moments of artistic rupture, forebears were quickly sourced. In 1972, McLaren had been excited by glam shamblers New York Dolls, while precedents could quickly be found for the messy musical and performance style that paraded incompetence as virtue: for example, in the shape of 1960s garage music (the garage/psych collection *Nuggets* came out in 1972), The Velvet Underground or Iggy and the Stooges. For John Savage, '*Nuggets* codified a critical idea that had been current in America since the turn of the decade. In the midst of hippie excess, writers such as Lester Bangs and Dave Marsh began to celebrate the unconscious, noisy pop of the mid-1960s'.[5]

Punk in Britain emerged after, not alongside, progressive rock and the stadium rock of The Who and Led Zeppelin. The historical context of urban and industrial decay might have been similar, but punk (as a phenomenon that affected how music was played and received) is exactly as 'English' as progressive rock is often thought to be. The same newspapers, such as the *New Musical Express*, that had previously promoted progressive rock, started to attack well-established bands. Punk claimed to be a return to rock's roots and to the source of rhythm, energy and authenticity that 'trained' musicians were no longer seen to provide. As well as the financial discrepancy between a rock band and the public, there was an ever-growing skill divide, which meant that dreaming of being on stage playing guitar was impossible without time, money and feasibly the right background. The caricature of progressive rock members all being from the English public school system might be a gross exaggeration (it applies really only to Genesis, and does not include Phil Collins), and the claim that the musicians were all middle class in origin is equally stereotypical. However, if class can be constructed rather than just inherited, then class is shaped by actions, skills and an acquired position within society. Having an education in music is a marker of class distinction that was much touted by music papers in Britain, even after 1977, in praise of the 'classically trained' musician or popular polls such as 'bass player of the year'. To a new generation that felt alienated where the previous generation had glimpsed liberation, this looked like collusion in search of social approval.

All of the above notions have combined into a critical consensus that progressive rock was in terminal decline in the second half of the 1970s and that its end was hastened by punk. Even writers such as Bill Martin and Edward Macan buy into this consensus. Paul Stump offers a variation that became the consensus for a more avant-garde public (for example, in the *Wire* magazine): that is, that most progressive rock deserved to be killed off, but we can acknowledge a certain type of prog as fit to be saved from the cleansing (Henry Cow, Soft Machine, Van der Graaf Generator and King Crimson). The critically acceptable variety would no longer even be associated with progressive rock, which could now be confined to a stereotypical blanket definition of a style gone to seed. Newer generations of journalists marvel at discovering that this is a caricature when they learn how many twenty-first-century groups use progressive music elements, as we discuss in later chapters of this book.

Why is this? The journalists of the mid- to late 1970s had a huge role in establishing this consensus.[6] What was most likely a genuinely held position gradually ossified into a dogma that needed constant reinforcement through affirmations of how much 'everything changed' in 1976–7. What now looks like part of standard rock history has had very grand claims made for it. This is not just cynicism, or even the privileged position of a certain generation of writers who loved punk and new wave at the time and continue to see the world through that filter. At least as important is the institutionalization of writing about popular music: it is now a regular feature in news outlets, it is taught in cultural studies and music departments, and the first stirrings of contextually grounded music discourse in the academy occurred with that generation of writers. Bill Bruford traces it back further, arguing that American music journalists had, by the 1970s, acquired an importance that led them to see themselves (and be seen) as participants in rock production.[7] This led to a spectacular development of writing styles, position-taking and a pressure to progress. This was the first phase of the professionalization of music discourse as something more than a description of the music and usually more analytic than the popular press. Ultimately, this has led to books such as this one, but the number of volumes that have been published on punk is vast and shows no sign of abating.[8] There is the sense that rebellion – even reheated rebellion – sells, but it is the claim of authenticity that drives this punk industry, propelled by constructions of authenticity that emerge from American writers such as Lester Bangs, Greil Marcus, Legs McNeil, Clinton Heylin, and, in Britain, the writers of the *NME* and, to some extent, *Sounds*.

It is not that punk went looking for such plaudits: the Sex Pistols were always about constructedness, parody and an unmediated anger that turned both inward and outward, while The Clash sought authenticity, which developed over time into a political philosophy that looked outward from Britain. Where we can identify a more realized type of authenticity is in the shape of individual expression – one that had barely been present in rock up to that point, at least the explicit expression of anger, anomie and anguish. Stewart Home questions even this, writing that any attempt to turn punk into conscious avant-garde rebellion is totally wrong. In fact, if this avant-garde impulse can be glimpsed in a band then it cannot, by definition, be a punk band: so, on this account, John Lydon is too arty to really be punk.[9]

We have noted the increasing distance between musicians and public in terms of instrumental skill, wealth and, quite literally, the large-scale format of the stadium concert. But it is not clear that this transition applies only to progressive rock, and certainly not to all of it. For all the success of Yes, ELP, Jethro Tull and, to a lesser extent at the time, Genesis, bands such as King Crimson and Van der Graaf Generator were not vastly wealthy. Myriad bands toiled away globally, often on independent labels or by playing free festivals with almost no possibility of making a living by that means alone. This is another reason prog faded away by 1976: many of the bands could not sustain playing avant-garde music over a period of years with little reward. Those that did continue were often at the more radical end of progressive rock, and were largely untouched by punk's intrusion. Huge-scale concerts were not just the province of Rick Wakeman's concept spectacles such as *Journey to the Centre of the Earth* and *The Myths and Legends of King Arthur and the Knights of the Round Table*. North American rock bands (or anyone successful in the US, such as Led Zeppelin) also played to huge audiences in arenas. Queen and David Bowie somehow avoided criticism for this, but it was also more middle-of-the-road acts such as Elton John or 10cc that dominated the concert world in the late 1970s. Needless to say, the 'middle of the road' (MOR) or 'adult-orientated rock' (AOR) modes reached their financial peak in the aftermath of punk, as did disco. The crime, especially for popular progressive acts, was not that they had lost their audience but that they had gained a mass public following, leading to showmanship that bordered on the ridiculous (as noted by Mont Campbell of National Health and Arthur Brown in the 2008 BBC documentary *Prog Britannia*).

As the 1970s wore on, concerts expanded in scale and time, bands explored and lengthened individual tracks in performance, and the individual solo came to be an integral part of not only the concert but also the fans' expectations. LPs reflected this, with triple albums such as Yes's *Yessongs* (1973) and Emerson, Lake and Palmer's *Welcome Back My Friends to the Show That Never Ends* (1974), although it would not be until 1985, and Bruce Springsteen's *Live 1977–1985* (five albums), that anyone would try to match the length of Chicago's four-album set *Chicago* (1971).[10] The sprawl of tracks was mirrored in heavy metal and hard rock, where the already important role of the solo was further enhanced. But what did the solo represent in the context of a highly communal group such as Yes? Certainly, solos showcase virtuosity and enable the individual musician to present their own material, but why in that form? We would argue that the combative group compositional approach, which often led to arguments and assertions of leadership, actually created a vacuum where individualism seemed lost in a holistic structure. The solo and the solo album offered a means of restating the place of the individual embodied in the lyrics of Yes and Rush, even as their music enacted a complex communal dynamic. Before Rick Wakeman left Yes, he had begun his series of mythical concept albums, while between *Relayer* and *Going for the One* (1975–7) every single member of Yes had released a solo album. Other group members often featured on these solo albums, but the lead artist was, for a time, just that. ELP went so far as to release two albums (*Works Volume I* and *Works Volume II*, both double, both 1977) that combined solo and group efforts, over a much more protracted scale than Yes's *Fragile* or even Pink Floyd's *Ummagumma*. *Works I* and *II* should be seen not merely as the sign of compromising competing ideas but also as an attempt to occupy a particular kind of individualism that accurately represented how the band had been playing live for some years, where lengthy solos had always formed part of the set.

If Yes's multiple solo albums represent an assertion of individual freedom, then Emerson, Lake and Palmer's solo projects and *Works* albums need to be seen more as the competing autonomies of big business, where the market encourages exuberance and then hopes that profit and social progress emerge as a result. Lester Bangs has pointed to the extravagance of ELP, almost admiring it for its excess, but essentially he detests what looks and sounds like an emphasis on quantity over raw musical power.[11] Oddly, given the power of the punk music he praises, Bangs even complains that the extreme volume of an ELP show drags us into a coldly technologized world where the band dominates from above and afar.[12] Although all rock bands had acquired huge amounts of material that needed transporting, and required large crews to do so (thereby acting as actual businesses), as we noted in Chapter 7, ELP won the competition for most ambitious tour in 1977–8, with its three iconic trailer trucks, a band member's name emblazoned on the roof of each. As a new visualization of archaic, large-scale land art that could be seen only from the sky, these trucks symbolized the greedy individualism that progressive rock was now seen to represent. At the same time, they are also what Walter Benjamin saw in the 1830s Paris arcades, a dream of the future: in this case, the 1980s dominated by the right-wing politics of Ronald Reagan and Margaret Thatcher.

Punk sought to restore an individuality that could be accessed by everyone, whereas the mass-audience rock band worked only as a model or display of an aristocratic individuality. Punk offered the prospect that all could express themselves in the present moment, not after years of training or

EMERSON LAKE&PALMER

Publicity still of Emerson, Lake and Palmer (1977).

after the keyboard player had finished with his solo. Any anger progressive rock offered (say, in Van der Graaf Generator or Henry Cow) dissipated in prowess and in developmental time, whereas punk would instead happen in the moment, at speed and with repetition. Reviewing punk and Oi! anthologies, Lester Bangs proclaims that the best kind of musical immersion comes from locating 'a whole LP side by one band, eight songs in a row that possess only hair's breadth differences between them *yet still are not boring!*'.[13] The Ramones would exemplify this theory, as would many other punk groups. The LP itself was under threat from the return of the 7-inch single (affordable to produce or buy), and a band did not have to wait to create a whole album or bother working on the relation between tracks. A multitude of bands would release only one or two singles and vanish in the new spread of independent labels and self-produced albums that echoed but far outstripped a similar growth in folk and progressive independent labels in the late 1960s up to the mid-1970s. But the LP could not easily be killed off, and record companies could usually pull together enough material for albums.

This is a familiar tale, as is the argument that punk disposed of a caricature of progressive rock once and for all. The stylistic differences between prog and punk are stark. To generalize, punk is musically simpler, with more emphasis on the song (although not necessarily on advanced lyrics). It is faster and shorter, and any changes in key or tempo are unlikely to derive from virtuosity. A typical punk song is, paradoxically, a call to order – verse, chorus, verse, chorus, solo, chorus, or small variations thereon (especially when punk went ultra-short in Oi! – or on Wire's *Pink Flag*, in the case of avant-punk). If progressive rock attained band unity through group composition or improvisation, then punk bands did so by a massing of the sound as a unified attack. Punk made many progressive rock bands rethink the length and multipart structures of tracks, but there is also a more interesting and almost certainly unconscious place where punk addresses progressive rock on its own ground, in the form of the long track. Such strategies affected a renewed progressive rock that emerged alongside new wave and in relation to the art rock of Magazine and Brian Eno. There are very different models of a 'long punk track', but each one operates a reduction or removal of what could be expected from a 10-minute progressive rock track.

Alternative TV opens *The Image Has Cracked* (1978) with 'Alternatives'. At over 9 minutes and beginning with 'a Moog-assisted progressive rock overture', this track moves away from the basic punk model of what a song should be.[14] Its synth introduction segues into a long section where the group asks audience members on stage to speak over simple instrumental riffing. Ultimately, singer Mark Perry gets annoyed and complains about people not using their chance well or intelligently and, after a collage of different tape sections, he warns of the need for punk not to be triumphalist or derivative. The purpose of the song is to establish what social alternatives there are, and how to behave differently from current expectations; its distinguishing feature is that the band eschews exploring its own freedom in favour of giving space to the listeners. Although Perry acts as a temporary leader, the purpose is to hand over authority, implicitly criticizing progressive and hard rock for the maintenance of elite control through the distance established by virtuosity and large-scale showmanship.

In a similar fashion, long tracks within or close to punk tend to simplify and minimize. There is probably no better example of this than Suicide, but Television and Public Image Limited also take the time customarily associated with progressive rock tracks to remove, cut and hone. The length of a track can indicate the lack of repertoire of a band, as in the early Siouxsie and the Banshees take on 'The Lord's Prayer', stretching up to 20 minutes (including a 14:09 version on the 1979 album *Join Hands*). This is not the same as the 'stretching out' identified as the hallmark of the move to progressive rock in the late 1960s; rather, it is an emptying out, approaching an awareness of the time of performance and the time occupied by music.[15] Such emptying had been heard in the 1960s in the shape of American minimalism, or of The Velvet Underground and The Stooges. The stripping away of content was accompanied by a heightening of volume and a concentration of power. Suicide did not even really seem to be playing anything very much, let alone playing rock instruments badly. Vocals, synth and drum machine form virtually the entire palette of *Suicide* (1977). With this album, it was not only virtuosity that was removed but also instrumentation itself, along with variation. 'Frankie Teardrop' relates the life of Frankie, 'trying to survive', over 10:24 of an unvarying drum-machine beat and marginal changes in the synth sounds. The harshness of Frankie's life and the actions to which he is driven are undercut by the metronomic backing track, which transports us from the authentic misery of the blues to a world at the periphery of Kraftwerk's futuristic social models. Sporadic yelps disrupt the integrity of the story even as they emphasize it, moving away from the idea that the events can be clearly narrated with artfulness. For all that 'Frankie Teardrop' is far from progressive rock, it uses time to build narration, as Frankie's tough life and descent need time to be adequately conveyed.

The long tracks enabled punk bands to reclaim and reuse the time taken by progressive rock, often wasting time but always diminishing it as they sought to make an aesthetic out of 'less'. Television's *Marquee Moon* (1977) also emerged, as Suicide did, from an American lineage of minimalizing as a technique of experimental rock. Its title track (restored on the 2003 remastered CD to its 10-minute length) is closer than Suicide to progressive rock, and for all its proto–new wave credentials it marks a return to the dominance of vocals and guitars, builds up to an instrumental crescendo, and tries to develop a story in lyrics and a narrative through guitars.[16] The title track, 'Marquee Moon' (10:40), is a response to punk as much as to bloated rock music, and signals future developments of progressive rock in the 1990s (see Chapter 12). It is also in a strange place between genres, where rhythm is restored – the whole track builds rhythm, recycling and returning to guitar motifs as the percussion slowly evolves. The predictability of the rising instrumental section is precisely where it derives its power, recalling the closing 'Würm' section of Yes's 'Starship Trooper' (1971). Critically, the extended tracks of Television continued to meet with approval; the individual sounds were cleaner and simpler than progressive rock typically attempted, and with no hint of multitracking. This approval was not without its doubters in the wake of punk – certainly in Britain, where 'art rock' was probably too close to progressive rock in its sophistication and cadences. Reynolds writes that 'post-punk *was* progressive rock' but stripped down, leading to complaints that it was 'lapsing back into . . . rock elitism'.[17]

John Lydon had quickly tired of how Malcolm McLaren's prioritizing of image and shock had reduced the scope of what the Sex Pistols could do musically and lyrically. *Public Image: First Issue* (1978), the first album of his band Public Image Limited (PiL), addressed punk's shortcomings, as well as those of disco. More implicitly, the opening track, 'Theme', is a demolition of progressive rock that uses its methods. Instead of a theme, it is just 'Theme' – its content, dominated by the line 'I wish I could die', and other expressions of anomie and loss, is stated through repetition rather than narrative development. The music never varies or falters, washing cymbals over pulsing bass lines and a small range of guitar chords and merging into a mass of undifferentiated sound. Filtered by dub, this musical mode permeated PiL's second release, *Metal Box* (1979), initially a triple album (although only about 60 minutes long) in a metal box. The packaging does the same work as 'Theme', adopting the emphasis of progressive rock on visual presentation and scale but emptying it out. There is very little information, no track titles on the records and a box engraved with the PiL logo but nothing else. Where a progressive rock album signals its content through its visual and material features, this album displays content as a removal of content. Its focus on materiality calls attention to the status of packaging, a philosophy that is taken even further and made more literal on PiL's 1986 *Album*, *Cassette*, *Compact Disc*, *Single* releases.

Metal Box, like the Clash's triple album *Sandinista!* (1980), is an attempt at post-punk fusion. It combines *kosmische* repetition with the separated sounds of dub, while maintaining a furious critique of society and individual behaviour arising as a result of alienation. Lydon himself famously liked reggae and experimental rock (especially Captain Beefheart and Peter Hammill), and he played a selection of this wide range of interests on London's Capital Radio while still in the Sex Pistols.[18] From the opening, side-long 'Albatross' through to the elegiac closing instrumental 'Radio 4', *Metal Box* strips down punk and rock alike, and does so in a dub style where even the sparse dramatics of dub are lost in their encounter with something like the residue of punk. 'Albatross' is a pure entropy of rock, not minimal enough to settle into, while the second half of the near 8-minute 'Poptones' is a non-building instrumental free of exploration, a static wash with vocals echoing on a distant machine. Other tracks play out the rhetoric of punk from a distance, as an observer from within but at one remove. This is not to claim that early PiL is progressive rock, but its oppositional force is a direct deconstruction of progressive narratives: in other words, it happens in the place of progressive rock in a way that straightforward versions of punk do not do.

Progressive and punk did meet, notably in the free festivals of the late 1970s and early 1980s, but although we could say that Hawkwind, for example, combined both musical modes they did not merge them. Another festival band, Here and Now, went some way towards this (as did The Cardiacs); their sound brought together punk vocals and lyrical concerns, progressive rock time signatures and keyboard flourishes, free improvisation and reggae. Here and Now released recordings of concerts with both Alternative TV and Gong, but they showed that progressive rock did not have to revolve around the performance of musical prowess. As we discussed in Chapter 8, mainland Europe was already familiar with a radicalized left-wing version of progressive rock, and Britain would never quite see this connection without many years of hindsight. In England, following Henry Cow (as a progressive band with an avant-rock and free music background) was This Heat, whose sound-world of distortion and often minimalist soundscapes on the debut album belied a hidden complexity. This was progressive rock that somehow sounded like punk, something that Peter Gabriel would also aspire to in his early solo career, and evident in different ways in Peter Hammill's and Robert Fripp's records of the period.

This Heat brought a European avant-garde approach that lay between punk and prog, echoing the experimentation of Italian group Pierrot Lunaire, Richard Pinhas' Heldon project, and some of the odder offerings to be found on Nurse With Wound's list.[19] This Heat used tapes, looping, samples and the studio as an instrument more akin to a psychopathic gardener in a shed than The Beatles' producer George Martin – just as Cabaret Voltaire, Throbbing Gristle and others were doing in the mid-1970s. Taking a position outside of both punk and prog, Reynolds describes the band's sound as 'abstract protest music'.[20] The stark first album, *This Heat* (1978), empties punk just as PiL was emptying out prog. This would be a complex minimalism that used the DIY ethic for other ends, without falling into the trap of it being an end in itself. The 12-inch single 'Health and Efficiency' combines a sinister bureaucratic title with a cheery song about sunshine, albeit one that squalls to a halt over breaking glass, only to riff without development for close to 6 minutes. (The B-side of 'Health and Efficiency' features tape loops that can be played back at any speed.)

With its second album, This Heat took a stance on the world around it, combining the fever of jangling dissonance with lyrics about controlled consumer society and the public's complicity in it. Reynolds correctly calls *Deceit* (1981) 'almost a concept album', as this theme of self-devouring power infiltrates the whole album, from the sleepwalking consumers of the opening track, 'Sleep', to the premonitions of world destruction in 'A New Kind of Water'.[21] The deceit of the title is that of freedom through consumer choice and also with the individualistic protest against it. Drummer and vocalist Charles Hayward describes the failing consumer world of 1970s Britain as 'Hitler-lite'; in positioning itself against everything, punk merely allowed the controlling forces of society to continue as before.[22]

This Heat's take on power is not Marxist but closer to a subtle anarchism that echoes Michel Foucault's notion of the carceral society. In this model, power permeates all, affecting our actions and activities even when not bearing down on us in the form of force.[23] The track 'S.P.Q.R.' on *Deceit* associates rationalism with imperial power and domination, but essentially it is also within us as 'we are all Romans'. This is not the same as saying everyone is guilty or brainwashed, but that our every move is circumscribed by the power of control and manipulation. After This Heat intones 'pax romana', there is an almost sardonic rattle around the drum set to demonstrate the illusion of peace bought through acceptance of force. After the opening of the American Declaration of Independence on 'Independence', we arrive at the penultimate track, 'A New Kind of Water'. The opening section is a chant fed through tape

This Heat, Cold Storage (c. 1980).

and probably reversed several times. This indicates that the alienation of the masses leads to decadence or nihilism and that the world collapses because of greed and wastefulness. At the end of the first verse, the pounding drum is joined by crashing cymbals and the guitar increases in volume to announce a moment of resolution by means of a single voice saying 'I don't know either, what is the answer?' before outlining the public's perpetual demand for more. This section closes with a heavier version of the earlier guitar, and more expansive drumming punctuates line and verse. The third section comprises four verses outlining an ambiguous position where progress and the welfare state are to be admired, but the pursuit of progress has become blind and culminates in destruction. Nuclear power and the threat of warfare loom, and all we can do is 'hope we've got good men on the job'. This critical fatalism concludes with the blame lying not only with those in positions of power, or of unthinking science, but with everyone: 'You know from experience/ The creature comforts, a house that's warm/Your body would choose all this'. Although the track refers to innate selfishness, it would seem that we have been led to believe in the necessity of selfish comfort and consumer ease, and have been made to forget that this is not without cost.[24]

Late 1970s avant-garde rock returns firmly to the alienated worldviews of earlier progressive rock. In the case of Pink Floyd, alienation increased in line with Britain's combination of traditional values, decline as a world power and embrace of consumerism, leading to a hardening of the lyrics on *The Dark Side of the Moon* (starting with the spoken line 'I've been mad for fucking

years, absolutely years'), *Animals* (1977) and *The Wall* (1979). As we discussed
in Chapter 7, it is really the latter album that finally brought threatening and
malevolent anger to progressive rock, and the lavish production is largely
overwhelmed by Roger Waters' focus upon the alienating collision of the
personal and political. *The Wall* is so gargantuan a project and arguably too
self-absorbed on Waters' behalf; it captures the spirit of punk with unerring
precision, but it does not represent the shift into a new type of progressive
rock suggested by This Heat and the RIO groups.

Peter Gabriel's first two albums can be situated similarly to *Animals*. There
is a restlessness with 1970s rock gestures that seeps through his music and
lyrics alike, but still no further progression. In fact, Gabriel's first two albums
represent a turn to the pomp rock of 10cc, Queen or Elton John, especially
in the lavish production and feel of a band under a leader's instruction. This
changed as Gabriel began to master the studio and started to incorporate
non-Western percussion styles, sometimes with physical percussion and at
other times through drum machines. It should be noted that before Genesis
attempted a sort of 'pop prog', the band initially became more progressive
after Gabriel left, stretching out the songs again and relating tales of whimsy
on *Trick of the Tail* and *Wind and Wuthering* (both 1976). Long instrumental
sections turned the band's sound into something keyboard-heavy and lush
with guitar. Ultimately, this turned into a mannered set of moves that neo-
progressive bands developed in the 1980s (see Chapter 10) and, as the Genesis
songs shortened on *And Then There Were Three* (1978), so the prog moves
were even further attenuated. Gabriel slowly stripped all that back on his first
two albums, *Peter Gabriel* (1977) and *Peter Gabriel* (1978), but the production
would hold back the process that is hinted at in the slowly tragic 'Humdrum'
until albums three and four, *Peter Gabriel* (1980) and *Peter Gabriel* (1982).
The uniform titling is a refusal of both the commercial angle of the music
business and the arguably over-elaborate titles and concepts of prog albums.
All four albums feature Gabriel's face distorted or under attack; having made
himself the content of the albums, through his choice of a recurring self-
referential title, this new focus is one that is there to be stripped away. It is
with the third album (also known as '3' or 'Melt'; fans have insisted on giving
pseudonyms to the albums) that this process yields properly new progressive
elements. Its subject matter is nearly exclusively marginal, criminal, deluded
or isolated individuals who exist outside the confines of normalized human
existence, most of whom, such as on 'Intruder' and 'No Self Control', are
narrated in character by Gabriel. The exceptions to this theme are the political
'Games Without Frontiers', which recasts international relations as a version
of the slapstick European game show *Jeux Sans Frontières* (also known as *It's
a Knockout* in its British version), and 'Biko', the brooding meditation on the
prison murder of South African anti-apartheid activist Stephen Biko.

Musically, this album marks Gabriel's embrace of technology as spur and
material of experimentation. Instead of complexity, the inventiveness of the

third and fourth albums relies on rhythm and the consequent reorganizing of the band dynamic – a musical mode that Gabriel takes further into his experimentation with voice as a noise below the level of words, which he demonstrated on ITV's *South Bank Show* (1982) while recording the fourth album. The third album features powerful, solid drumming that sounds unusual because of the removal of the cymbal as punctuating device or colour; given that one of the drummers, Phil Collins, was well known for precisely this type of percussion, this is a major rethinking of the place of the drum-kit. The result is redolent of non-Western music and is certainly a departure for rock music. Gabriel had recently become interested in world music, and he tried to incorporate it as rock fusion, not as colour but as a structural and instrumental framework. The concurrent use of drum machine and computer-generated sounds means this is not just an exercise in finding a more authentic form.[25]

The closing track, 'Biko', recounts the murder of Stephen Biko in 1977 with straightforward lyrics framed by African chants and songs. The whole is driven by the combination of a slowly pulsating synthesized rhythm track and Jerry Marotta's ultra-heavy repetitive drumming. This direct subject matter reveals Gabriel to be reacting to the challenge of punk to reconnect, to be more direct and to simplify. But it also maintains the virtues of progressive rock: its value unfolds over a long duration (the single version of 'Biko' is actually extended to 9 minutes); it self-consciously uses form to convey content, hinting at Gabriel's future soundtrack work later in the decade, such as *Birdy* (1985) and *Passion* (1989); and it uncompromisingly aims for new forms. The fourth album takes up where 'Biko' left off, with two long, minimal, slow-building tracks, which can be heard at their most effective on *Plays Live* (1983) that documents the 1983 tour.

Gabriel's first solo tour in 1977 was very much a rendition of the first album but had a much simpler sound than Genesis had produced live or in the studio. He played only one Genesis track, 'Back in NYC', from *The Lamb Lies Down on Broadway*, which stressed the break with prog even more firmly than if he had performed none. In choosing part of the old repertoire, Gabriel emphasized that the task of progressive music is to move on, and one way in which that happens is to reassess the past. King Crimson did the same, and in various reincarnations kept only 'Red' and 'Larks' Tongues in Aspic Part II' from the pre-1974 period. Gabriel's 1983 tour was very different and was dominated by his third and fourth albums; the sound was deep and the rhythm the essential part. Concerts opened with the lengthy 'The Rhythm of the Heat' and closed with 'Biko'. In between, he played songs that, while not entirely focused on bass and drums, highlighted that this was a new hybrid form of the rock band (in line with synth groups and the 1980s version of King Crimson). Gabriel also developed a new way of performing a show as a minimized commentary on what it means to be in a show (wearing simplified face paint and a white suit), and he featured the innovation of crowd surfing on 'Lay Your Hands on Me' which, although it is depicted on the cover of *Plays Live*, is not on the album itself.

While Gabriel was reconfiguring the potential of the rock band, Peter Hammill was also moving to a variation on progressive rock that used new technology as the means of experimentation. By *A Black Box* (1980), Hammill was willing to construct a side-long track where he would play almost everything. 'Flight' was accompanied by a side of shorter songs with almost abstract backings, as if rock was being wiped away. Punk itself had little bearing on this change, perhaps except in sweeping away as a necessary process. In a small way, Hammill had already written his punk album, *Nadir's Big Chance* by 1975 (this was the album Lydon played part of on the Capital Radio show), and by 1980 the possibilities of new sound and structuring from increasingly computerized instrumentation appealed to Hammill and gave room for the more minimal aesthetic.

The peak of prog minimalism, though, could be found in the newly convened King Crimson, in the shape of the trilogy *Discipline* (1981), *Beat* (1982) and *Three of a Perfect Pair* (1984). Robert Fripp was joined by Tony Levin on bass stick; Adrian Belew on guitar and vocals; and Bill Bruford who incorporated a full electronic drum-kit. The resemblance of this music to the American new-wave group Talking Heads is no accident; Belew had played guitar on their album *Remain in Light* (1980), as had Fripp on the preceding *Fear of Music* (1979). King Crimson's strategy was to pare back their sound and make from it a precision-based metallic minimalism based on repetitions, phasing between guitars, and a rhythm section that did not act as a backing unit but rather contributed to the overall structure and the melodic development of tracks. The Talking Heads connection was not one way; hints of its sound (and of vocalist David Byrne himself) can be heard on Fripp's solo albums of 1979–80 and also in his short-lived no-wave/new-wave band The League of Gentlemen. The key to the newly disciplined King Crimson was a virtuosity that was based on meshing. Incredibly complex parts hide their difficulty in tracks that seem almost circular. These are punctuated by fierce rock tracks, wherein the loud parts would themselves be punctuations of a very steady state music: 'Thela Hun Ginjeet' and 'Indiscipline' on *Discipline*, for example.

These three albums form a coherent sound-world, one that critics have noted is highly reminiscent not only of 1960s Western minimalism but also of Javanese gamelan.[26] The key structuring concept is the 'discipline' of the first of the albums; Discipline had been the original name for the band when it started playing live in 1981. At the end of his *The League of Gentlemen* album (1981), Fripp established that this was not just one theme among many: a recording of spiritual guru J. G. Bennett declares the virtue of discipline, just as the run-out groove announces 'the next step is discipline'.[27] Fripp had also begun developing a model for how musicians would interact that could work within the group, as well as within the marketplace and towards the public, with the liner notes of *God Save the Queen/Under Heavy Manners* (1980) presenting a lengthy manifesto. Included in that statement is a hint of how Fripp saw the developments within 1970s progressive rock, citing the loss of contact with the audience (because of the scale of events) and the passivity of audiences (overwhelmed by the showmanship that came with those events). Fripp wrote a statement to accompany the release of *Discipline*: 'the musical movement of which King Crimson was a founding force went tragically off course'.[28] Despite this being the reason for the disbanding of King Crimson in 1974, something about that moment pushes him to suggest that progressiveness can be resuscitated but by very different means.

These means are as listed above in this chapter, but we need also to consider the self-reflexiveness as manifested on *Discipline* and then more implicitly on the two following albums. This is a music of punctuation, circling and stasis that vies with detailed variation. The gamelan element lies not just in the minimalism or the feel of these records but also in the percussiveness of the playing. Levin's bass is literally tapped; Fripp's ultra-fast arpeggios, where the overall range of notes is purposely limited (again, literally, in the areas used on the guitar or in the number of notes used), mean that he does not 'express' in a rock manner; Bruford's drumming is likewise reined in on the instruction of Fripp, as well as through playing techniques, the electronic drum-kit and the sparing use of cymbals. Only Belew roves consistently away from the

King Crimson, *Discipline* (1981). Knot logo by Steve Ball.

primary drive of rhythm. On the key tracks 'Discipline' and 'Frame by Frame', Belew joins with Fripp in and out of phase. 'Discipline' is highly repetitive and is probably the best example of what Eric Tamm refers to as the illusion of harmonic activity: 'there are changes or shifts, but no real sense of gravitational motion through tonal space'.[29] 'Frame by Frame' is similar but features short verses, which, although seemingly about psychoanalysis, can best be thought of as the band's analysis of its own activity: 'Step by step (suddenly)/ Doubt by numbers (from within)'. 'Indiscipline' acts as the counterpart to the title track, with the latter closing the album (and thereby asserting itself as the dominant idea) and the former closing side one. 'Indiscipline' is the paradigm for the explosive elements of this early 1980s incarnation of King Crimson, and is also about punctuating moments. It concerns the fascination with an unnamed object that links directly to the band's strategy of interlocking micro-movements of complexity into the minimalist whole of *Discipline*: 'No matter how closely I study it/No matter how I take it apart/No matter how I break it down/It remains consistent'.[30] Belew's spoken lyrics are quiet and calm until the closing line of the second verse. When the track was played live in 1982 and 1984, the ends of both verses were shouted following Belew's pause and the withholding of them. The track might be meant to be about a sculpture by Margaret Belew or Fripp's view of Bruford's drumming.[31] However, in concert it is transformed into a test of turning concentration into numbers, into the precise moment the whole band comes in; only when that is assured is the space for relative indiscipline possible.

This might sound like lab music, and to some extent it is: a clinical dissection of the epic sprawl of progressive rock into narrative, showmanship and virtuosity. Here skill is almost hidden, emerging only as an awareness of the complexity of constituent parts. It is no longer important that virtuosity be heard. This is not just music of logic, though, as the purposely limited instrumentation and instrumental strategies give the music an organic feel, even if often inhuman. The power of metal-style tracks such as 'Thela Hun Ginjeet' ensure this is not just music for a gallery, and King Crimson ultimately would fully combine the mid-1970s heavy-trio sound with cyclical elements in the late 1990s and 2000s. *Beat* has an even stronger metallic edge, driving its thematic of beat poetry, but *Three of a Perfect Pair* drifts somewhat through its expanded sound-world, with the minimalist power of the first two albums appearing only fleetingly. The last track of this version of the group, 'Larks' Tongues in Aspic, Part III', continues the reflection on progressive rock and King Crimson's place within it, fading out just as the group merges into a more harmonic and steadily building crescendo.

In these three early 1980s King Crimson albums, progressive rock becomes a possibility again through radical reimagining. Many would disagree with Fripp's stance on what happened to progressive rock in 1974, but what is curious is how he adopts exactly the position of the critic of prog in order to start it all over again from somewhere else. Writing ten years later, David

Tibet wrote in *Sounds* that 'King Crimson have managed to produce a sort of modern manual to what used to be called progressive music'.[32]

Notes

1. Greil Marcus, *Lipstick Traces* (London: Faber and Faber, [1989] 2001) and Stewart Home, *Cranked Up Really High: Genre Theory and Punk Rock* (Hove: CodeX, 1995). The Anglocentric view of punk as being an exclusively English adoption of continental European avant-gardes is challenged by Clinton Heylin, *From the Velvets to the Voidoids: The Birth of American Punk Rock*, 2nd edn (London: Helter Skelter, [1993] 2005). According to Heylin, we should not try to construct one lineage but should instead work out parallel genealogies.

2. Captain Sensible, 'Foreword Two', in Alex Ogg, *No More Heroes: A Complete History of UK Punk from 1976 to 1980* (London: Cherry Red, 2006), 10–11.

3. As Keith Emerson puts it, 'for the high-rolling bands, English taxation had become way out of order . . . But where to go?' (Keith Emerson, *Pictures of an Exhibitionist*, London: John Blake [2004], 292). Many musicians would join Emerson in Switzerland.

4. Home, *Cranked Up Really High*, 13.

5. Jon Savage, *England's Dreaming: Sex Pistols and Punk Rock* (London: Faber and Faber, 1991), 81.

6. Simon Reynolds argues that the 'prominence of music papers . . . began with punk', *Rip It Up and Start Again: Postpunk 1978–1984* (London: Faber and Faber, 2005), xxvi.

7. Bill Bruford, *The Autobiography* (London: Jawbone Press, 2009), 119.

8. As of December 2010, Amazon.com lists seventeen new books on punk bands, the punk phenomenon and punk art due out by the first half of 2011. The UK version of the site has fifteen for the same period, with some but not all included in the US listing.

9. Home, *Cranked Up Really High*, 14, 19.

10. It should be noted that Bruce Springsteen's box is more of a premonition of multiple CD box sets, and also that multi-album releases were far from confined to stadium-level bands: Throbbing Gristle's *24 Hours* (1980) was a 26-cassette release.

11. Lester Bangs, 'Blood Feast of Reddy Kilowatt! Emerson, Lake and Palmer Without Insulation!', *Mainlines, Blood Feasts and Bad Taste* (London: Serpent's Tail, 2003), 47–55 (55).

12. Ibid., 47.

13. Lester Bangs, 'If Oi Were a Carpenter', *Mainlines, Blood Feasts and Bad Taste*, 125.

14. *The Image Has Cracked*, reissue, liner notes.

15. One notable exception is side three of The Damned's *Black Album* (1980), which consists of the 17-minute 'Curtain Call'.

16. The track would also be stretched when played live, to as long as 15 minutes (Heylin, *From the Velvets to the Voidoids*, 273).

17. Reynolds, *Rip It Up and Start Again*, xx, xvii.

18. See Phil Strongman, *Metal Box: Stories from John Lydon's Public Image Limited* (London: Helter Skelter, 2007), 31.

19. See Nurse With Wound, *Chance Meeting on a Dissecting Table of a Sewing Machine and an Umbrella*, liner notes. Released in 1979, this avant-garde improvisational album provided an extensive list of influences, or music to aspire to, culled from group leader Steven Stapleton's collection. This Heat features on the list.

20. Reynolds, *Rip It Up and Start Again*, 212.

21. Ibid., 212.

22. This Heat, *Out of Cold Storage*, liner notes, 23.

23. See Michel Foucault, *Discipline and Punish: The Birth of the Prison* (London: Allen Lane, [1975] 1977).

24. This Heat drummer and vocalist Charles Hayward would continue the musical and lyrical direction in his band Camberwell Now, and, later, in his solo work, which largely concerns technological surveillance and other new modalities of power.

25. In 1982, Peter Gabriel formed WOMAD to promote world music, and he later worked with many musicians from Africa and released albums from musicians around the world on his Real World label. This exoticist take on music can doubtless be addressed by postcolonial critiques, but we would claim instead that Gabriel's version of global music is already a properly postcolonial take on it: see Neil Lazarus, 'Unsystematic Fingers at the Conditions of the Times: "Afropop" and the Paradoxes of Imperialism', in *Postcolonial Discourses: An Anthology*, ed. Gregory Castle (Oxford: Blackwell, 2001), 232–50 (248). For a good example of the critical uncertainty on Gabriel and world music, see Charles Keil and Steven Feld, *Music Grooves* (Chicago: University of Chicago Press, 1994), 270–2. For a more dismissive critique, see Timothy D. Taylor, *Beyond Exoticism: Western Music and the World* (Durham, NC: Duke University Press, 2007). According to Taylor, Gabriel uses collaboration as a smokescreen for exploitation (127) and perverts Nusrat Fateh Ali Khan by channelling his music away from a sacred context (148).

26. See Smith, *In The Court of King Crimson*, 231 and Tamm, *Robert Fripp*, 138–9.

27. J. G. Bennett was himself inspired by spiritual leaders G. I. Gurdjieff and P. D. Ouspensky.

28. *Discipline* (2004 CD issue), liner notes, 5.

29. Tamm, *Robert Fripp*, 144.

30. For connections between complexity and reductive strategies as an arcane device to read the three King Crimson albums of the 1980s, see Jonathan Sheffer, ed., *Perceptible Processes: Minimalism and the Baroque* (New York: Eos, 1997).

31. See Smith, *In the Court of King Crimson*, 229.

32. Review of *Three of a Perfect Pair*, *Sounds* (24 March 1984). Reproduced on *Three of a Perfect Pair* liner notes (CD issue, 2001), 3.

Chapter 10

Neo-Progressive

Edward Macan begins his chapter on Emerson, Lake and Palmer's first sabbatical from each other with the following line: 'during the early 1980s, no musical style was more desperately unfashionable than progressive rock; and no progressive rock band was more desperately unfashionable than Emerson, Lake and Palmer'.[1] As Macan notes, the splintering of ELP happened just as Yes was struggling to find a new vocalist after Jon Anderson had temporarily left the band; Pink Floyd was close to meltdown; Camel lost direction after the 1981 concept album *Nude*; Barclay James Harvest and the three remaining members of Genesis were veering towards album-oriented rock (AOR); and the recent deaths of Keith Moon and John Bonham marked the demise of The Who and Led Zeppelin respectively, the latter which might have been close to a renaissance following two high-profile shows at Knebworth in 1979. Popular American stadium bands such as Journey, Boston, Styx and Kansas had taken the place of progressive rock, shifting between versions of the musical complexity traced in the first half of this book and direct, radio-friendly songs dealing with relationships and lifestyles.[2]

This transition can be exemplified on two Journey singles that shift from the jazz-rock fusion of their first three albums (1975–7) to the stadium-rock outfit of the early 1980s. The single 'Wheel in the Sky', taken from *Infinity* (1978), is a tightly composed 4-minute song that alternates between verse and chorus, with a delicate acoustic introduction and mournful vocals by the band's new vocalist, Steve Perry, that combine mystical resonances ('The wheel in the sky keeps on turning') with a reflection on fate and the need to forge a spiritual passage onwards. In contrast, Journey's best-known single, 'Don't Stop Believin'', on *Escape* (1981), is more direct: a song about young lovers from humble backgrounds who meet by chance by night in a big city (probably Los Angeles), featuring a memorable opening piano hook, Neal Schon's wind-up guitar, Perry's extensive vocal range and a sing-along chorus.[3] The dominance of white rock bands and performers at the turn of the 1980s – including Foreigner, REO Speedwagon and Bob Seger – meant that groups that could be classified as prog in their early guises, such as Kansas or the American-sounding but mostly British Supertramp, veered towards a marketable identity and song structures that could maximize radio airplay and record sales, such as Supertramp's 1979 album *Breakfast in America*, with its tourist's view of New York City on the front cover (an air hostess parodies the Statue of Liberty, and cereal packets make up Manhattan) and its four hit singles released in the US. In Britain, groups such as Queen and the Electric Light Orchestra (ELO) attained commercial success through epic and highly orchestral rock, energetic live performances, and melodic yet extravagant singles, with Queen's 6-minute 'Bohemian Rhapsody' (1975) a contender as a progressive rock song in its contrasting moods, three-part structure, and lack of chorus.

The early 1980s can be seen as a watershed for progressive rock, as bands from the 1970s broke up or splintered to form a new generation of watered-down supergroups. Asia is perhaps the best known example of a 1980s supergroup formed from members of Yes, King Crimson, ELP and The Buggles – what Paul Stump calls 'the black hole' of progressive rock.[4] Asia found instant radio and chart success in 1982 with its single 'Heat of the Moment', taken from their first, eponymous album. Rather than interweaving voice and music, as was a hallmark of 1970s progressive rock, John Wetton's clear vocal delivery is pushed into the foreground and pivots around a catchy guitar riff and repetitive harmonic chorus. 'Heat of the Moment' is perhaps most interesting because it positions itself in a precise cultural moment when music markets were in transition – and not in the direction that most rock bands wanted. The singer looks back to a better time and bemoans cultural decline: 'and now you find yourself in '82/The disco hotspots hold no charm for you'. We might look to the vermillion sea-serpent with open wings on *Asia*'s cover, and its rising from a tempestuous sea and staring towards a distant planet, as a symbol of rock music's coming back to life. But it was actually a mixture of old and new. Although Asia's line-up changed regularly over the years, the band continued to use prog-rock cover art designed by Roger Dean and experimented with jazz riffs and interesting vocal arrangements on 'Time Again' from the first album, as well as on extended tracks on *Arena* (1996), including the 9-minute track 'The Day Before the War'. On the whole, though, Asia moved away from complexity and conceptual unity towards 4- and 5-minute songs with an eye to the American market and drive-time radio (even though they had fan bases in mainland Europe and East Asia). This radio-friendly trend was also true of Yes's 1983 number one US single 'Owner of a Lonely Heart', which favoured repetition rather than complexity, offsetting Jon Anderson's alto voice with a sparse and distorted guitar riff (produced by Trevor Horn) that might have fitted into a number of early 1980s musical genres.

The 'neo' in neo-prog suggests a movement beyond progressive rock, as well as a return to an originary conception of the term. 'Neo' suggests less of a

break than 'post', but it is hard to pin down if we are looking for this revision-
ing among records by bands such as Asia or GTR (formed by Steve Hackett
and Steve Howe but lasting only two years), or the collaboration between Jon
Anderson and Greek keyboardist Vangelis (which lasted from 1979 to 1991) that
developed from the splintering of 1970s groups. The beginnings of neo-prog
are also hard to determine. We might choose 1980 as a key year when a number of new bands emerged, or when tunics, robes and long hair were replaced
by formal jackets and shorter hair-styles (evident in Led Zeppelin's 1979
Knebworth concerts, by which time Jimmy Page had abandoned his moon and
star costume for a conventional blue shirt and slacks), or when a distinctively
progressive band such as Rush shifted its attention towards shorter, keyboard-
oriented songs and a broad palette of musical styles and influences, such
as The Police-inspired reggae riffs on its 1983 album *Grace Under Pressure*.

Neo-prog has typically been characterized by groups such as Marillion,
IQ, Pendragon, Pallas and Twelfth Night, which all began to release records
at the beginning of the 1980s. This new generation of bands wanted to play
extended rock songs with prominent keyboards and dramatic soundscapes
underpinning complex lyrical themes. Neo-prog was, in many ways, a
reaction to punk and a rebuttal of the dogma that what was good until 1976
was now banned forever. But it was also a positive reaction to the punk
assault on progressive rock, particularly as songs became more personal or
politically committed and less bound up in esoteric mythologies. Neo-prog
regenerated the more expansive gestures of Genesis and Yes in the shape of
dramatic reprises, interplay between guitar and keyboard, syncopated drumming, bass that does more than hold rhythm, and complex lyrical themes and
structures propelled towards ecstatic musical climaxes.[5] In this way, neo-prog
was a condensation of prog themes and techniques to create a newer form of
rock, albeit one that in progressive rock terms was not very progressive at all.
Importantly, the neo-prog 'movement' in Britain was built largely from the
bottom up, with independent releases, lengthy tours and connections with
the 'New Wave of British Heavy Metal' being more prominent than explicit
associations with established progressive rock bands.

One problem for 1980s neo-prog was its perceived lack of originality –
the singers of Marillion and IQ even adopted face paint in homage to (or
in parody of) Peter Gabriel. The melodiousness of neo-prog threatened to
undermine its new lyrical directions, admittedly after some early exaggerated
takes on 1970s epic tracks such as Marillion's 17-minute 'Grendel' (1982). But,
for all the questionable attitude to early 1970s progressive rock, it is important
to note that the 1980s bands consciously adopted prog as a palette from which
to work, just as in the late 1960s psychedelic or prog bands had looked to jazz
and to classical and South Asian music. These bands also demonstrated that
the musical aims of progressive rock were not necessarily confined to very
wealthy virtuoso players in large stadia, such as Emerson, Lake and Palmer.
This generation contained talented musicians, but there was more willingness

to retain roughness, especially on early albums. Group composition still held sway, but the division of labour was clearer than in Yes, King Crimson or Van der Graaf Generator, as recognizable solo passages occurred more often than collectively composed or improvised sections where everyone seems to be playing a lead instrument.

While a clear progressive style can be identified in the early 1980s approach, we can find similar examples of the use of prog as a genre in the 1970s, which leads us to argue that neo-prog styles run parallel and are fused with progressive compositions. On its self-titled 1976 album, for example, the American band Starcastle combined the sounds of Kansas and Journey with an almost engineered set of references to Yes. The vocals are often multipart harmonies (just as Yes had borrowed from Crosby, Stills and Nash) with a Jon Anderson-inflected lead vocal, the heavy yet high-pitched bass performs similar lead lines to Chris Squire, and the keyboards recall Tony Kaye and *Fragile*-era Rick Wakeman. Although the songs often comprise several sections, the complexity operates at the level of the entire song rather than in its individual instrumental phases, reinforcing the almost unrelenting positivity in the use of space, fantasy and self-help lyrics. As with 1980s neo-prog, there are virtually no instances of dissonance, atonality or breakdowns between parts. Reprises become more literal, as in the opening 'Lady of the Lake' on *Starcastle*. The band even reused its own strategies in opening *Fountains of Light* (1977) with the only long (10-minute) track of the album. It would be easy to dismiss Starcastle as simply derivative or formulaic, but the band stretched out the form of mid-1970s American rock, and the explicitness of its borrowing makes at least the first album feel like a postmodern take on prog. Despite the relative absence of home-grown progressive bands (the mostly instrumental Happy the Man is a notable exception), European prog was at the height of its commercial success in the US and may have been adopted as a style by new bands to launch their careers. While the overall feel is that of making recognizable prog methods more direct, the combination of influences in Starcastle is distinct and explicit. To take another example, the opening track, 'Midnight Madness', on the British band England's 1977 proto-neo-prog album, *Garden Shed*, combines the keyboard sounds of Tony Banks, the guitars of Brian May, and vocal and lyrical structures reminiscent of Gentle Giant and Steely Dan. On this album, we can hear how neo-prog is not just a derivation but a recombination of prog elements, so much so that it seems to be a self-conscious 'copy' of progressive rock but, we would argue, not necessarily a weak or bastardized one.

Traversing the period of 1970s prog is Robert John Godfrey's group The Enid, which took the idea of fusing classical music with rock music in the way of ELP, The Nice and, in particular, the discordant sounds of Egg. Like Keith Jenkins (one-time member of Soft Machine), The Enid was not interested in the current directions of modern classical music; rather, the band members can be aligned with Michael Nyman in their interest in chorus-based instrumental music that, in turn, owed something to rock and minimalist structures. The Enid sought to revive an epic yet light-hearted form of the pastoral, notably in its career centrepiece 'Fand', first released on *Aerie Faerie Nonsense* (1977) and later extended from over 17 minutes to nearly 30 minutes when re-released as *Fand* in 1985. The Enid would not be the first or last in progressive rock to bear the traces of Ralph Vaughan Williams.

The early 1980s marked the emergence of a number of bands whose longevity survived the label 'neo-prog'. Three bands discussed here – Marillion, Pendragon and IQ – are still recording and performing thirty years later, while other singers with progressive tendencies – Kate Bush, Peter Gabriel and Roy Harper – cannot easily be defined by a stable musical style or discrete period, despite releasing key albums in the 1980s. Genesis was much criticized in the mid-1980s (and parodied in Bret Easton Ellis's 1991 novel *American Psycho*) for throwaway songs such as 'Land of Confusion' (1985), with its *Spitting Image* music video involving puppet versions of the three band members alongside national leaders Margaret Thatcher and Ronald Reagan. But the singles success enjoyed by Genesis and Phil Collins in the mid-1980s hid lengthier and more interesting tracks on the *Invisible Touch* album (1986), such as 'Domino', which explores the domino effect on musical and lyrical levels. After his first four studio albums, Peter Gabriel also moved to more direct songs on his most commercially successful album to date, *So* (1985), but he mixed socially conscious tracks such as 'Red Rain' with the playful lyrics of 'Sledgehammer' and 'Big Time' (two singles played regularly on MTV); the ambient minimalism of 'We Do What We're Told (Milgram's 37)'; and the avant-garde collaboration 'This is the Picture', composed as a call and response between Gabriel and performance artist Laurie Anderson.

We might wish to characterize neo-prog as postmodern pastiche rather than pursuing a distinct line of influence and development. On this reading, the loss of master narratives that had hitherto structured society, self and history (as Jean-François Lyotard discussed in *The Postmodern Condition*) was reflected on a stylistic level by compressing song lengths and reining in mythical and allegorical resonances. This reading suggests that neo-prog not only recycles musical styles but also (more positively) reflects a growing interest in non-Western musical traditions, a trend that is crucial for explaining Peter Gabriel's passion for world music, as well as inflecting the Middle Eastern riffs on Marillion's tracks 'Incubus' and 'Assassing' on *Fugazi* (1984) and the East Asian ambience of Rush's 'Tai Shan' (1987).

For 1980s neo-prog bands, concepts loosened up as songs became shorter and unified narratives were replaced by albums based on melodies, moods or diffuse themes. Cover art still played an important role in projecting a particular image to suit the album's lyrics and musical reach: take the adolescent boy on Hugh Syme's cover art for Rush's *Power Windows*, who is caught between the media (an old-fashioned television and wireless radio) and an electrical storm outside his bedsit window, or the three red geometrical balls suspended on a red colour field on *Hold Your Fire* – an image carried through on its 1987–8 tour brochure as an abstraction of the three band members. Rush found other ways to tell narratives, perhaps most successfully on the Fear song-cycle, which began with part three of Fear, 'Witch Hunt' on *Moving Pictures* (1981), and continued in reverse order through part two, 'The Weapon' on *Signals* (1982), and part one, 'The Enemy Within' on *Grace Under Pressure* (1993), before its return as part four, 'Freeze' on *Vapor Trails* (2002), nearly twenty years later. Neil Peart claimed that he was inspired by a man he met who said that his life was ruled by fear, and Peart devised a series of three songs, or 'theaters of fear', which related 'how fear works inside us ('The Enemy Within'), how fear is used against us ('The Weapon') and how fear feeds the mob mentality ('Witch Hunt').[6] This suggests a movement outwards from self to society, but the cycle was composed in reverse order – partly because Peart found it easiest to write a song about persecution and scapegoating first, and partly because he wished to trace the social effects of fear back to their psychological roots. The Cold War context gives the second and third tracks particular resonance, but Peart's interest in psychology and biology is clearly evident on 'Freeze'. The song shifts from its social setting ('The city crouches, steaming/In the early morning half-light') to focus on a figure who is pursued by his fears through darkened streets. Perhaps the most conventional of the four songs, 'Freeze' moves evenly between verse and chorus ('Sometimes I freeze . . .'); recalls the 'flickering light' that twists the faces of the mob on 'Witch Hunt'; and echoes another track on *Grace Under Pressure*, 'Between the Wheels', where a rabbit is blinded by headlights, 'frozen in the fatal climb' and caught under spinning car wheels (the consequences of being blinded and trapped on 'Between the Wheels' are linked directly to the 1980s political climate, 'the wars of our time' and 'the big-time world'). This technique of echo and development, both within and beyond the Fear song-cycle, exemplifies a subtle shift in the use of prog concepts.

Concept albums were still possible in the early 1980s. Pink Floyd's final album in the group's 1970s guise (before reforming in 1987 as a three-piece without Roger Waters), *The Final Cut* (1983), reflects the demise of the band, but it is also a diatribe against politicians who were responsible for the loss of 'The Post War Dream', the title of the mournful first track. We indicated in Chapter 8 that social critique was embedded in progressive music as far back as the early 1970s; but in the 1980s we find more direct references to the shared world, rather than contemporary issues refracted through myths and alternative social structures. *The Final Cut* searches around for personal and social answers through self-questioning ('Was it you, was it me, did I watch too much TV?'), social observation (reflecting on the loss of industry and problems of immigration), and interrogating the last forty years of British history. Margaret Thatcher is in the firing line: she is name-checked in the first track, 'Maggie, what have we done?', and, after the sound of a bomb dropping, she is indicted along with General Secretary of the Soviet Communist Party

Leonid Brezhnev and Israeli leader Menacham Begin on 'Get Your Filthy Hands off My Desert', as Thatcher tries to reclaim the Falklands from the Argentine leader General Galtieri. But rather than a sustained political attack on national leaders (there is marked nostalgia for a British national past) or the forces of globalization (an invective against the Japanese), the album collapses into the punk anger of 'Not Now John' ('Fuck all that, we've got to get on with this') and the initially gentle but apocalyptic closure of 'Two Suns in the Sunset', which prompts the singer to reflect mournfully that perhaps 'the human race is run'.

Waters continued his interest in concepts and narratives into his solo career with *The Pros and Cons of Hitchhiking* (1984) and *Radio K.A.O.S.* (1987), the latter of which revives the progressive interest in idiosyncratic protagonists by suggesting (not entirely convincingly) that technology can be a means to overcome disability. Twelfth Night offered a Waters-esque take on a society oppressed by the abuse of power and hamstrung by passivity and moral control on *Fact and Fiction* (1982), which ends on a positive note on the final track ('Love Song'), where the band suggests utopian thinking is not only possible but also necessary if we are resist the weight of conformity. This period of Twelfth Night offers a rare coming together of the more anarchistic Here and Now with the intricate critique and sound of early Marillion. More often bands were happy to look for distinctive moods, images and themes that could keep together a selection, such as Magnum's *On a Storyteller's Night* or Rush's *Power Windows*. Jethro Tull exploited the sword-and-sorcery craze of the early 1980s on *Broadsword and the Beast* (1982), with a cartoon version of Ian Anderson on the cover looking like a Tolkien character; but the band opted for evocative and more abstract cover art as a ploy for marketing a rockier sound on *Crest of a Knave* (1987), *Rock Island* (1989) and *Catfish Rising* (1991), after unsuccessfully experimenting with a heavily synthesized sound on *Under Wraps* (1984). This return to the lead guitar in the late 1980s paralleled Rush's decision to lessen the emphasis on synthesizers on *Presto* (1989) and *Roll the Bones* (1991); Jethro Tull even won a Grammy in the hard-rock category for *Crest of a Knave*, which has been likened to the guitar rock of Dire Straits rather than to progressive or heavy rock. Arguably, mythology and concepts became the property of heavy rock bands in the 1980s, with Iron Maiden, Dio and Queensrÿche experimenting with song lengths and narrative structures, which fed into a later form of prog rock that includes the genre of progressive metal, as we discuss in Chapter 14.

One of the most distinctive British neo-prog bands of the 1980s, bridging experimentalism with mainstream success in the middle of the decade, was the Buckinghamshire band Marillion, which was formed in 1980 and was named after Tolkien's posthumously published Middle Earth book *The Silmarillion* (1977). In the band's first few years, it was often derogatively compared to the early incarnation of Genesis, with Mark Kelly's keyboard style echoing that of Tony Banks and the propensity of the Scottish lead singer, Fish, to wear grease-paint on his face in the shadow of Peter Gabriel. The fact that Marillion's early concerts contained versions of 'I Know What I Like (in Your Wardrobe)' and songs from *The Lamb Lies Down on Broadway* gave weight to these claims.[7] Jon Collins notes that their longest early track, the multipart 'Grendel', which retells the *Beowulf* legend from the monster Grendel's perspective, caused the band some concern because it was structurally quite similar to Genesis's 'Supper's Ready'. However, 'Grendel' is in fact very different, maintaining a consistent point of view within the parameters of a well-known myth and building claustrophobic intensity through Fish's dramatic vocal delivery, rather than the ontological and geographical shifts that 'Supper's Ready' makes. Indeed, if Marillion was a new incarnation of Genesis, then the band could also be seen as reviving the early experimentation of 1970s progressive rock at a time when Collins, Rutherford and Banks were focusing on shorter, more radio-friendly songs and looser album concepts.[8] Despite these comparisons and the occasional echo (such as the lyric 'baptized in tears from the real', which mutates into the vocal 'drowning in the rael' on 'Fugazi' and recalls the protagonist of *The Lamb Lies Down on Broadway*), in the early years Fish's delivery was closer to that of Alex Harvey and Peter Hammill than to Gabriel's more soulful style, and Marillion made liberal use of samples, recitation and spoken dialogue more in common with Pink Floyd of the late 1970s. If early Marillion is a version of postmodern pastiche, then it injected a rockier element into the motifs and style of Genesis, together with the punk attitude of Fish's modulated delivery, which could move swiftly from aggression to tenderness.[9]

It is worth discussing the band's first four albums in some detail, partly because they offer interesting thematic links and different versions of the 1980s concept album, and partly because they mark the first phase of Marillion up to the point Fish left the band for a solo career in 1988. After Fish's departure, Marillion went on to produce many albums with new lead singer Steve Hogarth and continued to work with mood pieces such as *Season's End* (1989), concept pieces such as the 1994 album *Brave* (based on a report of a girl found on the Severn Bridge who could not remember her past) and the 2004 album *Marbles*, as well as a cover of Rare Bird's 1969 prog track 'Sympathy' (released as a single in 1992). However, the first four albums with Fish as the lead singer and primary lyricist – *Script for a Jester's Tear* (1983), *Fugazi* (1984), *Misplaced Childhood* (1985) and *Clutching at Straws* (1987) – all interrelate and work with concepts on different levels. The thematic unity of these four albums links to their cover art, in which the jester, who melancholically plays the violin as he tries to compose a song in a gloomy bedsit on the cover of the first album, becomes a strung-out rock star lying on a hotel bed on *Fugazi*; we see the jester jumping out of the window on the back cover of *Misplaced Childhood*, to be replaced by the image on the front cover of a young drummer-boy holding a magpie and wearing a heart pendant instead of a war medal; and then we see the jester's costume hanging out of the young man's coat pocket in the foreground of the bar scene on *Clutching at Straws*.[10] The artist Mark Wilkinson also used the jester motif variously on the band's 7-inch and 12-inch releases. The jester removes his actor's mask on 'Market Square Heroes' (1982) to reveal a grotesque and bloodshot eye behind it; the mask is violently torn away to expose a 'manic, kohl-streamed face' on the cover of the album's second single, 'He Knows You Know'; the jester is masked by bourgeois pretension complete with monocle on 'Garden Party'; he mutates into a bourgeois puppet on the cover of 'Punch and Judy' (with a boxing glove aimed at a miniature Judy); and he becomes a Vietnam War veteran with a 'thousand yard stare' on 'Assassing', tempted by the Ace of Spades card offered to him by a devilish inquisitor, a concept inspired by Edgar Allan Poe's gothic story 'The Masque of the Red Death' and by soldiers' accounts of the Vietnam War.[11]

Wilkinson's technique of airbrushing, his highly symbolic style and his literalist rendering of the song's characters were quite different from Roger Dean's often character-free landscapes on Yes album covers, or from the surrealism of Hipgnosis. The artwork was sometimes prepared in advance and directly inspired the music, gathering 'images and symbols around themes, playing games and creating layers of allegory that the fans would revel in', as Fish described it.[12] Wilkinson did not simply focus on the mutating and

Mark Wilkinson's artwork for Marillion's 'Assassing' single (1984),
www.the-masque.com/shadowplay

mutable character of the jester; he included symbols that dramatized songs and lyrics, such as a chameleon on *Script for a Jester's Tear*, a Walkman on *Fugazi*, and a rainbow and magpie on *Misplaced Childhood*. The image of the jester was reprised by Wilkinson much later in Marillion's career on the live archives sets *Curtain Call* (2004) and *Early Stages* (2008), but the iconography was also reinforced in 1980s performances by Fish who sometimes wore a jester's garb on stage, among other costumes, such as a straitjacket for 'He Knows You Know' and an army jacket for 'Forgotten Sons' in 1983.

Jon Collins notes that the title track from Marillion's first album stemmed from an earlier song, 'The Crying Jester', which Fish wrote on the night The Who's drummer Keith Moon died.[13] If Moon was the initial stimulus for the figure of the jester, then 'Script for a Jester's Tear' is neither biographical (of Moon) nor autobiographical (of Fish), although it is shot through with regret and melancholy. The song (8:42) is composed around four contrasting parts, a progressive composition but one that suggests that psychic release cannot occur until the primal roots of neurosis are uncovered. It starts with a bare whisper, 'here I am once more/In the playground of the broken hearts . . ', and a few broken piano chords accompany Fish as he contemplates 'abandoning the relics in my playground of yesterday'. A nursery rhyme setting of swings and roundabouts becomes a cry of excruciating torment as the singer realizes his loss and entrapment in the 'playground of the broken hearts'. The rock sequence that forms the song's second part gives way to a more ambient section of acoustic guitar, keyboard and whispers, in which the jester strikes the pose of a poet who tries to channel his well of emotion through words. But this dream-like reverie does not last, and his attempt to 'examine the shadows on the other side of morning' forces him to confront his loss. In the final section of the song, the jester's tear stands as a double symbol, fusing the loss of his lover with the realization that childhood innocence has gone forever.

The first side of the album is an extended psychomachia in which an isolated male protagonist contemplates drug-related psychosis and an inability to hold down a job and a relationship on 'He Knows You Know'. He vainly tries to break free of an imprisoning past on 'The Web', on which desire is refracted through mythological images of the 'Cyclops in the tenement', 'celluloid leeches' and 'fateful dice', as the protagonist weaves a psychic web of his own entrapment. The second side moves out of this solipsistic world but continues to explore isolation. The first track on side two, 'Garden Party', signals a different musical mood, opening with a sample of birds tweeting and lyrics that satirically mock the pretentious roles that middle-class socialites play at public engagements, before sinking back towards the melancholia of 'Chelsea Monday', in which an ageing female actress is locked within a 'cellophane world' of fading beauty and a failing career, drifting 'through the labyrinth of London' and enacting scenes from her past to an imaginary audience.

The final track, 'Forgotten Sons' (8:23), is the most dramatic and compositionally ambitious song on the album. It is also highly performative, with Fish

Mark Wilkinson's artwork for Marillion, *Script for a Jester's Tear* (1983), www.the-masque.com/shadowplay

enacting the twin roles of perpetrator and victim of the 'Troubles in Northern Ireland', including a sequence where he mimes a rapier and machine gun at the Hammersmith Odeon in 1983, captured on the video release *Recital of the Script*. Like the title track, 'Forgotten Sons' was inspired by a real-world event: Fish's cousin was injured in a riot in Belfast, and Fish was concerned that the 'Irish situation had been lowered in the agenda of the media'.[14] Whereas 'Chelsea Monday' begins with samples of a firing-squad march and the cries of a newspaper boy, the social world of 'Forgotten Sons' is marked in the first few seconds by the tuning of a radio dial. We hear snatches of radio channels mixing news and music, but none long enough to be recognizable except for a fragment of 'Market Square Heroes', before the song returns to the very end of a news broadcast and the words '... to you'. These first 15 seconds of samples identify the media as a central theme and indict a desensitized public that skims over serious news in search of entertainment; they are reprised at 2:38, as the representative middle-class father sits in the 'safety of his living room chair'. The high-tempo keyboard, military drumming and staccato lyrics ('Armalite/Street lights/Night sights/Searching the roofs for a sniper') presage a song that deals with political and military violence at the expense of young 'boys baptized in war'. Rather than the four distinct sections of the 'Script for a Jester's Tear' track, the musical transitions of 'Forgotten Sons' are swifter and more integrated, combining different vocal styles and the dramatic use of echo at two points: the first, a spoken indictment of the mother and father overlaid by a radio newsreader's voice, and, the second, a demonic prayer (4:14) containing vitriol levelled at 'the nameless, faceless watchers that parade the carpeted corridors of Whitehall', where Fish speaks both parts through different audio channels, ending with the quasi-blasphemous 'Amen' (5:21). The persona of Death arrives to surprise the military patrol and shifts the song at 5:46 towards its elegiac conclusion.

This closing section contains some of Fish's most acute lyrics, set against Steve Rothery's soaring guitar and Kelly's ecclesiastical keyboards to project the limited opportunities for young Britons in the early years of the Thatcher government – 'from the dole queue to the regiment a profession in a flash' – with little to protect them from politically sponsored terrorism. The final moments echo the lost childhood of the title track. Fish's declamatory, almost punk-like vocal delivery is softened by the tender intonation of 'forgotten son' at 7:26, and then this moves to the social invective of the chanted 'forgotten sons' before shifting tone again to the mournful line 'Mother Brown has lost her child', often linked to the nursery rhyme 'Ring a Ring of Roses' and a line from 'Rule Britannia' in the extended coda of live performances. The 1983 Hammersmith Odeon rendition of 'Forgotten Sons' ends with Fish's tracing a huge imaginary cross in the sky, before clasping his hands above his head and slowly lowering them to mime a loaded gun in his mouth. He pulls the imaginary trigger as the music ends and the stage goes black.

This layered mode of composition is reflected on the closing title track of Marillion's second album, *Fugazi*. This 8-minute track begins softly with the isolation of a 'bleeding-heart poet in a fragile capsule' who is trying hard to remain conscious and to keep his social faculties sharp. This is another version of the poet who tries to find new language to express what he sees in the world, but who is also the conscience of his generation. 'Fugazi' reveals a dystopian vision of London as the protagonist tries to prevent himself from drowning 'in the liquid seas of the Piccadilly line rat race' only to see robbery, violence, pornography, neo-Nazism and vandalism all around him. Mythical and religious imagery fuse with social and political turbulence, reflecting the generational collapse of 'Forgotten Sons'. Released the same year that the Doomsday Clock was reset at three minutes to midnight, when the Cold War reignited with the escalation of the arms race between the United States and Soviet Union, the album projects an apocalyptic vision ('Pandora's box of holocausts') tinged with Cold War paranoia ('waiting for the season of the button'). After Fish repeats 'Do you realize . . .' three times (each time with more menace), the band concludes that 'this world is totally Fugazi' – a term used by US servicemen during the Vietnam War to mean 'Fucked Up, Got Ambushed, Zipped In'.[15] Whereas *Script for a Jester's Tear* ends with the fusion of invective and mourning on 'Forgotten Sons', *Fugazi* closes with a vision of social insanity and the realization that there are no prophets, poets and visionaries left in the mid-1980s to prevent total destruction. The seemingly joyful piping that closes the song belies a loss of moral centre; this piper is more likely to draw us to our doom than towards a new dawn.

These disturbing visions return to haunt the next two albums, *Misplaced Childhood* and *Clutching at Straws*, which both follow different narrative arcs but circle around themes of lost innocence, isolation and social unease. Released in 1985 to popular acclaim and the UK chart success of the album's first single, 'Kayleigh', *Misplaced Childhood* is one continuous piece of music that narrates the story of a young boy growing up, refracted through the self-analysis of his adult self. Although *Misplaced Childhood* is written in a confessional mode, mixing Fish's life story (his Scottish childhood and his failed relationships) with fictional elements, the protagonist is less engulfed in the cloying emotion experienced by many of the characters on *Script for a Jester's Tear*. The prelude track, 'Pseudo Silk Kimono', takes us into a nocturnal adult world of 'nicotine smears' and 'long, long dried tears', and from there into the unnamed singer's past, as 'the spirit of a misplaced childhood' appears as a ghostly apparition to jolt him from his mournful neurotic state into reverie, signalled by the first line ('Do you remember?') of the second track, 'Kayleigh'. The album follows a psychotherapeutic arc, but this is self-analysis (the singer is both the 'I' and the 'you' of the narrative) that reflects upon broken relationships, rather than interrogating the family romance (there are no fathers or mothers) in an attempt to free the protagonist from the controlling hand of the past; a demo version of 'Kayleigh' (available on the 1998 remastered version of the album) uses echo to suggest that the singer is talking to himself across time and space. The vision of the ghostly child in 'Pseudo Silk Kimono' does not transport us to a world of untrammelled innocence but offers a double vision of adult and child, where the past is paradoxically both entrapping and freeing. 'Kayleigh' is about young love, in which the adult self is the observer and the younger incarnation the participant, while the third track, 'Lavender', begins with a ponderous piano refrain as the singer is jolted into the past by 'children singing' and 'running through the rainbows'. The lyrics shift to a childlike chorus and simplistic sentiments that echo closely the seventeenth-century English folk song 'Lavender Blue', contrasting with the emotional complexity of the present.

The most successful musical elements of *Misplaced Childhood* are the transitions between tracks (the gentle guitar chords of 'Kayleigh' arrive seamlessly after the spoken words 'safe in the sanctuary, safe', as the organ-like ambient keyboard of 'Pseudo Silk Kimono' slowly fades out) and in the song-cycles 'Bitter Suite' (7:56) and 'Blind Curve' (9:29), which make up the middle passages of the two sides, containing three and five distinct musical elements respectively. The continuity of these multiple tracks not only emphasizes the plenum of experience that cannot be subdivided into separate phases but also suggests that the boy's sexual awakening and disappointment push us back towards the adult neuroses of 'Pseudo Silk Kimono', both on 'Bitter Suite' (which ends with the recognition of life's detours in the lines 'On the outskirts of nowhere/On the ring road to somewhere/On the verge of indecision/I'll always take the roundabout way') and in the isolation of singledom, alcohol and sleeping pills on 'Blind Curve'. The slowly building middle section of 'Blind Curve' ('Perimeter Walk') begins at 5:11 with a murmured whisper and builds to a bitter crescendo at 6:24 ('Childhood/The childhood/Misplaced childhood') as the protagonist realizes that the past is in desperate need of reclaiming. This self-realization leads to the visionary sequence of 'Threshold' (the last section of 'Blind Curve'), in which the singer observes a host of social ills, focusing on 'children with vacant stares/Destined for rape in the alley ways' and 'children bleeding with outstretched hands/Drenched in napalm'. The guitar at 8:46 reprises one of the uplifting solos from the earlier track 'Heart of Lothian' and then segues into the final two optimistic songs, 'Childhood's End?' and 'White Feather', on which the rebirth of morning replaces the dystopian night-time vision and optimism follows neurotic gloom. The realization on 'Childhood's End?' is that 'the answers to the questions' are not out there in the world but 'were always in your own eyes', and that the imaginative exuberance of childhood (symbolized by the 'magpie in a rainbow' in the cover art) can be harnessed once the singer finds 'direction' to lead him away from broken relationships. The optimism of *Misplaced Childhood* is in direct contrast to the closing tracks of the previous two albums: the flag-waving of 'White Feather' is not nationalistic – the white feather is a declaration against war – but emphasizes individualistic pride and a communal childhood that might usher in 'the dawn of the sentimental mercenary' otherwise out of reach without the poets, prophets or visionaries in the coda of 'Fugazi'.

The fourth album, *Clutching at Straws*, again explores the relationship between past and present but this time filtered through the character of Torch, who appears in colour on the cover propping up the end of the bar with the jester's costume hanging from his pocket, along with a host of other literary drinkers, drawn in monochrome, who represent shades from the past. In toned-down *Sgt. Pepper* style, the drinking figures include Dylan Thomas, Robbie Burns, Truman Capote and Lenny Bruce on the front cover and, on the reverse, a ghostly Jack Kerouac, James Dean and John Lennon join the band members in a game of bar pool (Kerouac is credited at the beginning of the after-hour drinking song 'Torch Song' for putting Torch 'on the track' in a lyric that follows a faint bell for last orders, drunken laughter and the popping of a champagne cork). Artist Mark Wilkinson described Torch as 'the pivotal figure, a guardian angel at the end of the bar', but Torch lacks the heroic stature that we would associate with legends, and his social acuity is blurred by alcohol.[16] Torch is not even a wounded hero. He is consumed by alcohol and the psychology of drinking as he tries to make sense of his own life and of social intolerance, linked to the epigram from Erasmus on the back cover, which ends with the line 'Thus all things are presented as shadows'.[17] Haze, alcohol and shadows permeate the album and do not make for clear reflection. Song sequences are replaced by shorter tracks (only two tracks are over 6 minutes), mixing drunken musings with the fragmented visions of 'Fugazi' as the singer frets about the loss of national identity and envisages invidious forms of nationalism rising to fill the void.

The album moves in circles to reflect the subject matter: from the 'warm wet circles' of the opening track to the first line of the final song, 'The Last Straw', 'hotel hobbies padding down hollow corridors' (which recalls the first track's title, 'Hotel Hobbies'), and the realization that despite the twin illusions of self-growth and social development things still remain the same.[18] The album's longest track, 'White Russian', begins with the refrain 'Where do we go from here?' and transports us to a nightmarish police state filled with terror and violence ('Uzis on a street corner') and the neo-Nazi fears that featured on the previous two albums. 'White Russian' is punctured by two reflective sections at 2:15 and 3:53, in which the singer recognizes that he has fewer answers than he once had and that his reflex is to try 'to shut it out' through alcohol. However, he also realizes that this dystopian vision cannot be quelled by sedatives. This leads to the elegiac final section, at 4:33, where the singer reaches some sort of self-understanding; although he would rather be 'out of this conspiracy', he sees this bleak social reality 'is going to come back another day'. Similarly, the final track, 'The Last Straw', does not end with the optimism of 'White Feather' but draws the audience into a dark epiphany emphasized by the refrain 'We're clutching at straws/We're still drowning'; the closing sequence pivots around this couplet involving singer Tessa Niles and Fish in a nihilistic call-and-response exchange.

Marillion might be the most interesting of neo-prog bands to emerge from the UK in the 1980s, continuing into the 1990s and 2000s with Steve Hogarth as singer and with a more collaborative (and arguably less poetic) approach to lyrics, while Fish continued his soul-searching on *Vigil in a Wilderness of Mirrors* (1989) and later albums such as *Field of Crows* (2004) and *13th Star* (2007). Three other British bands, Pallas, IQ and Pendragon, helped push progressive rock in new directions. These groups clearly worked from a 1970s sound palette, but they eschewed the sword-and-sorcery dimension of Jethro Tull's *Broadsword and the Beast* and Magnum's *On a Storyteller's Night*, preferring to focus on a mixture of personal and mythological themes, and chose distinctly British (or non-American) vocal styles despite the pressure of the US market.

The Scottish band Pallas's second album, *The Sentinel* (1984), relied heavily on synthesizers, bass and percussion; a quasi-operatic vocal style enhanced by studio techniques of sustain and echo; and artwork by Patrick Woodroffe in the cosmological style of Roger Dean's *Yes* covers. Conceived as a Cold War concept album and initially titled 'Atlantis Suite', in which a new civilization emerges from the clash between East and West, the released album mixes up the intended sequence to juxtapose radio-friendly tracks with longer, more conceptual pieces ('Atlantis Suite' was performed live in the mid-1980s in the originally conceived order).[19] The directly accessible tracks include the opening song, 'Eyes in the Night (Arrive Alive)', and the best of the Atlantis tracks is the 10-minute 'Rise and Fall', originally composed as two shorter pieces written to open and close the first side. This track begins with a slow drum-roll, a siren, and a dramatic staccato section with keyboard, bass and drum, followed by the arrival of the song's main theme (0:55) and Euan Lowson's vocals (1:07). Later in the song, there are spoken passages in which Lowson adopts a bardic role as he oversees the battle from afar; an ecclesiastical section begins at 6:04, promising hope, and a soaring guitar at 9:20 closes the piece. The track tells of the clash in Atlantis between the 'once proud and mighty' civilizations of the East and West that risk destroying a thousand years of peace. There is a chance that the Sentinel (the computerized 'keeper of the peace') can prepare the ground for a future race, but it is too late to save the ancient civilizations as Atlantis 'crumbles upon itself' and sinks into the ocean.

Whereas Pallas is very much part of the mid-1980s (its next album, *The Wedge*, appeared in 1986 with a different vocalist, and then there is a gap of twelve years before their third album), IQ and Pendragon have sustained their output over thirty years.[20] The artwork of IQ's first album, *Tales from the Lush Attic* (1983), displays a montage image of faces and characters in different poses arranged in a monochrome spiral with a blue border, suggesting a type of pastiche – echoed by a similar spiral, this time in colour with a

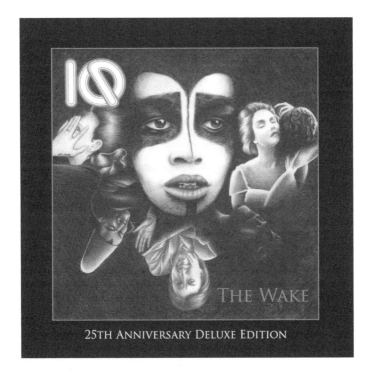

IQ, *The Wake* (25th Anniversary Edition, 2010). Artwork by Peter Nicholls.

grease-paint-masked face as a centrepiece (inspired by primitive face painting in the 1981 film *Quest for Fire* and reflecting Nicholls' own stage persona), on its second release, *The Wake* (1985).[21]

There are parallels between IQ and the 1970s manifestations of Genesis, Pink Floyd and King Crimson on *Tales from the Lush Attic*; the use of 'tales' echoes Yes's *Tales from Topographic Oceans* in exploring ideas and themes from a number of interrelated angles, and the reliance on Martin Orford's bank of synthesizers may suggest a band in thrall of others, not least synth-based new-wave bands such as the Human League. However, the opening, almost 20-minute track 'The Last Human Gateway', on *Tales from the Lush Attic* (as featured in IQ's live set in the early 1980s), reveals a band in search of its own sound as a combination of old and new. The experimental use of synthesizers is a key element, but so too is the restless shifting between styles and moods in a loosely conceptual song about a journey to the 'gateway' of death (death is personified at the bottom left-hand corner of the album cover).

The track begins almost inaudibly with waves lapping on the shore, before a gentle flute melody is introduced at 1:19 and Peter Nicholls' plaintive vocal – which is reminiscent of early 1970s Peter Gabriel – enters at 1:43.[22] The track begins with a dim feeling that nature has been disturbed and that the singer feels isolated from his family and society. A ghostly force then disturbs the relative calm ('Out of shadows something takes my hand/To lead me homeward through a foreign land') to take him to the gateway of death. An intrusive synth riff at 3:21 signals the protagonist's activity on 'the other side', where he encounters a number of visions and feels the urge to 'smack the enemy'. Neither a messianic hero nor a victim in a hellish underworld, the protagonist realizes that his 'bad half' might be dead but that he has the spirit and resilience to stay half alive. The twin assertions of identity in the song – 'I'm still alive' and 'It's only me' – suggest a psychomachia in the vein of *The Lamb Lies Down on Broadway*, internalizing the clash between elements that Pallas externalized on *The Sentinel*. By the end, though, the singer contemplates bleakly that 'the future's all gone' and 'There's none to carry on'. This bleak view is reprised on the last track on the original album, 'The Enemy Smacks' (the fifth track of six on the re-release). In this song, the protagonist is held down by weeds and enclosed in a 'rocking-horse room' from which he cannot escape. Echoing the entrapment and ghostly presences in 'The Last Human Gateway', 'The Enemy Smacks' provides a twist towards the end: the assertion that 'I still got second sight/I still can see at night'. This theme of second sight looks backwards to *Tommy* and *The Lamb Lies Down on Broadway* and forwards to *Snow* (2002) by Spock's Beard, with its 'freak boy' protagonist who has the special power to look beyond appearances.

Pendragon's first album, *The Jewel* (1985), followed its EP *Fly High, Fall Far* (1984) and a number of years touring as a neo-progressive live act, often supporting Marillion. Pendragon's early album covers straddled the cosmologies of Roger Dean and the character-based artwork of Mark Wilkinson, with an angelic figure gesturing towards a burnished sunset on *Fly High, Fall Far* and a disorienting grey grid with fractured lines on *The Jewel*, the latter image also featuring a precious stone and an indistinct figure lying face down but striking a similar pose to the angelic figure on the earlier record.[23] Dominated by lush keyboards, *The Jewel* combines short songs of immediate impact, particularly the opening track, 'Higher Circles', with more conceptually interesting and haunting tracks such as 'Circus' and 'Alaska', but without the grand concept of *The Sentinel* or the sustained narrative of 'The Last Human Gateway'. The second longest track, 'Alaska' (8:39), with its two contrasting parts ('At Home with the Earth' and the instrumental 'Snowfall'), foreshadows more cohesive and sustained experiments with multipart tracks: *Not of This World* (2001) explores the mid-world between everyday reality and mythology, and *Pure* (2008) is structured around the three-part Comatose suite in the middle of the album. Lyrically, 'Alaska' shuttles between high and low, eliding a frozen landscape with a frigid relationship; switches between perspectives (I, you, we); and includes weak punning by vocalist Nick Barrett on 'Alaska' and 'why don't you ask her'. The track builds slowly, with keyboards taking over the vocal role at 4:15, shifting tone and reducing tempo at 5:30, and then regaining speed and taking on jazz inflections at 6:10 to close out the track. Reminiscent of Pink Floyd early in 'Alaska' and Yes later on, the track (and album) holds up as a distinctive melodic contribution to progressive rock, consolidated after Pendragon founded its own label in 1991 and moved to more narrative artwork, such as on the double album *The Masquerade Overture* (1996), with its cast of global, historical and mythological characters.

When considering the work of neo-prog bands that emerged in the 1980s (even if often formed before), we need to note the persistence of progressive rock styles. While Marillion, IQ and Pendragon continued to record and perform despite key band members leaving, there were other second-generation progressive rock bands offering a different type of neo-prog, such as the pop prog of It Bites; Abel Ganz's concept album *The Danger of Strangers* (1988), which focuses on child abduction and endangered innocence in more direct ways than Marillion; or the King Crimson-tinged instrumental music of the American band Djam Karet, as an early form of math rock meeting post-rock. As an attempt to reformulate progressive rock, to recognize the richness of prog instrumentation and composition, and to self-consciously maintain a meaningful musical heritage, neo-prog has a surprisingly long afterlife. Amid this persistence, many 1970s bands reformed or brought out records after a long hiatus, together with the emergence of a plethora of tribute bands based on Genesis, Yes and Pink Floyd in particular (the current touring singer with Yes, Benoît David, was formerly the singer in a Yes tribute band, Close to the Edge).

Neo-prog also needs to be contextualized alongside a third generation of prog, or, more accurately, a second generation of neo-prog, which includes Spock's Beard, The Flower Kings, Magenta, Echolyn, Mostly Autumn, Glass Hammer, The Tangent, Jadis, and Frost', as well as offshoots such as Transatlantic (formed by members of Spock's Beard, Dream Theater, The Flower Kings and Marillion). As this generation became active, IQ was searching for the perfect extended progressive track; perhaps their best long song is 'Harvest of Souls' on *Dark Matter* (2004), which brings together 9/11 and a failing relationship in subtle and unsentimental ways, as the transitions between near-acoustic and epic sections drive together the connections. Other bands, though, such as Marillion and Pallas, moved away from the sound template that defines neo-prog. With new vocalist Steve Hogarth's arrival in 1988, Marillion adopted a more mainstream rock (or pop) identity and wrote shortened songs, but in 1997 they returned to archetypal prog track structures on *This Strange Engine*, while for Pallas this can be similarly dated to their return with *Beat the Drum* (1998).

By the mid-1990s, neo-prog groups had begun to expand on the CD format just as their forebears did with the vinyl album, and releases reached new lengths over the course of a double CD. In 1997, IQ released its dystopian fantasy *Subterranea*, which deals with a mind-control experiment and an individual's attempts to discover what is being done to him; the final, 20-minute track, 'The Narrow Margin', is dwarfed by the whole album. The

Flower Kings released a sequence of double studio albums, with many long tracks, with the longest, 'The Garden of Dreams', on *Flower Power* (1999), clocking in at 59:57 and comprising eighteen sections (see Chapter 13). The first CD is essentially an album conceived as a song, and many of the individual parts have their own choruses and several reprises, forming a fractal model of the album.[24] Spock's Beard took on the challenge of large-scale composition on *Snow*, which relates the path of an albino outsider who helps redeem the lives of the down and out, only to risk falling too far himself on the second part of the double CD. Snow is essentially an updated Christ-figure, as the opening track 'Made Alive' makes clear:

> From a world that's never ending
> From a sky beyond the skies
> A child is born
> And love is made alive

If we were in any doubt about Snow, having watched him fall into human temptation and failure, the finale that precedes 'Made Alive Again' turns to a mounting resolution once we hear 'and God said/"Welcome back my friend"'. The liner notes relate the story of Snow, but it is clear that this album is about reconciliation with the Christian God: He is the 'you' addressed in the outro or finale of each of the two albums. There is some interesting doubling on this double album: each CD has an overture; each ends with the constantly rising 'Wind at my Back', with its repeated choruses (there an extra soaring to Neal Morse's voice on the second CD); and 'Open Wide the Flood Gates' on the first CD is immediately followed by 'Open the Gates Part 2'. Biography is a key driver to the reading of this and of subsequent albums by Morse, particularly because he became a born-again Christian in 2002, leaving Spock's Beard to release a series of long Christian concept albums, such as the double *Testimony* (2003), *One* (2004) and a musing on Martin Luther on *Sola Scriptura* (2007). Morse has stayed largely within a neo-prog mode, but there are many heavier passages, not all of which are restricted to the pitfalls of a non-religious life. The Flower Kings also offer a very Christian vision, notably on *Adam and Eve* (2004), with their retro-hippie vision centred on God.

Transatlantic reflects The Flower Kings' interest in stretching out, echo and reprise on its first two albums, *SMPTe* (2000) and *Bridge Across Forever* (2001), and push it to extravagant lengths on their 2009 release *The Whirlwind*. Comprising a 77-minute, twelve-part single track, the album is based on the concept of the whirlwind and figured through the eschatological narrative elements of destruction, uncertainty, energy, a biblical voice in the tumult, and final redemption. The concept is literally represented on the steampunk-style cover (Transatlantic's trademark emblem is the zeppelin) and links to the topical creationist dismissal of evolution. While one layer of 'The Whirlwind' is the hectic pace of life, it is equally an assertion of God as a creative force. It also connects to what Macan and Martin identify as the church tradition that is a minor strain in 1970s English progressive rock, but comes through more strongly in the Christian tendencies of neo-prog in the promise of redemption for good behaviour and the perfect qualities of melodious musicianship. With hindsight, the transitions and resolutions of mainstream progressive bands such as Yes and Genesis also lend themselves to a recasting of late Protestant traditions in offering the listener redemption through tightly integrated musical form and ensemble performance.

In addition to these two groups of neo-prog bands, there is also a younger group of musicians (a fourth generation of progressive rock), releasing fully fledged concept albums and interested in reviving progressive styles. This group would include, to take two examples, Vienna Circle, whose World War I album *White Clouds* (2008) traces the story of a young British man who moves to Berlin on the eve of war, and Aquaplanage, whose self-named debut album (2008) works as a homage to the early 1970s musical styles of Jethro Tull and Yes (Aquaplanage emerged from another Yes tribute band, Fragile). However, a cycle of generations is perhaps not the most productive way to view the transition of progressive styles. Although prog becomes more diffuse in the 1990s and 2000s, these examples suggest a layering or self-renewal rather than a chronological sequencing. As we discuss in the following chapters, recent developments and fusions of prog styles with other musical sources mean that progressive, neo-progressive and post-progressive cannot be placed within a neat lineage.

Notes

1. Macan, *Endless Enigma*, 447.

2. In 1981, this group of bands was described as follows: 'at best, the music is a sophisticated test of its own limits; at worst, it's musical junk food, overly sweet and utterly non-nutritious' (J. D. Considine in 'AOR Rock', *Musician Player and Listener: The Year in Rock 1981–82*, ed. John Swenson [Farncombe: LSP Books, 1981], 11).

3. For Journey's transition as a band, see John Hotten, 'Escape to Victory', *Classic Rock Presents AOR* (December 2010), 34–43, and the review of their first two albums, 110.

4. Stump, *The Music's All That Matters*, 258.

5. Macan briefly discusses the neo-progressive style in *Rocking The Classics*, 202–6.

6. Neil Peart, *Rush Backstage Club Newsletter*, January 1994.

7. Jon Collins, *Marillion: Separated Out* (London: Helter Skelter, 2003), 18.

8. Peter Gee of Pendragon commented (in an interview with Collins) that in the early years of Marillion 'not many of the press took them seriously. There was this big Gabriel/facepaint/voice rip-off thing levelled at Fish most of the time. Many journalists' attitude was, we buried all that Genesis stuff in the 70s, the last thing we want is for it to come back. There was the anti-long song lobby, and the fact that Marillion were themselves and not trying to be overly commercial' (Collins, *Separated Out*, 41).

9. Marillion quickly established a rapport with a mixed fan base including prog fans, punks and squaddies. The band crossed over into heavy rock (appearing in 1982 on Tommy Vance's Rock Show on BBC Radio and featuring in *Kerrang* that same year) and migrated

from playing at small venues to larger concerts at the Marquee and the Reading Festival even before the release of its debut album.

10. Self-referentiality was central to Marillion's early covers. The bedsit scenario on the cover of *Script for a Jester's Tear* reveals posters for 'Market Square Heroes' and 'He Knows You Know' on the reverse, together with prog records on the floor; copies of *Sounds*, *Kerrang* and the *Daily Mirror* on a grubby bed; and a pillow crumbled into a skull shape, which echoes the skeleton on the inside cover of the gatefold sleeve. The Punch puppet gesturing from the TV set on *Script* comes to life on the 'Punch and Judy' single, while the chameleon that blankly watches the jester on the front cover mutates into the song 'She Chameleon' on *Fugazi*, and is then seen again with its mouth agape imprisoned in a bird cage by a magpie on the reverse cover of *Misplaced Childhood*.

11. Mark Wilkinson, *Shadowplay* (Brusen/Fantasmus-Art, 2009), 24, 29.

12. Ibid., 12.

13. Collins, *Separated Out*, 39.

14. Cited in Collins, *Separated Out*, 40.

15. Ibid., 52.

16. Mark Wilkinson interview (January 1999): www.marillion.com/music/albums/cas. htm.

17. Collins, *Separated Out*, 73.

18. There is another coda to *Clutching at Straws*, 'Happy Ending', but there is no substance to the song, just a faint 'Help' heard in the background, which, perhaps, echoes the more dramatic close-out 'don't give me your problems' from 'He Knows You Know', on *Script for a Jester's Tear*.

19. Short-lived Welsh neo-prog band Multi-Story pursued a similar angle on *East/West* (1985).

20. Pallas released *XXV*, their follow-up to *The Sentinel*, in 2011 after a gap of twenty-seven years.

21. *Tales from the Lush Attic* and *The Wake* were actually IQ's second and third albums, following a cassette-only release, *Seven Stories into Eight*, in 1982. For a discussion of *The Wake* twenty-five years on, see Rich Wilson, 'IQ's *The Wake*', *Classic Rock Presents Prog*, 18 (October 2010), 58–61.

22. Peter Nicholls left the band in 1984 to form his own band, Niadem's Ghost, before returning to IQ in 1990. In the mid-1980s, the replacement singer Paul Menel pushed the band away from long progressive songs towards a broader palette of melodic rock interspersed with neo-prog such as the two long tracks 'Human Nature' and 'Common Ground' on *Nomzamo* (1987).

23. *The Jewel* was remastered in 2005 and re-released on Pendragon's own label, Toff Records, with a new, more immediately arresting cover.

24. Roine Stolt of The Flower Kings had also produced some early examples of neo-prog with his heightened involvement on Kaipa's third album, *Solo* (1978).

Chapter 11

The Female Voice

The late 1960s and early 1970s gave rise to a number of female vocalists in progressive bands: in the US, Grace Slick of Jefferson Airplane; in the UK, Sandy Denny of Fairport Convention, Jacqui McShee of Pentangle, initially Jane Relf and then Annie Haslam of Renaissance, Sonja Kristina Linwood of Curved Air, and Bobbie Watson of Comus; and, in Ireland, Clodagh Simonds and Alison Williams of Mellow Candle. This is not to conflate a range of vocal styles, though. Despite Jefferson Airplane's forays into psychedelia in the late 1960s, Grace Slick was in the mould of a straight rock vocalist, while Denny and McShee brought layered vocals to two bands experimenting with modes of folk fusion (see Chapter 3), and Renaissance and Curved Air used the female voice to balance classical, blues and folk elements.

Female vocalists form a distinct strand of progressive rock, largely one that sees folk mutate into more complex styles, but the fact that Geddy Lee of Rush and Jon Anderson of Yes have alto tenor singing voices (and that Phil Collins sang countertenor in post-1975 Genesis) suggests that progressive bands were drawn to pitches and timbres that could enhance complex instrumentation. It can be argued, as Jennifer Rycenga does, that these vocalists, along with the incorporation of more acoustic elements into prog (as compared to heavy rock), offered an open and encompassing sexuality and an almost queerly gendered position.[1] But this view all but removes the space for female participation. Women appeared in the guise of backing singers in Hatfield and the North and National Health (notably including Barbara Gaskin), and Mike Oldfield regularly used the female voice to complement his pastoral sound-worlds. The voice was largely the only access for women to progress-ive rock, with the even rarer exceptions of female singers who were also musicians: Gilli Smyth, Miquette Giraudy, Mireille Bauer of Gong, or singer Dagmar Krause and multi-instrumentalist Lindsay Cooper of both Henry Cow and Slapp Happy. These rare inclusions sometimes involved virtuosity, but the near absence of women in progressive rock is true for all rock music of the time – and, despite improving in the 1980s and 1990s, this situation is far from transformed today. By way of contrast, women had significant roles as pop singers and, increasingly, as singer-songwriters in the 1970s; the exception, where women formed a larger minority, was in non-rock avant-garde music, where electronic pioneers Pauline Oliveros, Eliane Radigue and Delia Derbyshire have successors in industrial music, noise and avant-rock.

The problem here is not one of progressive rock demanding complexity and abrasiveness, or even that women prefer tunefulness over musical expansion. Nor is it one of innate nature, where men can display inherent tendencies through virtuosity; as we have argued, for all the skill in prog, it tends towards group improvisation and composition. Instead, the issue pivots on gender expectations and the absence of many female role models in the early history of rock. The real problem is that in exploring (and often problematizing) traditionally masculine traits, progressive rock largely excluded or limited the role of women. In order to claim a space within the band – and in rock in general – female singers often displayed their sexuality. Grace Slick and Sonja Kristina projected sexualized images to enhance the theatricality of their contralto voices, but female lead singers more often offered compositional balance rather than driving an explicit gender politics (as in Henry Cow, the punk band Crass and, to some extent, Gong). Even when this chapter arrives at its central focus – the female solo performer as singer, composer, multi-instrumentalist, producer, and user of new media (for example, video in the 1980s) – we do not always encounter a gender politics that feminist critics would necessarily recognize.

Sheila Whiteley is partially right in *Women and Popular Music* (2000) in asserting an ambivalence within the 1960s counterculture towards women: 'both the lifestyle and the musical ethos of the period undermined the role of women, positioning them as either romanticized fantasy figures, subservient earth mothers or easy lays'.[2] However, the range of female vocalists in predominantly male bands in the 1970s means we have to look beyond the 'victimized' tragic figures of Janis Joplin and Cass Elliot, on the one hand, and the 'authentic' folk singers Joan Baez and Joni Mitchell, on the other, to gauge the place of women in progressive rock. This also moves beyond writer and musician Charlotte Greig's claim that prog rock quickly became a 'boys' club' and that Joplin and Slick tried too hard 'to be one of the boys'.[3] As this chapter discusses, it was not until the 1980s and 1990s that women practitioners, often as solo performers rather than as lead singers of otherwise male bands, found ways of bridging the expressive and performative dimensions of their art. This is not to sideline the important role of female vocalists when they did feature in 1970s progressive music, and it is worth looking back at two distinct examples – Renaissance and Curved Air – to assess this contribution.

Renaissance was formed in 1969 by guitarist Keith Relf and drummer Jim McCarty, after the fragmentation of The Yardbirds. The sound was defined by Relf's and McCarty's interest in blues and classical composition, and by the voice of Relf's sister Jane, even though on the band's debut album, *Renaissance*

(1970), she performs a supporting vocal role. This is evident in the sequencing of songs: following the dramatic piano opening of the instrumental 'Kings and Queens' and the bluesy 'Illusion' (sung by Keith Relf), 'Island' (released as a double A-side with 'The Sea') exemplifies the early Renaissance sound as a version of English pastoral. A classical piano provides the opening chords of 'Island' (5:57) before a blues guitar and soft drums come in at 0:16, followed by Jane Relf's mellifluous vocals at 0:37. Her alto voice yearns for a pastoral island where she can be free 'for the rest of my time', almost a prog version of W. B. Yeats' lyric 1888 poem 'The Lake Isle of Innisfree'. Her brother provides backing vocals in the first chorus, before the song moves into a classical section at 3:35; Jane Relf's wordless voice joins again, veering between choral purity and jazz rock, harmonizing around riffs in a manner that Dutch progressive band Focus would develop on 'Hocus Pocus' (1971).

Annie Haslam featured more consistently as the band's lead singer after the departure of Jane and Keith Relf in 1971. Haslam was the focal point of Renaissance from 1972 onwards, but many songs contained increasingly long and seemingly improvised instrumental passages, such as the 9-minute opening track, 'Running Hard' on *Turn of the Cards* (US 1974; UK 1975), where the vocals do not arrive until the third minute. Although Haslam was a soprano, she could sing at a lower pitch than Jane Relf for narrative songs; Haslam had an unusual five-octave range and an operatic reach from her classical training, by which she could inject drama and emotion. This is exemplified on 'Ashes are Burning', the title track of Renaissance's 1973 album, developed to nearly twice its original length at 23 minutes when performed on tour in 1975–6. The 20:13 version of 'Ashes are Burning' played at Nottingham in January 1976 (captured on *British Tour '76*) begins with a classical piano and tympani before Haslam invites the listener to join her to travel 'the days of freedom' and follow the paths that the burning embers create. The musical mode is distinctly folk rock, with harmonized choruses, jazz piano and a touch of melancholy as the singer follows the smouldering path while the 'past is still turning'. The harmonized chorus gives way at 2:31 to Haslam's singing scales as a prelude to an extended instrumental jam of piano, bass and drums (and a keyboard section at 10:09), which eventually diminishes to create an ambient backdrop at 11:55. Haslam's vocals re-enter and build slowly to a screamed crescendo at 13:19. When she reaches the line 'ashes are burning the way', it is not a path into the future we see but a trail of devastation leading back into the past, much as the final crane shot in *Easy Rider* (1969) pulls back to leave the burning devastation on the Louisiana road as a graphic reminder of the carnage of Vietnam. The piano soon returns to weave a sustained melody around the vocal flights for the remaining 7 minutes, before drums round out the song with an ominous military march. Although the evocative lyrics, stretching into both past and future, are an important aspect of the first third of the song, the final third privileges the expansive sonic qualities of the voice as a counterpart to the piano.

Renaissance's primary mode was a fusion of rock and classical music, but the band made extensive use of poetic lyrics (many of them written by Cornish poet Betty Thatcher), Haslam's melodic voice for ballads such as 'I Think of You', and female-associated modes of storytelling and iconography, evident in the five tarot cards held in a woman's hand on the album cover of *Turn of the Cards*, the title of the band's next album, *Scheherazade and Other Stories* (1975), and the cover image of a songstress-storyteller on *Novella* (1977). Reworking themes from Nikolai Rimsky-Korsakov's symphonic suite *Scheherazade* (1888), 'Song of Scheherazade' is the band's most ambitious song-cycle; three vocal tracks celebrating Scheherazade's beauty, cunning and imagination punctuate the nine-song suite comprising the album's second side. Although female motifs are often brought to the fore in lyrics and narrative perspectives (such as on 'Ocean Gypsy'), Renaissance drew on a broad range of storytelling, including 'Mother Russia' (1974), which responded to the deportation and exile of Soviet writer Alexander Solzhenitsyn that same year. The song recounts Solzhenitsyn's hard labour in a Siberian gulag ('Working blindly, building blocks/Number for a name') and beseeches Mother Russia to hear the writer's cry as representative of an oppressed nation.[4]

Storytelling and musical virtuosity combine in Curved Air, which formed in 1970 to practise a similar fusion of rock, folk and classical elements to Renaissance. The band developed as a progressive act over its first three albums, *Air Conditioning* (1970), *Second Album* (1971) and *Phantasmagoria* (1972); via its improvisation and revisiting of classical music (the violin pieces 'Vivaldi' and 'Vivaldi with Cannons', which rework Antonio Vivaldi's *The Four Seasons*); and through Sonja Kristina's powerful vocals on the 1971 singles 'It Happened Today' and 'Back Street Luv'. Sonja Kristina had performed on the London stage in *Hair* and had her own musical act before joining the band, and she brought with her a theatrical style that bordered on the operatic. Although Curved Air was not as adept at storytelling as Renaissance and other 1970s progressive bands, on a track such as 'Marie Antoinette' (1972), Sonja Kristina's delivery evocatively captures the drama of the French Revolution and the storming of the Bastille, as well as the plight of the Queen of France as her 'shadow' falls 'along the land'.[5]

Although these bands are the most prominent to feature female vocalists in the 1970s, other female voices were used, often very creatively, in what was undoubtedly a male-dominated industry. Mike Oldfield was drawn repeatedly to female vocalists to inflect and extend the range of his complex instrumentation. Oldfield had experimented with guttural non-words on *Tubular Bells*; on his next two albums, *Hergest Ridge* and *Ommadawn*, he used high-pitch chants to develop primary musical themes, but the vocals often fly above the music without the symbolic weight of recognizable words. In his autobiography, Oldfield recalls that he asked Clodagh Simonds to write something nonsensical in Gaelic for *Ommadawn*, including the word 'amadán', meaning 'idiot' or 'fool', reflecting the title of the album.[6] The evocation of the idiot in the title pushes the listener to reflect on the pre-linguistic nature of sounds rather than the social signification of words. Reflecting Oldfield's interest in the layering of sounds, Simonds' vocals were recorded several times and mixed down to create a single, multitracked vocal. A haunting background vocal begins the album, blending sustained notes with cadenced choral voices for the first three and a half minutes. The background vocal returns at 11 minutes, and then moves into Simonds' 4-minute open-vowel 'ommadawn' chant, which lurks behind synthesizer and glockenspiel turned high in the mix, before a discordant electric guitar banishes the vocals to the background again. Simonds' voice extends the musical range of *Ommadawn*, works to empty out the album's content (which signifies less than the explicit connection to the Herefordshire topography on *Hergest Ridge*), and offers a pagan spirituality through orality, allowing the music to soar without reverting to the vogue for rock-style lead guitar, as exemplified by Pink Floyd on 'Shine On You Crazy Diamond', which opens and closes *Wish You Were Here* (1975).

Oldfield returned periodically to ambient voices through his career, from his fifth album *Platinum* (1979) to *Music of the Spheres* (2007). But in his pop-orientated music of the 1980s he used a variety of female vocalists: the Scottish singer Maggie Reilly on the singles 'Moonlight Shadow' (1983) and 'To France' (1984); the Welsh vocalist Bonnie Tyler on the rock-pop fusion 'Islands' (1987); and, in 1998, the Irish folk singer Cara Dillon for the pop-orientated vocal of 'Man in the Rain', a track written some years earlier. His consistent choice of vocalists shows that he was drawn to singers with a Celtic timbre and of a certain pitch, as evident in his collaboration with Jon Anderson on 'Shine' (1986) and 'In High Places' (1987).

Oldfield began his career collaborating with his sister Sally Oldfield in The Sallyangies. This collaboration did not last long, but the pair received the endorsement of John Renbourn and recorded one album, *Children in the Sun* (1969), in which Sally Oldfield's ethereal, virtually choral vocals inflect the album's folk and mystical songs. Although she was not a major influence on 1970s music, Sally Oldfield re-emerged as a recording artist in 1978 with *Water Bearer*, the first of a series of solo albums released at a moment when disco and punk seemed to give little space for other types of female singers. *Water Bearer* echoes the classical elements of Renaissance and the folk fusion of Pentangle but adds interesting syncopation, harmonies, mythical and mystical elements. Renaissance turned to a more pop sound with its 1978 single 'Northern Lights', which purposely reined in Haslam's vocals, whereas *Water Bearer* offers complex vocal styles that weave through acoustic guitar, mandolin, marimba, glockenspiel, harp, harpsichord, bongo and electronic instruments (mostly played by the singer). The album contains the minor hit 'Mirrors' and explores Celtic folklore and Tolkien in a closely woven series of tracks, including a song-cycle, 'Songs of the Quendi', which narrates an elven quest, with classical tenor Brian Burrows providing readings from Tolkien's *The Silmarillion*.

The year 1978 also saw Kate Bush emerge as a teenage singer-songwriter-performer, marking an important link to, but also movement beyond, the tenets of progressive rock. A major difference between Bush and other female vocalists in 1970s progressive bands is that she has been her own songwriter throughout her career, pushing beyond the singer-songwriter model of Joni Mitchell through her interest in film, theatre, novels and dance; the ability to flex and improvise her voice to fit words to music; and her feel for the texture of language (as evident from an early age in poems and songs such as 'The Man with the Child in his Eyes', written when she was thirteen). David Gilmour was highly influential at the outset of Bush's career, connecting her to EMI and asking his fledgling band Unicorn to play on her demo tape. Gilmour became a regular collaborator through her career, and by the early 1980s the two were working on a more equal basis: he provided backing vocals on Bush's 'Pull Out the Pin' (1982); Bush sampled helicopter sounds from Pink Floyd's *The Wall* on 'Waking the Witch' (1985); Gilmour played lead guitar in a 1987 performance of 'Running Up That Hill' and on the recording of 'Love and Anger' (1989); and the pair performed a version of Pink Floyd's 'Comfortably Numb' at the Royal Festival Hall in 2002.

Like many progressive rock bands, Bush's influences were eclectic and combined various musical and performance styles: in her early years as a recording artist she cited Elton John as a major influence on her piano playing; she was a fan of Bryan Ferry's and David Bowie's vocal delivery; there are glimmers of Patti Smith and post-punk performers in her stage persona; and she later noted her interest in Frank Zappa and Captain Beefheart. While Marillion and IQ reconfigured progressive styles and themes in a neo-progressive mould, Kate Bush is perhaps more authentically progressive in her approach, especially from 1982 onwards. As well as Gilmour, she worked with Roy Harper and Peter Gabriel in the late 1970s and 1980s: Harper provided the song 'Another Day' (1970), which Bush performed with Peter Gabriel on the BBC1 *Kate Bush Christmas Special* show (1979) as a stony-faced couple on the verge of separation, while an inset film emphasized what they had lost in their relationship; she dueted on 'You' on Harper's *The Unknown Soldier* (1980); and she featured again (with Gilmour) a decade later on the title track of Harper's 1990 album *Once*. The musical relationship with Peter Gabriel was the most visible link to 1970s progressive rock, and to the newly technologized version of prog rock that arrived in the wake of punk. Gabriel featured on keyboards for a solo performance of 'Here Comes the Flood' on the 1979 Christmas show, Bush sang backing vocals in 1980 on Gabriel's 'Games Without Frontiers' and 'No Self Control' (feasibly the occasion of her initial interest in using an electronic sampler), and the two recorded a duet, 'Don't Give Up' (1986).[7] The video of 'Don't Give Up' (played extensively on MTV that year) shows a tenderly embracing couple who revolve as a sun goes through an eclipse; the sun reappears at the end of the video as the camera pulls away to show the couple silhouetted on a rocky hillside. Although 'Don't Give Up' is a ballad about economic hardship and Bush's vocals are more restrained than on many of her own songs, the visual performance linked to other videos she produced in the mid-1980s, which embraced subjects, concepts, visual motifs and sonic textures that displayed a kinship to progressive rock, although never a slavish devotion. Despite these connections to the 'classic phase' of prog rock, Bush's narratives and compositional complexity position her in a broader history of progressive music that does not revolve around any particular paradigm – unless it is her contribution to the pastoral tradition.

Storytelling and narrative are significant for women performers working within the framework of progressive music, enabling them to express and legitimate a creative female perspective. Unlike Joni Mitchell, who uses the personal pronoun 'I' in many of her early 1970s lyrics to emphasize the 'truthfulness of experience', Kate Bush wedded expressive lyrics to her fascination for other characters that linked to her interest in fantasy and drama.[8] As Deborah Withers points out, Bush constantly creates characters in order to drive a broad and heterogeneous subjectivity that flows across genders, times, locations and periods.[9] An unusually wide vocal range allowed her voice to express limited situations, transitions and different characters, and to express her subjectivity as multifaceted and sometimes exceeding control. Nonetheless, EMI released a series of publicity shots to launch Bush as an attractive young woman with an unusual beauty that contrasted much of the music and lyrics on her first album, *The Kick Inside* (1978). As early as her second album, *Lionheart* (1978), Bush took more control of her image; this album is at once English, exotic and otherworldly – drawing out the dramatic characters of her songs, which vary between the sensuous, the melodramatic, the outlandish and the macabre. Sheila Whiteley sees this combination reflected in the 'seemingly unnaturally high register' of Bush's debut single, 'Wuthering Heights' (1978), which 'assumes both childlike qualities in its purity of tone and an underlying eroticism in its sinuous melodic contours and obsessive vocalised femininity'.[10] The multilayered textures of Bush's vocal style attracted as many detractors as admirers in the press in 1978–9. Holly Kruse argues that

> one of the victories won by female singers in the punk era of the mid-seventies was the opportunity to experiment with a wider range of vocal sounds [through] a repertoire of unearthly shrieks and guttural whispers . . . to convey a disturbing breadth of emotion. Yet Bush's music was also a reaction against the one-dimensional angst and unorchestrated discord of punk, using melody and often frail vocals to create a surreal world of affect.[11]

Bush's vocal delivery linked to her late 1970s performances and video realiza-
tions in the 1980s. She contributed centrally to the videos, creating detailed
storyboards for singles such as 'Army Dreamers' (1980) and directing videos
for singles taken from her later albums. 'Wuthering Heights' compressed
Emily Brontë's 1847 gothic novel into a 5-minute dramatic 'songscape' in
which Bush plays Catherine Earnshaw (she is called Cathy in the song,
reflecting Bush's own childhood name as a strange form of postmodern
self-referentiality); Cathy returns from the dead to haunt Heathcliff with
their unrequited love. In her piercing vocals and sweeping arm gestures, Bush
expresses the intensity of the lovers' emotions and dramatizes the 'wild and
windy' Yorkshire moors. Although 'Wuthering Heights' has a pop structure,
the vocals and instrumentation are multilayered, and a slowly fading guitar
solo provides a lengthy coda, which Whiteley reads as progressive in its
'modulation, compression, extension and transposition'.[12]

Bush's interest in choreography began before her first recordings. In the
mid-1970s, she trained as a dancer and with mime experts Adam Durius
and Lindsay Kemp (who had previously worked with David Bowie). Kemp's
melodramatic performative style can be seen in a number of Bush's early
videos, particularly in the chorus of 'Wuthering Heights', on which she mimes
the pressing of the window pane as the ghostly Cathy tries to enter. This
interest in performance provided a means to explore different versions of
sexuality, which Withers argues is coextensive with the 'sonic cross-dressing'
of her voice, which can go low as well as high and can move from a whisper
to a shriek.[13] Within this performative mode, many of Bush's videos use
dance to link lyrics and visual presentation, exemplified by her only live
tour. The tightly choreographed Tour of Life (1979) comprised a series of
two-and-a-half-hour shows across Europe, structured into three acts with
an ever-changing stage set complete with theatrical curtains on either side of
the stage, dramatic lighting, dance and mime, and a series of slides and films
shown through the evening.[14] Bush changed frequently into new costumes
to represent her diverse characters, interacting with stage props, and playing
the piano for pared-down ballads that punctuated more theatrical songs such
as 'Violin', which in its gothic extravagance echoed the punk singers Toyah
Wilcox and Siouxsie Sioux. In the ambitious theatricality of Tour of Life, Bush
echoed the stage sets and costumes of progressive rock bands and the desire
for a 'total experience' that had excited proto-prog musicians in the late 1960s.

Bush's dancing style and combination of childlike and sensual poses
linked to her interest in beginnings and natality. When questioned on a
BBC Nationwide special, Kate Bush on Tour (1980), about what she might do
next after two albums and a successful tour, the twenty-one-year-old Bush
responded, 'I haven't really begun yet. I've begun on one level, but that's
all gone now so you begin again'.[15] This interest in natality is evident on a
conceptual level. At the Hammersmith Odeon concert in May 1979, Bush
performed 'Room for the Life' inside a large padded drum, which rocked,

Kate Bush's Tour of Life, Carré Theatre, Amsterdam (29 April 1979).

womb-like, from side to side in a song that celebrates the double-life of pregnant women with 'room for a life in your womb' – imagery that carries over to the title track on her first album, 'The Kick Inside'. Bush was to return to birth, from the mother's perspective, in 'This Woman's Work' (1989), and foetal development is dramatized in the video for 'Breathing', the first single from her third album, *Never for Ever* (1980).[16] Bush appears in the video in a semi-transparent costume, an umbilical cord connecting her to the amniotic sac that encases her and, initially, rocks reassuringly. Dramatic opening chords give way to a tender song of an embryo breathing inside her mother, but the singer becomes increasingly fraught as the embryo also breathes in the harmful substances of nicotine and plutonium. During the instrumental break, the embryo escapes from the womb in a dramatic birth sequence, only to be confronted by a nuclear landscape emphasized by a slowly intoning voice explaining the spectacle and nature of bomb blasts. Bush now appears in another guise, wearing a nuclear-fallout suit as one of five scientists wading through what appears to be contaminated water. Rather than a celebration of birth and primal purity, the song turns into a quasi-protest song about radiation poisoning, including a reverse mushroom cloud and a strange coda in which Bush sits with her fellow scientists and turns to look straight at the camera, the embryo nowhere to be seen. More often than not, birth and growth are positives, but love, desire and relationships continually loop back to danger, including 'The Man with the Child in his Eyes' (1978), 'The Infant Kiss' (1980) and 'Mother Stands for Comfort' (1985), in which parent-child relationships always prove problematic.

Bush balanced her interest in literary and mythical references, usually English or Irish in origin, with versions of an Anglicized pastoral that connect her to early 1970s folk rock. Literary intertexts appear from 'Wuthering Heights' through the figure of Peter Pan on *Lionheart*; a re-creation of Tennyson's 'The Coming of Arthur' (1869) on *Hounds of Love*; a reworking into song of the final chapter of Joyce's *Ulysses* (1922) on her 1989 album *The Sensual World* (an album that Bush composed as a short-story cycle); and into the realm of film, with a reimagining of director Michael Powell's Hans Christian Andersen ballet fantasy *The Red Shoes* (1948) for her 1993 album of that name.[17] Sometimes the references are more suggestive, such as the implicit evocation of Sylvia Plath's 1963 poetry collection on the double album *Aerial* (2005), combined with the sonic meaning of 'aerial' on the second disc (as discussed later in this chapter) and a painting of a fishing boat with the same name as part of the artwork. Although some of these references are often diluted, refracted or mediated (in a 1978 interview with Michael Aspel, she admitted that 'Wuthering Heights' was influenced by a TV adaptation rather than Brontë's novel), Bush's ability to transform the source texts into innovative musical versions – and a self-directed film version of *The Red Shoes* in the 1994 extended music video *The Line, the Cross & the Curve* – suggests that literary texts provided her with musical touchstones. While not exclusively the domain of progressive rock, such literary and mythical intertexts offer a symbolic layering not dissimilar to those of major mid-1970s groups. This literary sensibility is inflected in Bush's interest in English pastoral, most obvious in the delicate nostalgia of 'Oh England, My Lionheart' (1978) but also on the fantasy song 'Delius: Song of Summer' (1980), written about the English composer Frederick Delius in his later life when he was unable to speak properly (echoing Mike Oldfield's interest in the wordless voice), and in references to Ralph Vaughan Williams and Edward Elgar on *Aerial*. Although Ron Moy over-emphasizes Bush's Englishness (particularly given her interest in Irish and world music), he rightly sees her musical reimaginings as versions of the 'classical song suite or tone poem', which echo progressive rock.[18]

Bush is drawn to imagery and stories emanating from the natural world, and to the connectedness of human emotion, sexuality and life stories to natural cycles. This is reflected in her interest in natality and the elemental nature of *Hounds of Love*, in its exploration of hills, sky, clouds, ice and water. Her previous album, the self-produced *The Dreaming* (1982), was experimental in terms of song structure, vocal accents (working-class London on 'There Goes a Tenner' and Australian English on 'The Dreaming') and use of instruments (tribal drums, didjeridu, uillean pipes and bouzouki). *The Dreaming* was marked by the use of the Fairlight sampler, halfway between synthesizer and studio, which expanded the range of sounds and textures available. This is the moment that Bush fully developed an authentic solo version of progressive rock, because she also took control of production. Earlier in the chapter we noted the difficulty in finding a place for women performers in progressive rock; one answer lies in supplanting the band to become a studio performer or band leader, where the musicians are brought in for their particular sound rather than for their compositional contribution. Bush (and a few female musicians after her) structured her own sound-world entirely and inhabited supposedly masculine technologies in order to present narratives that focus on physicality, sexuality and nature.

In the same year that Donna Haraway published her 'A Cyborg Manifesto' (1985), extolling the virtues of feminist interaction with technology and hybrid existence, Bush released *Hounds of Love*, which, in its stretching of narratives and soundscapes, provides the clearest example of her interest in song-cycles and conceptually based stories.[19] The album falls into two halves: a group of five songs (four were singles) collectively called 'Hounds of Love', and a seven-song cycle 'The Ninth Wave', named after Tennyson's Arthurian poem cycle *Idylls of the King*, which is quoted on the album sleeve. Two of the tracks on the first side – 'Hounds of Love' and 'Cloudbusting' – are high-concept songs: the first begins with a line from Jacques Tourneur's supernatural horror film *Night of the Demon* (1957), and the second takes Peter Reich's *A Book of Dreams* (1973) as its source to elaborate a family psychodrama around a revealing glimpse of his father Wilhelm Reich's experimental and controversial psychology. The two songs also introduce elements – water and sky – that become central motifs on 'The Ninth Wave', as well as blurring temporality through emotional regression (on 'Hounds of Love') and dreams and fantasy (on 'Cloudbusting').[20]

'The Ninth Wave' is the first of the two self-contained song suites, preceding 'A Sky of Honey' on *Aerial* by two decades, but each leaks into the other half of the album: the elemental foreshadowing on the first side of *Hounds of Love* and the counterpart first disc 'A Sea of Honey' on *Aerial*, which is visually reflected by the symmetry of sky and sea in the honey-coloured artwork on the cover. While 'A Sky of Honey' adopts a painterly aesthetic (realized in the appearance of Rolf Harris as the artist's voice on 'An Architect's Dream') and initially approaches nature from a contemplative distance, when experienced close up nature can be threatening and frightening ('The Ninth Wave') as well as enticing and surprising ('The Big Sky'). 'The Ninth Wave' uses the quest narrative from Tennyson's version of the Arthurian myth and a complex layering of temporal moments. Rebirth through water imagery is central to the song, combining with Bush's interest in natality and the elusive search for an authentic self that echoes the narrative of *The Lamb Lies Down on Broadway*. The opening track, 'To Dream of Sleep', moves from the comfort of drifting off to sleep to a threatening icescape ('Under Ice') in which it is difficult to tell whether the subject is trapped beneath the water trying to get out or skating on the ice to elude threats from below. The subject is unanchored in the hallucinatory middle sections of the song-cycle: it is unclear whether she is an observer or the victim in a witchcraft trial on 'Waking the Witch', and when she sings 'I'm not here' on 'Watching You Without Me' her voice sounds disembodied as she drifts between indistinct ontological states. The contrast with the next song, 'Jig of Life', is stark: an Irish jig disrupts the somnambulistic mood of 'Watching You Without Me', and a familiar-looking old lady advises the sleeper that she is at a crossroads – what Holly Kruse describes as 'the place where past, present, and future converge, where she must choose between physical and spiritual existence'.[21] Kruse reads 'The Ninth Wave' in Jungian terms: the singer merges with a collective unconscious to see the earth from afar on 'Hello Earth', before the diminished voice returns with a stronger physical existence in 'The Morning Fog'. At the end of the song-cycle the singer renews family bonds within a domestic awakening that contrasts with Tennyson's messianic 'The Coming of Arthur', which closes with the future king's birth.

The narrative elements of 'The Ninth Wave' are highly developed, but the sampling of radio noises, helicopters, the overlapping of voices and other indistinct sounds (created by the Fairlight), and the inclusion of traditional Irish instruments on 'Jig of Life' and a German choir on 'Hello Earth' (adapted from Werner Herzog's 1979 film *Nosferatu, Phantom der Nacht*) lends the cycle a rich sonic texture that, according to Ron Moy, is 'classically prog in its willing experimentation and eclecticism'.[22] Bush did not try anything as conceptually ambitious as 'The Ninth Wave' on her next two albums, and her sparing use of electric guitar and drums, reserved for tracks such as 'Experiment IV' (1986) and, later, 'How to Be Invisible' (2005), disconnects her from the neo-progressive music of the time and pushes her towards post-progressive styles that prefigure post-rock (see Chapter 12). The central focus on love and passion across her eight albums also distinguishes her from the male-orientated subject matter of many progressive rock songs. In a 1989 VH-1 interview, Bush acknowledged this gender perspective as a major influence behind *The Sensual World*, which focuses on a range of physical and emotional experiences. Her exploration of gender, sexuality and creativity provided an unmistakably female perspective for her songs, reflected in the chaotic swirl of fantastic images that emerge from her dress on the front cover of *Never for Ever*, on which Bush collaborated with artist Nick Price.[23] But this interest did not limit the range or scale of her audience, and she influenced experimental band Coil and a host of post-progressive artists. Her choice of collaborators has been broad, ranging from important figures in progressive rock (Gabriel, Harper, Gilmour) and other 1970s musicians (Eric Clapton, Lol Creme, and Gary Brooker from Procol Harum) to more surprising artists such as Prince, Nigel Kennedy, Michael Nyman, Eberhard Weber, and the Bulgarian female vocal group Trio Bulgarka – an eclecticism that also marked Björk's choice of producers and musical collaborators in the 1990s. Bush's progressive inheritance is diffused across experiments with concepts, sounds and instrumentation, her diverse musical and literary interests, and her attempts to organically integrate dance, performance and film with her music.

In the 1980s and early 1990s, as Sheila Whiteley notes rather sweepingly, Bush was 'one of the few alternatives to girl pop'.[24] Another would be Laurie Anderson, who worked on extending the creative balance between music and performance, evident in the 1977 compilation *New Music for Electronic and Recorded Media*. Anderson turned from an avant-garde performer in the late 1970s (working with John Cage, William Burroughs and Allen Ginsberg) to a recording musician after the success of her 8-minute single 'O Superman' and her album *Big Science* (1982). Anderson worked frequently with violin, percussion and innovative recording techniques using tape loops and vocoders, but she had more in common with the electronic performers Kraftwerk and Brian Eno than any kinship with progressive rock, even though *Big Science* has been grouped with Peter Gabriel's fourth solo album and Bush's *The Dreaming* as the most experimental albums of 1982 (and Anderson recorded with Gabriel a few years later).[25]

Bush opened the way for female performers who would not be constrained by the gender constraints of rock. Punk and no wave also cleared a path into more challenging roles, enabling Lydia Lunch and Diamanda Galas to develop their own avant-garde music in its wake. In goth music, Siouxsie Sioux showed a highly assertive (if not politically feminist) role was possible; others followed, down to the heavily goth-inflected symphonic metal of the 1990s and 2000s. In industrial and avant-garde music, the possibilities marked by Bush are mirrored by Cosey Fanni Tutti in Throbbing Gristle, Danielle Dax, Rose McDowell, and Kim Gordon in Sonic Youth. The involvement of women as instrumentalists and vocalists spread globally across alternative rock, shoegaze, neo-folk, and noise bands.

In the late 1980s, Canadian Jane Siberry made a journey familiar in the history of progressive rock towards increased complexity and the fusion of genres. Like Bush, she also took charge of writing, singing, playing numerous instruments and producing. Her 1987 album *The Walking* offers a series of sustained reflections on emotion and its connectedness to physical experience and nature. The opening 'The White Tent the Raft' is a contemporary pastoral, using synths over its 9:10 to complement the multi-layered and multi-sectional journey across emotional states and changing relationships. 'Lena is a White Table' sets out a surreal domestic space that troubles and interferes with domesticity as a container for femininity. Also in surrealist vein, the closing 10-minute track, 'The Bird in the Gravel', does not tell a story as such but has different vocal and musical styles to represent a range of characters with class-bound attitudes. This compositional complexity reached its height on *Maria* (1995), which is divided into two parts, with the first nine songs a loosely connected song suite about growing love and shared domesticity. The second part is 'Oh My My', which has as many micro-sections in its 20:15 length as a long Henry Cow track but returns repeatedly to overlapping musical refrains, its backing a slowly mounting tonal jazz. The track looks back to birth and forward to bleak despair, a much repeated appeal to the mother (in the 'mama mama' verse-length refrains), reiterations of the fragile beauty and goodness of life (the 'precious candles' refrain), a list of (numbered) observations of decline (1–12) and life-advice suggestions (13–24), nursery-rhyme fragments, and a journey into and out of addiction. The 'Oh My My' refrain expands to end in 'My Mother', as something both withheld and awaiting the end of a cyclical journey of self-realization. As we near the end of the lyrics (at 13:02), Siberry, as the first-person narrator, asks, 'am I healing or dying, I can't tell', and, after a brief moment of self-awareness, she closes on the repetitive 'here I go', indicating freedom but also the difficulty of achieving such a state.

A group of performers in the early 1990s – notably Tori Amos, Björk and P J Harvey – offered a challenge to the commercial imperatives that stimulated female singer-songwriters in the 1980s. Whiteley exaggerates the emphasis on authenticity and truthfulness of this group of singers compared to the 'artifice' of commercially driven acts (particularly given Amos's increasing interest in costume and Björk's esotericism), but this group of female musicians challenged gender stereotypes by exploring sexuality and lyrical perspectives, enabling them to straddle mainstream (or chart) music and avant-garde experimentation.[26]

Tori Amos is often cited as the natural heir to Kate Bush, largely because of their idiosyncrasies, vocal ranges and use of piano but also because of the relative scarcity of such autonomous female performers and the tendency of critics and fans to fix on superficial similarities.[27] They have both been eager to assume control over their careers; Bush did so from her fourth album onwards, whereas Amos had to wait until she left her first label, Atlantic Records, in 2001 and joined Epic before she felt she had control over her output.[28] Both Bush and Amos have grasped the means and mode of production by building their own studios in the country; we would claim that this is the final stage in completing the move into an autonomous realm supposedly the preserve of the male musician.

Amos has been reticent when it comes to her musical relationship with Bush, claiming not to have heard any of her albums before *Hounds of Love*, reminiscent of the similar disavowal made by Marillion about the band's Genesis influence. Amos stated in *Q* magazine in 1998 that she had been wary of copying Bush's style, but she noted that their song structures and arrangements are very different. Although the cover design of Amos's first album, *Little Earthquakes* (1992), is vaguely reminiscent of Bush's *The Kick Inside*, in many ways they are very different performers. Amos has developed an interest in disguise, dramatic personae and concepts that stem from the mix of surreal imagery and confessional lyrics on her early albums, which differ in tone from the songs Bush was writing in 1979–80. Amos has been increasingly self-conscious over her assumed split personality: her authorized biography begins 'there is more than one Tori Amos. The carefree little girl, the Tart, the provocative performer, the poet, the minister's daughter', and it notes that she often refers to one or other aspect of herself as 'she'.[29] This has become part of Amos's marketing strategy, carefully balanced with a musical range that moves between rock and a pared-down ballad format of singer and piano. Her playing style has been described as 'prog rock piano' because of her ability to mix gentleness with a thumping bass sound; in performance she often turns round to half face the audience in a quasi-rock stance as she plays the piano, or straddles a stool to play piano and keyboard at the same time (such as on her 2007 single 'Bouncing off Clouds'). In concert she sometimes wears dramatic clothing – such as the cloak she donned for a 2003 West Palm Beach concert which was reminiscent of Rick Wakeman. This 2003 tour, released as part of *Welcome to Sunny Florida*, saw Amos perform with a full rock band, include experimental interludes, and use an electronic tape loop to introduce a druggy version of her debut single, 'Crucify' (1992).

Much more prolific than Bush in terms of her creative output, Amos is both consistent in the texture of her voice and willing to use guitars, bass and drums, but at times she also pares back her instruments to only piano and percussion. The artwork on her albums has usually focused on her body, such as her provocative poses on the cover of *Boys for Pele* (1996): on the front, she sits on a Southern rocking chair with a shotgun; on the reverse, she hugs a piglet to her breast, her right hand between her legs barely hidden by a blanket. The gender-bending performance that Deborah Withers sees in Bush's *Lionheart* could equally apply to Amos, although despite her shape-shifting it is hard to recuperate her as a queer performer because her narratives tend to pivot around heterosexual desire. Both artists are interested in internal and external spaces. The artwork for *From the Choirgirl Hotel* (1998), for example, features images of Amos in various intimate and theatrical poses juxtaposed with a crudely drawn map including a standing stone, orchard, troll bridge and 'Mr Grumpy's Maze'. At times esoteric and bizarre, Amos has conjured up the spirits of her Native American ancestry, and on *Boys for Pele* she evokes the goddess Inanna from Sumerian mythology. Her interest in costume and alter egos is evident on the extensive artwork of the covers album *Strange Little Girls* (2001) and of *American Doll Posse* (2007), but her most fully realized concept album is *Scarlet's Walk* (2002), which Amos described on a number of occasions as a 'sonic novel'.

Written in the wake of 9/11, *Scarlet's Walk* charts a circuitous journey across the US, where differently coloured lines on a national map in the CD artwork link directly to the songs: from the Californian road trip of 'A Sorta Fairytale' to 'I Can't See New York', which responds obliquely to the bombing of the World Trade Center, and onwards to the Southern journey on the album's title track – echoing a more famous Scarlett from *Gone with the Wind*. Reflecting Amos's road trip through all fifty states in 2001, the album is at once personal, as Amos tries to recover her Cherokee roots, and archetypal, as her persona Scarlet travels through urban and rural areas and meets a diverse cast of characters. Rather than the classic East–West US road trip or the international leisure travel of Frank Sinatra's *Come Fly with Me* (see Chapter 4), this is a darker travel narrative full of discovery, anguish, estrangement and passing moments of ecstasy. The music is dominated by piano played at mid-tempo, and many of the tracks have identifiable verse-chorus structures, occasionally broken with slower tracks, such as the spare 'I Can't See New York', 'Scarlet's Walk' (which recounts the forced relocation of Native Americans after the Indian Removal Act of 1830), and the orchestral 'Gold Dust', which provides a self-reflective coda. Amos's stream-of-consciousness lyrics are more restrained than on her previous albums, but the density of the sleeve notes (the lyrics are printed in lower-case and songs flow into each other) and her consistently lengthy albums suggest that the control Amos has latterly exerted over her output, artwork, merchandising and web presence undermines Sheila Whiteley's distinction between authenticity and commerce.[30]

Whiteley's argument is increasingly tenuous given the access to digital technology for the composition, mixing and production of albums. Amos and Bush use technology not only to create complex recorded works but also to develop images for their narratives and for their narrating and performing personae. Peter Gabriel has followed a similar path, as have many musicians discussed in the following chapters of this book, but here the most relevant case might be that of the Icelandic musician and singer Björk. She has developed an increasingly dense and digitized sound-world with carefully selected co-producers and collaborators, and this has also played out at a visual level. With her 1997 album *Homogenic* Björk began a fusion of digitally driven music that over subsequent albums stretched across many techno and dance styles yet never lost the dramatic arc of song form. On *Homogenic* a continually shifting set of sampled sounds hover over complex beats. Amid this floats the Icelandic String Octet, which is supposed to anchor the album in a polar sensibility; the pulsing, cracking and shifting digital sounds are the dramatic conditions that alternate with the calm of the octet's ice.[31] Perhaps Björk's most conceptually organic album is the 2004 release *Medúlla*, consisting mostly of voices and of samples, beats and sounds from vocals. On this album the voice as a potential cyborg is brought to the fore (visually, Björk has been having cyborg dreams since her 1997 collaboration with Chris Cunningham for the video of 'All Is Full of Love'), but *Medúlla* does not have an unfolding narrative or much connection to other progressive elements. Nonetheless, Björk directly bears on Radiohead and post-progressive music in her combination of styles, technologies and voices, and can be heard in dance-prog hybrids such as Pendulum. Björk's music is an important source for progressive rock of the last decade or so, occupying a similar position to the 1960s examples of proto-progressive rock found in psychedelic rock, blues rock and jazz. As discussed in Chapter 13, Californian singer-harpist-pianist Joanna Newsom is a contemporary performer who continues the female lineage outlined in this chapter, and we could add Natasha Khan's Bat for Lashes and the pomp pop of Florence and the Machine.

At the same time, a new wave of neo-prog centred around a female voice can be found in bands such as Karnataka, Mostly Autumn and Odin Dragonfly, whose lead singer Heather Findlay (in both of the latter two bands) works with both electronic and traditional acoustic instrumentation. Other bands across the prog spectrum have emerged recently, such as Touchstone, Panic Room, the doom-metal outfit Blood Ceremony, the Dutch goth-rock band Epica, and the Finnish power-metal group Nightwish. We should also take note of the distinctive sound of the Shanghai group Cold Fairyland, which combines musical virtuosity with an interest in mythic storytelling and the clarity of lead singer Lin Di's voice (also in Chapter 13). Although an Anglo–Celtic–American axis marks the major contribution of women to progressive rock, examples from Holland, Finland and China suggest that, like modes of neo-prog discussed in the previous chapter, the form has grown laterally more than linearly.

The danger of positioning the autonomous female performer into an expanded history of progressive rock could be, paradoxically, to reduce the contribution of Bush, Siberry, Amos and Björk to a distinctive set of practices that construct complex works and lengthy narratives. Conversely, the return of the female voice (in folk, neo-prog, symphonic metal and goth rock) normalizes the female rock performer by privileging the expressive voice over other forms of musicality. Our discussion of autonomous performers in this chapter affirms yet also challenges and extends these points: the performers discussed here introduce a critical female voice into prog, heighten explicitly emotional content, explore socially constructed roles, and re-emphasize the need to constantly renew the pastoral as a central component in the history of progressive rock.

It is in the return of Kate Bush on *Aerial* after a hiatus of twelve years that we can hear the domestic connection to nature (such as bird calls) as well as nature on a much wider ecological scale (as heard on Yes albums between 1970 and 1977). *Aerial* brings together Bush's earlier moves by following characters such as the figure in 'π' (who thinks in complex numbers) and 'Joanni' (about Joan of Arc) and by rethinking domestic spaces in 'Mrs. Bartolozzi' (with its 'washing machine' refrain) and 'Bertie' (about her son). As noted above, the album splits into two: the songs of the first CD form 'A Sea of Honey', and the second CD comprises the multipart, 42-minute track 'A Sky of Honey', which follows the sounds and impressions of a day, from one morning to the next. This mirrors the structure of The Moody Blues' *Days of Future Passed*, separating natural time from the clock-time of work and presenting a natural cycle that includes humans in its ambit.

The song suite begins and ends with birdsong (including a blackbird and a woodpigeon), which merges with Bush's voice, suggesting a connectedness to nature that builds over the following sections. Light is a recurring motif (temporal transitions are identified by the relation to light throughout) that requires perceiving beings to imagine the passage of a day in terms of light and dark; the first few sections of the track focus on looking as the day progresses. The painter attempts to achieve this in 'An Architect's Dream', but the 'colours run' on 'The Painter's Link' to match the effects of the arriving sunset. The first of these two tracks introduces the refrain 'all the time, the light is changing', which recurs in part eight, 'Nocturn', while part five, 'Sunset', introduces the 'sea of honey, sky of honey' couplet, which also recurs in 'Nocturn'. Most of the sections end in a chorus, although this is not always a chorus in the sense of a refrain – the momentum builds to the end of a section, mirroring the growth of the song-cycle as more instruments join in; the drums become more powerful; and Bush's vocals are more frequently part of a chorus.[32] As we cross over to sunset (the time of 'somewhere in between'), we lose track of time and begin to lose our observational distance of the opening five sections. The night announces freedom as 'we tire of the city'; this is an immersive freedom – 'we become panoramic' (the 'we' and 'our' of the song connect singer and listener) – and gives way to the depths of the night sky and to excitement as dawn begins to show. When 'the sky's above our heads/ The sea's around our legs', we have become conductors between these spheres: an ecstatic and joyful connection that marks the closing section 'Aerial'. On the one hand, we surrender the rational skill of observation to experience being part of nature in a way that is both embodied and ecstatic; on the other hand, the nature we experience seems to require the presence of an observer ('the aerial') for it to exist. The closing two parts are by far the longest (8:34 and 7:52 respectively) and form a double finale that builds slowly through 'Nocturn' into the fully climactic 'Aerial', broken only briefly by Bush's chuckle and the return of the blackbird. As on *Days of Future Passed*, the night and its transition to dawn are the most revealing phases of time; we are far from the world of work, clock-time and the city, and we are restored to an awareness of the surrounding wider reality. But the track is not empty of urban and industrial imagery: 'we go driving' into the night on 'Nocturn', and the album is named after a machine built to receive radio waves. Whereas the waves we normally receive are transmitted, the radio waves of the song-cycle are the universal conditions that provide the ground for our smaller-scale waves.

Ultimately, this song-cycle demonstrates the viability of a progressive worldview, mediated by familial concerns and the small details of nature, as well as the larger natural setting that is formally mirrored in the narrative of 'A Sky of Honey'. Through these means, Kate Bush challenges the idea of the large-scale rock composition as the exclusive province of male musicians. As such, *Aerial* provides the most obviously progressive musical meditation on nature since *Days of Future Passed* in 1967 and Yes's *Close to the Edge* in 1972.

Notes

1. Jennifer Rycenga, 'Tales of Change Within the Sound: Form, Lyrics and Philosophy in the Music of Yes', in *Progressive Rock Reconsidered*, ed. Holm-Hudson, 143–66 (159).

2. Sheila Whiteley, *Women and Popular Music: Sexuality, Identity and Subjectivity* (London: Routledge, 2000), 23.

3. Charlotte Greig, 'As Good as Their Words', the *Guardian* (19 April 1993), 30–1.

4. For interviews with Annie Haslam and keyboardist John Tout and multiple reviews of Renaissance albums, see www.nlightsweb.com/lib/reviews.htm.

5. Jeanette Leech discusses Sonja Kristina's later re-engagement with psychedelia (which she first experienced when working at the Troubadour, in Earl's Court, London, as a teenager) on *Songs from the Acid Folk* (1991) and the 'folktronica' album *Harmonics of Love* (1994): Leech, *Seasons They Change*, 207–9.

6. Mike Oldfield, *Changeling*, 177.

7. Rob Jovanovic makes this claim in *Kate Bush: The Biography* (London: Portrait, 2005), 109.

8. Whiteley, *Women and Popular Music*, 82.

9. See Deborah M. Withers, *Adventures in Kate Bush and Theory* (Bristol: HammerOn Press, 2010). Withers calls this the 'Bushian Feminine Subject'; she notes that it develops through 'the invention of characters and identities which often push the boundaries of gendered and sexual correctness' (5). A queer Kate Bush, emerging from performances and albums, rather than biography, is a well-developed idea in Withers' book, but she seems disappointed that Bush sometimes adopts personae that are problematic from a leftist-feminist perspective.

10. Whiteley, *Too Much Too Young: Popular Music, Age and Gender* (London: Routledge, 2003), 9.

11. Holly Kruse, 'In Praise of Kate Bush', in *On Record: Rock, Pop, and the Written Word*, eds Simon Frith and Andrew Goodwin (London: Routledge, 1990), 455.

12. Whiteley, *Too Much Too Young*, 67.

13. Deborah Withers, 'Kate Bush: Performing and Creating Queer Subjectivities on *Lionheart*', *Nebula*, 3 (2–3) (September 2006), 127. Accessible at www.nobleworld.biz/images/Withers.pdf.

14. Jovanovic, *Kate Bush: The Biography*, 99. See also Graeme Thomson, *Under the Ivy: The Life and Music of Kate Bush* (London: Omnibus, 2010).

15. *Kate Bush on Tour*, *Nationwide* special (Laurie Choal, BBC, 1980).

16. Whiteley describes 'Breathing' as having a 'Floyd-like outro': Whiteley, *Too Much Too Young*, 9, 70.

17. Kate Bush interview: *The Sensual World of Kate Bush* (VH1, 1994).

18. Ron Moy lists 'an English sense of the pastoral', 'weighty lyrical concerns with metaphysics, fantasy narratives or histories and mythologies', the careful 'sequencing of tracks', and use of experimental studio techniques: Ron Moy, *Kate Bush and* Hounds of Love (Aldershot: Ashgate, 2007), 70–1. Moy discusses classical influences on Bush, including Delius, Vaughan Williams and Elgar (61).

19. Donna Haraway, 'A Cyborg Manifesto: Science, Technology and Socialist Feminism in the Late Twentieth Century', in *Simians, Cyborgs and Women: The Reinvention of Nature* (New York; Routledge, 1991), 149–81. On the latter point, see Ann Powers' forthcoming book *Kate Bush's* The Dreaming (New York: Continuum, 2012).

20. Kruse, 'In Praise of Kate Bush', 459–60.

21. Ibid., 462.

22. Moy, *Kate Bush and* Hounds of Love, 71.

23. Jovanovic, *Kate Bush: The Biography*, 121.

24. Whiteley, *Too Much Too Young*, 78.

25. See New Gibraltar Encyclopedia of Progressive Rock: http://www.gepr.net/am.html.

26. Whiteley, *Women and Popular Music*, 196.

27. For a comparison of Amos and Bush, see www.hereinmyhead.com/musicians/bush.html.

28. See, for example, a BBC *HARDtalk* interview with Tori Amos (2 June 2009).

29. Kalen Rogers, *Tori Amos – All These Years: The Authorized Illustrated Biography* (London: Omnibus, 1994), 1.

30. A limited-edition CD of *Scarlet's Walk* provides a hyperlink to an exclusive website, 'Scarlet's Web', which helps to elucidate the various legs of the journey and also offers Tori Amos merchandise.

31. See Mark Pyklit, *Björk: Wow and Flutter* (Toronto: ECW Press, 2003).

32. Only 'Somewhere in Between' (part seven of 'A Sky of Honey') has a recognizable verse-chorus structure.

Chapter 12

Post-Progressive

As Robert Fripp was all too aware, we cannot keep referring back to 1974, either negatively or positively, in order to find out what progressive rock later became. If we do refer back, then we should not use the classic phase of progressive rock as a fixed point to determine what was to follow. King Crimson, Peter Gabriel and Peter Hammill all heeded this lesson in their own music as they developed what they considered to be a departure from progressive rock. In the meantime, experimental bands ranging from This Heat through Throbbing Gristle to Nurse With Wound recovered obscure progressive groups, many from continental Europe, in the late 1970s and early 1980s. As we have discussed in previous chapters, Rush, Yes, Genesis and Renaissance reinvented themselves as pop versions of progressive rock, in different ways and for different lengths of time, taking the rich layering of progressive rock and epic development and condensing them into shorter rock or pop songs. By the mid-1980s, Genesis had become the most commercially successful of these bands and had had a string of US number one singles. At the same time, neo-prog shifted from being a radical anti-fashion recuperation of prog (just as the music industry was championing the authenticity of punk) to become a clearly definable style.

These, then, are variants of progressive rock with clear connections to the late 1960s and early 1970s. We have already seen how a less literal reworking of prog occurred in the music of Kate Bush in the 1980s and early 1990s, and in that of later female artists; other rock bands moved in relative unison away from rock, making direct use of the studio and computer technology and incorporating non-rock elements. This particular progression led to what Simon Reynolds defined in 1994 as 'post-rock'.[1] For Reynolds, the late 1980s saw a type of music (with its roots in the earlier part of the decade) that filled the place of rock and refined and exaggerated its ecstatic drive, often to the exclusion of grounding elements such as a steady beat, verses, choruses and clear distinctions between instruments.

Not all post-rock is progressive rock, or even post-progressive, but in early moments of 'post-rock' – in the shape of David Sylvian, Kate Bush and Talk Talk – we can see that a version of post-rock is entirely consonant with the idea of progressive rock. It may seem to have little reference to 1970s music, but this is the point: to reinvent progressive rock in 1983 or 1990 meant starting from somewhere else and seeking a new mode of fusion. Even 1980s neo-prog began as a reaction to progressive rock (both as a movement beyond and a form of recuperation of prog in the face of punk, rather than a weakly derivative copy) and did not derive directly from the psychedelia, folk and jazz of the late 1960s, discussed in the early chapters of this book. The explicit reference points of post-progressive music are ambient music, folk rock, forms of jazz, *kosmische* or Krautrock, the minimalism of New York art rock, and electronic music.[2] This is the set of formative elements that represented a secret new approach to progressive music that refused the stylistic conventions of the 1970s. However, we would argue that refusal belies the actual connections to progressive rock.

The term 'post-progressive' is designed to distinguish a type of rock music from the persistence of a progressive rock style that directly refers to 1970s prog. The 'post' also refers to that which has come after other forms of avant-garde and popular music since the mid-1970s. It is not a synonym for 'postmodern', which arguably could be applied to neo-prog in light of its citation and pastiche of 1970s gestures, or, equally, could be applied to more recent bands such as The Mars Volta that blend prog with other styles. Rather, post-progressive identifies progressive rock that stems from sources other than progressive rock. This does not spread the net to include all avant-rock from the 1980s and 1990s. Instead, as we discuss in this chapter, there are direct affiliations between post-progressive and early progressive forms: the presence of musicians involved in 1970s prog, lengthy tracks, overarching narrative aims, complexity, section changes, communitarian group structures of playing, and more implicit reiterations of how progressive rock relates to other music. These are key identifiers of a musical mode that shares with progressive rock an awareness of temporal relatedness to other music and to its own temporal development.

It is tempting to stretch the net as far as Julian Cope, or to all the shoegaze bands of the late 1980s and early 1990s. We could envisage an argument where Cope's use of 1960s garage, 1970s *kosmische*, 1980s keyboard technology and grand narratives based on pagan reimagining represent a version of progressive rock. But there is a repetitive lumpiness at the heart of some of Cope's best albums that puts him more in line with the anti-prog of Public Image Limited's first two albums (see Chapter 9). The Cocteau Twins could also be construed as progressive: the band's oceanic songs almost always include a dramatic prog-style key-change oddly akin to its regular use in neo-prog; the imagining of a whole world incorporating artwork recalls the importance of art for 1970s bands; and the vocal language known only to vocalist Elizabeth Fraser is a move away from rock into experimentation.

However, this is actually more the case of pop adrift in the avant-garde soundscape. This is also the case for Ride and My Bloody Valentine. The latter's *Loveless* (1991) might be so progressive that nothing else will ever match it, but too many components of prog are absent – its stretching out is purely musical, taking us back to free jazz, not to the impulse that drove changes in late 1960s rock. Many critics of prog would no doubt be happy at the idea of progressive music being embodied in My Bloody Valentine, or in other avant-rock bands at different moments. But it is not simply about being avant-garde, and to be in any way meaningfully progressive there must be a route – albeit increasingly indirect – to several of the characteristics of the main phase of progressive rock. Another way of looking at this is to remind ourselves that the last label anyone credible in critical or commercial terms would adopt in the 1980s was that of progressive rock.[3] Few groups would imagine themselves in this way, even those that were straining to push back the boundaries of genre and form. Only in the mid- to late 1990s did this change at a discernible level of sales through The Smashing Pumpkins, Super Furry Animals, Sigur Rós and, most significantly, Radiohead. We contend, though, that progressive rock is far from hidden (as the previous three chapters illustrate), and that post-progressive rock feeds a more explicit return to prog: in other words, a return that is not one. This trend is best exemplified by two British avant-rock acts of the 1980s and early 1990s: David Sylvian and Talk Talk.

David Sylvian's original group, Japan, gradually overcame its over-reliance on references to Roxy Music and David Bowie to release the exotic minimalism of *Tin Drum* (1981). Peppered with visual, lyrical and musical nods to China, it presented a repetitive, almost machinic equivalent to the rhythms of both King Crimson and Peter Gabriel. Like King Crimson, there is an amorphous Western take on Eastern thought, expanded on Japan's live album *Oil on Canvas* (1983), which signals the ambient element Sylvian went on to develop on several of his albums. Rob Young notes that Sylvian interwove various strands of jazz and brought in musicians to develop his sound far beyond pop and more or less outside of rock. This fusion recalls the early moments not only of prog but also of jazz fusion itself: 'in a similar fashion to the way jazz elements lubricated folk and rock in the late 1960s, Sylvian's solo albums were aerated by additives from beyond the pop sphere.'[4] Young underestimates Sylvian's construction of post-progressive music because the fusion Sylvian sought combined the jazz of Miles Davis and the ECM label, the ambient music of Brian Eno, the guitarscapes of Robert Fripp (with whom Sylvian worked extensively into the 1990s), and a nascent rock appropriation of non-Western (notably East Asian) music. His albums have a mission, a questing for spiritual fulfilment, and a knowingly philosophical take on sometimes mundane subject matter. Sylvian's website says of his second album, *Gone to Earth* (1986), that it 'intermingles the personal with the themes of gnosticism and alchemy'.[5]

His first album, *Brilliant Trees* (1983), established a marker for post-progressive and, to some extent, post-rock, trading in rock instrumentation for a wide range of acoustic instruments – combined with electronic fragments, drones and soundscapes – and using drumming that introduces 'oriental' patterns to the repetitive circling of *kosmische*.[6] *Brilliant Trees* is laden with references to literature, philosophy and art of the twentieth century, as well as with imagery that continually returns to the soil. The album's twin approach to profundity reveals high and low elements working across each other. Furthermore, the entirely European (mostly French) selection of references is not just a summoning of a repertoire of existential truth through gloom and art, but also the first indication that this album is about place. This is a wider sense of locatedness than that of Eno's *On Land* (1982) or Virginia Astley's *From Gardens Where We Feel Secure* (1983), but it owes its philosophy to the presentation of sound and place on those recordings. Astley's album is even more resolutely localized than Eno's early 1980s albums; its soundscapes of piano and sampled natural sounds create a pastoral that is both experimental and harmonious, albeit occasionally disturbed through treatments of samples. Each track has its source locations provided, and the title and marshalling of sounds convey security through awareness of place. Sylvian attempted a similar move, but to a generalized place or location. As such, *Brilliant Trees* is a meditation on locatedness: behind the veneer of limp Sartre and Cocteau references, the album is actually more in tune with the thought of Martin Heidegger. The key to Heideggerian thought is Sylvian's references to the soil and the album's acoustic instrumentation, especially the breathy phrasing of Jon Hassell's trumpet. This search for lost authenticity is clearest in the title track, where 'every step I take leads me so far away', a distance that is overcome with the realization of the chorus: 'My whole life/ Stretches in front of me/Reaching up like a flower/Leading my life back to the soil'. The soil here is a threefold Heideggerian earth or ground. First, it is the authentic connection to the land (the peasant shoes in Heidegger's mid-1930s essay 'The Origin of the Work of Art'); second, it is the awareness of death that structures an authentic existence (as developed in Heidegger's *Being and Time*); and, third, it is the sense that only in the bringing of awareness back into contact with the world does the world come to be (an understanding developed in 'The Origin of the Work of Art').[7]

Gone to Earth covers much the same ground, but the place of spiritual guidance grows over the album, as it did increasingly over Sylvian's career. Musically, though, *Gone to Earth* takes the same ideas as *Brilliant Trees* and separates them out, with the first part of the double album being more recognizably in a rock idiom, even if it is experimental in a stately way (except the title track, dominated by Fripp's harsh guitar playing, which deviates from the search for self to a consideration of the self as something lost). The second record is entirely instrumental, consisting of drones, repetitive guitar playing and electronic sounds. Again, the exception is Fripp's playing at the close of

'Upon This Earth', where a long, transcendent and yet muted solo (recalling jazz guitarist Pat Metheny's more expansive excursions on the ECM label) counters 'Gone to Earth' by offering a form of musical redemption (this mirroring is somewhat lost on CD format). The second album acts as the ground for the breath of spirit on the first album, so the whole operates as much more than a division of stylistic approaches.

Sylvian was not averse to such separation; between these two albums, he had brought out a fully instrumental set on the cassette-only *Alchemy: An Index of Possibilities* (1985), and he would release two more in the same vein with Can's Holger Czukay (who had already been involved on *Brilliant Trees*), *Plight and Premonition* (1988) and *Flux and Mutability* (1989). On these albums, improvisation and composition come together as the acoustic meets the electronic, with a rock sound squeezed into an inconsequential middle. *Alchemy* also marks the beginning of Sylvian's engagement with sound art, particularly on side two, 'Steel Cathedrals', which was made as part of a film to be shown in galleries. Although these works had been made possible by the idea of Eno's ambient music, they are closer to the slowly building improvisations of AMM and therefore retain the fusion of progressive rock, now bringing together free improvisation, ambient music, modal jazz, sampling, and moving on from the early 1980s use of synths in rock and pop.

This last move characterizes the trajectory of Talk Talk from synth-pop to pioneering post-rock artists. The album *The Colour of Spring* (1986) marks Talk Talk's break into a complex, multi-instrumental type of rock, disguised by moments that seem to be simply pop music, such as 'Life's What You Make It' (which sold well as a single in the UK). This is a lush album with acoustic non-rock sounds adding to the rock dynamic. However, the lyrics display a nagging discontent and anomie on 'Happiness Is Easy', and the prospects in 'Life's What You Make It' seem limited during a period of rampant individualism in Britain and the US during the Thatcher and Reagan governments. Mark Hollis's snarled vocals slowly bury themselves in the mix, taking us away from the solidities of the rock and pop song. In 1988, Talk Talk released *Spirit of Eden*, on which the vocals literally become absent, sparse and hard to make out, and the lyrics often highly abstract. Side one is a single track in three parts ('The Rainbow') and development is slow throughout, which gives the blasts of guitar and group noise a powerful punctuating effect. For all of the stasis of *Spirit of Eden* and the following album, *Laughing Stock* (1991), the music signals contrast rather than settlement. Instead of deploying the studio as instrument, *Spirit of Eden* uses the recording itself: the array of musicians, including a choir and orchestral instruments, were recorded together through the air – in contrast to separate studio booths, where the unity is created via the mixing desk. Young argues that 'Hollis equated the artificiality of modern studio techniques with the pervasive dishonesty of his times'.[8] Talk Talk worked from numerous jazz styles, ambient music and the darker side of early 1980s music. As in Sylvian's music, we can see a move to a more authentic practice of something like rock and nostalgia for a lost world that has been brought into being as lost. The stretching out of the rock form is more extreme than on *Brilliant Trees* and is recognizably an heir to the stretching out of the late 1960s and early 1970s. That this sounds almost nothing like most prog rock (except perhaps for King Crimson's *Islands*) should not distract us from realizing that for Talk Talk's music to be progressive it needs to move away from a recognizable prog sound and to emerge from musical currents of the mid-1980s.

Spirit of Eden maps out the lostness of the contemporary individual, with themes of injustice, alienation and the thirst for a promised or glimpsed spiritual core needed to re-establish the integrity of the subject. But the songs themselves are only parts of more substantial reveries, variously adrift in music, anchoring it, or emerging like atolls above the waves. The 'Eden' of track two is not much of a paradise: 'summer bled of Eden' is the opening line, and it closes on the refrain of 'everybody needs someone to live by/Rage on omnipotent'. The Christian tinge to *Spirit of Eden* and *Laughing Stock* is heretical, or at least circles around a faith full of doubt shot through with passing cynicism towards the Christian God. The lines quoted above suggest a need for faith, rather than a discovered truth. The despairing repetition of 'Everybody needs someone' is a sign of the possible weakness of having faith, but the final line of 'Eden' twists 'impotent' into a reflection of a God still impotent even with total power. This turning in and out of Christian belief also informs the closing track, 'Wealth', which centres on a reversal of 'the love of wealth' into this song's 'wealth of love'. The lyrics suggest that the alienation of capitalism turns in on itself and does not totally debar some sort of redemption. At the same time, the song gestures towards a rediscovery of the sacred through physical and emotional connectedness to another person, before switching back to a closing meditation on the holy: 'take my freedom for giving me a sacred love'. Hollis captures a multiple perspective here: the taking of freedom is a willed surrender and recognition of the power of the other, whether a human or a god. But 'sacred love' can also be seen as the removal of freedom in a more negative light, linking to a type of religious faith that limits and alienates. The ambiguity of the album is both undecidable and purposeful because of the literal turns of phrase in Hollis's lyrics.

The lyrics are not a manifesto, of course, and float in or burst over the music: for example, the shouted 'that ain't me babe' on 'Desire'. But the lyrics and music work in tandem to suggest that wholeness is briefly attainable, although only after periods of self-doubt or by tackling barriers imposed by materialistic society – this is the case on 'Inheritance', with its critique of progress perverted into gain. The battle that rages amid this ostensibly abstract and sometimes deviant pastoral sound-world is played out in the disappearance of the lyrics; even though the lyrics are provided on the liner notes, the script is not always very clear and Hollis is hard to follow – his words roll into one another, are distorted, mumbled and swallowed. That they are important is shown by their presence on the sleeve; that they elude the listener's mastery is their purpose. The vast array of instruments used on these two albums is also in danger of being lost – sounds flicker in and out as if barely present, and when the volume is louder and veers towards rock the instruments often merge into a purposeful indeterminacy. This is what Simon Reynolds identifies as the central features of post-rock that play out, around 1990, in the epic shoegazing of Ride, Lush, Chapterhouse, Bark Psychosis and Swervedriver, as well as the ultra-dense imploding of that style on My Bloody Valentine's *Loveless*.

Laughing Stock inhabits the same sound-world as *Spirit of Eden* and so seems much less of an experiment. Where *Spirit of Eden* displays the discovery of a raw exploration, *Laughing Stock* moulds those sources by extending similar practices. This is not just settling into a style; the dwelling in the sound-world enables changes to be made. The album opens and closes with tape hiss; in 'After the Flood', the cymbals merge with the frequencies of the hiss, and otherwise clean sections of guitar and vocals on 'Taphead' are earthed by the sound of the recording medium. The interventions become increasingly fleeting, and the percussion is relentlessly and statically repetitive. That the changes to the overall sound are minimal is significant, giving a sense of gradual and almost occult development along a spiritual path – in this way, *Laughing Stock* is properly hermetic. The ambiguous relation to higher forces is heightened while the vocals become even more muted, the words slipping into a realm where the voice is not an instrument but a medium.

The opening 'Myrrhman' is the first of several tracks to call for help to recover the self from a sense of inadequacy and failure; with 'faith one path and the second is fear', the music a slow, declining drone. The second track, 'Ascension Day', worries that fate rather than a godhead or secular individualism shapes the world. It opens with chiming, thrashing guitar chords, and these return at the end of the lyrics to build into repetitive dissonance for over a minute before cutting out abruptly. This is not just an overly literal reading of fatalism but a reminder of the narrator's position as one of resistance to fate. In fact, the cut-out could be read as a reassertion of providence – the submission to the seemingly arbitrary will of the Christian God (here in the shape of a willed edit). 'After the Flood' might be seen as a response to Peter Gabriel's 'Here Comes the Flood' (1977), hinting at a new beginning that starts to emerge later on side two of the album but here connects the awareness of being beyond the human to the degradation of the lost human: 'Shake my head/Turn my face to the floor/Dead to respect'. 'Taphead' begins within 'After the Flood' and is more personal because of its stripped-down guitar and vocals, but it marks out a journey through pain and knowledge of finitude towards rebirth in the lyrics 'born again' and 'nascent/Naissant'. This is mapped musically as the song introduces wind instruments, keyboards, more guitar and some percussion, and then fades back down to guitar, vocals and tape hiss after the lines 'dust to dust/Consume'. 'New Grass' is almost jaunty; the opening line, 'lifted up', is brought in by a melodic guitar line and is then sustained by sheltering and static percussion for most of its 9:46. The percussion anticipates both the retrieval of the moment and of a greater time beyond the mortal individual, linking with an open narrative that moves towards a plea for salvation. The closing track, 'Runeii', is astonishingly slow-moving, a kind of discordant grace where the spiritualization of the world has either not happened or will not happen.

Despite their heavy use of Christian imagery, *Spirit of Eden* and *Laughing Stock* together offer a complex take on the claims of Christian salvation and divine purpose. This is illustrated by the cover art by James Marsh, which reflects on the lyrical and musical concerns in a less literal way than, say, Mark Wilkinson did on early Marillion albums. Simon Reynolds notes that the cover of *Spirit of Eden* replicates the absence of Eden in the music, with the whole 'a lament for paradise lost and an attempt to conjure the "spirit of Eden" in this "world turned upside down"' (the opening line of the album).[9] We would not argue that *Spirit of Eden* tries to re-establish an Eden – or, if it does, then it knows it will fail. If the cover art could be said to depict a tree of knowledge, then it is complicated by the sea-shells, puffin and penguin hanging from the tree that push us towards a drifting Noah's Ark experience, from which there is no way back to Eden – or perhaps it gestures towards a failure of faith in a fallen world that is no longer or never had been Eden. The cover of *Laughing Stock* also depicts a tree, this time with groups of colourful birds (all of them endangered) that form the globe's continents, throwing into relief the otherwise bare branches and the barren ground on which the tree stands. Marsh's artwork draws the two covers together conceptually through an environmental theme, but it also functions aesthetically in a midzone between pure abstraction and cultural reference. It is as if the belief expressed on the albums becomes as abstract as the vocals, instrumentation, structure and cover art.

Talk Talk is a good example of a band in the 1980s and 1990s that developed extended musical forms to explore grand themes across a range of genres, including industrial (which also had its concept albums, such as Foetus's 1985 album *Nail* and Nine Inch Nails' 1994 album *Closer*), gothic, indie and electronica. A place could be found for The Cure's *Disintegration* (1989) or *Bloodflowers* (2000) as some sort of prog – they are, after all, connected concept albums reflecting on mortality and the passing of love. But these albums never reach a point of reflective complexity that mirrors the move to 1970s progressive rock. For our purposes, even if the sound sources, instrumentation and lyrical concerns of a band are absolutely different in 1990 than they were in 1975, they should still arrive at a recognizably similar point. A stronger case can be made for The Smashing Pumpkins, particularly the 1995 album *Mellon Collie and the Infinite Sadness*, which is 120 minutes long and divided into day and night sections. The album contains many lengthy tracks

Talk Talk, *Spirit of Eden* (1988) and *Laughing Stock* (1991).
Artwork by James Marsh, www.jamesmarsh.com

and represents a stretching out of the band's sound that had begun on *Siamese Dream* (1993), which makes sense within a prog framework, particularly as vocalist and guitarist Billy Corgan has admitted his formative learning of the entirety of Rush's '2112'.[10] Similarly, Sonic Youth's epic *Daydream Nation* (1989) or *Washing Machine* (1995) might be progressive-style expansions, but these albums develop within their own sound, as opposed to the marked departure of Radiohead's *OK Computer* (1997), which also incorporates musical approaches from a variety of sources, including prog. A hint of this can be found in Levitation, formed by Terry Bickers, previously (and since) guitarist with The House of Love, and in music that follows the aesthetic of the 4AD label, such as A. R. Kane and No-man.

A. R. Kane is at the centre of Reynolds' idea of 'oceanic music', and he argues that the band reaches new heights of rock experimentation on its album 69 (1988), in which it found 'unprecedented connections between jazz, dub, acid rock, Sonic Youth-style "reinvention of the guitar", the Cocteau Twins of *Head Over Heels*'.[11] This album is all about the ocean, Reynolds claims, in word and sound: it uses the sea, both internally and externally, as a concept, and it foreshadows trip hop in the meeting of dub and rock. The album also features Ray Shulman, from Gentle Giant, on bass. There is certainly a post-progressive quality here, even if it ends up being 'post-pop' too. But while 69 is soaked in reverb, its ocean is not the trippy bliss that Reynolds sees as bathing us in a lost unity.[12] This liquid soundscape is not fully immersive but one where instruments clash and where vocalist Alex Ayuli drifts, Wyatt-like, in, over and often underneath a swirl of guitars. Where other forms of 'oceanic rock', often featuring Robin Guthrie's trademark production, had turned the guitar into a machine emanating lines of sound as part of a greater whole, for his band Cocteau Twins or for Lush, on 69 the individual sounds fight submersion. The ecstasy of 69 is not without conflict or awkward complexity: guitars play against each other in different metres on many tracks.

This recovery of the guitar as an ecstatic device permeates alternative music around 1990. It is reminiscent of the inexorable build from isolated jangling to overwhelming group unison on the title track of Television's 1977 album *Marquee Moon* (see Chapter 8), with a return to ground in the reprise of the opening riff. As we have argued above, this relentlessness is best thought of as 'anti-prog', which occupies the same space as prog but counters it. Alternative, indie, goth and shoegaze bands, together with My Bloody Valentine, all include examples of this, but at moments there are clear echoes of prog in mounting sound as a type of narrative, ironically recalling the more straightforward prog of post-Gabriel Genesis as much as the free power of King Crimson in the mid-1970s. A simplified reiteration of prog can be heard in Fields of the Nephilim's *Elizium* (1990), but Levitation not only reiterates structures and approaches of prog via a set of references that merges 1980s British rock, Hawkwind and the rock elements of This Heat but also prefigures the chaotic reconceptualizations of prog by Radiohead or The Mars Volta. This is progressive rock returning at a distance, self-aware, ironic and resistant to canonical musical references.[13] Levitation's *Need For Not* (1992) presents itself via a fractured mandala cover image and an updating of psychedelic imagery that connects to the excitement about fractals that came with the spread of Ecstasy as the recreational drug of choice in the late 1980s and early 1990s. The refrain of the closing track, 'Coterie', makes this apparent: 'In the last chaotic wave/Only the human condition/Could be so out of touch'. It also mounts to a climax after 5:10, only to dissipate in a long fade and then return as an already faded, ghostly coda. The album alternates themes of paranoia, isolation and loss with upbeat sentiment, such as 'without grief/Without fear' on 'Arcs of Light and Dew'. This alternation is worked out musically by the contrast between sudden changes of time and tune and multitracked calm vocals, although this is not mapped over-literally onto the lyrics.

Side two of the *After Ever* EP (1991), 'Bedlam', is perhaps Levitation's most explicit updating of progressive rock. Over its 9:25, it develops its idea not of madness, as such, but of how thought without limit can be overwhelming ('don't question everything' ends each verse), and how madness is unquestioningly located and confined within the asylum.[14] In fact, the song veers between suggesting that not questioning is the best way to behave and criticizing wilful ignorance for being an oppressive restriction. The second verse calls on the listener to open himself or herself to thought without limit, with 'you're a flood/That washes everything through your soul/Come and sing/Without hope'. As might be expected from a song about uncontrolled thoughts, there is an increasingly discordant middle section, 3 minutes long, where the vocals drift in and out but are always submerged in the tide of the band's mounting volume and dissonance. This is followed by a quiet return and a verse that is pure resolution: massed chords and slowed, heavy percussion announce a last verse where awe is all. In the end, though, loss becomes everything, in a creative merging of Nietzsche and The Beatles' 'Tomorrow Never Knows'.

So far in this chapter we have identified musicians who seemed to be recovering or uncovering something hidden, lost or excluded from consumer society and from the culture industry model of rock. There are many shifts away from rock instrumentation and forays into the self-conscious use of technology, but there is another dimension to post-progressive music to be found in the explicit embrace of new computer technologies and sounds. At a time when ambient music was migrating to the dance hall or at least to the 'chill-out' room, No-man offered a post-progressive take on synthesized beats, sounds and samples, bringing them towards rock – much as Björk was beginning to do – without ever quite returning to the rock of the time. Steve Hillage resurfaced with Gong partner Miquette Giraudy in the trance of System 7's music; The Future Sound of London conjured exotic, sprawling post-world music; while The Orb was on a mission to stretch dance music and ambience alike – for example, in its updating of Pink Floyd and Tangerine Dream in the 19-minute single 'A Huge Ever Growing Pulsating Brain That Rules from the Centre of the Ultraworld' (1989). This was music looking to the future as source material, and No-man used it to rethink the romantic songs of 1980s experimental rock.

No-man's earlier releases, from 1989 onwards, possess an ultra-clean sound, as Steven Wilson's music joined with Tim Bowness's yearning yet cool voice. Like those of The Red House Painters, No-man's simple songs are oddly structured and see slowness used as a compositional tool. But Wilson injects the ecstatic rock blasts we can also hear in Levitation. The early single 'Days in the Trees' (1991) uses sampled, slowed beats, deep bass sounds and synth to break out after 4:48, as the violins provide an aggressive guitar-like focus. The last 2 minutes (from 7:11) fall away, leaving the surging section as an interlude in a sound-world that parallels trip hop, which had started to come out of Bristol by 1991. Many of the longer tracks use this contrast to highlight the more serene passages, taking No-man's sound away from that of The Blue Nile. No-man's 21-minute song 'Heaven Taste' is a heightened version of the twin euphoria of the slow-building song part with the epic rising break – a mutually reinforcing duality to be found on many of Wilson's Porcupine Tree releases. After an initial period of post-Julian Cope songs on the 1992 release *On the Sunday of Life*, Porcupine Tree spent the remainder of the 1990s immersed in an extreme version of rock ambience, with ultra-lengthy tracks dominating (see Chapter 14). But all the ecstasies, recoveries and embraces discussed here can arguably be seen as preparing the way for the discordant appropriation of new machinery in the form of Radiohead's *OK Computer*.

Although Radiohead had encountered inner alienation on the debut single, 'Creep' (1992), and on the second album, *The Bends* (1995), this became ever more exposed on *OK Computer* and subsequent releases. As we have discussed, from the mid-1960s onwards progressive rock relied on the latest technologies for playing, recording and performing, linking closely to a new relation to visual-media technologies and new attitudes to live spectacle. In the 1980s and early 1990s, Peter Gabriel and Kate Bush used the studio as an instrument that they themselves could play through computer technology, at the same time as Brian Eno was developing music software for the most complete abdication of control in his distinctive form of generative music. The musical mode we recognize today as techno rethought the use of vinyl, and digital recording and formats progressed to the point that record companies convinced consumers to buy the same album for a third time in the form of the remastered CD. All these trends are relevant contexts for *OK Computer*. Along with its rock merits and prog credentials, this makes *OK Computer* a pivotal moment in progressive rock in its mobilization of histories that derive from the rejection of prog. Guitarist Jonny Greenwood stated that the album was not progressive rock, and that progressive rock was wrong in trying to merge classical and rock forms.[15] Despite this view, the connections to Pink Floyd, dissonant strategies, the extended take on alienation, the use of visuals to augment the music and the structuring of the album as a coherent whole, to name but a few relevant characteristics, suggest that *OK Computer* might well be progressive rock.[16] For us, the album is as much about the state of the reception of prog as it is about the development of, or a return to, progressive rock. While a generation of music journalists was still insisting that 1976–7 was the most important period ever, many musicians writing and perform-ing in the 1990s had forgotten that or had never known it. Equally, they did not need to refer back to the sounds or styles of 1970s prog rock in order to make authentic progressive rock. Radiohead increasingly brought in practices much more familiar to electronica or dance music, such as those found on the Warp label or its mainland European techno equivalents. Paradoxically, though, it was Radiohead's reintegration of rock into a post-progressive context that created a new wave of progressiveness.

OK Computer is thematically linked as a series of meditations on the state of the individual in a highly technologized consumer society run for the benefit of a small group of its members. The album also returns repeatedly to the notion of travel and transport, beginning with the car crash of the opening track, 'Airbag', a plane crash in the penultimate track, 'Lucky', and the instruc-tion to 'slow down' on the closing 'The Tourist'. According to Tim Footman, transport in *OK Computer* represents 'the various kinds of movement that modern life imposes on humanity'.[17] In so doing, transport stands as the paradigm for the increasingly decentred individual who is manufactured as a by-product of capitalist informatics. If Hawkwind and Kraftwerk offered a 1970s take on J. G. Ballard, then Radiohead matches Ballard's later obsessions with shopping malls, holiday resorts, and the seething madness that increased uniformity and a desire for security bring about.[18] *OK Computer* also recalls Gabriel's third *Peter Gabriel* album (1980), with its vignettes of those driven outside society's norms and forced to adopt a micro-oppressive attitude to society: for example, the competing paranoid visions in 'Paranoid Android', the housebreaking in 'No Surprises', or the needling abusiveness of 'Climbing Up the Walls'. Dai Griffith argues that one of the strengths of *OK Computer* is its attention to 'novelistic detail', as the small aspects of the album signal a wider concern, such as the crash and the airbag of the opening track.[19] Seemingly trivial controls, breakdowns, nastiness and limited hopes illustrate the surgical incision of power that has replaced 'the system', which imposes itself from above. 'Airbag' is a microcosm of the album itself, 'an agenda-setter for the album to follow: the voice, words, noise breaks, guitar solos, carefully positioned motivic bass and drums, the details'.[20]

As there already exist two book-length studies of *OK Computer*, we will not work through every part of the album, but we should note the shock value of the dissonant three-part track 'Paranoid Android', which was not only released as a single but also became a huge commercial success. We also note Griffith's neat way of linking together the album as a carefully measured interplay between vocal and instrumental sections, with returns of musical parts and a balancing throughout of vocal and instrumental that serves to unify the album.[21] We should also mention the ironic use of Bob Dylan's 1965 'Subterranean Homesick Blues' in the title of 'Subterranean Homesick Alien', with its banal setting ('I live in a town/Where you can't smell a thing') and the repetition of 'uptight', as well as the diseased version of Pink Floyd's 'Breathe' reprise, at 5:54 of 'Time' from *The Dark Side of the Moon*, on 'Exit Music (For a Film)'. 'Exit Music' is another song about being short of breath and is accompanied on the CD liner notes by the stick-figure version of the businessmen on the cover of Pink Floyd's *Wish You Were Here*. 'Lucky', the penultimate track, brings together key motifs, combining the rapturously melodic vocals in the soar of Thom Yorke's announcing 'a glorious day' with the David Gilmour styling of Greenwood's elevating guitar solo. If *OK Computer* updates the alienation of *The Wall*, then it also tells of a world more compromised and less clearly polarized than that in the 1970s. The despair of being 'lucky' enough to survive leads to a demand that will not go away and the cry to 'pull me out'.

Footman and Griffith identify the possibility in 'The Tourist' that the line 'hey man, slow down' is so far outside Yorke's lexicon as to be the voice of another character, as is the case on many other tracks on the album. The two critics do not pursue the implications of this phrase, though: the 'hey man' call to chill out is exactly part of the problem of conforming to social norms, and the seemingly soporific musical backing is a clear sign that any chance of escaping into death or to freedom has been extinguished. The song also completes the narrative of speed and travel, with 'where the hell im going?? at 1000 feet per second' [*sic*]. It is not quite the speed of sound, but a common enough speed for air travel – the narrator of 'Lucky' has been caught in a time loop without escape and with only palliative care on the unwanted journey.

OK Computer is significant as an album. Footman argues that it is the end of the indie album, marks the indie move into the mainstream, and blows apart the genre of 'alternative rock' through Radiohead's synthesis of so many non-indie approaches and sounds.[22] More importantly, it is the beginning of Radiohead's attempt to salvage the album form – which continued with the experimental unity of *Kid A* (2000) and, to a lesser extent, on the accompanying album *Amnesiac* (2001). As internet downloading of music spread in the early 2000s, the notion that the prime unit of music was the album rather than the song came under threat. The practice of maximizing the form with filler or 'bonus' tracks and remixes further reduced the sense of an album as a composed, purposely organized statement, even for albums that did not work with concepts. But many pop musicians resorted to the hitherto derided idea of the concept album in the 2000s, from Beyoncé and Madness to Kanye West and The Streets. Radiohead made the simpler assertion of the meaningfulness of a suite of songs by varying the length of albums and never trying to fill up the time. The final assertion of this trend was the self-release of *In Rainbows* (2007), initially as a download, where the purchaser would choose how much to pay for it (it was technically available for nothing but still subject to a credit-card fee). Later, there was a double-vinyl, double-CD box set of *In Rainbows* that could be ordered at the same time as the free or cheap download. Radiohead continued the 'download album' format for *The King of Limbs* (2011), but fixed the cost of the download to bring it roughly into line with iTunes prices – arguably a step backward, or, at least, a step back into the culture industry.[23] Other pioneers of technology as a producing device and a means to connect with fans can be seen elsewhere in progressive rock: for example, Gabriel constantly sought to develop new technologies, such as his involvement in and promotion of streaming technology in the shape of 'We7', or the various internet strategies Marillion have developed since the mid-1990s.[24]

Radiohead not only made progressive rock an acceptable component of contemporary music; *OK Computer* marks a moment in the slow decline of the critical consensus about punk's banishing prog forever. From this point on, artists did not seem to care about the possibility that certain sounds, ideas or presentational strategies would recall a taboo type of music. Indie bands such as Super Furry Animals, The Flaming Lips and Gorky's Zygotic Mynci happily recalled a panoply of unacceptable 1970s sounds within newer frameworks; stadium rock adopted U2's style and approach in the shape of Coldplay, Elbow, Kings of Leon and neo-Radiohead band Muse; post-rock could stretch out and stretch back into songs by the Icelandic post-rock band Sigur Rós. Newer progressive rock bands such as Spock's Beard adapted their approach to incorporate these new sounds, and Porcupine Tree moved back from electronica after 2002 in an attempt to resuscitate rock from the outside. Radiohead dismantled its own sound on *Kid A*, an album of electronica tinged with rock – particularly if we view it as an example of the extended instrumentation of progressive rock. Paul Morley regards this album as something of a luxury, a whimsy permitted to an already successful band; he claims that although 'this is not entirely Radiohead's fault', the band's financial and artistic security make it 'a fabrication, a copy, a tribute'.[25] For Morley, *Kid A* is neo-experimentalism, a borrowing rather than a progression, in which we detect musical techniques analogous to T. S. Eliot's use of poetic fragmentation in 'The Waste Land' or to William Burroughs' neo-Dadaist cut-up technique. We would argue that *OK Computer* is the more progressive album, and that the oddness of *Kid A* is overstated by a public unfamiliar with the wilder shores of experimental rock, as Morley correctly notes.[26] The problem he never quite identifies is that albums such as *Kid A* give mainstream listeners the chance to engage with experimental and difficult music. Here we see the *NME* anti-prog stance creeping back in distrust of Radiohead's change of approach. A similar criticism could be made of Radiohead's chosen means for disseminating *In Rainbows*, because not everyone is in the financial position to make such a decision. But Radiohead had choices not to move towards electronica on *Kid A*, or not to offer *In Rainbows* as a more or less free download.

In between the two 2000–1 albums and *In Rainbows* was *Hail to the Thief*, which, in aural terms, is a much closer follow-up to *OK Computer* than those other releases.[27] The theme of alienation, the critique of capitalism and the hesitant acknowledgement of technology suggest that *Hail to the Thief* (2003) is something of a return, and the instrumentation, while incorporating the sounds of *Kid A*, recalls Pink Floyd filtered through a post-punk lens. If it is a successor to *OK Computer*, then *Hail to the Thief* is even more conceptually focused and outward-looking in its take on the failings of contemporary society. This is evident in its title in its explicit criticism of Republican candidate George W. Bush's controversial win over Democrat Al Gore in the 2000 US presidential election: in doing so, the album attacks the claims of the United States to represent the ideal society and to have the right to impose itself globally. Each track has an alternative title, as does the album itself (in the guise of 'The Gloaming', which appears as a track at the centre). Instead of providing ambiguity, the alternative titles indicate a separation between subject matter and narrator. The 'I' of the album recounts events, takes positions, and hovers above the wars of the twentieth and twenty-first centuries. 'The Gloaming' makes this explicit; on this track, Yorke's voice is spatially separated and almost distracted in tone. It is clear that contemporary society damages the mind of the individual so that he or she is lost in a morass of deadening insignificance amid signs of power and wealth, but the mental anguish is a direct result of ideological manipulation (on the opening track, '2+2=5'), ultimately leading to the collapse of boundaries between the individual and mass capitalist society (on the closing track, 'A Wolf at the Door'). As well as the distancing achieved in the ghost titles of each track, the multipart and often complex songs stand as a set of techniques to resist social brainwashing. The seeming failure of the final track, where the wolf never leaves the door, is a call to stay vigilant. Yorke ends the album by telling 'you' to 'turn this tape off', which means that this is no triumphalist or sloganeering release.

This critical position, imbued with the possibility of its failure, distinguishes post-progressive music from the utopian bent of 1970s progressive rock. The restoration of something lost or hidden can go only so far. Crucially, post-progressive music starts from a different place to the classic phase of progressive rock in the late 1960s, a place that may well be a site of richer philosophical meditation on social, economic and political alienation, where punk attitude is transformed into something more constructive. This does not make post-progressive music a mid-point between progressive rock and its successor styles but a new fusion, one that is mirrored in a revivification of folk.

Notes

1. Reynolds, 'Post-Rock', in *Audio Culture: Readings in Modern Music*, eds Christoph Cox and Daniel Warner (New York: Continuum, 2004), 358–61.

2. Rob Young, *Electric Eden: Unearthing Britain's Visionary Music* (London: Faber and Faber, 2010), 5–7, 567.

3. In an interview with Paul Morley in April 1984, Marillion's lead singer at the time, Fish, insisted on the newness of the band's sound and its unrelatedness to Genesis, in Morley, *Ask: The Chatter of Pop* (London: Faber and Faber, 1986), 39, 41.

4. Young, *Electric Eden*, 574.

5. See David Sylvian's website: www.davidsylvian.com/discography/albums/david_sylvian_gone_to_earth.html.

6. As with Peter Gabriel, there is a potentially problematic side to this appropriation of 'the Eastern' in David Sylvian's music, and reference to Sylvian's connections with Japan (the country) may not be enough to help. The exception could be Ryuichi Sakamoto, with whom Sylvian has worked for nearly thirty years. This is not because he provides a Japanese alibi but because Sakamoto is keenly aware of cultural appropriations through his band Yellow Magic Orchestra, which not only ironically celebrated the stereotyping of Japan but also had a worldwide hit with 'Firecracker' (1979) – a remake of a track by Martin Denny, who pioneered the use of 'exotic sounds'.

7. Martin Heidegger, *Being and Time* (Oxford: Blackwell, 1962) and 'The Origin of the Work of Art' in *Basic Writings* (London: Routledge, 1993), 143–203: see, in particular, 172 and 180.

8. Young, *Electric Eden*, 578.

9. Reynolds, *Blissed Out: The Raptures of Rock* (London: Serpent's Tail, 1990), 132.

10. Interview on *Rush: Beyond the Lighted Stage* DVD (2010).

11. Reynolds, *Blissed Out*, 128.

12. Ibid., 129.

13. Press release accompanying the vinyl issue of Levitation's *Need For Not* (1992).

14. Rock had been slow to adopt the 12-inch single developed as part of the rise of disco in the mid-1970s. New Order demonstrated that the format could be used to fuse rock, electronic and dance styles (particularly on New Order's 1982 single 'Blue Monday'), and the advent of the CD single doubtless applied pressure to make EPs, which flourished in the late 1980s and early 1990s. Marillion's 17-minute 'Grendel' notwithstanding, groups such as Levitation and My Bloody Valentine took the opportunity to stretch the format in ways that used emerging technology to experiment with rock forms.

15. Jonny Greenwood interview from 1997, quoted in Tim Footman, *Radiohead: Welcome to the Machine – OK Computer and the Death of the Album* (New Malden: Chrome Dreams, 2007), 53–4.

16. Footman argues that progressive rock was one component of Radiohead's new sound, along with techno, jazz rock and 'atonal composition' (Footman, *Radiohead*, 185). Dai Griffith also concedes that 'it's possible to see some elements of progressive rock in Radiohead', in Griffith, *OK Computer* (New York: Continuum, 2004), 44. However, both critics resist seeing it as more than a component, implying progressive rock is a fixed and homogeneous musical mode.

17. Footman, *Radiohead*, 120.

18. This is the landscape of J. G. Ballard's later novels, from *Cocaine Nights* (1996) onwards.

19. Griffith, *OK Computer*, 49.

20. Ibid., 51.

21. Ibid., 90–3.

22. Footman, *Radiohead*, 235.

23. The download of *The King of Limbs* was released in February 2011; CD, vinyl and 'newspaper' versions of the album were released six weeks later.

24. See Collins, *Marillion/Separated Out*, 147–51.

25. Paul Morley, *Words and Music* (London: Bloomsbury, 2003), 324.

26. Ibid., 330.

27. Thom Yorke identified the album as '*OK Computer 2*', cited in Joseph Tate, '*Hail to the Thief*: A Rhizomatic Map in Fragments', in *The Music and Art of Radiohead*, ed. Joseph Tate (Aldershot: Ashgate, 2007), 177–97 (194).

Chapter 13

The Return of Folk

Has progressive folk returned? Or perhaps it never went away? There was certainly a resurgence of interest in folk and roots music in the early 2000s, particularly in the UK and US, promoted by new documentaries about Appalachian music and the tangled roots of British folk.[1] This revival was partly orchestrated at a grassroots level and linked to a renewed interest in local cultures and small-scale performances, but it was given an institutional push in the US and prompted major artists such as Bruce Springsteen to record a batch of Pete Seeger songs on *We Shall Overcome* (2006), which emphasized both musicians' sensitivity to American folk history. The Smithsonian Institute's 1990s repackaging of John and Alan Lomax's field recordings from the 1940s and 1950s established the historical importance of roots music, and producer T. Bone Burnett brought folk music to a wider audience through a range of Hollywood soundtracks, from *O Brother, Where Art Thou?* (2000) and *Cold Mountain* (2003) to the musical dramas *Crazy Heart* (2010) and *Ghost Brothers of Darkland County* (2012), after what felt like twenty years in the folk wilderness. None of these ventures showcased progressive folk as such, although Burnett's role as producer on Robert Plant and Alison Krauss's album *Raising Sand* (2007) experimented with structure and vocals, mixing subtle harmonies with bluegrass, folk and rock. What all this hybrid musical activity confirms is that, as Benjamin Filene argues, there is no such thing as 'pure' folk. This is especially true over the last thirty years, as musicians have straddled 'the boundaries between "folk" and "commercial", "old-fashioned" and "modern"', often returning to the early 1960s folk revival, and further back, to revive or reinvent traditional songs.[2]

In the UK, the popularity of folk festivals has, if anything, grown since the 1970s, with a range of traditional, hybrid, progressive and contemporary manifestations of folk on the festival circuit. The prime example is the annual Cropredy Festival in Oxfordshire, which, since 1976, has been organized by Fairport Convention and showcases a wide variety of music over three days, including Wishbone Ash, Strawbs and Show of Hands in 2007 and Little Feat,

Rick Wakeman and Status Quo in 2010. BBC Radio 2 has capitalized on the Cambridge Folk Festival (established in 1964 and now running over three days), which combines traditional folk music from Ralph McTell, Christy Moore, Joan Baez and Eliza Carthy with the folk rock of The Levellers and The Waterboys, together with more divergent strains including Joe Strummer in 2002 and an acoustic set from Scottish indie band Idlewild in 2005. Although some festivals, such as Sidmouth Folk Week, are more conservative in taste and lean towards family entertainment, other festivals have developed laterally, such as (in the UK) the Green Man Festival in the Brecon Beacons, which has grown from modest beginnings in 2003 into a three-day festival showcasing an eclectic mix of music and culture (The Flaming Lips and Joanna Newsom headlined in 2010), and (in the US) the Bumbershoots International Music and Arts Festival in Seattle (established 1971) and the multimedia South by Southwest Festival in Austin, Texas (established 1987) – even the Newport Folk Festival (established 1959) has diversified over the last decade. Closer to the prog mainstream, the summer concert circuit often features special events, including the Doncaster Rocks Festival in July 2009, at which Jethro Tull played a mixture of blues, progressive rock, folk and jazz, performing alongside folk and folk-rock performers Julie Felix, Steeleye Span, Strawbs and The Popes.[3] There was less space for progressive folk at the first High Voltage Festival held in Victoria Park, London, in October 2010: the headline acts were ZZ Top and a reformed Emerson, Lake and Palmer, as well as a dedicated prog stage featuring Transatlantic and Marillion. However, the combination at High Voltage of Steve Hackett, Wishbone Ash and Focus, on the one hand, and metal prog band Bigelf and rock guitarist Dweezil Zappa, on the other, emphasizes how eclectic progressive rock concerts have become.

These different trajectories suggest that progressive folk – or the combination of progressive rock and folk – never went away. It was certainly harder to detect in the 1980s, when high-tech synthesizers were prominently on display, but through the 1990s a number of musicians started to re-engage with folk-acoustic forms, representing what Rob Young in *Electric Eden* calls 'scattered links of the silver chain'.[4] Young detects a more complex vision of 'Poly-Albion' in the 1980s and 1990s than in earlier versions of folk, but he barely mentions progressive folk and does not venture outside Britain. If he had done so, then he might have reflected on the long-running folk publication *Sing Out!* (established 1950) or on Pete Seeger's interest in the inherent hybridity of folk music through which regional and national strains can co-exist – a belief Seeger held despite his purist attitude towards Bob Dylan going electric at the 1965 Newport Folk Festival.[5]

Young might also have detected a great deal of progressive folk activity in the 1990s. Anthony Phillips and (more periodically) Steve Hackett continued to write albums for acoustic guitar well beyond their stints with Genesis, and Peter Gabriel explored his ongoing ambivalence towards nature on *Us* (1992), from the dream-like ritualistic union of 'Blood of Eden' to the masochistic self-analysis of 'Digging in the Dirt' to the puzzles of presence and absence on 'Secret World'. Roy Harper had moved away from the long folk compositions of 'Me and My Woman' (*Stormcock*, 1971) and the grand concepts of 'The Game (Parts 1–5)' (*HQ*, 1975), but in the 1990s he collaborated with David Gilmour and Kate Bush on *Once* (1990) and worked with conceptual material on his autobiographical-mythical fusion album *The Dream Society* (1998). Peter Hammill returned to the introspective melancholy of mid-1970s songs such as 'Alice (Letting Go)' on his 1992 *Fireships* album, during the long break from Van der Graaf Generator; Rush occasionally forayed into folk territory, most obviously with 'Resist' (*Test for Echo*, 1996), which regularly featured in live performances as a break in the band's electric set; and Neil Young released a full-scale concept album about a northern Californian town, *Greendale* (2003), and embarked on an environmentally friendly tour. Another distinctive mode is the stripped-down formula popularized by *MTV Unplugged* in the 1990s and exemplified by Wishbone Ash's *Bare Bones* (1999) and Marillion's *Less is More* (2009) as acoustic explorations of their back catalogues. This stripped-down mode was developed as an acoustic-electric hybrid by Marillion guitarist Steve Rothery's and vocalist Hannah Stobart's band The Wishing Tree, providing a vehicle for tapping into mystical-natural themes on the 2009 album *Ostara*.

Some contemporary progressive bands such as Mostly Autumn have continued to extend and fuse Celtic folk forms, particularly 'Flowers for Guns' and 'Tearing at the Faerytale' on the 2008 album *Glass Shadows*. But neo- and post-progressive bands more often incorporate folk elements piecemeal into their repertoires. The Swedish group The Flower Kings are a good case in point. Their 1999 double album *Flower Power* contains the 60-minute song suite 'Garden of Dreams', discussed in Chapter 10. It follows a familiar progressive arc, moving from 'Dawn' to 'Shadowland' to 'The Final Deal', where the life cycle and the temporal movement of the day and seasons entwine. This is emphasized on the album cover, on which a fractal human image is presented against a psychedelic circle of light, with 'A Journey to the Hidden Corners of Your Mind' printed beneath. 'Garden of Dreams' is more eclectic than The Moody Blues' *Days of Future Passed* and more adventurous than *The Seven Ages of Man* (see Chapters 3 and 5), including the operatic-ambient fusion of 'Dungeon of the Deep' and the soulful jazz-piano and vocals on 'Indian Summer' (parts 12 and 13). The eighteen parts of 'Garden of Dreams' allow the band space to shuttle between simplicity and complexity, where disarmingly simple songs segue into heavily structured compositions, often using the Mellotron to layer sounds. For example, following the prelude 'Dawn', where we hear an orchestra and an operatic vocalist warming up and a slowly building march led by organ and percussion, we move into the acoustic second part, 'Simple Song'. Roine Stolt's melodic voice recalls the 'primal days' where summer sun, green meadows, everyday activities and laughter characterize prelapsarian childhood innocence. The song is wistful, though, using the past tense to suggest that this innocent state no longer exists or can be glimpsed only in dreams, particularly the last line: 'speeding the wheels of evolution, set the industrial heart in motion'. This line shifts the tempo and mood into the long electric prog opening of 'Business Vamp', which yearns to reclaim a 'private Eden' in a chaotic world full of 'tattered tongues' and 'human factories'.

The garden is under periodic threat from the relentless machinery of industry and business represented by harsher guitar-playing or brooding, keyboard-led instrumental parts. The lyrical centrepiece of 'Garden of Dreams' (part eight, which takes its name from the song-cycle) echoes the threats to nature that run through 1970s progressive rock. Here the garden is a surreal dreamscape ('Puppets and prunes in the world of balloons') where pastoral sanctuary is questionable ('Flowers and trees in the garden of dreams, can we touch it all?') and does not fully mask the singer's solitude and his fear of the void. The song is gently lyrical, the music lush and seductive – until the final 45 seconds, when it disintegrates into a clock-work unwinding and meandering vocal noises before moving dramatically to an up-tempo electric track, 'Don't Let the Devil In'. In part fifteen, the instrumental 'Gardens Revisited', a folk melody on piano jostles with indistinct noises reminiscent of seagulls or static interference, before drums, guitar and whistle join at 0:30. The final two tracks shift away from the acoustic mode, only to return in a quiet interlude of 'The Final Deal', at 1:45. This reintroduces the theme of dreaming in the pastoral land of 'Evermore', where life's complexities are calmed by angelic singing and the promise of homecoming before gently fading out.

The Flower Kings continued to use acoustic-folk modes within their broader musical palette, such as 'End on a High Note' (10:44), the last track of the first disc of their double concept album *Paradox Hotel* (2006). The harmonious chorus and a sense of upbeat festivities in the first 4 minutes move into a more complex set of themes and musical currents for the next 5 minutes; return to the folk opening; and then fade out with an electric and acoustic guitar complementing each other. Tracks such as 'Giant Minor Steps' (12:13), which opens the second side of *Paradox Hotel*, is an electric folk track that embraces the paradox (both 'giant' and 'minor') at the heart of the album, while a number of songs on *The Sum of No Evil* (2009) use folk melodies and motifs piecemeal without dedicating a whole track to them.

A similar acoustic folk mode has been adopted by Manning, a band based in the British West Midlands headed by multi-instrumentalist Guy Manning, who had previously played alongside The Flower Kings' Roine Stolt and Jonas Reingold in the early days of the eclectic neo-prog band The Tangent.[6] Manning does not fit easily into the category of progressive folk, but the band does blend folk and progressive rock elements. To take one example, Manning's 'Lost in Play' on *Songs from the Bilston House* (2007) is a pastiche of Marillion (the yearning for lost innocence), Jethro Tull (the vocal delivery and the extensive use of flute), and Mike Oldfield (the playing of different instruments in turn to inflect the central melody). The overall concept is the topos of the dilapidated Bilston House near Wolverhampton, on which is hung the sign 'Do not enter here! The last person died', and through which Manning revives 'stories, observations and atmospheres' that have long been lost in dilapidated rooms and empty corridors. The nostalgia of 'Lost in Play' finds other resonances, such as the opening of the penultimate track, 'Pillars of Salt' (10:35), which reflects on the passing of 1960s counterculture, combining the lyrics 'retrospect and contemplation/In places now hard to find' with the refrain 'which way did the sixties go?', complemented by posters of The Beatles' *Let It Be* and Jimi Hendrix in the CD booklet. A rhythm of loss and recapture pulses through *Songs from the Bilston House*, pushing it towards the self-searching and imaginative acts of recovery on Fish's post-Marillion albums.

There are other routes to the melancholia of 'Lost in Play', such as the title track on The Tangent's second album, *The World That We Drive Through* (2004), which combines flute, piano and guitar to create a deeply emotional song: the singer and his lover lose themselves at dusk to discover that the city has lost its familiar shape, the natural world looks strange, and dreams and reality have fused together. 'The World That We Drive Through' blends folk, jazz, ambient and new wave with an extended version of prog rock reminiscent of the early 1970s incarnations of King Crimson and Genesis, brought together in a long track (12:58) that is impossible to categorize. Guy Manning's vocals are earthier than those of his former band member Andy Tillison, and 'Lost in Play' (7:05) is a tighter song than many of The Tangent's compositions. It opens with an image of a child playing, oblivious to the 'midnight blues', and then shifts into the first person in the second verse, where 'worries are far away' from this pastoral playground. The third verse is more ominous: the child is pursued by the (possibly imaginary) 'catcher man'; although the child cannot be caught as he runs through the rivers and mountainside, there is a sense that time is catching up with him. This is reinforced in the fourth verse – now it is 'sometime later as the sun goes down on me' – and we move to an adult perspective in which the singer must call on 'dreams and fantasy'. The repeated refrain 'please don't fade away' suggests a desperate attempt to hold on to memories, but the adult singer can console himself with this dream-like past ('still not faded away') and lose himself in musical play.

On another tangent, the engagement with folk music by alternative rock bands of the mid-1990s was preceded by what is widely known in continental Europe as 'neo-folk'. This is a variegated genre not really accepted by many of its practitioners as an adequate description, particularly as it is connected variously to goth, folk and industrial music. Rob Young writes about English groups such as Coil and Current 93 as part of a 'diaspora from the industrial scene of the late 1970s', arguing that their interest in shamanic practice, occultism and other submerged religious traditions echoes earlier folk traditions in England.[7] Young goes on to note Current 93's turn to acoustic, non-Western instruments and the band's retention of industrial musical sources such as tapes, drones and arrays of percussion, together with an interest in resuscitating English mystic and visionary thinkers who are largely outside of any movement or tradition.[8] He also sees visual and musical references to The Incredible String Band and Comus in the late 1960s and early 1970s (both are present in the visuals and text of Current 93's 1988 album *Earth Covers Earth*), but, other than commenting on the instrumentation, Young never clearly indicates why Current 93 should be labelled as 'folk'. He echoes David Keenan's study *England's Hidden Reverse* (2003) by arguing that the band taps into a hidden stream of radical illumination from England's past, but he does not link the aims of progressive rock to folk on any meaningful level.[9] This is crucial because Current 93 fuses earlier radical folk music with themes from industrial music in a properly progressive fusion. Rather than leaving behind industrial music (partly because they were never really in it), albums such as *Soft Black Stars* (1998) explicitly demonstrate that there is a knowledge, a set of practices, and ways of living hidden in the noise of consumer society.

This trend is shared by Death in June, Sol Invictus, Fire and Ice, Blood Axis, and The Moon Lay Hidden Beneath the Clouds, as well as a range of groups across Europe that followed in the wake of Current 93. The violence that is deemed inherent to nature, humanity or society is also hidden away, to the detriment of authentic living (in an echo of Georges Bataille's theory of the

Current 93, *Earth Covers Earth* (1988). Artwork by Ruth Bayer.

'accursed share', wherein the universe is based on a principle of waste, death, sacrifice and eroticism).[10] It is hidden away by the pernicious violence of rationalized capitalist society, and hence the ambiguous use of Nazi imagery by these bands as a means of opening a crack through which shock value can expose widespread social violence. Current 93 is not in this category, though, and its use of swastikas on *Swastikas for Goddy* (1987) is a return to the Hindu meaning (the swastika reversed is a Hindu sacrament and lucky charm) and is often couched in ways that deflate its fascist co-option, even when the rest of the arcane imagery is serious.

David Tibet, the driving force, lyricist and conceptualizer of Current 93, combines so many influences and traditions that it is impractical to favour some over others. Young discusses some of these connections, and we would add the specific reworkings of folk songs along with the sixteenth- and seventeenth-century music of John Dowland and William Lawes, which most strikingly informs Current 93's recordings of the early to mid-1990s. In this period, the many progressive interests of David Tibet surfaced tangentially in the form of long narrative and conceptual works. The mid-1990s also saw Current 93 present its version of the traditional Scottish song 'Tam Lin', following earlier renderings by Fairport Convention, Steeleye Span and The Watersons. This fable of metamorphosis, violence and redemption was part of the darker side of folk probed by Comus, Dave and Toni Arthur, The Watersons, and June Tabor, as well as by Pentangle, the Irish group Mellow Candle and, occasionally, Fairport Convention. This focus on the darker and more mysterious side of nature (exemplified by the 1973 British horror film *The Wicker Man*, which combined shocking visuals with a variety of folk tunes played by multi-instrumental band Magnet) meant that 1960s and 1970s folk was already a sort of neo-folk, and often linked closely to progressive rock as it sought a selective reference to the past that made the music into a new progressive intervention. The key to the term 'neo-folk' is that the music so described traps elements of folk to make something else of them. Even if the sounds might hark back to an instrumental past, this is a past that never was – or was never heard.

In 1994, Current 93 brought out two EPs, *Tamlin* and *Lucifer over London*, the second of which explores an arcane ghost that hovers either above or in wait, and also the colossal album *Of Ruine or Some Blazing Starre*, which brought together all the Current 93 tributaries mentioned above. This album documents a metaphysical quest to see what is beyond the here and now, a quest that contains both violence and the beholding of the face of God. Its narrator moves through space and time; its occasional references to specific places barely function as markers and do not ground the overall search in material reality. This is not just an individual quest but a sign of the greater existence of an earth that offers forth potentially apocalyptic knowledge, as indicated by the British outsider artist Charles Sims' paintings that frame the album, set centrally on the gatefold sleeve of the original vinyl release.

The first side of the album charts a process of spiritual quest, including false turns and a growing sense of the importance of locatedness; the range of specific locations gives way to the narrator's growing sense of being part of a reality that cannot be understood by using reason and physical senses. Part of the wrong path is a fall into an obsession with death, which by side two is revealed as a necessary stage, as visions of blood no longer drive a dark occult version of hopeless and permanent death but instead make up a universe throbbing with life ('All the World Makes Great Blood'). The narrator reframes the band's position on the created cosmologies and becomes capable of communicating some essence of the growth and quest of the universe on a post-cognitive level. The closing sequence of three sections proclaims the meaninglessness of death, and the prospect of hope in the shape of God's universe that awaits at the end of a long and difficult path. The penultimate track declares the meaninglessness of what we imagine to be the real world ('So, This Empire Is Nothing'), and the profane, properly mundane world gives way to the ocean, the sunset and canopies of stars on the closing 'This Shining Shining World'.

The album is undoubtedly a personal statement of coming to a Christian revelation of sorts. But, for those on the outside of this theological worldview, it conveys its message through the literal paratexts of apocalyptic yet hopeful art, the meditative music of the seventeenth century, and David Tibet's tendency to refer to songs or albums from earlier in his career. The returns and repetitions of acoustic guitar themes anchored by tidal drones indicate a deeper sense of time beyond human comprehension, reflecting the attempt to capture this time shared by many neo-folk and progressive folk bands discussed in Chapter 3. Most literally, this takes the form of traditional, acoustic or atypical instrumentation, together with many visual and auditory references to cyclical, geological or mystical time. So while we might question the term 'neo-folk', we can see a distinction between post-industrial folk and its 1960s and 1970s precursors in that the later bands look to universal, seasonal and cyclical elements without referring to specific histories with localized roots. Just as with many, if not all, progressive rock styles, this trend needs representing by the greater scale and ambition of releases such as *Of Ruine or Some Blazing Starre*, and by the stretching out of the ambitions of both industrial and folk music in the context of highly virtuosic and epic narratives.

The scene looks slightly different in North America, where a number of bands emerged in the 2000s to push progressive rock in very different directions to the neo-prog mode of the bands Asia, Spock's Beard and Transatlantic. Examples of avant-garde folk are scattered geographically across the US, from Boston's Sunburned Hand of the Man (the 2009 *A Grand Tour of Tunisia* album plays with noise, polyphony and performance poetry across extended tracks) and Baltimore's Animal Collective (the psychedelic folk of Animal Collective's 2004 album *Sung Tongs* was enhanced by the band's interest in live multimedia performances and by its members' habit of wearing masks and face paint on stage in the early 2000s) to 'new weird America' groups such as No-Neck Blues Band from New York and Davenport from Wisconsin. The most interesting American connections to progressive folk are through the Pacific Northwest indie scene in the early 2000s. These connections are not always obvious when first listening to groups from Seattle and Portland such as Fleet Foxes, The Shins, Band of Horses and others on the Sub Pop label (founded in the mid-1980s and best known for promoting grunge bands in the early 1990s). Their songs tend to have pop structures and lush vocal harmonies, but there are obvious links to The Byrds, Crosby, Stills and Nash, The Band and America in their musical textures and West Coast vibe – as well as unexpected elements. Fleet Foxes' self-titled album of 2008, for example, focuses on the natural world ('Sun It Rises', 'White Winter Hymnal', 'Ragged Wood', 'Meadowlarks') and geographical sites (the Tennessee Mountains and Barringer Hill in Central Texas), but darker forces puncture the rural harmony. This is exemplified on 'Tiger Mountain Peasant Song', which begins as a gentle acoustic ballad. The singer wonders where a group of 'wanderers' are going as they pass by him in the 'cold mountain air', and he then shifts to a meditation on physical frailty and 'premonitions of my death'. The song lurches towards anguish in the repeated line 'I don't know what I have done/I'm turning myself to a demon' (this might mean 'turning towards a demon' or 'turning into a demon') and ends as mellifluously as it began. This complex and ambiguous pastoral is signalled by the choice of cover artwork: a detail from Dutch Renaissance painter Pieter Bruegel the Elder's *Netherlandish Proverbs* (1559) injects demonic and destructive forces into what at first glance seems a harmonious scene of village life.[11]

The Decemberists are the most obvious of the northwestern bands to explore large concepts through a fusion of folk and rock elements, although this can also be glimpsed elsewhere in mainstream US rock – in The White Stripes and REM and a number of indie bands and performers such as Devendra Banhart and Sufjan Stevens who are interested in revivifying the rhythms of roots music.[12] Based in Portland, The Decemberists draw extensively on English, Scottish and Irish folk tales, combining religious and pagan themes shot through with violence and transformations. The Decemberists deploy a wide range of traditional instruments (accordion, violin, upright bass, glockenspiel) and a mixture of regular and odd electronic instruments (theremin, Wurlitzer, Obermeier synthesizer, Hammond organ) that make the band difficult to classify musically. They do not cite progressive rock explicitly among major reference points, but 1960s British folk rock is a discernible influence on lyricist and lead singer Colin Meloy's vocals. Sounding more West Country than Pacific Coast in his timbre, Meloy cites British folk singer Shirley Collins as a particular inspiration. He revived Collins's 1959 ballad 'Barbara Allen' on his 2006 solo tour, but also references Norma Waterson's and Martin Carthy's versions of 'Barbary Allen' in his phrasing and delivery. This contact with the past is reflected in the sepia tones and retro artwork on the band's first two albums, *Castaways and Cutouts* (2002) and *Her Majesty The Decemberists* (2003) and inflected through the dramatic interchanges between male and female vocals. The past is also explored on *Picaresque* (2005) through old-fashioned songs about barrow boys, bagmen, mariners, bandit queens and engine drivers, and their interest in retelling old stories, such as the resuscitation of a Japanese folk story for the three-part title track of the 2006 album *The Crane Wife*. This tendency might be seen to reflect Shirley and Dolly Collins's influential album *Anthems in Eden* (1969) in rescuing lost tales and forgotten music, but The Decemberists challenge the audience's expectation of what constitutes a stable musical genre and what musical tradition might mean in the twenty-first century. On this level, they share connections with other neo-folk bands, as well as to a particular cultural milieu that gave rise to the Portland multi-artist collective Red 76, founded in 2000 with the mission to use local spaces creatively for 'gatherings, masking, and public dialogue'.[13] The pantomimic qualities of the artwork on *Picaresque*, the band members presenting themselves as a cast of characters, and Meloy's propensity for wordplay ('There are angels in your angles'; 'I'm a legionnaire, camel in disrepair, hoping for a Frigidaire') suggest an attempt to introduce rough humour into what might otherwise be reverence for the past. Concepts are mined with an eye to narrative detail and storytelling, but dark comedy often draws the band towards macabre and violent subject matter, such as the 11-minute 'Mariner's Revenge Song', on which the band acts out a pantomime whale on stage.[14]

The clearest example of this storytelling ambition is *The Tain*, a five-part, 18-minute track released on an EP in 2004. *The Tain* takes its subject from the pre-Christian Irish prose epic that relates a battle between Ulster and Connacht. The myth centres on Queen Maeve's cattle raid on Ulster and the young Hound of Culainn's defence of the scared bull. The Irish folk-rock band Horslips released a musical version, *The Táin*, in 1973, which moves between traditional Irish reels and jigs and electronic music akin to that of Hawkwind in order to explore the phases and textures of the epic story. Whereas Horslips retells the myth in the sleeve notes, acknowledges its centrality to Irish folklore and reverentially quotes W. B. Yeats, The Decemberists explore the text at some distance. The band released a video using silhouette animation by Andy Smetanka (deliberately echoing the style of Lotte Reiniger's 1926 pioneering animated film *The Adventures of Prince Achmed*) that visually links the song to its source text, particularly to Queen Maeve's supernatural raising of her army. However, the offbeat lyrics and various voices (crone, husband, captain, soldier and widow) construct a dramatic narrative of betrayal and conflict that refers obliquely to the Irish legend, with only occasional explicit references to the setting loose of the hound in part three and the mother's sow in part five.[15] Indexed by the EP's cover image of a rural Oregon with a heavy, opaque sky, it is impossible to re-create the original text from The Decemberists' version. The myth works merely as a catalyst to set off a series of lyrical and musical currents. We hear Black Sabbath in the opening bass riff in part one, Led Zeppelin in part two, a folk-rock elegy in part three, glimmers of Kurt Weill in the vocals and accordion of part four, and a complete musical mix in part five, before the coda returns to the opening bass riff. This is not pastiche or homage but a version of post-progression in which the source text is impossible to extract from its cultural mediations.

The Decemberists took the extended form further on *Hazards of Love* (2009), which relates a supernatural love story over a double album, its cover adorned by a thick tangle of branches and trunks that spell out the title against a plain black background. The narrative is carefully structured: a formal prelude, a traditional setting of 'Offa's Way' in which the 'true love' goes 'riding out', a choric narrator, familiar folk iconography, and a number of interlude pieces and reprises of the title track in different voices. The album's title derives from Nottinghamshire folk singer Anne Briggs' a-cappella EP *Hazards of Love* (1964), but, as Alexis Petridis notes, the project 'seems to have grown out of control', entangling the mythology of seduction and natality with themes of violence and revenge.[16] Meloy's act of creative extension gives rise to a story that is as entangled as the branches on the front cover. The music is similarly hybrid, but Petridis is not quite right when he notes that the folk and prog elements sit uncomfortably with 'tumescent blues-rock' and 'sludgy metal riffs' that remind him of an unconvincing take on Black Sabbath played 'dead straight'. Rather, the album is at once a profound meditation on the complexities of love and a wry take on a number of musical and lyrical styles, extending (as Petridis notes) the shape-shifting theme into the level of form.

Another American band that straddles avant-rock and progressive folk is the five-piece band Midlake, from North Texas. Midlake's first album, *Banman and Silvercock* (2004), mixes jazz, rock and electronica with the pastoral flute opening on 'Kingfish Pies' and Tim Smith's quasi-Radiohead vocals on 'I'll Guess I'll Take Care'. Midlake initially worked with DIY ensemble composition, but structured guitar and piano come to the fore on the next two albums, *The Trials of Van Occupanther* (2006) and *The Courage of Others* (2010). The former assumes the mythical character of Van Occupanther, who presides over the album without ever becoming the central character, even though he has his own track on which he wishes to 'stay out of sight for a long time', after being 'too consumed with this world'. The album offers a pastoral retreat from industrialism and capitalism. 'Roscoe', the opening track, is undergirded by a chugging bass and a lyrical lead guitar reminiscent of mid-1970s Fleetwood Mac, but the lyrics are more arcane; the singer imagines what his life would be like if he had been born in the late nineteenth century with the 'productive' name Roscoe. The focus is on a self-made abode in a remote village, repaired by mountaineers but now surrounded by chemicals. This pastoral reverie continues in the third and longest track, 'Head Home'

(5:45), which has a similar tempo to 'Roscoe' and yearns for pre-industrial 'honest work/And a roof that never leaks'. The organic instrumentation and harmonies are lush, the scene is of farming at harvest time, and the dominant emotion is desire for a 'comfortable bed' and a young woman who quietly reads Thomas Hobbes's 1651 political tract *Leviathan* to counter (it seems) Hobbes's famous claim that life is 'solitary, poor, nasty, brutish and short'.[17] The young woman returns on the folk-rock song 'Young Bride', but the narrator wonders why her shoulders are like those of 'a tired old woman' and her fingers are 'of the hedge in winter'. The relationship between the singer and the 'young bride' is not disclosed, but in a song inflected by a mournful violin it is clear that hard labour has shortened the youth and joy of this young woman (this is ironic, given the reference to *Leviathan*). There is no polluting industrialism here, but on the next track, 'Branches', it is clear that there will be no marriage, 'because she won't have me'. Time speeds up and slows down across the album; seasons change, and the past moves in and out of focus. Tim Smith reflects on 'We Gathered in Spring' that 'no-one lives to be three hundred years/Like the way it used to be', but from his hill-side vantage point (a hill now filled with greed and of which the singer has grown tired) he glimpses his house and wife as shades of the past.

Cover of Midlake, *The Courage of Others* (2010).

Midlake's follow-up release, *The Courage of Others*, is an even stronger contender as a progressive folk album. Musically, it harks back to Fairport Convention of the early 1970s, even though Smith's vocals are more plaintive than any of Fairport's singers, and his flute more melancholic than either Peter Gabriel's or Ian Anderson's, pushing the band towards Radiohead's post-progressive angst (they cite Radiohead as an early influence, along with Björk, Clinic and The Flaming Lips).[18] But the album is a distinct departure from Radiohead's aesthetics of alienation. The cover presents the band as a brotherhood of bearded and hooded druids in a wooded retreat; the mirror image doubles the number of band members and lends the pastoral retreat a mystical-psychedelic mood as the druids pass a totemic object between them, which might be a life-giving chalice or an urn symbolizing death and physical passing.

The lyrics of *The Courage of Others* work through a moral relationship with the earth and a yearning to be at one with nature. As on *Van Occupanther*, these 'trials' are brought about by the callous 'acts of men' (the title of the opening track), which 'cause the ground to break open'. However, the singer realizes that the quest for mystical unity cannot wait, because the natural world has already started to 'fade' and 'falter'. This deep ecology reflects the lyrics of Yes in the early 1970s but here leads to an explicit retreat from contemporary society in a quest to find the 'core of nature'. The melancholic lyrics are sometimes consumed by the rapturous quality of the music, with lapping waves of instruments and frequent transitions between acoustic and electric instruments offering an organic pulse that resonates through the album. However, although he is awe-struck in the face of nature and willing to align his values to the soil, the singer believes he does not have the capacity to fully commune with the natural world. On 'Small Mountain', Smith seeks a vanished 'land of gold' and tries to recapture 'a way of life that was common for all', but he realizes that he lacks 'the courage of others' and is hampered by his education (on the title track, he admits he has been 'taught to worry about . . . the many things [he] can't control'). The Gaia principle is evident on 'Core of Nature', in which the singer does more than just inhabit nature: he 'will wear the sun/Ancient light through these woods', even though he realizes that 'no earthly mind can enter'. This mystical union is complicated by spiritual and moral self-doubt, making the relationship simultaneously universal ('man', 'men' and 'rulers' are evoked; specific times and places are avoided) and intensely personal: the singer walks through the woods alone, he 'want[s] to be left to do [his] own ways' ('Rulers, Ruling all Things'), there is no young woman on this album, and he is isolated from a wider community – and this despite the depiction of the brotherhood on the album cover and the harmonies on 'Children of the Grounds', which suggest the group are in this quest together.

This questing motif and mystical connections to the natural world are also evident on Canadian folk band The Acorn's 2007 album *Glory Hope Mountain*.

Formed in 2003, The Acorn has a less direct route to progressive folk, but the band's music and themes refer back just as they are taken in new directions. *Glory Hope Mountain* draws its concept from lead singer Rolf Klausener's Honduran mother Gloria Esperanza Montoya, whose name translates as the album title. A travelling album, it tells of Montoya's journey through illness, abuse at the hands of her father, hardship, and diasporic passage from South America to Canada. This is not a complete narrative but takes vignettes from Montoya's life, moving from 1950s Honduras to present-day Montreal.[19] Linking in some ways to the Ottawa music scene, many of the songs possess a rhythm that veers between Paul Simon's Latin American album *The Rhythm of the Saints* (1990), David Byrne's self-formed music label Luaka Bop, and the kind of Native American quest narrative popularized by Kiowa Indian writer N. Scott Momaday, whose *The Way to Rainy Mountain* (1969) tells of a personal quest by retracing his tribal past and his grandmother's physical journey from Montana to Oklahoma. Like Midlake, The Acorn plays its music straight, without the wryness of The Decemberists and without the weight of explicit literary references.[20] Keyboards and drums are enhanced by a range of traditional instruments, including ukulele and marimba, propelled by traditional Honduran folk rhythms, Garifunan chants and West African influences that push The Acorn towards world music (although it is more discernibly indie folk on the 2010 album *No Ghost*). Many of the tracks on *Glory Hope Mountain* are 4 to 5 minutes long, but they have a conceptual and rhythmical unity that moves from the gentle piano and percussion that begin the first track, 'Hold Your Breath' (telling of Montoya's difficult birth); through the Honduran rhythms that give life to Montoya's brother Napoleon (who is unable to travel easily because of his polio-affected 'Crooked Legs'); and through the two-part 'The Flood', which forms the second and penultimate track of the album, making this an ecological album as well as a generational quest narrative.

Another example of the fusion of different national roots is the Shanghai band Cold Fairyland, which draws from the idioms of 1970s European progressive rock to inflect a dedication to traditional Chinese instruments and syncopation. Partly shaped by Shanghai's unique fusion of East and West and the distinctive 'Haipai' metropolitan style, which looks simultaneously to the past and the future, Cold Fairyland's dual interest is in Chinese legends and modernity in both their authentic and inauthentic forms.[21] This ambivalence is inflected in the band's name, which derives from Japanese author Haruki Murakami's 1985 magical novel *Cold Fairyland and the End of the World* (best known in translation as *Hard-Boiled Wonderland and the End of the World*). Band leader Lin Di describes the band's name as a reflection of not only how the world has 'materially developed and industrially developed' but also how it can easily become 'very cold and indifferent'.[22] This ambivalence is illustrated by the art-gallery scene on the cover of their first full album, *Kingdom of Benevolent Strangers* (2003), which emphasizes the surfaces of modernity as fashionable young Chinese women pass by older women in traditional dress. Musically, Cold Fairyland moves between tightly structured rock compositions, involving the five-piece band, and melodious folk songs pivoting around Lin Di's four-stringed lute. Together with a cello, the lute is the focal point on a series of tracks on *Seeds on the Ground* (2008) that reflect upon the natural world, not as a retreat from modernity but as a spiritual re-engagement along the lines of The Acorn and Midlake. Cold Fairyland's two styles of rock and folk were both on display during performances at the 2010 Shanghai Expo, whereas a fusion of folk and new age characterizes Lin Di's three solo albums, shifting between domestic and intimate reflections on *Meet in Secret Garden* (2009) and mythical quests conveyed by traditional Chinese instruments on *Ten Days in Magic Land* (2002) and *Bride in Legend* (2004).

If progressive folk tends to move outwards to world music and onwards away from the familiar reference points of 1970s progressive rock, then in our final example it moves inwards and downwards. Like Lin Di and Tori Amos, the Californian singer-harpist Joanna Newsom was classically trained and composes primarily for the harp, sometimes accompanied by piano, orchestral strings or unobtrusive percussion. The clearest reference points for Newsom's vocals are Joni Mitchell, Kate Bush and Björk, as heard on the three songs 'In California', 'Only Skin' and 'Cosmia' respectively, but Newsom also develops the folk styles of Vashti Bunyan, Mary Margaret O'Hara and Texas Gladden (who, as Jeanette Leech notes, accompanied folk collector Alan Lomax on his field recordings), and she knowingly echoes Joan Baez's 'Diamonds & Rust' (1975) in the phrasing of 'Sawdust & Diamonds' (2006).[23] Despite these echoes of earlier female vocalists and her work with producer Van Dyke Parks that loops back to the Beach Boys of the late 1960s, as well as to the feel of Van Morrison's *Astral Weeks* (1968) and Roy Harper's *Stormcock* (1971), Newsom relies on frequent changes of tempo, pitch, volume, rhythm and phrasing to create an idiosyncratic vocal that weaves through songs preoccupied with existential themes of life and death. Newsom's third, self-produced, triple album, *Have One on Me* (2010), is perhaps her most ambitious, but her second album, *Ys* (2006), offers the strongest links to progressive folk. This album self-consciously presents itself as a mythical construct, from the reference to the mythical lost French city Ys in the title and a still-life portrait of Newsom by Benjamin Vierling on the cover, which combines a Dutch Renaissance painterly style with 'a subtle radiance of tone', achieved through the use of oil and glaze, and rich symbolism that echoes Mark Wilkinson's artwork on early Marillion albums.[24]

Ys does not have an overarching narrative pattern, but Newsom describes the project as 'a fictional narrative. It was an effort on my part to organize and score and . . . articulate a year of my life [that began to assert] synchronicity and real shape'.[25] The album comprises five extended tracks (between 7 and 16 minutes each) with loose yet discernible structures that reflect Newsom's

Joanna Newsom, *Ys* (2006). Artwork by Benjamin Vierling, www.bvierling.com

interest in polyphony and the West African kora. These rhythms structure
elliptical stories, often framed within a pastoral tradition, with surprising
twists. For example, 'Emily' begins the album with a pastoral scene in which
the observer feels comfortable with the natural world and her companion,
Emily, possibly an imaginary or ghostly figure (even though the character
is named after her sister). Emily meets the singer by the river and teaches
her the power and the physical properties of the meteorite. This is a song
frozen in time but timeless in its symbolic reach. Occasionally jarring images
upset the natural order: Pharaohs and Pharisees enter from nowhere in the
first stanza; baboons are mentioned alongside farm and moor animals; the
ties that bind the singer and Emily are 'barbed and spined'; and the lyric
'hydrocephalitic listlessness' pushes Newsom's languorous delivery towards
an excess of fecundity and poetic meaning.

Desire, fantasy, loneliness and death are running themes through the
album, particularly on the longest song, 'Only Skin', and on the closing track
'Cosmia', which returns us to the river of the opening track. The river is a
complex symbol of loss, grief, cleansing and renewal that links to the singer's
request for assistance from the mythical Cosmia. We can read this deep

exploration of natural cycles as neo-folk and post-progressive at the same time, but it also exceeds generic conventions, as Leech argues about Newsom's next album, *Have One on Me*.[26] More specifically, the elemental force in 'Cosmia' parallels the summoning of angels Gabriel, Raphael, Michael and Uriel to protect the protagonist within a 'circle of fire' on Kate Bush's *The Red Shoes*, but Newsom changes the elemental focus to push us further back towards, and also deeper into, the water imagery and mystical ecology of Yes's *Close to the Edge*.

Notes

1. See *The Appalachians*, three parts (PBS, 2005), *Folk Britannia*, three parts (BBC, 2006), *We Dreamed America* (Brickwall Films, 2008) and *Folk America*, three parts (BBC, 2009).

2. Benjamin Filene, *Romancing the Folk: Public Memory and American Roots Music* (Chapel Hill: University of North Carolina Press, 2000), 3. Filene notes that in 1993 both Red Hot Chili Peppers and Soul Asylum claimed that they were reinventing folk idioms: ibid., 235.

3. Curved Air was also billed at the 2009 Doncaster Rocks festival but did not play.

4. Young, *Electric Eden*, 567.

5. Pete Seeger, 'The Purist vs. the Hybridist' (1957–8), in *The Incompleat Folksinger*, ed. Jo Metcalf Schwartz (New York: Simon & Schuster, 1973), 174–5.

6. The four long tracks on The Tangent's first album, *The Music That Died Alone* (2003), emphasize the eclecticism of some contemporary progressive bands, including a pastiche of the Canterbury scene on 'The Canterbury Sequence' (8.06). Prior to The Tangent, Guy Manning was a member of Parallel or 90 Degrees (Po90) – a band that claims that there is as much Radiohead and Nine Inch Nails in their sound as there is Pink Floyd or Van der Graaf Generator (www.po90.com) – and, with Andy Tillison, Manning released an album of Peter Hammill covers, *No More Travelling Chess* (2001).

7. Young, *Electric Eden*, 602.

8. Ibid., 602–3.

9. See David Keenan, *England's Hidden Reverse: A Secret History of the Esoteric Underground* (London: SAF Publishing, 2003).

10. See Georges Bataille, *The Accursed Share* (New York: Zone, [1947] 1991).

11. Tom Milway, 'DiScover', *Drowned in Sound* (2008): drownedinsound.com/in_depth/3442778. Fleet Foxes' use of Pieter Bruegel the Elder echoes the late 1960s American psychedelic folk band Pearls Before Swine: Bruegel's painting *The Triumph of Death* (c. 1562) features on Pearls Before Swine's anti-war concept album *Balaklava* (1968), following the Hieronymus Bosch cover of its debut album, *One Nation Underground* (1967).

12. Jack White appeared as a wandering Southern mandolin player in the Civil War period film *Cold Mountain* (2003).

13. See Red 76's website: www.red76.com.

14. *The Decemberists: A Practical Handbook* DVD (Kill Rock Stars, 2007).

15. For the music video for *The Tain*, see *The Decemberists: A Practical Handbook*, as well as the video of 'The Bachelor and the Bride', which uses the same silhouette animation.

16. Alexis Petridis, 'Sirrah, Wilt Thou Headbang?', the *Guardian*, Film and Music (20 March 2009), 9.

17. In a 2007 interview, Midlake's singer and lyricist, Tim Smith, claimed he did not know

Hobbes's *Leviathan* and this lyric references a random poem he was reading, but Hobbes's tract fits well as a contrast to the sentiment of 'Head Home': www.avclub.com/articles/tim-smith-of-midlake,14146/.

18. 'Gearwire goes SXSW: Midlake' (17 May 2006), www.gearwire.com/midlake.html.

19. Michael Barclay, 'Family Affairs', *On the Cover* (October 2007): exclaim.ca/Features/OnTheCover/acorn-family_affairs.

20. Ibid.

21. For discussion of the aesthetics of 'Haipai' or the 'Shanghai style', see Lynn Pan, *Shanghai Style: Art and Design between the Wars* (Hong Kong: Joint Publishing Co Ltd, 2008).

22. Interview with Cold Fairyland, www.coldfairyland.com/interview/20050329.htm.

23. Leech, *Seasons They Change*, 249.

24. Interview with Benjamin Vierling, www.fromamouth.com/milkymoon/specials/ysart.

25. 'Visions of Joanna', *House of Skronk* (6 November 2008): skronkadelic.wordpress.com.

26. Leech, *Seasons They Change*, 278.

Chapter 14

The Metal Progression

Heavy metal was spawned from overdriven blues, where guitar riffs and solos became structuring devices and where percussion took off from the polyrhythmic jazz drumming of Elvin Jones. The first wave of heavy rock emerged in the second half of the 1960s and featured The Jimi Hendrix Experience, Cream, Blue Cheer, The Who and Vanilla Fudge, followed at the end of the decade by a first wave of British heavy metal in the shape of Deep Purple, Led Zeppelin and Black Sabbath. In heavy metal and heavy rock we see clearly the decline attributed to progressive rock: a creative growth phase followed by a loss of direction in the mid-1970s in the face of commercial success and inflated virtuosity when playing to hundreds of thousands of fans in massive stadia. These bands all followed the road to excess, but they also extended the rock format, often containing a strongly narrative and conceptual base and, initially at least, using instrumental skill for formal development. Just as Deep Purple splintered into Rainbow, Whitesnake and Gillan, Black Sabbath replaced vocalist Ozzy Osbourne with Ronnie James Dio in 1979, and Led Zeppelin faltered and then disbanded with the death of John Bonham in 1980, so the New Wave of British Heavy Metal (NWOBHM) emerged as an outcrop of punk's reaction to stadium rock. This period also mirrored new developments in progressive rock, with neo-prog bands and NWOBHM emerging at the same moment and playing on shared festival bills. But as the progressive rock of the mid-1970s fell away from public attention, so metal began to diversify, infiltrate and expand on different rock forms, just as prog had done around 1970. By the 1990s and 2000s metal had given rise to many new subgenres that contained progressive elements.

Among thrash, death, doom, symphonic, black, ambient and other metals is an amorphous category of 'progressive metal', which refers to progressive rock but indicates that it has grown from a process of convergent evolution: in other words, its forms and practices resemble those of prog, but its ancestor is the darker and less obviously socially progressive heavy metal. Progressive metal covers a range from Dream Theater (a band that is both metal and progressive) through Tool, The Mars Volta, Porcupine Tree, black metal, some parts of symphonic metal, math rock, hardcore variants of metal, and post-rock precision music. The term is too capacious to usefully identify emergent types of progressive rock; it serves more as a marker within metal that indicates a crossover to prog audiences. This chapter discusses how similar processes of 'progressing' occur both in metal and in the classic phase of progressive rock: increasing complexity in musical content, form and lyrics; tendency to narration; group composition and improvisation; multiple changes of key, rhythm and song form; and albums composed as organic wholes, integrating artwork, lyrics, music and even the recording format. Metal is almost as interested as prog in narratives, and shares many of its characteristics. But instead of looking for shared roots, in this final chapter we will track progressive rock both in and as metal from the late 1980s onwards.

This mode began gradually at first, as Iron Maiden started to expand its lyrical horizons from *Piece of Mind* (1983) onwards to include war, horror and science-fiction stories, although not with the same reflective purpose as Rush. Side one of Iron Maiden's 1984 album *Powerslave* mostly concerns war, whereas side two is dominated by the title track's evocation of ancient Egypt (as depicted on the cover art) and the 'Rime of the Ancient Mariner' (13:32), which includes a reading of part of Samuel Taylor Coleridge's 1798 narrative poem in the middle. Iron Maiden developed its progressive side on the 1988 album *Seventh Son of a Seventh Son*, linking together tracks through the theme of the album title and making more extensive use of synthesizers, and the band continued to play with concepts and extended tracks up to *The Final Frontier* (2010). Halfway between NWOBHM and neo-prog were Magnum and the short-lived Saracen, whose *Heroes, Saints and Fools* (1982) showed the way forward for progressive metal in emphasizing riffs and building instrumental landscapes around them. Diamond Head was more influential on metal, disinterring the drawn-out power riffs of Black Sabbath in a lyrical world dominated by fantasy and medieval themes (accompanied by the fantasy artwork of Rodney Matthews, who also created the cover art for Magnum's *On a Storyteller's Night*). By the time of the *Canterbury* album of 1983, Diamond Head's sound was more literally reminiscent of prog, sometimes more pop-orientated or continuing with the riffs of *Borrowed Time* (1982). *Canterbury* is the first marker of progressive rock's re-emerging from a genuinely metal starting point in its hybridity and fusion of rock forms. As the 1980s went on, metal bands often alternated between heavier tracks and radio-friendly singles (Van Halen, for example) or combined a return to stomping glam rock with newer metal approaches and lyrical interests, but this is not quite the same as fusions that keep several genres in play.

An essential moment in the late 1980s version of progressive metal was Seattle band Queensrÿche's concept album *Operation: Mindcrime* (1988). This album punctuates the choral guitars of Iron Maiden, the bass riffs of Diamond Head and the pop of hair metal with sound collages, together with an ambience and paranoid suspicion of authority redolent of Pink Floyd's *The Wall*. Queensrÿche also looks forward to Dream Theater and sideways to the concerns about mind control frequently addressed in industrial music. The album's concept is that the narrator has been brainwashed into murdering people, with the intent to bring about a revolution that will destroy the corrupt world of capitalism and religion. As the story progresses, the narrator develops a conscience and experiences an emotional awakening. For all the violent futility of his unwanted killing mission, the narrative is sharply critical of American society: 'Spreading the Disease' not only attacks US military interventionism, capitalism and hypocrisy around prostitution but also delves into clerical abuse. The lyrics on the album's first half are as politically transgressive as much industrial music, the music becoming more experimental in the longer tracks at the centre. Where the album is not so politically radical is in the love interest, Mary, who goes from being a prostitute to other exploitations, becoming the narrator's fantasy before she is killed. This figure has a more interesting role (and voice) as a ghost in the 2006 sequel *Operation: Mindcrime II*, which has a very complex centrepiece where brainwasher 'X' and narrator-assassin Nikki confront each other, raising questions of guilt and complicity, even though the theme of redemption crossed with revenge is underdeveloped. The music, too, while acknowledging newer types of metal, harks back to the earlier album, perhaps purposefully but not particularly creatively.

The 1980s saw the growth of dense virtuosity in metal, as thrash, speed and death metal sped up, and as it crossed into and out of hardcore. The journey out of hardcore also led to doom metal, with Neurosis's *Souls at Zero* (1992) taking a dual route on tracks that amalgamate and cut between styles, and others that settle into circling, punishing band riffs. The lyrical focus of metal became harsher, attacking political, social and religious limitations on action and thought, and gradually those forms stretched, most notably in the guise of Atheist and Voivod, both of which began to produce albums combining a range of musical genres.[1] Atheist's second album, *Unquestionable Presence* (1991), develops the lyrical concerns of thrash, death and metal: the need to expose the hypocrisy, power and corruption of organized religion, politics and the common-sense ideas of the masses, in favour of total individual freedom. Musically, stop-start punctuations are framed by riffs reminiscent of King Crimson's mid-1970s period. Although none of the tracks are particularly long, styles are mixed at a fierce pace, from fleeting Iron Maiden dual guitars to hardcore and black metal (the title track is a good example of these crossings), and even structures that recall the harsher end of free jazz. Atheist's third album, *Elements* (1993), pushes this further, even featuring a samba track and arguably overdoing the eclecticism of *Unquestionable Presence*. But on both albums, the closest point to jazz is not the 'jazzy' sounds of the slap bass but the emphasis on change as the central structuring device. As with the progressive rock of the late 1960s, Atheist stretched out the thrash form of the mid-1980s and created a fusion that maintains rather than merges genres: the combination becomes a musical, compositional device, not just a method or style.

The post-thrash sound of Atheist (from Florida) and Voivod (from Quebec) is principally an extension of hardcore stop-start strategies in Black Flag and Nomeansno. Working backwards from math rock, post-rock and later metals, we can detect the slowly emerging prog qualities in the changing genotype. The radical punctuations of math rock and post-thrash are not just a mutation of hardcore; they also contain references to This Heat, Henry Cow and 1970s Italian prog, as well as a reminder that even the more pastoral Gentle Giant explored the idea of punctuation alongside the extended linear development of songs. But the purpose of punctuation in stop-start and rapid key and tempo changes divided by sharp, delineated pauses is quite different. Whereas 1970s prog used these devices as way stations within the musical and lyrical narrative, these were increasingly disrupted in the late 1980s and early 1990s. The punctuation is not just structure but also anti-structure that comments on the concept of structure. Harsh divisions, chopped chords and clustered drum-beats link closely to lyrical purpose, just as content and form were brought together in earlier progressive rock. This technique indicates alienation as well as the prospect of attacking alienation head on; or, in terms of 1980s science fiction, it can be seen as a form of hacking or gene-splicing that aims to expose social ills or to explore future potentials.

In 1989, Voivod took a quantum leap on *Nothingface* from virtuosic thrash to a sound that strongly echoed King Crimson's *Three of a Perfect Pair*: heavy bass (sometimes slapped), complex drumming, and guitar that alternates between competition and combination within the whole musical effect. The share of instrumental space is egalitarian and the singing close to the punk prog of Here and Now or the grimier end of indie music, thereby disdaining the virtuosity of the death-growl singer or the highly skilled 'straight' singer. As with Atheist's albums, the narrative of *Nothingface* is a sequence of short sections and bursts of syncopated cuts and restarts. Voivod's debt to prog is signalled directly on the band's cover of Pink Floyd's 'Astronomy Domine', but more telling is the self-reflexivity of the subsequent 'Missing Sequences', which push the stop-start approach to an extreme point. The complexity of linear construction and the shifts between sections of long prog tracks are replaced by a heightened sense of time as monadic, occurring in autonomous moments or clusters. This is a time that is hard to dwell in or settle into; it also connects to what went before in progressive rock and twists the ongoing concern with time as the crux of organic and holistic development. For progressive metal bands, time itself becomes complex, whereas 1970s progressive rock linked complexity to temporal development and alteration.

The putative math rock of *Nothingface* is not so much about mathematics as about an audible take on the structures of time. We see another important moment in the development of metal progressive rock in increasing lyrical abstraction; the disruptiveness of what seem to be random sequences of words is essential and not peripheral (in the case of the death growl or other metal vocal styles that push the voice to its limits, the voice itself becomes the message and conveyor of the lyrical purpose beyond the words themselves). Themes emerge from Voivod's songs on this album, but the lyrics are used as riffs as much as melodies, such as on 'Into My Hypercube':

> Transient illusion
> Clairvoyant suspension
> Translucid condition
> Principal connection

Even as the lyrics tend towards abstraction, thematic concerns emerge beyond the critiques of power, most notably an interest in science and its connections with alchemy and non-Christian religions. Progressive rock of the 1970s largely shunned the vocabularies of science (even if bands were happy to use science fiction), whereas progressive metal bands find in science an expressive tool that brings together content and form – an interest that stretches from Muse to The Dillinger Escape Plan.

From this point, there is further diversification. Pittsburgh band Don Caballero brought a fascination with precision into play in the mid-1990s; the build and release through staccato sections return to a complex narrative, but one that is entirely turned inward, without vocals. This is perhaps at its most striking on the long tracks of *Don Caballero 2* (1995), such as 'Please Tokio, please THIS IS TOKIO', where a multiplicity of pulsing riffs and section changes push the music close to classical sonatas and Abstract Expressionist painting: the interest in pure form, aggression, volume, alternations, and carefully scripted battles between instruments creates a sense that something is being expressed, even if the content is elusive or absent. In this highly hermetic music, the expression itself becomes content. The radical difference between Don Caballero and the evocative instrumentals of Godspeed You! Black Emperor, Sigur Rós and Tortoise becomes clear only if we place them within a story of unfolding prog approaches, not least because King Crimson and Henry Cow can be restored as possible influences in the 1990s. Further, we need to remind ourselves that everything to be found in the build-up and ecstatic release of math rock was already evident in the late 1980s in the form of instrumental progressive band Djam Karet.

The fascination with technical ecstasy permeates later rock that opts for a combination of sonic dissonance; dissonant structuring; stop-start as developmental model; and audible conflict between instruments, metres and keys. In the late 1990s, Pacific Northwest band Botch was not afraid to return to a version of hardcore that has a chugging death metal core and flailing prog limbs in the form of unexpected saxophone interventions and pastoral sections breaking through powerfully riffed progressions. We can see

Botch's *American Nervoso* (1998) as a marker of prog strategies reseeding the genres that had initially fed a new, harsher progressive rock.[2] Differentiating the majority of music in this chapter from 1970s prog is the strong emphasis on heavy or dissonant music, and the heightened aggressive take on subjects that had been addressed in that earlier period. The Dillinger Escape Plan, from New Jersey, is superficially similar to Botch but more clearly part of a resuscitation of the purpose of progressive rock in harsher form. *Calculating Infinity* (1999) shows The Dillinger Escape Plan at its best. Ferociously fast drums are battered by the punch of the stop-start guitar or fast riffing, broken up by sharply defined dissonant quiet sections or synthetic soundscapes. The shouting vocal style eschews the scream in favour of relentlessness, and the constant message of anger, misanthropy and jaundiced fatigue is conveyed through an unwavering, barked vocal. The sameness of the voice illustrates two aspects: first, the shrinking of the world to a vision of damaged emotionality, and, second, the voice as part of the percussive whole, so that the music partakes of the dense vocal monomania, even though the music changes incessantly.

The other path that leads away from Voivod is less about a display of precision and more about the stretching of aggression into longer and more clearly conceptualized tracks reminiscent of black metal. Black metal itself shares some of the characteristics with the metal forms dealt with here, but it should be seen as a tributary of the fusion of styles; it is highly conceptual in its focus on the pernicious influence of Christianity on all Western morals and practices, and often takes the view that absolute freedom would be the ideal. There are actual conceptual albums, such as Burzum's instrumental take on Norse legend in *Daudi Baldrs* (1997) and Bathory's mythologizing of Viking culture in *Nordland I* and *II* (2002–3). There is virtuosity in black metal, in the drumming, the vocals and the rapid scale-based guitar-playing. The complexity is often shallow, though, or purposely lost in low-grade production that flattens and lowers to a primordial level, revealing a potentially authentic darkness that has been hidden away by Western art and society. The deep-throated growling vocals of black metal can also be found in music that is essentially progressive, as in Opeth, Cynic, Cathedral or Mastodon. However, instead of flattening or densification, the music of these groups moves towards clearing and contrast.

On the 1993 album *Focus*, Cynic returned to a theme not so far from the concerns of Yes and Pendragon. The opening track, 'Veil of Maya', establishes a spiritual quest that is aware that the truth it seeks might well be the truth of nothingness (the veil of Maya is the stuff of the world that distracts us from contemplating the real universe). The lyrics concentrate on a quest to find what has been lost or hidden, but the music tells a different story, especially the vocals, which alternate between clear-voiced singing and metal growled verses. These alternations do not map simply onto a lyrical contrast between the alienated world and the true reality, but they are accompanied by appropriate changes in music. Alienation (oddly missing from the lyrics) is signalled through the use of the clear voice, accompanied by fewer instrumental effects and the use of brighter production for pastoral moments. There is also a third vocal style: a lightly processed and almost buried choral voice on 'Veil of Maya' and 'Sentiment' that appears to be the voice of the quest, punctuating the conflict but not seeking to dominate through new knowledge.

Cathedral proposes a harsher but equally developed vision of humanity's earthly existence on *Garden of Unearthly Delights* (2005). Loosely based on Hieronymus Bosch's painting *The Garden of Earthly Delights* (c. 1500), the anti-pastoral 'The Garden' (26:56) moves from an Edenic opening (acoustic instrumentation, female voice, drones) to more violent sections before returning to the pastoral. Cathedral charts the disappearance of the Christian vision of earthly paradise, and is sanguine about it, for this is a bloody, death-ridden, corrupt land. In section 2b, the guttural male narrator says the serpent has 'chosen to pervert God's land'; but by section 2c (the seventh part of the song and a return to the refrain of 2b), 'we have chosen to accept God's land' as it is, full of death, physicality and free of the 'chains of morality'. Humanity has reached this place by understanding the materiality of death-filled nature: 'in earth's garden nature sings man's requiem', and 'all life's beauty is its end'. The supposed loss of paradise is the source of our freedom, and this is clearly marked out in the heaviest riffs of the song, filling 22:31 to 25:39 before giving way to the return of the opening sequence – this time with the full awareness of our precarious yet free place in nature. This track, and the album as a whole, is a sort of utopia, despite its garden being the polar opposite of the one found on The Flower Kings' *Flower Power*, as discussed in the previous chapter (Cathedral would say it is the same garden, but seen clearly). This is a utopia based on the creative rejection of the Christian view of humanity, in favour of knowledge, self-awareness and savage harmony with the earth.

Swedish band Opeth alternates strong riffs, fast drumming and growled vocals with acoustic sections, often accompanied by a clear or clean voice. This vision is a brooding meditation on death, but is less perverse than those of Cathedral. Like Cynic's *Focus*, but unlike the very clear narrative purpose of musical changes on Cathedral's 'The Garden', these changes are not explicitly linked to lyrics. On Opeth's *Morningrise* (1996, widely issued in 2000), tracks ranging from 10 to 20 minutes frequently enact alternations, often for only short time spans. The opening 'Advent' (13:46) takes us from a quiet beginning into pummelling double-bass drumming, and then quietness again, followed by the song's key riff accompanied by growled vocals. This all happens in the space of not much over a minute and occurs across the whole of the album, except on the closing 'To Bid You Farewell'. The guiding theme is the loss of a female lover, who becomes more ghostly as the album proceeds, while the narrator slowly comes to terms with loss and searches for an easier relationship with death (following a 20-second scream 19 minutes into 'Black Rose Immortal'). Individual songs are not divided into sections but shift from electric to acoustic, or, less frequently, the vocals become clear rather than growled. Whereas Voivod or The Dillinger Escape Plan play with time as chaotic densification or approaching collapse, Opeth dramatizes time in a manner that is not quite a return to narrative. Opeth's take on relentless change grows in scale and expands to match the interest in death that informs its lyrics. The two styles hammer into one another, life into death, and vice-versa, separate but embracing.

The bludgeoning differential of *Morningrise* becomes a more complex series of interactions on *Blackwater Park* (2001). Although the sense of a divided world remains, the two approaches flow into one another and develop across more minimal instrumental parts, on occasion dominated by piano. The album integrates acoustic, melodic and more obviously metal parts into clearer musical-narrative development. This is at its height on 'Bleak', its riff-backed melodic sections split with harsher moments. There are clear choruses on several songs, for the most part sung by Mikael Åkerfeldt in a clear rather than growled voice. Only the title track reverts to the alternation model of *Morningrise*, an alternation taken to the extreme of two albums recorded together, with *Deliverance* (2002) almost entirely metal and *Damnation* (2003) mostly melodic. Opeth does not display references to 1970s prog (even if there are passing hints in the medievally tinged acoustic passages) and the sound derives from metal; oddly, it is when adopting a structure that is easier to follow that Opeth comes closer to the developmental stretching of earlier progressive rock. However, the playing of *Blackwater Park* in its entirety in 2010 (the core of *In Live Concert at the Royal Albert Hall* DVD) almost overdoes the references to 1970s prog: its cover is a homage to Deep Purple's *Concerto for Group and Orchestra* (1969, recorded at the same venue); its subtitles of 'Observation One' and 'Observation Two' reference the subtitle of *In the Court of the Crimson King*; and the discs are a near facsimile of EMI prog offshoot Harvest. Lyrically, *Blackwater Park* presents us with a panorama of death in its physical form that signals a complete turn to progressive rock, even if more recent albums have not extended the references to prog in direct musical terms.

Opeth is far from being the only European band to produce music at the interface of progressive rock and metal. While North America saw thrash, hardcore and metal reference points twisted into harsh complex forms, pro-gressive metal in Northern Europe developed a stronger narrative feel, both in its lyrics and its musical development, across a plethora of conceptual and thematic albums. Metal of the symphonic variety fosters a gothic sensibility in metal, one that references not only Romantic tropes of death, sex, nature and paganism but also the gothic music of the 1980s and 1990s. The symphonic element of Nightwish, Kamelot, Within Temptation, Epica, Stratovarius, Sonata Arctica and Ayreon recalls the aspiration of progressive groups to incorporate classical music. Although this is less dominant in progressive rock than has often been presumed, orchestral passages (by means of key-board or digital technology) in progressive symphonic metal are pushed to the fore, building effects over song suites into what aspires to be an irresistible sublime, such as on Kamelot's *Epica* (2003). Like the post-thrash progressive parts of metal, this aims to present an impression of strength, often using double-bass drumming and effects-laden guitar.

This type of progressive metal is a subtle alternative version of neo-prog: a pastiche of musical styles and structures already in place and grounded in more contemporary metal styles. What makes one album a pastiche where another is a more authentic take on prog is in the use of complexity as con-notation rather than as a building device. Swedish group Pain of Salvation epitomizes this contrast in their two-part concept album *The Perfect Element, Part 1* (2000) and in *Scarsick* (2007). The first of these albums develops the idea of hardship and misery creating monstrous behaviour. The sound is a harshening of second-wave neo-prog bands The Flower Kings and Spock's Beard, and also a recombination of metal elements, many of which are simple when taken in isolation. The message of *The Perfect Element* veers between promoting a simplistic moral and the troubled entwining of victimhood and aggressor, as the music in its second half becomes a dense metallic version of prog (although, technically, the album is written in three parts). *Scarsick* pursues a weary grumble about the state of the world through an array of styles that almost parodies the fusion of progressive rock, but we can nevertheless see this as an echo of the search in the mid-1970s for ever more complex compositions.

This direction of metal progressiveness stands out, though, for featuring female vocalists within bands.[3] The style of voice and dramatic presentation emphasizes the connection to gothic metal, and is much more sexualized than female vocalists of progressive bands in the 1970s. There is still a strong suggestion of folk vocal styles, along with hints of operatic style which were common to metal from its inception. The role of the female singer in sym-phonic metal is often as a counterpart to the lead guitar or within a duo of singers (as with the current neo-prog group Mostly Autumn). This counter-part is substantial, though. Far from making the female figure ancillary, it puts the female singer at the centre, as she alternates between fighting and communing with the metal instrumentation, representing a figure of excess both within and outside of the whole.

Within Temptation combines orchestral sounds with a full metal line-up, completed by singer Sharon den Adel. The band's epic pop sound offers little by way of complex lyrical narrative, focusing on emotion and smaller-scale personal stories. Nor is there much in terms of compositional development; rather, Within Temptation achieves a rich density by incorporating orches-tral instrumentation that relies heavily on the percussive attack of choir and instruments heard in Carl Orff's *Carmina Burana*. The integration is most clearly evident on the 2008 live DVD *Black Symphony*, where what can often sound decorative on symphonic metal drives the melody and structure.[4] Den Adel emphasizes her femininity through costume changes and a fluid gothic dance style. The DVD also highlights the large number of women in the audience. This is not about attracting a heterosexual male audience but an attempt to alter the notion that rock is an exclusively male preserve. In appealing to an idea of gender balance, Within Temptation adds a layer to its implicit critique of over-masculinized rock. The concert emphasizes certain types of virtuosity, not just in the skill of orchestral players but also in timing, the combination of instrumental approaches and digital visuals, and more traditional stadium-rock displays. This is in marked contrast to the effect of Orff-style orchestral bursts used for colour on Within Temptation's studio albums.

Epica is a harsher proposition, despite mobilizing similar elements, notably in the shape of a full choir and chamber orchestra on *The Phantom Agony* (2003). The singer is not credited as a vocalist, but as mezzo-soprano Simone Simons. Her approach brings together the folk singing of Renaissance and Fairport Convention with 1990s neo-folk and Lisa Gerrard. *The Phantom Agony* is thematically linked; the whole album is focused on the idea of a hidden truth repressed by organized religion, political power and consumerism. The album alternates between attacking agents of repression and finding a way out through self-reflection ('Cry for the Moon'), a physical coming to self-awareness ('Musine Consensus'), or recognizing the double nature of reality – the ubiquity of corrupt power and the enigmatic excess of the universe. The album heads towards heightened consciousness of this world and its possibilities, but along the way the searching voice of Simons is periodically interrupted by the growled vocals of Mark Jansen. His voice represents a more negative take on existing powers, driving a dialectic through which Simons moves further along the path to knowledge. In the title track, 'The Phantom Agony', both voices try to break through the veil to another level of existence. Even with a few extended tracks, a narrative connectedness to the album and the presence of chamber orchestra, there is not much space for instrumental development. This could be seen to represent the questioning position Epica takes on God: the beginning of 'The Phantom Agony' queries the existence of an unnamed interlocutor ('I can't see you/I can't hear you/ Do you still exist?'); this is more than a human addressee, as the existence (or otherwise) of 'you' will determine the nature of our existence. We later hear the multi-voiced demand or wish to 'free the disbelief in me/What we get is what we see'. As such, the belief in the possibility of God and the fear of his absence combine. This seeming contradiction is reflected in the almost constant presence of vocals; even the framing instrumental tracks feature a choir, while voicelessness represents the empty cosmos.

Dream Theater also deals with religious themes, but in a different way. Musically, the band resembles Opeth's development of a new progressive mode by recombining metal styles, with the clear influences of Metallica,

Megadeth and Slayer. Unlike Opeth, Dream Theater also references previous prog and neo-prog styles that pivot on the function and style of the keyboards. Mike Portnoy's virtuosic drumming is an excessive take on thrash, doom and death metal and covers a vast array of drums (Portnoy even has two complete drum sets on the *Score* DVD). Dream Theater thus performs a very specific extension of metal into a progressive approach, broadening the range of sounds and connecting the key changes into longer musical narratives than those of math rock groups. We would also argue that although it is not immediately noticeable, the neo-prog sounds and highly melodic parts disguise a hidden affinity with post-thrash, post-hardcore progressive rock.

Starting with *Metropolis Pt. 2: Scenes From a Memory* (1999), a double-CD concept album, Dream Theater's compositions extend, and the title track of the following release *Six Degrees of Inner Turbulence* (2002) is a 42-minute, eight-part suite. Later albums invariably feature multi-section songs of over 20 minutes, with most single-section tracks reaching 8 to 10 minutes. 'Six Degrees of Inner Turbulence' introduces six different modes of mental withdrawal from the world (the last of the six is a potentially more positive reprise of the first). This disconnectedness is ironically echoed in the title, which refers to the six degrees of separation that apparently connect any one individual to any other. The piece opens with a genuine overture that introduces all the musical themes that will be developed in the track, reiterated in the closing eighth part. The overture introduces martial elements that metal has always picked up on in classical music, filtered through the keyboard

Mike Portnoy of Dream Theater performing at Fields of Rock, The Netherlands, (June 2007).

simulation of the full range of the orchestra in a manner that strongly recalls The Enid. The different mental states of each section are allocated different metal styles (from the big riffs of part three, through the fast thrash metal take on Dio of part four, and into the booming rock of part five) or neo-prog elements framed within the group's quasi-orchestral crescendo sections. These could represent the chaotic world that stimulates withdrawal, but the connection to the upbeat sense of recovery in parts seven and eight suggest a rebalancing of mental energy where complexity can be managed. The lyrics of the closing part ('Losing Time/Grand Finale') suggest that the retreat from socially sanctioned behaviour is not just a defence mechanism but also an apt one that holds out the hope for controlled escape from worldly problems.

Dream Theater's songs are nearly always thematic, with just enough ambiguity to let the music work at a narrative level rather than being a vehicle for the stories. This band, like the majority of groups discussed in this chapter, is also willing to take up positions – an ideological robustness that was much less prevalent in 1970s prog. Dream Theater's perspective is, however, not driven by the industrial music-inspired anti-religiousness or fear of mind control to be found in much recent metal. When the group does criticize power, religion, consumerism or alienation, it is from a more liberal perspective and with more than a hint of Christian influence. In 'The Great Debate', on the first CD of *Six Degrees*, Dream Theater discusses the ethics of stem cells, medical experimentation and IVF, focusing on the creation of 'spare' embryos and speculating on the effects of biotechnology on what it means to be human and whether one can be 'justified in taking/Life to save life', which is reiterated in the shouted chorus. Just as lyricist John Petrucci has decided that IVF embryo-making necessarily involves 'taking life', so the song reveals a 'pro-life' perspective on when human life begins, and presumes that the non-implantation of 'spare' embryos is 'taking life'. The debate about rights or wrongs transforms into a discussion about whether good ends can come from bad means. This stance is echoed in this song in the first of several references in Dream Theater's work to 9/11 and associated acts of violence ('Poised for conflict at ground zero'). The September 2001 attack on the World Trade Center is the entire subject of 'Sacrificed Sons', on the 2005 release *Octavarium*. There is no disguising the band's sympathy for the victims in the World Trade Center ('Towers crumble/Heroes die'), nor the suggestion of who or what is to blame:

> Who would wish this
> On our people
> And proclaim
> That His Will be done
> Scriptures they heed have misled them
> All praise their sacrificed sons.

No doubt some will read this as Dream Theater's secret pro-American government Christianism, and that bemoaning a mass attack on your fellow citizens is somehow ideologically suspect. The band suggests that the fault lies in Islamic belief, but by the last verse it seems more that the fanatical use of scripture has led people to righteously sacrifice themselves in order to kill others ('God on High/Our mistake/Will mankind be extinct'). Ultimately, Portnoy's lyrics vigorously challenge the use of violence for supposedly ethical or holy purpose: 'Sacrificed Sons' becomes about all religions and all victims of religious-inspired aggression, and, implicitly, argues against the righteousness of revenge. Dream Theater offers a very early non-right-wing meditation on al-Qaida that does not seek to apportion blame to the West but looks to the psychology of religious manipulation found in more controversial form in Martin Amis's 9/11-themed literary collection *The Second Plane* (2008). Musically, the refrain of Dream Theater's 'Sacrificed Sons' (cited above) is sung chorally, illustrating solidarity. After the closing verse, which universalizes potential blame for religious violence, there is an epic, minor chord-led instrumental ending, indicating the possibility of violence to come, emphasized by the sudden ending.

The theme of religious corruption in the quest for power returns on 'In the Presence of Enemies', a two-part, 25-minute track that opens and closes *Systematic Chaos* (2007). The title suggests an 'enemy within' and the threat of values being inverted, which is perhaps a reference to the United States feeling under threat, although little in the track pursues this. The protagonist is offered a Faustian bargain, where he can trade his soul for unlimited power. The 'Dark Master' (affiliation unknown) demands immediate worship, which entails committing violence in his name. Although the inspiration derives from the fault-line of 9/11, Petrucci's lyrics detect that the problem cannot be confined to a single belief system. Much in the song actually suggests that the Dark Master perverts Christian beliefs. The prelude is harsher than the band's other overture sections and signals the wider chaos of the album's title. It is interrupted by the slow, clean guitar theme after 2:10, signalling the prospect of truth amid danger. In section two ('Resurrection'), the Dark Master entices the potential heretic with the prospect of immanent power, and speaks of the saviour's being awaited by 'the fallen' 'on this wicked day'. The saviour here is a false one (feasibly the Christian Antichrist), and the following part recounts the heretic's worshipful killing in the name of the Dark Master. As the conflagration builds with metallic riffs and shouts in part four, the heretic gradually sees the evil of his actions and by the end achieves the capacity not only to resist but also to triumph. The protagonist welcomes the Christian God ('Lord/You are my god and shepherd'); the second part of the fourth section pronounces judgement on 'the damned' (a judgement, which if it is supposed to be from a good god, seems vindictive, involving mass slaughter for most and redemption for only the protagonist); and he recognizes the inevitability of violent behaviour due to 'the beast/That lives in all of us'. 'The Reckoning' sees guitar, keyboards and drums building together and also against each other; like the battle in Yes's 'Gates of Delirium', 'In the Presence of Enemies' ends in bloodied redemption following the climactic group resolution of 'The Reckoning'. The most recent album, *Black Clouds & Silver Linings* (2009), continues Dream Theater's interest in religious violence, particularly the opening track, 'A Nightmare to Remember', which focuses on the human cost of arbitrary violence (a bomb attack on a wedding) and the shared recovery of the wounded. Tracks on *Systematic Chaos* and *Black Clouds & Silver Linings* display a subtlety lacking in the earlier references to 9/11, and also demonstrate how musical complexity and variation can drive the message to become less simplistic and more nuanced.

It is not possible here to trace Dream Theater's multiple musical sources but, in addition to working with the structure of albums, the band connects tracks, most obviously in Portnoy's 'Twelve Steps' sequence, which builds over five albums. Paradoxically, this strategy strengthens the idea of the 'album' because it shows the need for longer narrative development than a single release permits. The sequence carries more weight because it nestles in more structures than if it were free-standing, although the temptation might be to bring them together, as Canadian prog band Saga did with the Chapters sequence (starting in the late 1970s and reprised in 1999).[5]

So far, this chapter has focused on extensions of metal that become forms of progressive rock, but there are also prog moves towards metal, such as in Porcupine Tree, a band that tests several post-progressive fusions by incorporating trance and new-wave soundscapes. Porcupine Tree does not shy from long tracks where the shifting structure carries lyrical meditation: for example, 'The Sky Moves Sideways' (1994, reworked in 2003) echoes Pink Floyd's 'Shine On You Crazy Diamond'. Like Wilson's other main project of the 1990s, No-man, Porcupine Tree shifted towards a take on progressive music that often moved a long way from rock and mutated the dynamics of prog tracks. From 2002 onwards, Porcupine Tree began to develop a sound more reliant upon overdriven guitar chords, which anchors a group density that does not exclude the development of bass, drums, atmospheric keyboards and samples. This sound is only partially evident on *In Absentia* (2002); it comes into clearer definition on the 2005 album *Deadwing*.

The other facet of this distinctive reordering of metal into a progressive rock is the presence of acoustic guitar-led sections in alternation with the power-centred parts (and, as with many moments identified in this chapter, Neurosis lurks here as a ghostly reference point). As with Opeth, it is not that the split conveys a specific message or tone; rather, it is the split itself that is important and, in the case of Porcupine Tree, informs the ambiguity and often troubling changes of perspective within the lyrics. 'Blackest Eyes' opens *In Absentia* with an explosive riff carried by the band as a whole and then leaks into a quieter section where the story of a swiftly maturing narrator shifts from third to first person, including a sexual awakening where he makes a woman cry 'under the trees' while walking with her in the woods. The chorus outlines a mantra of alienated statements ('I got a place where all my dreams are dead') that shows the isolation and unconcern of a narrator who deviates from social norms. The track cuts immediately into the acoustic opening strum of 'Trains', a song full of melancholy for lost childhood ('Always the summers are slipping away') and the parallel threat of sexual abuse of the narrator's cousin as trains pass by. But the lyrics are not simply about destructive violence, despite following on from the predatory words of 'Blackest Eyes'. In the closing verse of 'Trains', sung over acoustic guitar, there is complicity:

> When the evening reaches in
> You're tying me up
> I'm dying of love
> It's OK

The uncertainty is not about whether the narrator takes pleasure in this act but about why he might do so. It could be that the overheard cousin's experience in the first verse (the voice is plaintive and masked by passing trains, suggesting that the cousin's experience is invasive) has determined an acceptance of social control. Equally, it could be that this submissive situation, however dangerous or possibly sadistic, has been actively sought out.

In Absentia marks the start of the close relationship with Danish visual artist Lasse Hoile, who has created visuals for Porcupine Tree concerts, videos and cover photography as a collaborative enhancement of Wilson's lyrical preoccupations. Hoile documents a world near to ours, but one where all the colours alter and the landscapes feel haunted, not least by the young who inhabit or drift through them. Similarly, the characters in Porcupine Tree's tracks are adrift, not quite able to attain reality but strongly imposing their impressions.

Deadwing presents a more unified aesthetic than the previous album, and atmospheres cede to power-chord sequences and into softer passages and back again, on a more consistent but not structurally predictable order. The opening title track returns us to an outsider who has turned their isolation into venom and fear. From the nameless threat of the first verse, we move towards the narrator, who declares his misanthropy via multiple generalized social threats. All the while, loss underpins the outsider's outlook. In the first verse of 'Deadwing', 'the precious things I hold dear' have been taken away; the environment holds constant threats of cancer and poison; in the last two verses, the narrator tells of his fear that intimacy inevitably leads to loss; and, in the end, he has to leave through a window, which could symbolize suicide or the complete sociopathy hinted at earlier. Claustrophobia is heightened by the narrowing of the band's sound dynamic, dramatic shifts occur through tone, cataclysmic eruptions lead into riff-led passages, and older prog strategies of contrasting instruments and frequencies are dampened. The final

'stepping through' lyric is launched after an instrumental section that gradually resolves into a return of the opening section, its separation from the rest
of the song echoing that of the narrator, who is dismissed even as the lyrics
offer some sympathy. Further multiple signals await us in 'Lazarus', which
is ostensibly a positive song about recovery or salvation, conveyed through
the chorus's call to 'follow me down' and the warmth of keyboard and guitar
tones. This narrator has 'survived against the will of my twisted folk' and is
on a journey away from home. But the song encourages the listener to follow
the narrator 'down to the valley below', and the song ends with 'come to us
Lazarus/It's time for you to go'. This sounds like a return to selfhood after
living death, but it could also be a suicide threat and a call to stop playing
the reborn Lazarus. Wilson's lyrics explore the confused emotions that might
result from trauma, and it is important to resist hearing his words simply as
compromising positive outcomes.

The persistent non-judgemental drift of *Deadwing* (acts or thoughts of
violence are not aggressively sung or framed) moves between sinister inten-
tions, threatening settings, and psychological escape routes, as later heard
on *Fear of a Blank Planet* (2007). Above all, *Deadwing* contains defiance in
the face of alienation and disturbance, even if this might take violent turns.
Amid the anger and staccato chords of a failing relationship in 'Open Car',
we return to the image of the narrator driving alongside a companion who
wears a summer dress and whose hair is blowing. The singer clings on to this
memory, or perhaps expresses annoyance that this fleeting moment has been
tainted. 'Arriving Somewhere but Not Here' dwells on life's direction (or lack
of it) in its multiple and rapid musical changes; the psychology of travelling is
always to be located, even as the traveller moves on to a new place. The singing of the title and bridge to the chorus signals death, and also a journeying
without consciousness. The chorus evokes the thwarting of desire ('All my
designs, simplified/And all of my plans, compromised/And all of my dreams,
sacrificed') in a choral voice, leading into a languid solo guitar that reveals a
pocket of self-awareness even as the lyrics hit their most maudlin.

From the individual reflections of *Deadwing*, Porcupine Tree moves to
sustained social critique on *Fear of a Blank Planet*, framing similar ideas in
a concept album based upon a shared social malaise. Unlike Public Enemy's
Fear of a Black Planet (1990), this is not a world based on strict social segregation with clearly identified authorities to be toppled and that live in fear of a
changing order. The fear of the blank planet is double: the concern about the
receding of thought and action in bloodless anomie, and the fears that those
'of the blank planet' have had induced in them. One of the album's strengths is
its avoidance of judging a young generation entrapped by technology, the culture industry and prescription drugs. Rather than depicting this generation
as lost victims identified by a superior viewer, Wilson avoids moralizing by
approaching the alienation of youth close up; in fact, the lyrics grow increasingly responsive to the plight of its young subjects as the album develops.

The title track establishes the critique of personalized multimedia ('TV, yeah it's always on', 'X-box is a god to me') against a background of parental and social neglect. Wilson captures both distaste for what is happening ('My face is mogadon') and empathy (the quietly voiced 'bipolar disorder/Can't deal with the boredom'). People are gradually emptied, as they are in Radiohead's world, implying that what in the 1970s might have been a radical withdrawal has now become normalized. 'My Ashes' mitigates the critique, making it clear that the blank planet people are not to blame for their condition. The song identifies parental indifference as driving the need to be safe in more easily controlled worlds, rather than fostering interpersonal empathy across generations.

Over rolling drums, the opening section of 'Anesthetize' (17:43) announces the increasing failure to communicate. The words are not entirely sympathetic ('I'm saying nothing/But I'm saying nothing with feel'), but the incapacity to think is neither praised nor blamed. The second and longest part of the track becomes harsher, the heavy chords leading to the judgement of the chorus ('Only apathy from the pills in me') on both the individual and society at once. Throughout the album, the lyrics return to the mundane details of contemporary alienation linked to technology or to the limited scope of activities. This works simultaneously as critique, as fatigued recognition of how this situation

Porcupine Tree, *Fear of a Blank Planet* (2007). Photography by Lasse Hoile.

came about, and as assertive defence of the energetic rendering of the 'only apathy' refrain. The last of three vocal sections on 'Anesthetize' is more meditative, musing on the memory of a beach in the sun. This plaintive section, looking to recall or attain something beyond social indoctrination, also signals a dawning realization of the corroding effects of the machine-culture industry. This is emphasized by the absence of musical change following those verses, with a slow fade into a short atmospheric ending.

The emphasis of 'Sentimental' on avoiding adult responsibility extends the focus beyond an appraisal of contemporary youth.[6] The two remaining tracks look beyond mundane consumerism and a denial of human contact, albeit from the stunted perspective of those caught within mechanisms of social control. The ecstatic surges of 'Way Out of Here' that launch the refrain offer the prospect of a way out; but as the opening verses cross to those that follow the first chorus, we hear about loss, hatred ('I'll burn all your pictures/ Cut out your face'), and even possible murder ('And I've covered my tracks/ Disposed of the car'). Freedom is bound up with loss and destruction, and the final return to the chorus fades, just as the chorus speaks of 'fading out'. This echoes one of Radiohead's many songs about contemporary anomie, 'Street Spirit (Fade Out)' from 1995, where fading out might be either the consequence of alienation or an escape strategy from it. The last track on *Fear of a Blank Planet*, 'Sleep Together', is the most obvious of the album, taking sex as a quietly despairing attempt at intimacy. Irregularly pulsing keyboards dominate the track, along with a sense of winding down, even as the lyrics seem to suggest a minimal heightening of contact. Nonetheless, there is resistance and a belief that options can be actively chosen. The closing lyric, 'let's leave together', seems to refer not to death but to the need to escape – even if all destinations look similarly unappealing.

The album as a whole is designed to be oppressive, with bursts of anger-fuelled energy, both musically and thematically. The vocals are often treated, as they are on other Porcupine Tree albums, here echoing the distancing of the lyrics. The album ends with an isolated drum burst closing off the escape of 'Sleep Together'. As a whole, *Fear of a Blank Planet* focuses on power as a complete control system, internalized so that political power has no need to overtly oppress or attack. Even the pernicious influences of family and friends are caught within a wider web of power. Like Michel Foucault's examination of covert methods of social control in *Discipline and Punish* (1975), here circuits of intergenerational apathy, tranquillizers, computer games and other distractions function to control individuals through indirect means. This proves to be oppression without purpose, as power, too, is empty.

The development of Porcupine Tree's music provides a bridge to avant-rock that emerged in parallel with post-hardcore, post-rock and existing forms of metal. We have already discussed in Chapter 12 how 'post-progressive' opens onto instrumentally based post-rock, whereas avant-rock (or 'out rock') describes a more aggressive noise- or metal-based approach to experimentation. Both terms succeed in downplaying or ignoring the connections between progressive rock and experimental rock of the 1990s and 2000s, in favour of a continuum that includes Krautrock, no wave, the experiments of early industrial music, Japanese noise rock, and American art rock that preceded grunge. Some, if not all, of 'out rock' is a reinvigoration of progressive rock, particularly the fusion of forms and genres that underpins any progressive project. Some avant-rock is not even regarded as particularly avant because of its commercial success. This has largely been the fate of Los Angeles band Tool, which moved from its early 1990s combination of grunge and industrial metal to develop a harsh minimalism on *Lateralus* (2001) and *10,000 Days* (2006) that finds its source in equal measure in Swans and King Crimson. The relentless slow build of Tool's tracks, circling around repeated bass and guitar motifs, could perhaps even be thought of as a kind of maximalism based on repetition as the source of power. The instruments are clearly separated out in the mix, but their functions cross over. The bass often provides both rhythm and melody and the guitar supplies a punctuating force, as Tool bursts away from delayed resolution into a full group explosiveness. Complex time signatures are held as we edge towards changes, rather than embracing the developmental change common in 1970s prog. Maynard James Keenan's lyrics, like those of Steven Wilson, gradually build a worldview, without explicitly conceptualizing the whole album. Conversely, the otherwise rich album sleeves of *Lateralus* and *10,000 Days* do not contain lyrics, as if Keenan wants the vocals to be part of the instrumentation and not the primary point of focus.

'The Grudge' sets the tone for *Lateralus*. Its pacing, instrumentation and arpeggios recall post-1981 King Crimson, harnessed to lyrics about negativity. But Tool also introduces more cosmic elements that announce a wider view about individuals relating to the broader universe, mythology or alchemical combinations. The title track reiterates this, with its reference to the hermetic idea of layers of reality mirroring each other: 'as below, so above and beyond'.[7] 'Lateralus' goes further, specifying that embodiment must be central to our situatedness in the cosmos and should not be lost in the error of reflection: 'over thinking, over analyzing separates the body from the mind' (these lyrics are delivered above the sound of a full group attack). It goes further still in raising a deistic model of the universe and individuals in harmony with one another, where divinity is possible through a merging of layers or fusion; this occurs formally through the build of tracks, instrumental roles, the alternation between cyclical near-repetitions, and metal power chords. And it goes further again in referring to the spiral, identifying the connectors in chaotic patterning: the form might be hard to discover, but it can nevertheless be revealed. Each of these stages is present in the cover art. The CD booklet is a transparent layering of pages, a human body delayered or stripped on each page, combined with chaotic patterns of eyes and mandalas. Eyes fill the last page, as the body is replaced by a blazing symbol from which eyes radiate. Tool's videos add yet another dimension to the multiplicity, bringing together machine and body through animation, alterations and a kind of fleshy cyberspace. Despite Keenan's exhortation to let go of reflection, the sequence of 'Parabol' and 'Parabola' explores how individual embodiment becomes conscious in the close presence of another, linked to the realization that mortality defines the ambit of life. 'Parabola' explores the experience of subjectivity identified by Martin Heidegger in *Being and Time*, where awareness of mortality plays off the recognition that every moment is experienced as infinite ('Feeling eternal').

This sense of being part of patterns that lie beyond human perception also informs *10,000 Days*, especially 'Wings for Marie (Part 1)' and '10,000 Days (Wings Part 2)'. In this sequence, the lyrics and music develop and alter across tracks. The song '10,000 Days' concerns Keenan's mother, who was paralysed for roughly this length of time, up to her death. This biographical information inflects how we listen to the track, which essentially recounts the goodness of a saintly individual who becomes the emotional centre of the narrative and whose presence taps into the mysteries of the universe. To others, the mother is entirely embodied, but to herself she is almost without a body. Similar concerns about multilayering of reality and experience permeate this album, but the lyrics adopt an external position as well as slightly odder perspectives, such as the drug nirvanas and panics of 'Rosetta Stoned', or angels musing on the stupidity of the endlessly warring human monkeys on 'Right in Two'. Perhaps we can read this distance in the album cover, with its mandalas and stereoscopic images that require a viewer to see them as a quasi three-dimensional image. This confirms that vision and perspective are the primary foci of *10,000 Days*.

By the 2000s, Guapo had also developed a style based on cycles of near-repetition – recalling a more metallic Magma – as well as a harnessing of the free music of the late 1960s. *Five Suns* (2004) centres on the 46-minute title track, a sequence of ever-opening crescendos, returns and purposeful meanderings. Guapo is interested in the parallel world of science, where there is no distinction between chaotic maths and the speculations of alchemists. Musically, this is conveyed through group unity; the bass, keyboards and drums rarely fight with each other. The overall sound does not so much recall Magma or other Rock in Opposition bands as it replicates the location those bands found themselves in – somewhere arcane, a sort of fusion that eludes definition. This use of repetition as a structuring device does not come close to the almost static yet powerful work by the duo Om, as exemplified on their first release, *Variations on a Theme* (2005). As we have seen, repetition often signifies an attempt to address spiritual and universal themes explored (somewhat differently) by Midlake and some contemporary progressive folk bands (see Chapter 13). This is due to the meditative space gained by players and listeners through percussion and long duration – trance properties that are also found in Indian ragas and world music. This is not to counter the spirituality in free jazz. The key is extremity, whether it is the near total freedom of late Coltrane or the discipline of recurrent patterns that frees the mind.

Om's spirituality most likely connects to chemical assistance, as evident on the 60-minute-plus 'Dopesmoker' (released in 2003) by Sleep, the band from which Om emerged. But Om has increasingly used Christian imagery and included references to Indian religions from the start. *Variations on a Theme* begins with 'On the Mountain of Dawn' (21:18), which quickly reveals the irony of the title – there is precious little variation at the macro scale, even if locally the drums and bass create a slew of sound that combines harsh jazz and metal. The lyrics play with repetition as lines and verses recur; first lines become last lines as words and music bind in a knot. Al Cisneros's deadpan vocal style is part of the binding, with lyrics that are abstract to the point of arbitrariness, intoned according to syllable position in the line and not for meaning or emphasis ('Anchorite beacon to sentient ground/Platform witnessed to diffuse tomorrow – screen'). The sound and overall mood count for more than a clear message or a rational narrative; where Jon Anderson varies his delivery to remain within the group drive of Yes, so Cisneros matches words to the compacted non-drive of Om. The two remaining tracks offer more significant variations on the initial sounds of 'On the Mountain of Dawn', but subsequent releases follow the same pattern, where tracks more or less stay where they begin ('Bhima's Theme' on the 2007 album *Pilgrimage* is an ultra-rare exception, but each section is free of variation). So we could say that Om builds a narrative that far exceeds the album form, and its mission becomes clear the more we encounter Om's music.

Despite the emergence of Guapo and Om in the early 2000s, not all that was new came from freshly formed bands. The prime exponents of complex repetition in prog had not disappeared: King Crimson returned in 1994 with *Vrooom*, much of which was reconstituted for *Thrak* (1995), and the band continued releasing albums up to 2003, with *The Power to Believe*, and sporadically toured up to 2008 (including a tour with Tool in 2001). This period, though far from homogeneous in the band's membership or overall sound, saw an increase in the number of tracks based on power metal progressions, combined with an updated use of atmospherics based on new digital technologies. This was to some extent a revisitation of previous material for King Crimson, but it was in tune with many metal styles outlined in this chapter. Other bands from the classic phase of progressive rock also toughened their sound, such as Rush, with *Vapor Trails* (2002), and the trio version of Van der Graaf Generator, both live and on *Trisector* (2008). We would argue that this confirms metal in its many guises as the location of authentic progressive rock of the 2000s.

If the fusion of styles is what makes a metal band progressive, then we need also to consider other avant-rock that has explicitly returned to prog styles as well as moving towards metal. A clear example of this is the Finnish group Circle, formed in 1991. In common with so many others, Circle moves towards metal, reincorporating both harshness and strong riff sequences into its experimental sound. Circle reworks the prog of Can and Neu!, as well as the messier world of Samla Mammas Manna or even Frank Zappa. The soundscapes of post-rock are present, as are the cosmic explorations of Hawkwind: for example, on 'Puutiikeri' (24:13), which closes *Tulikoira* (2005). The drive towards free music is also evident, with improvisation, the live situation and concert releases confirming Circle's jazz sensibility. More recently, groups such as Kayo Dot and Genghis Tron (formed in 2003 and 2004 respectively) have extended this fusion into progressive rock informed by free music and extended techniques facilitated by digital technology.

Perhaps the most extreme version of fusion combined with a move to metal and progressive rock is that of the Texas-based band The Mars Volta, which grew out of the post-hardcore band At The Drive-In, whose last album, *Relationship of Command* (2000), displays the emerging direction of core Mars Volta members Omar Rodriguez-Lopez and Cedric Bixler-Zavala. *Relationship of Command* is a complex version of hardcore; The Mars Volta begins to emerge in the breaks, as well as in the atmospheric tracks that close the album. Its debut album, *De-loused in the Comatorium* (2003), fuses The Mars Volta's own styles within individual tracks: the metre, rhythm, genre and relation between group and guitarist change with breath-taking speed as the group alternates between fast-paced staccato sections, riffs, atmospheres, jazz, Latin approximations, and song parts that vary just as much vocally as musically. The band does not develop the math rock approach of post-hardcore but includes it as one of an excess of styles. The Mars Volta also connects to the 'metal fusion' of funk and metal that came about on the West Coast in the mid-1980s, in the guise of Red Hot Chili Peppers, Faith No More and Jane's Addiction (in ascending order of relevance and experimentation). Faith No More took an early grunge approach in a metal direction, and lead singer Mike Patton has since had a long career of experimental projects, from the Zappa-esque palsied rock of northern Californian band Mr. Bungle to a host of collaborations with John Zorn and noise musicians. Jane's Addiction established a fusion template that connects proto-punk US art rock, alternative rock, funk and metal. Group climaxes puncture rolling bass rhythms and detailed guitar-playing to create an ecstatic and dynamic whole. Jane's Addiction even developed longer pieces, and side two of *Ritual de lo Habituel* (1990) contains a lyrically connected song suite. The Mars Volta transplants Jane's Addiction whole (and often features musicians from Red Hot Chili Peppers) and thus sits at the heart of a properly metallic fusion that recalls the first Mahavishnu Orchestra album, just as it summons the group playing of Yes, albeit in a way that is more persistently dissonant.

The musical narrative of *De-loused in the Comatorium* is anything but a fusion; its constant changes and interruptions structure a lyrical descent into the dream-world of a coma. With the aid of the accompanying 20-page story, initially available only via the band's website, we follow the post-Beat surrealist journey of Cerpin Taxt through an otherworld (or inner world) that might be seen to mock the patterning of the cosmos in Tool's music, especially as it constantly falls into confusion and scene-changing. In a world replete with monsters, danger and incomprehension, there are similarities in style and content with Peter Gabriel's writing on *The Lamb Lies Down on Broadway*. The ending sees Cerpin Taxt emerge from the coma only to repeat his suicide attempt, this time successfully. On this and on all Mars Volta albums, the lyrics echo William Burroughs (or perhaps David Cronenberg's take on Burroughs in his 1999 film of *The Naked Lunch*), because bodies and language are always porous, even though images abound suggestively. Cut-ups vie with Joycean reconfigurations ('an internal hemorrhaging made aware by the animonstrosity of his frankenstatue presence' is an early line), while lyrical connections offer sense only to withhold it in ways that channel surrealism, particularly in the partial and fragmentary rendering of the story in the actual lyrics.[8] The combination of fractured music and words functions far more suggestively when more obscure, and the ghost of filmmaker David Lynch drifts through this album to form a surrealist cut-up Book of the Dead. As well as reworking the details of the journey recounted in the story, the crossing points between realities and worlds within other realities are marked by instrumental passages, or by the dissipation of a track's momentum in atmospheres that suggest sinister activity. Tracks not only break and crack, but fissures appear within these cracks on 'Drunkship of Lanterns' and 'Take the Veil Cerpin Taxt'. This is a disassembled progressive rock that applies hardcore musical logic to prog, just as it pushes a range of alternative rock styles in a direction that overtly reiterates sounds, dynamics, and developments of earlier types of progressive music.

The second album, *Frances the Mute* (2005), explicitly performs progressive rock. Both albums feature the art of Hipgnosis, but *Frances the Mute*, with its red-curtained heads (represented on the cover of this book), makes the Lynchian core visually present. Where the first album had lengthy songs, but only one track over 10 minutes long, *Frances the Mute* has only five tracks over 77 minutes, one of which, 'Cassandra Gemini', is 32 minutes long. The title track's lyrics are listed, but the track is not present on the album, featuring only on 'The Widow' single and on the limited four-disc vinyl set; the three-album standard vinyl issue makes a point of omitting it: side six has an etching where the track could have been.

The Mars Volta has made a strong claim on these and succeeding albums to be part of the material, as well as the musical inheritance, of progressive rock, using coloured vinyl, gatefold sleeves, and surrealist imagery that flows into the album contents. *Frances the Mute* extends the section splits of the first album: in many ways, the second album is a stretching of the first. This is a Lynchian narrative of transitions, visions, violence and lost spaces that can be glimpsed only in peripheral vision. Sections of complex brute power alternate with longer improvised sections and atmospheres that build over time, to be finally disrupted. The opening track, 'Cygnus . . . Vismund Cygnus', even opts for different production levels in the transition from the opening section, emphasizing disruption. The opening 'Sarcophagi' also closes the album, a circularity heightened on the vinyl version, where sides one to four end in locked grooves. Tracks one and four also end with sections titled 'Con Safo', charting the movements of the Miranda character from 'L'Via L'Viaquez' to 'Miranda That Ghost Just Isn't Holy Anymore'. The first of these tracks has an internal dualism, as sections of guitar rock take turns with slow Latin parts, with no obvious verse-chorus hierarchy between them.

Circularity structures the narrative to unify tracks, as well as crossing between them. This is not a spiral patterning but an undoing of the very linearity that long tracks ostensibly provide. Despite these circular structures, individual song parts presage the more direct style of The Mars Volta's succeeding releases, *Amputechture* (2006), *The Bedlam in Goliath* (2008) and *Octahedron* (2009). The songs on these albums are simpler and the lyrics more linear, but the interest in time, tempo and metre remain as narrative devices, as well as the intrusion of staccato bursts. As the older Mars Volta interrupts the new, it is as if, with this band, we are witnessing an accelerated take on the history of progressive rock.

Notes

1. The extreme condensation found in Napalm Death and Extreme Noise Terror, as songs collapse into a few seconds, can be seen as an ironic stretching out of the metal song form.

2. This reseeding is updated by Canadian band Mare, which recombined a math aesthetic with black metal. It should be noted that within metal the word 'technical' is used as surrogate for something similar to progressive rock: hence 'technical black metal'.

3. A rare example of a female musician who is not a vocalist in this period is Eva Gardner, who played bass in the first incarnation of The Mars Volta. Chloe Alper is a multi-instrumentalist and one of the vocalists of Pure Reason Revolution, so should also be considered differently to female singers in prog bands.

4. Other notable releases that bring band and orchestra together are Yes, *Symphonic Live* DVD (2002), Dream Theater's *Score* (2006), and Michael Kamen's collaboration with Metallica, *S & M* (1999).

5. Among contemporary groups, Epica's two recurring sequences, 'A New Age Dawns' and 'The Embrace that Smothers' should be noted. Looking further back, we find Rush's *Fear* song-cycle and King Crimson's 'Lark's Tongues in Aspic' instrumental series, as discussed earlier in the book.

6. Porcupine Tree's *Nil Recurring* EP (2007) features the track 'Normal', which centres on the same chorus as 'Sentimental'; in reframing the track, it takes a rueful distance from the problems of youth on *Fear of a Blank Planet*.

7. For lyrics and reflections on Tool, see toolshed.down.net/lyrics/lateraluslyrics.php.

8. For the story of *De-loused in the Comatorium*, see tmvfr.info/miscfiles/DeLoused_storybook.pdf.

Coda

The Future Now

Progressive rock needs time: time to arrive, time to develop, time to fulfil its historical reach and musical range. When we first started thinking about writing this book in the mid-1990s progressive rock had reached a nadir. Neo-progressive bands were breaking up or struggling to sustain record deals, while groups from the 1970s occasionally reformed in different configurations or splintered off to release solo albums of varying quality. Even those that stayed close to their roots, such as Rush and Jethro Tull, struggled for direction in the mid-1990s; in 1996, Phil Collins left Genesis after twenty-five years in the band; Pink Floyd marked the end of the post–Roger Waters phase with the tour album *Pulse* (1996); and the best offering from Yes in that period was the largely live two-album project *Keys to Ascension 1* and *2* (1996–7).

The mid-1990s also gave rise to three book-length assessments of prog rock that helped to legitimate its place within the history of popular music: Paul Stump's *The Music's All That Matters* and Edward Macan's *Rocking the Classics* in 1997, and Bill Martin's *Listening to the Future* in 1998. In his final chapter, Macan pays attention to the 'modest revival' of neo-progressive rock, but he and Martin are nostalgic, to differing degrees, for the 1970s classic phase with all its musical complexity, conceptual innovation and countercultural politics.[1] On this view, the music that came afterwards, in the 1980s and 1990s, was a pale shadow of what went before, rather than simply the next temporal phase in a longer sequence. It is easy to say with hindsight that the end point of this sequence extended far beyond the mid-1990s, even though new directions might have been detected with the release of Current 93's *Of Ruine or Some Blazing Starre* in 1994, King Crimson's *Thrak* in 1995, and Radiohead's *OK Computer* in 1997. Macan acknowledges some of these directions with his brief reference to post-progressive music and 'bands who have sought to fertilize the "classic" progressive style with entirely new influences such as minimalism and ethnic music', noting that the 'offshoots' of prog rock 'may eventually prove important'.[2] Despite Macan's acknowledgement, the three authors shared the tacit sense that this was the end of an era of progressive rock as 'a cultural force' and that we could now fully trace its arc from the late 1960s to its demise in the face of punk, before its neo-prog afterglow burnt briefly in the 1980s.[3]

It is tempting to adopt models such as Raymond Williams' emergent–dominant–residual dynamic to trace the trajectory of a musical form, or to borrow a paradigm from language development in which overused words turn into clichés and eventually dead metaphors, perhaps to be revived only as historical curiosities.[4] Used as paradigms for progressive rock, these models would suggest a slow rise and terminal fall, from which the only return is through nostalgia for an ever-receding past. Williams' emphasis on the 'complex interrelations between movements and tendencies both within and beyond a specific and effective dominance' links closely to the methodology of this book.[5] However, we would resist appropriating either model wholesale for two reasons: first, because these models are better applied to the development of a cultural form or language structure over a much longer historical period, and, second, because the recycling of popular musical styles from the 1980s onwards strains against a narrative of linear development or dialectical change. In the second half of this book, we have identified a sequence of generations of progressive rock since the late 1960s, but these could be conceptualized as a series of backward, inward, sideways or radial movements rather than a sequential development.

Such multiple directions are encoded in Storm Thorgeson's artwork for The Mars Volta's 2005 *Frances the Mute* album, represented on the cover of this book. The artwork depicts the meeting of past and future as two identical classic cars, one shown from the inside, the other from the outside, passing in opposite directions. There is something indecipherable about the picture: the identical red carpet-bags prevent the motorists from seeing where they are driving, thereby raising questions about freedom and autonomy and prompting us to wonder whether they are in fact pranksters or hostages. It also, perhaps, references the famous bag into which French Dadaist Tristan Tzara encouraged us to place cut-up words before shaking and randomly rearranging them to create new modes of expression.[6]

A better model is to be found in Marjorie Perloff's reconceptualization of modernism as a subterranean cultural mode that rose to prominence at certain moments in the twentieth century (1920s, 1940s, 1960s) but that can also be identified in cultural practices between and beyond these decades.[7] Progressive rock can usefully be seen as a late modernist flowering that continues to persist beyond its most visible phase of the early 1970s. As such, the ambition of musicians to fuse high and low musical styles, to extend and stretch forms, to borrow and appropriate material from other cultural modes, and to experiment with recording technology moves us far beyond conventional conceptions of progressive rock as a tightly encoded genre.

Nor does it mean that avant-garde experimentation arrives only at an early moment before ossifying into a fixed cultural form: experiments with composition, sonic range, performance and multimedia can occur at any point on this longer trajectory when elements are rearranged into new configurations. The tendency for the music industry to swiftly absorb new musical styles often gives rise to a processed or predictable sound that lacks the organic development of moments such as the late 1960s, when the possibility of fusions between blues, folk, jazz, pop and classical music seemed limitless. But, as we have discussed in the previous three chapters, elements of new wave, post-punk, electronica, industrial, trip hop and heavy metal have all been similarly deployed and stretched in recent versions of progressive rock. These elements help us to identify a continual forward movement, even as we spot spirals of connections between different periods and styles of prog. In the case of progressive metal, for example, we speak not simply of a linear development but also of reappearances, mutations and appropriations with complex temporal relations to the original. As we have shown, the high phase of progressive rock in the 1970s had myriad beginnings and influences and has given rise to other expansions and combinations of musical forms. And yet, progressive rock of the 1970s established a horizon for what was to follow. In order to see this horizon clearly and to account for the multiple returns of progressive rock, we need to identify two broad trends. First, although progressive rock was not critically acceptable between 1976 and 1997 (broadly between Sex Pistols and Radiohead), groups continued to reference 1970s prog while engaging in apparently separate and new musical forms. Second, the return to an avant-garde as a multilayered reference point alters how we listen to the high phase, as well as to its later versions. Sometimes straight and ironic musical borrowing is so tightly fused on an album or track that it is tricky to separate out homage from deliberate discordance and a speaking back to the past.

'Time Flies' from Porcupine Tree's *The Incident* (2009) is a good case in point. *The Incident* extends the critique of the media on *Fear of a Blank Planet*, and this track is the long (11:41) centrepiece of a fourteen-part song-cycle that takes as its concept the frequent use of 'the incident' as a media-friendly phrase that often masks the dramatic consequences for those involved in a shared experience or sequence of events. As Steven Wilson notes, the process of writing takes him inwards, to reconsider 'incidents in my own life, both good and bad, that had affected me as a person and changed the path of my life, sometimes for better and sometimes for worse'.[8] We might associate an autobiographical style with a consistent point of view and a stable register, but *The Incident* is eclectic in its musical range, as signalled on the opening track, 'Occam's Razor' (1:58), by the thrashing drums and reverberating electric guitar that surround an acoustic guitar before fading into sampled noises, whispers and grunts. These styles clash and meld throughout the album (such as on 'Great Expectations' and 'The Incident') but settle into an identifiable progressive sound on 'Time Flies'. Blending nostalgia for childhood with a meditation on time as it experientially shifts across a life cycle, the track checks the melancholy often associated with the loss of precious moments with the pace and momentum of time. This is literally rendered on Lasse Hoile's video for 'Time Flies', which uses accelerated, rewound and halted motion to explore a single life moving simultaneously forwards and backwards, where luminescent memories intertwine with raw experience. The song begins in classic autobiographical mode – 'I was born in '67' – accompanied by acoustic guitar. But it is not clear whether the 'suburb of heaven' into which the singer is born is a safe haven or an anodyne environment that contrasts unfavourably with two iconic albums released in 1967 that are name-checked in the first stanza: *Sgt. Pepper* and *Are You Experienced*.

The other layer of potential irony is the self-conscious adoption of the time signature and guitar sound from Pink Floyd's 1977 album *Animals*. Wilson's guitar work is almost identical to David Gilmour's on the opening of 'Dogs' (17:08), the second track on *Animals*. But the lyrics move in different directions, despite sharing the same transitional phrase: 'after a while'. Roger Waters' lyrics on 'Dogs' seem to warn the listener to prepare for a cynical dog-eat-dog world ('You gotta be crazy', 'You gotta sleep on your toes', 'You gotta strike when the moment is right'). It soon becomes clear, though, that these battle strategies are harder to sustain over a lifetime; that paranoia can easily set in ('You gotta keep one eye looking over your shoulder'); and that loneliness, 'creeping malaise' and illness might be inevitable consequences of a self-serving lifestyle. As the track progresses, it is clear that the lyrics are a warning to the listener (as well as to the band members) not to follow this pattern, for fear of being 'dragged down by the stone' – as emphasized by the sustained echo on this line for almost a minute in the middle of the track. The long sequence of lines that begin with 'Who was', which closes out the song, is deeply fatalistic: the protagonist (no longer in the second person) is born into 'a house full of pain' and is 'ground down in the end' before being 'found dead on the phone'.

Porcupine Tree's advice to the listener is much less cynical. On 'Time Flies', it is not the singer but a female figure (perhaps a mother or a girlfriend) who advises the singer and listener to make their own luck, to try to make things happen, and to 'take whatever comes to you'. The track is more experientially expansive than 'Dogs', evoking 'summer showers', laughter and dancing, before shifting to darker elements in a brooding passage from 3:50 to the delayed bridge at 8:12, when time suddenly breaks down and we realize that families can harm rather than nurture. However, 'Time Flies' resists the cynical turn of 'Dogs' by ironically referencing another Pink Floyd track, 'Have a Cigar', from *Wish You Were Here* (1975), in which the young musician is offered a cigar and the promise that he will 'go far, fly high' and 'never die'. Rather than accepting this devil's bargain, the singer on 'Time Flies' asks us to 'stop smoking your cigar', perhaps because he fears that this marker of capitalist success could be at the expense of purer experiences and simpler memories. The last image in the song is the memory of a coat that 'she' wore at Alton Towers (the West Midlands theme park). This could be read as a Proustian moment that forces its way into the present, or as the mourning for simple childhood pleasures no longer accessible to the adult singer. Whichever reading we pursue, the song preserves a space for immediate experience in the face of social, familial and temporal threats.

We should note that 'Time Flies' is a special case on *The Incident*, representing the only sustained bright moment on what is otherwise a dark and brooding album. But it does provide a strong example of a song that is a pastiche of musical and lyrical sources, pieced together with a recuperative irony that rescues it from the cynicism of *Animals* – an album that reflected Pink Floyd's struggle with industry pressures and the trappings of fame. As well as blurring boundaries between progressive, neo-progressive and post-progressive as a sequential progression of styles, on a broader aesthetic level this reading of 'Time Flies' collapses what Fredric Jameson sees as one of the chief stylistic differences between modernism and postmodernism by fusing irony and pastiche.[9] It also takes us back to Perloff's theory that modernism has a much longer arc than is often recognized, taking in stylistic elements that critics were confidently claiming in the 1980s and early 1990s marked a break from the past.

The Decemberists' 2004 EP *The Tain* could be used as another case in point, but, as we argue in Chapter 13, the EP moves too far away from the source text to offer more than an impressionistic version of the founding Irish

Porcupine Tree in concert, New York (September 2010).

myth. A better example is the Oklahoma psychedelic band The Flaming Lips'
re-recording of *The Dark Side of the Moon* (2009), which blends homage,
pastiche and irony, pushing Pink Floyd's best-known album into a different
musical register just as it shows reverence for the original. The Flaming
Lips – collaborating with Stardeath and White Dwarfs, as well as with Henry
Rollins (primarily for Roger Waters' spoken interjections) and Peaches (who
performs singing duties on 'The Great Gig in the Sky') – try to re-create
the album: it stays incredibly close to the original, even echoing the use of
sound effects. Unlike Dream Theater's live virtuoso rendition of the album
in October 2005, the faithfulness of The Flaming Lips version is heavily
mediated by a resistance to instrumental and studio skill. There is actually
a huge amount of skill, but the album strives instead to display ramshackle
authenticity. As such, this is a reimagining of *The Dark Side of the Moon* that
has not been painstakingly constructed over many tracks on the studio desk.

The album often replicates sounds by replacing them. Instead of beginning
with chiming clocks, 'Time' starts with a loud alarm, coughing and running
(playing with 'On the Run', which is curtailed in the 2009 version), thereby
dispersing the epic and crystalline introduction to Pink Floyd's 'Time'. But The
Flaming Lips do not eschew the epic, as the track explodes into overdriven
power riffs and screaming electronics, and then cuts to an acoustic ballad
for the vocals. For 'The Great Gig in the Sky', this new version of *The Dark
Side of the Moon* goes back to a different 1973, with acoustic guitar, flute, and
Peaches' treated take on the original vocal presented over a funk back-drop.
On 'Brain Damage', we are taken back firmly to psychedelic-era Pink Floyd as
a reverbed voice sings plaintively over synthesizers until a messy crescendo
emerges, straining against the faded vocal. The Flaming Lips bring not only
a post-punk sensibility to the album but also a greater sense of dissonance;
the closing 'Eclipse' has vocals very similar to those of Roger Waters, but the
music is a jerky, stop-start blast that is more 1987 than either 1973 or 2009.
In short, The Flaming Lips have very purposefully recast the album as a set of
conscious references to what Pink Floyd set out to do; the 2009 album takes
critical positions and plays with details in order to work very closely with the
original. It is as if the album has been perfectly replicated but also, somehow,
started anew. Like Porcupine Tree's 'Time Flies', The Flaming Lips' *The Dark
Side of the Moon* scrambles our ideas of whether a musical mode is subject
to parody, pastiche and irony, and this in turn renews how we should hear
Pink Floyd's *The Dark Side of the Moon*.[10]

A further example is The Orb and David Gilmour's collaboration *Metallic
Spheres* (2010). Famous for its extended electronic tracks in the 1990s (such
as their 1992 single 'Blue Room', at nearly 40 minutes), The Orb references
Gilmour's signature guitar style ('Shine on You Crazy Diamond' and 'Run
Like Hell' can be heard in the opening section) but incorporates it in a wash
of ambient electronica. Rather than playing on the clash of progressive styles
in the vein of Porcupine Tree, *Metallic Spheres* is an extended progression

over two old-fashioned album sides ('Metallic Side' and 'Sphere Side'), blending an eclectic style that links back to mid-1970s progressive rock, early 1980s systems music and early 1990s trip hop but also moves forwards and sideways to club culture, electronic sampling, and experiments with sound technology.[11] The Orb's wide-ranging use of vocal and musical samples and the bridging of progressive, electronic and punk influences (Pink Floyd, Brian Eno, Tangerine Dream, Killing Joke) help us to look beyond the neat alignment of musical genres and performance styles into which progressive rock is usually placed. These examples from Porcupine Tree, The Flaming Lips and The Orb tempt us to suggest that the 'beyond' and 'before' of progressive rock are in the 'now', rather than in the future or the past. This might also represent an essential change in what progressive rock is, insofar as new variants of it – whether uncannily doubling the past or explicitly referencing 1970s prog – might no longer be about the avant-garde in any meaningful sense. Instead, contemporary progressive rock seeks to live in the 'now', reflecting its currency as a multifaceted cultural resource.

We have taken recent returns to Pink Floyd as a key to the time of progressive rock as it is now. References have themselves become complex, adding to the multiplicity of prog time. These returns do not just look back to music of the 1970s; as we have discussed, neo-prog of the 1980s became a cultural reference point for later bands, as has post-progressive, folk and metal. These strains are in a time of the present that is constantly evolving into new combinations and fusions. We see this functioning at the interface between rock and electronica opened up by Radiohead, Björk and No-man, and, earlier still, by Peter Gabriel and Peter Hammill. It also extends into the merging of prog and early 1990s rave in the shape of Enter Shikari or Pendulum. Enter Shikari's first album, *Take to the Skies* (2007), brings together hardcore and prog structuring (reprises and bridges between tracks) where the crescendos are driven by a wilfully dated early rave keyboard sound. Pendulum features Steven Wilson and The Prodigy's Liam Howlett on its 2010 release *Immersion*, which builds prog crescendos out of techno, rave and drum and bass patterns. Pure Reason Revolution continue to incorporate electronic elements into an already eclectic sound and, on *Hammer and Anvil* (2010), rhythmical synth-driven tracks alternate with returns to the more experimental reaches of 1990s alternative rock. American stadium rock band Linkin Park has explored beats and electronic atmospheres on *A Thousand Suns* (2010), with the explicit aim of creating a unified sound-world. The English electronic artist Squarepusher, somewhat unusual in that domain for playing bass and drums live at ferocious pace, as well as for using electronics and digital sound, began to reveal the secret prog heart of complex dance music on *Just a Souvenir* (2008), which suggested not only 1970s progressive rock in its bass playing and its acoustic passages but also the future as envisaged by The Buggles, who joined Yes for the *Drama* album in 1980.

If the past is always returning in new forms of progressive rock, or in the revival and return of older bands, then we also have to note that the future is already with us – not just the currents that we have identified in this book but also future ones that will be seen only with hindsight.[12] It is, finally, as if all of the times and potentials of prog exist now, in the present.

Notes

1. Macan, *Rocking the Classics*, 220.

2. Ibid., 12, 10.

3. Ibid., 10.

4. Raymond Williams, *Marxism and Literature* (Oxford: Oxford University Press, 1977), 121–7.

5. Ibid., 121.

6. This indecipherability is confirmed by further images of the motorists on the inside artwork: one image has the second driver's arm protruding threateningly from the car; a second image shows the two figures wearing red carpet-bags on the back seat of the same car; and a third a close up of the covered head of a single driver wearing a checked shirt. This theme of loss of identity and muted transformation is emphasized in the search for biological parents that provides the narrative spine of the album; the fusion of English and Spanish lyrics; and the text on the back page of the CD booklet, which begins with 'i think i've become like one of the others' (repeated three times) and ends with 'no there's no light no there's no time you ain't got nothing your life was just a lie'.

7. See Marjorie Perloff, *21st-Century Modernism: The New Poetics* (Oxford: Wiley-Blackwell, 2002), 1–6, 154–200.

8. 'Porcupine Tree Interview', *The Aquarian Weekly* (September 2009), www.theaquarian.com/2009/09/24/interview-porcupine-tree-behind-the-incident-steven-wilson.

9. Fredric Jameson varies between parody and irony as the distinctive modernist style, and describes postmodern pastiche as a 'neutral practice . . . a blank parody, a statue with blind eyeballs . . . a kind of blank irony' (Jameson, *Postmodernism*, 17).

10. The Flaming Lips' previous release was a full-length film on DVD with an accompanying CD, *Christmas on Mars: A Fantastical Film Freakout* (2008), which also reprised and paid homage to earlier works, in this case, corny Christmas films, psychedelic visuals and science fiction. Like The Flaming Lips' *Dark Side of the Moon*, this is a lo-fi take on the space visions of the past; the entire time on Mars involves repair, salvage and potential failure, in a cheery yet sinister vein.

11. See Dom Lawson, 'Gilmour's Adventures in the Ultraworld', *Classic Rock Presents Prog* (September 2010), 42–5.

12. We could imagine a future prog that looked to techno, drum and bass, or its more recent variants, just as late 1960s bands turned to jazz, blues and folk, all of which were themselves undergoing revival, regeneration and recuperation. This also occurs in the far reaches of electronic dance music: in the 1990s, Drexciya's aquatic, Burroughs-inflected worlds on the Underground Resistance label; X-102's *Discovers the Rings of Saturn* (1992), including a journey inward to the planet; A Guy Called Gerald's *Black Secret Technology* (1995); Goldie's double CD *Timeless* (1995) and the less successful and more explicitly conceptual *Saturnz Return* (1998); and Plastikman's *Bladerunner*-noir album *Closer* (2003).

Discography

This list is of musical works cited in the text, and so is not designed as a comprehensive guide to progressive rock releases. Where the version discussed is significantly different, the first date refers to the original date, and the second to the date of reissue.

A Stereo Introduction to the Exciting World of Transatlantic (Contour Records, 1972)

Abel Ganz, *The Danger of Strangers* (Abel, [1998] 2008)

The Acorn, *Glory Hope Mountain* (V2, 2007)

The Acorn, *No Ghost* (Bella Union, 2010)

Alternative TV, *The Image Has Cracked* (Get Back, [1978] 2009)

Tori Amos, *Boys for Pele* (Atlantic, 1996)

Tori Amos, *From the Choirgirl Hotel* (Atlantic, 1998)

Tori Amos, *Scarlet's Walk* (Sony, 2002)

Tori Amos, *Welcome to Sunny Florida* (Sony, 2004)

Jon Anderson, *Olias of Sunhillow* (Atlantic, 1976)

Laurie Anderson et al., *New Music for Electronic and Recorded Media* (New World, [1977] 2006)

Laurie Anderson, *Big Science* (WEA, 1982)

Ange, *Au-delà de mon délire* (Philips, 1974)

Animal Collective, *Sung Tongs* (Fat Cat, 2004)

Aphrodite's Child, *666* (Vertigo, 1972)

Area, *Arbeit macht frei* (Edel, 1973)

Area, *Crac!* (Edel, 1975)

A. R. Kane, *69* (Rough Trade, 1988)

Asia, *Asia* (Geffen, 1982)

Asia, *Arena* (Inside Out, 1996)

Virginia Astley, *From Gardens Where We Feel Secure* (Rough Trade, [1983] 2003)

At the Drive-In, *Relationship of Command* (Grand Royal, 2000)

Atheist, *Unquestionable Presence* (Relapse, [1991] 2005)

Atheist, *Elements* (Relapse, [1993] 2005)

Atomic Rooster, *Death Walks Behind You* (Repertoire, 1970)

Baker Gurvitz Army, *Elysian Encounter* (Mountain, 1975)

Bathory, *Nordland I and II* (Black Mark, 2002–3)

Les Baxter, *Ritual of the Savage* (Rev-Ola, [1954] 2006)

The Beach Boys, *Pet Sounds* (Capitol, 1966)

The Beatles, *Rubber Soul* (EMI, 1965)

The Beatles, *Revolver* (EMI, 1966)

The Beatles, *Sgt. Pepper's Lonely Hearts Club Band* (EMI, 1967)

The Beatles, *The Beatles* (Apple, 1968)

David Bedford, *Rime of the Ancient Mariner* (Virgin, 1975)

Björk, *Homogenic* (One Little Indian, 1997)

Björk, *Medúlla* (One Little Indian/Atlantic, 2004)

Tim Blake, *Blake's New Jerusalem* (Egg, 1978)

Botch, *American Nervoso* (Hydra Head, 1995)

David Bowie, *Ziggy Stardust and the Spiders from Mars* (RCA, 1972)

Bumpers (Island, 1970)

Burzum, *Daudi Baldrs* (Misanthropy, 1999)

Kate Bush, *The Kick Inside* (EMI, 1978)

Kate Bush, *Lionheart* (EMI, 1978)

Kate Bush, *Never Forever* (EMI, 1980)

Kate Bush, *The Dreaming* (EMI, 1982)

Kate Bush, *Hounds of Love* (EMI, 1985)

Kate Bush, *The Sensual World* (EMI, 1989)

Kate Bush, *The Red Shoes* (EMI, 1994)

Kate Bush, *Aerial* (EMI, 2005)

The Byrds, *The Notorious Byrd Brothers* (Columbia, 1968)

Camel, *Mirage* (Decca, 1974)

Camel, *Music Inspired by The Snow Goose* (Decca, 1975)

Caravan, *The Land of Grey and Pink* (Deram, 1971)

Walter Carlos, *Switched on Bach* (Columbia, 1968)

Cathedral, *Garden of Unearthly Delights* (Nuclear Blast, 2005)

Circle, *Tulikoira* (Ektro, 2005)

Cold Fairyland, *Kingdom of Benevolent Strangers* (Cold Fairyland, 2003)

Cold Fairyland, *Seeds on the Ground* (Cold Fairyland, 2008)

Ornette Coleman, *Free Jazz* (Atlantic, 1961)

Shirley and Dolly Collins, *Anthems in Eden* (Beat Goes On, [1969] 1999)

John Coltrane, *Ascension* (Impulse, [1965] 2000)

John Coltrane, *The Olatunji Concert: The Last Live Recording* (Impulse, 2001)

Comus, *First Utterance* (Dawn, 1971)

Country Joe and the Fish, *Electric Music for Mind and Body* (Vanguard, 1967)

The Cure, *Disintegration* (Polydor, 1989)

The Cure, *Bloodflowers* (Polydor, 2000)

Current 93, *Swastikas for Goddy* (Durtro, 1987)

Current 93, *Earth Covers Earth* (United Dairies, 1988)

Current 93, *Tamlin* EP (Durtro, 1994)

Current 93, *Lucifer over London* EP (Durtro, 1994)

Current 93, *Of Ruine or Some Blazing Star* (Durtro, 1994)

Current 93, *Soft Black Stars* (Durtro, 1998)

Curved Air, *Air Conditioning* (Rhino Encore, 1970)

Curved Air, *Second Album* (Rhino Encore, 1971)

Curved Air, *Phantasmagoria* (Warner, 1972)

Cynic, *Focus* (Roadrunner, [1993] 2004)

Miles Davis, *Kind of Blue* (Columbia, 1959)

Miles Davis, *Sketches of Spain* (Columbia, 1960)

Miles Davis, *In a Silent Way* (Columbia, 1969)

Miles Davis, *Bitches Brew* (Columbia, 1970)

The Decemberists, *Castaways and Cutouts* (Kill Rock Stars, 2002)

The Decemberists, *Her Majesty* (Kill Rock Stars, 2003)

The Decemberists, *The Tain* EP (Acuarela, 2004)

The Decemberists, *Picaresque* (Rough Trade, 2005)

The Decemberists, *The Crane Wife* (Rough Trade, 2006)

The Decemberists, *The Hazards of Love* (Rough Trade, 2009)

Deep Purple, *Concerto for Group and Orchestra* (Harvest, 1969)

The Dillinger Escape Plan, *Calculating Infinity* (Relapse, 1999)

Don Caballero, *Don Caballero 2* (Touch and Go, 1995)

Dream Theater, *Metropolis Pt. 2: Scenes From a Memory* (Elektra, 1999)

Dream Theater, *Six Degrees of Inner Turbulence* (Elektra, 2002)

Dream Theater, *Octavarium* (Atlantic, 2005)

Dream Theater, *Systematic Chaos* (Roadrunner, 2007)

Dream Theater, *Black Clouds & Silver Linings* (Roadrunner, 2009)

Egg, *The Polite Force* (Esoteric, 1970)

Egg, *The Civil Surface* (Esoteric, 1974)

Duke Ellington, 'Reminiscing in Tempo' (Columbia, 1935)

Duke Ellington, *A Drum is a Woman* (Jazz Track, 1957)

Duke Ellington, *Black, Brown and Beige* (Columbia, 1958)

Emerson, Lake and Palmer, *Tarkus* (Manticore, [1971] 2001)

Emerson, Lake and Palmer, *Pictures at an Exhibition* (Manticore, 1971)

Emerson, Lake and Palmer, *Brain Salad Surgery* (Sanctuary, 1973)

Emerson, Lake and Palmer, *Welcome Back My Friends to the Show That Never Ends* (Sanctuary, 1974)

Emerson, Lake and Palmer, *Works*, Volume 1 (Atlantic, 1977)

England, *Garden Shed* (Garden Shed, [1977] 2005)

The Enid, *Aerie Faerie Nonsense* (Operation Seraphim, 1977)

The Enid, *Fand* (fan club release, 1985)

Brian Eno, *Here Come the Warm Jets* (Virgin, 1974)

Brian Eno, *On Land* (Virgin, 1982)

Enter Shikari, *Take to the Skies* (Ambush Reality, 2007)

Epica, *The Phantom Agency* (Transmission, 2003)

Fairport Convention, *What We Did on Our Holidays* (Island, 1969)

Fairport Convention, *Unhalfbricking* (Island, 1969)

Fairport Convention, *Liege and Lief* (Island, 1969)

Fairport Convention, *Babbacombe Lee* (Island, 1971)

Fields of the Nephilim, *Elizium* (Beggars Banquet, 1990)

Fish, *Vigil in a Wilderness of Mirrors* (EMI, 1989)

Fish, *Field of Crows* (Chocolate Frog, 2004)

Fish, *13th Star* (Chocolate Frog, 2007)

The Flaming Lips et al., *Dark Side of the Moon* (Warner, 2009)

Fleet Foxes, *Fleet Foxes* (Bella Union, 2008)

The Flower Kings, *Flower Power* (Century, 1999)

The Flower Kings, *Adam and Eve* (Inside Out, 2004)

The Flower Kings, *Paradox Hotel* (Century, 2006)

The Flower Kings, *The Sum of No Evil* (SPV, 2009)

Focus, *Moving Waves* (Red Bullet, 1971)

Foetus (Scraping Foetus off the Wheel), *Nail* (Some Bizarre, 1985)

Robert Fripp, *God Save the Queen/Under Heavy Manners* (EG, 1981)

Robert Fripp and the League of Gentlemen, *Robert Fripp/The League of Gentlemen* (EG, 1981)

Peter Gabriel, *Peter Gabriel* (Charisma, 1977)

Peter Gabriel, *Peter Gabriel* (Charisma, 1978)

Peter Gabriel, *Peter Gabriel* (Charisma, 1980)

Peter Gabriel, *Peter Gabriel* (Charisma, 1982)

Peter Gabriel, *Plays Live* (Charisma, 1983)

Peter Gabriel, *Birdy* (Universal, 1985)

Peter Gabriel, *So* (Geffen, 1986)

Peter Gabriel, *The Passion* (Geffen, 1989)

Peter Gabriel, *Us* (Real World, 1992)

Peter Gabriel, *Up* (Virgin, 2002)

Marvin Gaye, *What's Going On* (Commercial, 1971)

Genesis, *From Genesis to Revelation* (Decca, 1969)

Genesis, *Trespass* (Charisma, 1970)

Genesis, *Nursery Cryme* (Charisma, 1971)

Genesis, *Foxtrot* (Charisma, 1972)

Genesis, *Genesis Live* (Charisma, 1973)

Genesis, *Selling England by the Pound* (Charisma, 1973)

Genesis, *The Lamb Lies Down on Broadway* (Charisma, 1974)

Genesis, *A Trick of the Tail* (Charisma, 1976)

Genesis, *Wind and Wuthering* (Charisma, 1977)

Genesis, *And Then There Were Three* (Charisma, 1978)

Genesis, *Invisible Touch* (Charisma, 1986)

Gentle Giant, *Gentle Giant* (Vertigo, 1970)

Gentle Giant, *Acquiring the Taste* (Vertigo, 1971)

Gentle Giant, *Octopus* (Columbia, 1972)

Gentle Giant, *In a Glass House* (WWA, 1973)

Gentle Giant, *Civilian* (Terrapin Trucking, 1980)

Goblin, *Profondo Rosso* (Cinevox, [1975] 2000)

Goblin, *Il fantastic viaggio del "bagarozzo" Mark* (Cinevox, 1978)

Goldie, *Timeless* (FFRR, 1995)

Goldie, *Saturnz Return* (FFRR, 1998)

Gong, *Flying Teapot* (Virgin, 1973)

Gong, *Angels Egg* (Virgin, 1973)

Gong, *You* (Virgin, [1974] 2004)

The Grateful Dead, *Grateful Dead* (Warner, 1967)

The Grateful Dead, *Anthem of the Sun* (Warner, 1968)

The Grateful Dead, *American Beauty* (Warner, 1970)

Guapo, *Five Suns* (Cuneiform, 2004)

A Guy Called Gerald, *Black Secret Technology* (Juice Box, 1995)

Steve Hackett, *Voyage of the Acolyte* (Charisma, 1975)

Peter Hammill, *Nadir's Big Chance* (Charisma, 1975)

Peter Hammill, *A Black Box* (S-Type, 1980)

Peter Hammill, *Fireships* (Fie, 1992)

Herbie Hancock, *Headhunters* (Sony, 1973)

Bo Hansson, *Music Inspired by Lord of the Rings* (Charisma, 1972)

Roy Harper, *Stormcock* (Cadiz, [1971] 2007)

Roy Harper, *HQ* (Cadiz, 1975)

Roy Harper, *The Unknown Soldier* (Science Fiction, 1980)

Roy Harper, *Once* (Line, 1990)

Roy Harper, *The Dream Society* (Science Fiction, 1998)

Hatfield and the North, *Hatfield and the North* (Virgin, 1973)

Hawkwind, 'Urban Guerilla' (United Artists, 1973)

Hawkwind, *The Space Ritual Alive* (United Artists, 1973)

Hawkwind, *Warrior on the Edge of Time* (United Artists, 1975)

Hawkwind, *Astounding Sounds, Amazing Music* (Atomhenge, [1976] 2009)

Hawkwind, *Chronicles of the Black Sword* (Atomhenge, [1985] 2009)

The Jimi Hendrix Experience, *Are You Experienced* (MCA, 1967)

The Jimi Hendrix Experience, *Electric Ladyland* (Polydor, 1968)

Henry Cow, *The Studio: Volumes 1–5* (ReR, [1973–8] 2009)

Here and Now, *Give and Take* (Charly, 1978)

Horslips, *The Táin* (Talking Elephant, [1973] 2009)

The Incredible String Band, *The Hangman's Beautiful Daughter* (Elektra, 1968)

The Incredible String Band, *Hard Rope and Silken Twine* (Island, 1974)

IQ, *Tales from the Lush Attic* (Giant Electric Pea, 1983)

IQ, *The Wake* (Sahara, 1985)

IQ, *Subterranea* (GEP, 1997)

IQ, *Dark Matter* (GEP, 2004)

Iron Maiden, *Piece of Mind* (EMI, 1983)

Iron Maiden, *Powerslave* (EMI, 1984)

Iron Maiden, *Seventh Son of a Seventh Son* (EMI, 1988)

Iron Maiden, *The Final Frontier* (EMI, 2010)

Bert Jansch, *Jack Orion* (Transatlantic, 1966)

Japan, *Tin Drum* (Virgin, [1981] 2006)

Japan, *Oil on Canvas* (Virign, [1983] 2006)

Jean-Michel Jarre, *Oxygene* (Sony, 1976)

Jean-Michel Jarre, *Equinoxe* (Sony, 1978)

Jethro Tull, *This Was* (Chrysalis, 1968)

Jethro Tull, *Stand Up* (Chrysalis, 1969)

Jethro Tull, *Benefit* (Chrysalis, 1970)

Jethro Tull, *Aqualung* (Chrysalis, 1971)

Jethro Tull, *Thick as a Brick* (Chrysalis, 1972)

Jethro Tull, *A Passion Play* (Chrysalis, 1973)

Jethro Tull, *Minstrel in the Gallery* (Chrysalis, 1975)

Jethro Tull, *Too Old to Rock 'n' Roll, Too Young to Die* (Chrysalis, 1976)

Jethro Tull, *Songs From the Wood* (Chrysalis, 1977)

Jethro Tull, *Heavy Horses* (Chrysalis, 1978)

Jethro Tull, *Broadsword and the Beast* (Chrysalis, 1982)

Jethro Tull, *Under Wraps* (Chrysalis, 1984)

Jethro Tull, *Crest of a Knave* (Chrysalis, 1987)

Jethro Tull, *Rock Island* (Chrysalis, 1989)

Jethro Tull, *Catfish Rising* (Chrysalis, 1991)

Journey, *Infinity* (Sony, 1978)

Journey, *Escape* (Sony, 1981)

Kaipa, *Solo* (Decca, 1978)

King Crimson, *In The Court of the Crimson King: An Observation* (Island, 1969)

King Crimson, *Islands* (Island, 1971)

King Crimson, *Larks' Tongues in Aspic* (Island, 1972)

King Crimson, *Starless and Bible Black* (Island, 1974)

King Crimson, *Red* (Island, 1974)

King Crimson, *Discipline* (EG, 1981)

King Crimson, *Beat* (EG, 1982)

King Crimson, *Three of a Perfect Pair* (EG, 1984)

King Crimson, *Vrooom* (DGM, 1994)

King Crimson, *Thrak* (DGM, 1995)

King Crimson, *The Power to Believe* (DGM, 2003)

Kingdom Come, *Journey* (Cherry Red, [1973] 2010)

The Kinks, *The Village Green Preservation Society* (Pye, 1968)

Kraftwerk, *Autobahn* (Philips, 1974)

Kraftwerk, *Trans-Europe Express* (Kling Klang, 1977)

Kraftwerk, *The Man Machine* (Kling Klang, 1978)

Led Zeppelin, *Led Zeppelin IV* (Atlantic, 1971)

Levitation, *After Ever EP* (Ultimate, 1991)

Levitation, *Need for Not* (Rough Trade, 1992)

Lin Di, *Ten Days in Magic Land* (Indys, 2002)

Lin Di, *Bride in Legend* (Indys, 2004)

Lin Di, *Meet in the Secret Garden* (Indys, 2009)

Linkin Park, *A Thousand Suns* (Warner, 2010)

Love, *Da Capo* (Warner, [1967] 2002)

Magma, *Magma* (Le Chant du Monde, 1970)

Magma, *Mëkanïk Dëstruktïw Kömmandöh* (Le Chant du Monde, 1973)

Magma, *Studio Zünd* (Le Chant du Monde, 2008)

Magnum, *On a Storyteller's Night* (Sanctuary, 1985)

Mahavishnu Orchestra, *The Inner Mounting Flame* (Columbia, 1971)

Mahavishnu Orchestra, *Birds of Fire* (Columbia, 1973)

Mahavishnu Orchestra, *Apocalypse* (CBS, 1974)

Manning, *Songs from the Bilston House* (F2 Music, 2007)

Marillion, 'Market Square Heroes'/'Grendel', 12-inch (EMI, 1982)

Marillion, *Script for a Jester's Tear* (EMI, 1983)

Marillion, *Fugazi* (EMI, 1984)

Marillion, *Misplaced Childhood* (EMI, 1985)

Marillion, *Clutching at Straws* (EMI, 1987)

Marillion, *Brave* (EMI, 1994)

Marillion, *This Strange Engine* (Castle Communications, 1997)

Marillion, *Marbles* (Intact, 2004)

Marillion, *Less is More* (Earmusic, 2009)

The Mars Volta, *De-loused in the Comatorium* (Universal, 2003)

The Mars Volta, *Frances the Mute* (Universal, 2005)

The Mars Volta, 'The Widow/Frances the Mute' (Universal, 2005)

The Mars Volta, *Amputechture* (Universal, 2006)

The Mars Volta, *The Bedlam in Goliath* (Universal, 2008)

The Mars Volta, *Octahedron* (Warner, 2009)

Joe Meek, *I Hear a New World* (RPM, [1960] 2001)

Midlake, *Banman and Silvercork* (Bella Union, 2004)

Midlake, *The Trials of Van Occupanther* (Bella Union, 2006)

Midlake, *The Courage of Others* (Bella Union, 2010)

The Moody Blues, *Days of Future Passed* (Deram, 1967)

The Moody Blues, *In Search of the Lost Chord* (Deram, 1968)

Van Morrison, *Astral Weeks* (Warner, 1968)

Neil Morse, *Testimony* (Metal Blade, 2003)

Neil Morse, *One* (InsideOut, 2004)

Neil Morse, *Sola Scriptura* (Metal Blade, 2007)

Mostly Autumn, *Glass Shadows* (Nova, 2008)

Multi-Story, *East/West* (Kinesis, 1985)

My Bloody Valentine, *Loveless* (Creation, 1991)

Nektar, *Remember the Future* (Bellaphon, 1973)

Neurosis, *Souls at Zero* (Neurot, 1992)

Joanna Newsom, *Ys* (Drag City, 2006)

Joanna Newsom, *Have One on Me* (Drag City, 2010)

The Nice, *The Thoughts of Emerlist Davjack* (Immediate, 1967)

The Nice, *Ars Longa Vita Brevis* (Immediate, 1968)

The Nice, 'America' (Immediate, 1968)

Harry Nilsson, *The Point!* (RCA, 1971)

Nine Inch Nails, *The Downward Spiral* (1994)

No-man, *Flowermouth* (One Little Indian, 1994)

Nuggets (Rhino, [1972] 2006)

Nurse with Wound, *Chance Meeting on a Dissecting Table of a Sewing Machine and an Umbrella* (United Dairies, 1979)

Mike Oldfield, *Tubular Bells* (Virgin, 1973)

Mike Oldfield, *Hergest Ridge* (Virgin, 1974)

Mike Oldfield, *Ommadawn* (Virgin, 1975)

Mike Oldfield, *Platinum* (Virgin, 1979)

Mike Oldfield, *Music of the Spheres* (Mercury, 2007)

Sally Oldfield, *Water Bearer* (Sanctuary, 1978)

Om, *Variations on a Theme* (Holy Mountain, 2005)

Om, *Pilgrimage* (Southern Lord, 2007)

Opeth, *Morningrise* (Candelight, [1996] 2000)

Opeth, *Blackwater Park* (Music For Nations, 2001)

Opeth, *Deliverance* (Music For Nations, 2002)

Opeth, *Damnation* (Music For Nations, 2003)

The Orb featuring David Gilmour, *Metallic Spheres* (Sony, 2010)

Le Orme, *Collage* (Polygram, 1971)

Le Orme, *Felona e Sorona* (Polygram, [1973] 1998)

Pain of Salvation, *The Perfect Element I* (InsideOut, 2000)

Pain of Salvation, *Scarsick* (InsideOut, 2007)

Pallas, *The Sentinel* (EMI, 1984)

Pallas, *Beat the Drum* (InsideOut, 1998)

Pallas, *XXV* (Music Theories Recordings, 2011)

Pendragon, *Fly High, Fall Far* EP (EMI, 1984)

Pendragon, *The Jewel* (EMI, 1985)

Pendragon, *The Masquerade Overture* (Toff, 1996)

Pendragon, *Not of This World* (Toff, 2001)

Pendragon, *Pure* (Toff, 2008)

Pendulum, *Immersion* (Warner, 2010)

Pentangle, *The Pentangle* (Transatlantic, 1968)

Pentangle, *Sweet Child* (Transatlantic, 1969)

Pentangle, *Basket of Light* (Transatlantic, 1969)

Pentangle, *Cruel Sister* (Transatlantic, 1970)

Anthony Phillips, *The Geese and the Ghost* (Evangeline, 1977)

Pink Floyd, *The Piper at the Gates of Dawn* (EMI, 1967)

Pink Floyd, *A Saucerful of Secrets* (EMI, 1968)

Pink Floyd, *Ummagumma* (Harvest, 1969)

Pink Floyd, *Atom Heart Mother* (Harvest, 1970)

Pink Floyd, *Meddle* (Harvest, 1971)

Pink Floyd, *Obscured by Clouds* (EMI, 1972)

Pink Floyd, *The Dark Side of the Moon* (Harvest, 1973)

Pink Floyd, *Wish You Were Here* (Harvest, 1975)

Pink Floyd, *Animals* (Harvest, 1977)

Pink Floyd, *The Wall* (Harvest, 1979)

Pink Floyd, *The Final Cut* (Harvest, 1983)

Pink Floyd, *Pulse* (EMI, 1996)

Plastikman, *Closer* (Novamute, 2003)

Porcupine Tree, *On the Sunday of Life* (Delerium, 1992)

Porcupine Tree, *The Sky Moves Sideways* (Delerium, [1994] 2003)

Porcupine Tree, *In Absentia* (Atlantic, 2002)

Porcupine Tree, *Deadwing* (Atlantic, 2005)
Porcupine Tree, *Fear of a Blank Planet* (Roadrunner, 2007)
Porcupine Tree, *The Incident* (Roadrunner, 2009)
The Pretty Things, *SF Sorrow* (Snapper, [1968] 1998)
Procol Harum, *Shine On Brightly* (Salvo, [1968] 2009)
Public Enemy, *Fear of a Black Planet* (Def Jam, 1990)
Public Image Limited, *Public Image* (Virgin, 1978)
Public Image Limited, *Metal Box* (Virgin, 1979)
Pure Reason Revolution, *Hammer and Anvil* (Superball, 2010)
Q65, *Revolution* (Decca, 1966)
Queensrÿche, *Operation: Mindcrime* (EMI, 1988)
Queensrÿche, *Operation: Mindcrime II* (Rhino, 2006)
Radiohead, 'Creep' (EMI, 1992)
Radiohead, *The Bends* (EMI, 1995)
Radiohead, *OK Computer* (EMI, 1997)
Radiohead, *Kid A* (EMI, 2000)
Radiohead, *Hail to the Thief* (EMI, 2003)
Radiohead, *In Rainbows* (XL, 2007)
Radiohead, *The King of Limbs* (XL, 2011)
Rare Bird, *Rare Bird* (Charisma, 1969)
Renaissance, *Renaissance* (Island, 1969)
Renaissance, *Scheherazade and Other Stories* (BTM, 1975)
Renaissance, *Turn of the Cards* (Repertoire, 1975)
Renaissance, *Novella* (WEA, 1977)
Renaissance, *A Song for all Seasons* (Sire, 1978)
Return to Forever, *Hymn of the Seventh Galaxy* (Decca, 1973)
Return to Forever, *Where Have I Known You Before* (Decca, 1974)
Rush, *Caress of Steel* (Mercury, 1975)
Rush, *2112* (Mercury, 1976)
Rush, *A Farewell to Kings* (Mercury, 1976)
Rush, *Hemispheres* (Mercury, 1978)
Rush, *Permanent Waves* (Mercury, 1979)
Rush, *Moving Pictures* (Mercury, 1980)
Rush, *Signals* (Mercury, 1982)
Rush, *Grace Under Pressure* (Mercury, 1983)
Rush, *Power Windows* (Mercury, 1985)
Rush, *Hold Your Fire* (Mercury, 1987)
Rush, *Presto* (Atlantic, 1989)
Rush, *Roll the Bones* (Atlantic, 1991)
Rush, *Vapor Trails* (Atlantic, 2002)

The Sallyangies, *Children in the Sun* (Castle, 1969)
Pharoah Sanders, *Karma* (Impulse, 1969)
Santana, *Moonflower* (Columbia, 1977)
Saracen, *Red Sky/Heroes, Saints and Fools* (Escape, [1982] 2006)
The Seven Ages of Man (Rediffusion, 1972)
Jane Siberry, *The Walking* (Reprise, 1987)
Jane Siberry, *Maria* (Reprise, 1995)
Frank Sinatra, *Come Fly With Me* (Capitol, 1958)
Siouxsie and the Banshees, *Join Hands* (Polydor, 1979)
Smashing Pumpkins, *Siamese Dream* (Hut, 1993)
Smashing Pumpkins, *Mellon Collie and the Infinite Sadness* (Hut, 1995)
Soft Machine, *Volumes 1 and 2* ([1968, 1969] 1989)
Soft Machine, *Third* (Columbia, 1970)
Sonic Youth, *Daydream Nation* (Blast First, 1988)
Sonic Youth, *Washing Machine* (Geffen, 1995)
Spock's Beard, *Snow* (2002)
Squarepusher, *Just a Souvenir* (Warp, 2008)
Starcastle, *Starcastle* (Epic, 1976)
Starcastle, *Fountains of Light* (Epic, 1977)
Stormy Six, *Un biglietto del tram* (Warner, [1975] 2004)
Stormy Six, *L'Apprendista* (Warner, [1977] 2005)
Suicide, *Suicide* (Mute, [1977] 2002)
Sun Ra, *The Complete ESP-Disk' Recordings* (ESP-Disk', [1965–73] 2005)
Sunburned Hand of the Man, *A Grand Tour of Tunisia* (Pid, 2009)
Supertramp, *Breakfast in America* (A&M, 1979)
David Sylvian, *Brilliant Trees* (Virgin, 1983)
David Sylvian, *Alchemy: An Index of Possibilities* (Virgin, 1985)
David Sylvian, *Gone to Earth* (Virgin, 1986)
David Sylvian and Holger Czukay, *Plight and Premonition* (Venture, 1988)
David Sylvian and Holger Czukay, *Flux and Mutability* (Venture, 1989)
Talk Talk, *The Colour of Spring* (EMI, 1986)
Talk Talk, *Spirit of Eden* (EMI, 1988)
Talk Talk, *Laughing Stock* (EMI, 1991)
The Tangent, *The World That We Drive Through* (Inside Out, 2004)
Tangerine Dream, *Tyger* (Sanctuary, 1987)
Television, *Marquee Moon* (WEA, 1977)
This Heat, *This Heat* (ReR, [1978] 2006)
This Heat, *Deceit* (ReR, [1981] 2006)

Ton Steine Scherben, *Keine macht für Niemand* (David Volksmund, 1972)

Tool, *Lateralus* (Volcano, 2001)

Tool, *10,000 Days* (Tool Directional/Volcano, 2006)

Transatlantic, *SMPT:e* (Century, 2000)

Transatlantic, *Bridge Across Forever* (Century, 2001)

Transatlantic, *The Whirlwind* (Century, 2009)

Twelfth Night, *Fact and Fiction* (Cyclops, 1982)

Van der Graaf Generator, *H to He Who Am The Only One* (Virgin, [1970] 2005)

Van der Graaf Generator, *Pawn Hearts* (Virgin, [1971] 2005)

Van der Graaf Generator, *Trisector* (Virgin, 2008)

Vienna Circle, *White Clouds* (Vienna Circle, 2008)

Voivod, *Nothingface* (MCA, 1989)

Rick Wakeman, *Journey to the Centre of the Earth* (Universal IMS, 1974)

Rick Wakeman, *The Myths and Legends of King Arthur and the Knights of the Round Table* (Universal IMS, 1975)

Rick Wakeman, *The Gospels* (Stylus, 1987)

Roger Waters, *The Pros and Cons of Hitchhiking* (Sony, 1984)

Roger Waters, *Radio K.A.O.S.* (Sony, 1987)

The Watersons, *Frost and Fire: A Calendar of Ritual and Magical Songs* (Topic, 1965)

Jeff Wayne, *Musical Version of The War of the Worlds* (Sony, 1978)

Weather Report, *I Sing the Body Electric* (Sony, 1972)

Weather Report, *Heavy Weather* (Sony, 1977)

The Who, *Quadrophenia* (Polydor, 1973)

The Wicker Man (Silva Screen, [1973] 2002)

Tony Williams Lifetime, *Emergency!* (Polydor, 1969)

Brian Wilson, *Smile* (Nonesuch, 2004)

Wishbone Ash, *Argus* (MCA, [1972] 2002)

Wishbone Ash, *Bare Bones* (Talking Elephant, 1999)

Wishing Tree, *Ostara* (Absolute Marketing, 2009)

Robert Wyatt, *Rock Bottom* (Hannibal, 1974)

X-102, *Discovers the Rings of Saturn* (Tresor, 1992)

The Yardbirds, *Roger the Engineer* (Demon, [1966] 1998)

Yes, *The Yes Album* (Atlantic, 1971)

Yes, *Fragile* (Atlantic, 1971)

Yes, *Close to the Edge* (Atlantic, 1972)

Yes, *Tales from Topographic Oceans* (Atlantic, 1973)

Yes, *Yessongs* (Atlantic, 1973)

Yes, *Relayer* (Atlantic, 1974)

Yes, *Yesterdays* (Atlantic, 1975)

Yes, *Going for the One* (Atlantic, 1977)

Yes, *Tormato* (Atlantic, 1978)

Yes, *Drama* (Atlantic, 1980)

Yes, *90125* (Atco, 1983)

Yes, *Keys to Ascension* CD/DVD (Atlantic, [1996, 1997] 2010)

Neil Young, *Greendale* (Warner, 2003)

The Zombies, *Odessey and Oracle* (Repertoire, [1968] 2008)

Videography

Kate Bush, *The Line, the Cross & the Curve* (EMI, 1994)
The Decemberists: A Practical Handbook (Kill Rock Stars, 2007)
Dream Theater, *Score* (Rhino, 2006)
Easy Rider (Dennis Hopper, 1969)
Emerson, Lake and Palmer, *Pictures at an Exhibition* (Eagle Rock, [1970] 2010)
The Fall (Peter Whitehead, 1968)
The Filth and the Fury (Julian Temple, 2000)
The Flaming Lips, *Christmas on Mars: A Fantastical Film Freakout* (Warner, 2008)
The Isle of Wight Festival: The Movie (Castle Music, 1995)
Led Zeppelin, *The Song Remains the Same* (Warner, [1976] 2007)
Led Zeppelin, *Led Zeppelin: DVD* (Atlantic, 2003)
Lucifer Rising (Kenneth Anger, 1973)
Marillion, *Recital of the Script* (EMI, 1983)
Marillion, *Live from Loreley* (EMI, [1987] 2004)
Opeth, *In Live Concert at the Royal Albert Hall* (Roadrunner, 2010)
Pink Floyd: London 1966/1967 (Highnote, Peter Whitehead, 2005)
Pink Floyd, *Live at Pompeii: The Director's Cut* (Universal, [1972] 2002)
Pink Floyd, *The Wall* (Sony, [1982] 1999)
Prog Britannia (BBC, 2008)
Rush, *Beyond the Lighted Stage* (Rush Doc Films, 2010)
Tonite Let's All Make Love in London (Peter Whitehead, 1967)
Roger Waters, *The Wall – Live in Berlin* (Universal, 1990)
Jeff Wayne, *The War of the Worlds: Live* (Universal, 2006)
Within Temptation, *Black Symphony* (Roadrunner, 2008)
Woodstock: Three Days of Peace & Music (Warner, Michael Wadleigh, [1970] 1994])

Bibliography

Robert Adlington, ed., *Sound Commitments: Avant-garde Music and the Sixties* (Oxford: Oxford University Press, 2009).

Glenn C. Altschuler, *All Shook Up: How Rock 'n' Roll Changed America* (New York: Oxford University Press, 2003).

Paulo Alvarado, 'Guatemala's Alux Nahual: A Non-"Latin American" Latin American Rock Group', in *Rockin' Las Americas: The Global Politics of Rock in Latin/o America*, ed. Deborah Pacini Hernandez, Héctor Fernández L'Hoeste and Eric Zolov (Pittsburgh, PA: University of Pittsburgh Press, 2004), 220–40.

Jacques Attali, *Noise: The Political Economy of Music* (Minneapolis: University of Minnesota Press, [1977] 1985).

Philip Auslander, *Liveness* (London: Routledge, 1999).

Tony Bacon, ed., *Rock Hardware: The Instruments, Equipment and Technology of Rock* (New York: Harmony Books, 1981).

Philip Ball, *The Music Instinct: How Music Works and Why We Can't Do Without It* (London: Bodley Head, 2010).

Lester Bangs, *Mainlines, Blood Feasts and Bad Taste* (London: Serpent's Tail, 2003).

Tony Banks, Phil Collins, Peter Gabriel, Steve Hackett and Mike Rutherford, *Genesis: Chapter & Verse*, ed. Philip Dodd (London: Weidenfeld & Nicolson, 2007).

Paul Barotto, *The Return of Italian Pop*, 2nd edn (Milan: Vinyl Solution Music, 1998).

Georges Bataille, *The Accursed Share* (New York: Zone, [1947] 1991).

Andy Beckett, *When the Lights Went Out: Britain in the Seventies* (London: Faber and Faber, 2009).

Walter Benjamin, *Reflections: Essays, Aphorisms, Autobiographical Writings*, ed. Peter Demetz, trans. Edmund Jephcott (New York: Harcourt Brace, 1978).

—— 'The Task of the Translator', *Illuminations*, trans. Harry Zohn (New York: Random House, [1968] 2002), 70–82.

Graham Bennett, *Soft Machine: Out-Bloody-Rageous* (London: SAF, 2005).

Joachim E. Berendt, *The Jazz Book: From Ragtime to Fusion and Beyond*, 6th edn, revised by Günther Huesmann (New York: Lawrence Hill, 1989).

Harris Berger, *Metal, Rock, and Jazz: Perception and the Phenomenology of Musical Experience* (Hanover, NH: Wesleyan University Press, 1999).

Andrew Blake, *The Land Without Music: Music, Culture and Society in Twentieth-Century Britain* (Manchester: Manchester University Press, 1997).

Joe Boyd, *White Bicycles: Making Music in the 1960s* (London: Serpent's Tail, 2006).

Peter Brook, *The Empty Space* (London: Penguin, [1968] 1998).

Mick Brown, 'Man with the Vinyl Solutions', the *Guardian* (8 May 1980), 7.

Bill Bruford, *The Autobiography* (London: Jawbone Press, 2009).

Peter Bürger, *Theory of the Avant-Garde* (Minneapolis: University of Minnesota Press, 1984).

William Burroughs, 'Led Zeppelin Meets Naked Lunch', in *Very Seventies*, ed. Peter Knobler and Greg Mitchell (New York: Fireside, 1995), 120–7.

William Cameron, 'Is Jazz a Folk Art?', *The Second Line*, 9 (1–2) (January–February 1958).

Gary Carter and Mark Chatterton, *Blowin' Free: Thirty Years of Wishbone Ash* (London: Firefly, 2001).

Ian Chambers, *Urban Rhythms: Pop Music and Popular Culture* (Basingstoke: Macmillan, 1985).

Arthur C. Clarke, *Childhood's End* (London: Tor, [1954] 2010).

Ronald D. Cohen, *Rainbow Quest: The Folk Music Revival and American Society, 1940–1970* (Amherst, MA: University of Massachusetts Press, 2002).

Jon Collins, *Marillion: Separated Out* (London: Helter Skelter, 2003).

—— *Rush: Chemistry* (London: Helter Skelter, 2006).

Julian Cope, *Krautrocksampler*, 2nd edn (Yatesbury: Head Heritage, [1995] 1996).

Augusto Croce, *Italian Prog: The Comprehensive Guide to Italian Progressive Music, 1967–1979* (Milan: AMS, 2008).

Chris Cutler, *File Under Popular: Theoretical and Critical Writings on Music* (London: November, 1985).

Jim DeRogatis, *Kaleidoscope Eyes: Psychedelic Music from the 1960s to the 1990s* (London: Fourth Estate, 1996).

Andreas Diesel and Dieter Gerten, *Looking for Europe: Néofolk and Underground* vol I (Rosières-en-Haye: Camion Noir, 2008).

Jonathan Eisen, ed., *The Age of Rock* (New York: Vintage, 1969).

T. S. Eliot, 'The Hollow Men', *Collected Poems 1909–1962* (London: Faber, 1963).

Duke Ellington, 'The Race for Space' (1957), in *The Duke Ellington Reader*, ed. Mark Tucker (New York: Oxford University Press, 1993), 293–6.

Keith Emerson, *Pictures of an Exhibitionist* (London: John Blake, 2004).

Susan Fast, *In the Houses of the Holy: Led Zeppelin and the Power of Rock Music* (Oxford: Oxford University Press, 2001).

Benjamin Filene, *Romancing the Folk: Public Memory and American Roots Music* (Chapel Hill: University of North Carolina Press, 2000).

Tim Footman, *Radiohead: Welcome to the Machine – OK Computer and the Death of the Album* (New Malden: Chrome Dreams, 2007).

Hal Foster, ed., *Postmodern Culture* (London: Pluto, [1983] 1987).

Michel Foucault, *Discipline and Punish: The Birth of the Prison* (London: Allen Lane, [1975] 1977).

Steven and Allan Freeman, *The Crack in the Cosmic Egg*, 2nd edn (Leicester: Audion, 2005).

Ken Friedman, ed., *The Fluxus Reader* (Chichester: Academy Editions, 1998).

Bill Friskies-Warren, *I'll Take You There: Pop Music and the Urge for Transcendence* (New York: Continuum, 2005).

Paul Gallico, *The Snow Goose and The Small Miracle* (London: Penguin, [1941] 1967).

Charlie Gillett, *The Sound of the City* (London: Sphere, 1971).

Paul Gilroy, 'Soundscapes of the Black Atlantic', in *The Audio Culture Reader*, eds Michael Bull and Les Back (Oxford and New York: Berg, 2003), 381–95.

Jonathan Gould, *Can't Buy Me Love: The Beatles, Britain and America* (London: Portrait, 2007).

Charlotte Greig, 'As Good as Their Words', the *Guardian* (19 April 1993), 30–1.

Dai Griffith, *OK Computer* (New York: Continuum, 2004).

Donna Haraway, 'A Cyborg Manifesto: Science, Technology and Socialist Feminism in the Late Twentieth Century', in *Simians, Cyborgs and Women: The Reinvention of Nature* (New York; Routledge, 1991), 149–81.

Colin Harper, *Dazzling Stranger: Bert Jansch and the British Folk and Blues Revival* (London: Bloomsbury, 2006).

Mary Harron, 'The Hot Tip is a Cool Flavour', the *Guardian* (23 October 1981), 11.

G. W. F. Hegel, *Phenomenology of Spirit* (Oxford: Oxford University Press, [1807] 1977).

Martin Heidegger, *Being and Time* (Oxford: Blackwell, 1962).

—— *Basic Writings* (London: Routledge, 1993).

Clinton Heylin, *From the Velvets to the Voidoids: The Birth of American Punk Rock*, 2nd edn (London: Helter Skelter, [1993] 2005).

—— *The Act You've Known for All These Years* (Edinburgh: Canongate, 2007).

Michael Hicks, *Sixties Rock: Garage, Psychedelic and Other Satisfactions* (Urbana and Chicago: University of Illinois Press, 1999).

Brian Hinton, *Message to Love: The Isle of Wight Festivals, 1968–70* (London: Castle Communications, 1995).

Kevin Holm-Hudson, ed., *Progressive Rock Reconsidered* (New York: Routledge, 2002).

Kevin Holm-Hudson, *Genesis and* The Lamb Lies Down on Broadway (Aldershot: Ashgate, 2008).

Stewart Home, *Cranked Up Really High: Genre Theory and Punk Rock* (Hove: CodeX, 1995).

Andreas Huyssen, *After the Great Divide: Modernism, Mass Culture and Postmodernism* (London: Macmillan, 1986).

Richard Morton Jack, ed., *Galactic Ramble* (London: Foxcote, 2009).

Fredric Jameson, *Postmodernism, or, The Cultural Logic of Late Capitalism* (London: Verso, 1991).

Rob Jovanovic, *Kate Bush: The Biography* (London: Portrait, 2005).

Allan Kaprow, *The Blurring of Art and Life*, ed. Jeff Kelley (Berkeley, CA: University of California Press, [1993] 1996).

Will Kaufman, *American Culture in the 1970s* (Edinburgh: Edinburgh University Press, 2009).

Akitsugu Kawamoto, '"Can You Still Keep Your Balance?" Keith Emerson's Anxiety of Influence, Style Change, and the Road to Prog Superstardom', *Popular Music*, 24(2) (2005), 223–44.

David Keenan, *England's Hidden Reverse: A Secret History of the Esoteric Underground* (London: SAF Publishing, 2003).

Charles Keil and Steven Feld, *Music Grooves* (Chicago: University of Chicago Press, 1994).

Biba Kopf, 'The Autobahn Goes On Forever. Kings of the Road: The Motorik Pulse of Kraftwerk and Neu!', in *Undercurrents: The Hidden Wiring of Modern Music*, ed. Rob Young (New York: Continuum, 2002), 141–52.

Richard Kostelantz, *The Theatre of Mixed-Means* (New York: R. K. Editions, [1968] 1980).

Rosalind Krauss, *The Originality of the Avant-Garde and Other Modernist Myths* (Cambridge, MA: MIT Press, [1985] 1993).

Holly Kruse, 'In Praise of Kate Bush', in *On Record: Rock, Pop, and the Written Word*, eds Simon Frith and Andrew Goodwin (London: Routledge, 1990).

Harvey Kubernik, *Canyon of Dreams: The Magic and the Music of Laurel Canyon* (New York: Sterling, 2009).

Dave Laing, Karl Dallas, Robin Denselow and Robert Shelton, *The Electric Muse: The Story of Folk into Rock* (London: Eyre Methuen, 1975).

Neil Lazarus, 'Unsystematic Fingers at the Conditions of the Times: "Afropop" and the Paradoxes of Imperialism', in *Postcolonial Discourses: An Anthology*, ed. Gregory Castle (Oxford: Blackwell, 2001), 232–50.

Jeanette Leech, *Seasons They Change: The Story of Acid and Psychedelic Folk* (London: Jawbone, 2010).

Richard Leppert, *The Sight of Sound: Music, Representation, and the History of the Body* (Berkeley: University of California Press, 1993).

Aymeric Leroy, *Rock Progressif* (Marseille: Le mot et le reste, 2010).

Mike Levin, 'In *Downbeat*', in *The Duke Ellington Reader*, ed. Mark Tucker (New York: Oxford University Press, 1993), 166–70.

Graham Lock, *Blutopia: Visions of the Future and Revisions of the Past* (Durham, NC: Duke University Press, 1999).

James Lovelock, *Gaia: A New Look at Life on Earth*, 3rd edn (Oxford: Oxford University Press, [1979] 2000).

Jerry Lucky, *20th Century Rock and Roll: Progressive Rock* (Burlington, Ontario: Collector's Guide Publishing, 2000).

—— *The Progressive Rock Handbook* (Burlington, Ontario: Collector's Guide Publishing, 2008).

Jean-François Lyotard, *The Postmodern Condition: A Report on Knowledge*, trans. Geoffrey Bennington and Brian Massumi (Manchester: Manchester University Press, [1979] 1984).

Edward Macan, *Rocking the Classics: English Progressive Rock and the Counterculture* (New York: Oxford University Press, 1997).

Susan McClary, *Feminine Endings: Music, Gender and Sexuality* (Minneapolis: University of Minnesota Press, 1991).

Bruno MacDonald, *Pink Floyd: Through the Eyes of the Band, Its Fans, Friends and Foes* (London: Sidgwick and Jackson, 1996).

Chris McDonald, *Rush, Rock Music and the Middle Class: Dreaming in Middletown* (Indianapolis: Indiana University Press, 2009).

Ian MacDonald, *The People's Music* (London: Pimlico, 2003).

—— *Endless Enigma: A Musical Biography of Emerson, Lake and Palmer* (New York: Open Court, 2006).

Karen McNally, *When Frankie Went to Hollywood: Frank Sinatra and American Male Identity* (Urbana: University of Illinois Press, 2008).

Paul de Man, *Allegories of Reading: Figural Language in Rousseau, Nietzsche, Rilke and Proust* (New Haven: Yale University Press, 1979).

—— 'Conclusions: On Walter Benjamin's "The Task of the Translator"' (1985), in *The Resistance to Theory* (Minneapolis: University of Minnesota Press, 1986).

Greil Marcus, *Lipstick Traces* (London: Faber and Faber, [1989] 2001).

Bill Martin, *Music of Yes: Structure and Vision in Progressive Rock* (Chicago and La Salle: Open Court, 1996).

—— *Listening to the Future: The Time of Progressive Rock, 1968–1978* (Chicago and La Salle: Open Court, 1998).

Jonas Mekas, 'Movie Journals', *Film Culture: Expanded Arts*, 43 (Winter 1966), 10–11.

George Melly, *Revolt into Style: The Pop Arts in Britain* (Harmondsworth: Penguin, 1970).

Ian Middleton, 'Jethro Tull: "We're Really Human . . .", *Record Mirror* (12 October 1968): www.tullpress.com/rm12oct68.htm.

Richard Middleton, *Studying Popular Music* (Buckingham: Open University Press, 1990).

Edward Miller, *Emergency Broadcasting and 1930s American Radio* (Philadelphia: Temple University Press, 2003).

James Miller, *Almost Grown: The Rise of Rock and Roll* (London: Arrow, 2000).

Greg Milner, *Perfecting Sound Forever: The Story of Recorded Music* (London: Granta, 2009).

Allen Moore, *Rock: The Primary Text – Developing a Musicology of Rock* (Buckingham: Open University Press, 1993).

Paul Morley, *Ask: The Chatter of Pop* (London: Faber and Faber, 1986).

—— *Words and Music* (London: Bloomsbury, 2003).

Ron Moy, *Kate Bush and* Hounds of Love (Aldershot: Ashgate, 2007).

Andy Neill and Matt Kent, *Anyway Anyhow Anywhere: The Complete Chronicle of The Who 1958–1978* (London: Virgin, 2002).

Friedrich Nietzsche, *The Will to Power* (New York: Vintage, 1968).

Michael Nyman, *Experimental Music: Cage and Beyond*, 2nd edn (Cambridge: Cambridge University Press, [1974] 1999).

Alex Ogg, *No More Heroes: A Complete History of UK Punk from 1976 to 1980* (London: Cherry Red, 2006).

Mike Oldfield, *Changeling: The Autobiography* (London: Virgin Books, 2007).

Robert Palmer, *Rock & Roll: An Unruly History* (New York: Harmony Books, 1995).

Lynn Pan, *Shanghai Style: Art and Design Between the Wars* (Hong Kong: Joint Publishing Ltd, 2008).

Archie Patterson, *Eurock: European Rock and the Second Culture* (Portland, OR: Eurock, 2002).

Marjorie Perloff, *21st-Century Modernism: The New Poetics* (Oxford: Wiley-Blackwell, 2002).

Charles Perry, *The Haight Ashbury* (New York: Warner Books, 2005).

Joan Peyser, 'The Music of Sound, or The Beatles and the Beatless', in *The Age of Rock*, ed. Jonathan Eisen (New York: Vintage, 1969), 126–34.

Robin Platts, *Genesis: Behind the Lines: 1967–2007* (Burlington, Ontario: Collector's Guide Publishing, 2007).

Renato Poggioli, *The Theory of the Avant-Garde* (Cambridge, MA: Belknap, 1968).

Ann Powers, *Kate Bush's* The Dreaming (New York: Continuum, 2012).

Mark Pyklit, *Björk: Wow and Flutter* (Toronto: ECW Press, 2003).

Ayn Rand, *Anthem* (London: Signet, [1946] 1995).

Simon Reynolds, *Blissed Out: The Raptures of Rock* (London: Serpent's Tail, 1990).

—— 'Ecstasy is a Science: Techno-Romanticism', in *Stars Don't Stand Still in the Sky: Music and Myth*, ed. Karen Kelly and Evelyn McDonnell (New York: New York University Press, 1999), 198–205.

—— 'Post-Rock', in *Audio Culture: Readings in Modern Music*, eds Christoph Cox and Daniel Warner (New York: Continuum, 2004), 358–61.

—— *Rip It Up and Start Again: Postpunk 1978–1984* (London: Faber and Faber, 2005).

Kalen Rogers, *Tori Amos – All These Years: The Authorized Illustrated Biography* (London: Omnibus, 1994).

Will Romano, *Mountains Come Out of the Sky: The Illustrated History of Prog Rock* (Milwaukee, WI: Backbeat Books, 2010).

Harold Rosenberg, 'The American Action Painters', *Art News*, 51 (December 1952).

Neil Rosenberg, *Transforming Tradition: Folk Music Revivals Examined* (Champaign, IL: University of Illinois Press, 1993).

Joel Rosenman, *Young Men With Unlimited Capital: The Story of Woodstock* (New York: Harcourt Brace Jovanovich, 1974).

Dominic Sandbrook, *State of Emergency: The Way We Were: Britain, 1970–1974* (London: Allen Lane, 2010).

Craig Saper, 'Fluxus as Laboratory', in *The Fluxus Reader*, ed. Ken Friedman (Chichester: Academy Editions, 1998).

Jon Savage, *England's Dreaming: Sex Pistols and Punk Rock* (London: Faber and Faber, 1991).

Gerald Scarfe, *The Making of Pink Floyd:* The Wall (New York: Da Capo, 2010).

Nicholas Schaffner, *Saucerful of Secrets: Pink Floyd Odyssey* (London: Helter Skelter, [1991] 2005).

Roberta Freund Schwartz, *How Britain Got the Blues: The Transmission and Reception of American Blues Style in the United Kingdom* (Burlington, VT: Ashgate, 2007).

Pete Seeger, 'The Purist vs. the Hybridist' (1957–8), in *The Incompleat Folksinger*, ed. Jo Metcalf Schwartz (New York: Simon & Schuster, 1973), 174–5.

Jonathan Sheffer, ed., *Perceptible Processes: Minimalism and the Baroque* (New York: Eos, 1997).

David Sheppard, *On Some Faraway Beach: The Life and Times of Brian Eno* (London: Orion, 2008).

Bradley Smith, *The Billboard Guide to Progressive Rock* (New York: Billboard Books, 1997).

Sid Smith, *In the Court of the Crimson King* (New York: Helter Skelter, 2007).

Phil Strongman, *Metal Box: Stories from John Lydon's Public Image Limited* (London: Helter Skelter, 2007).

David Stubbs et al., *Krautrock: Cosmic Rock and its Legacy* (London: Black Dog, 2009).

Paul Stump, *The Music's All That Matters: A History of Progressive Rock* (London: Quarter Books, 1997).

Adam Sweeting, 'The Hair's Apparent', the *Guardian* (2 May 1997), 4.

John Swenson, *Musician Player and Listener: The Year in Rock 1981–82* (Farncombe: LSP Books, 1981).

Robin Sylvan, *Traces of the Spirit: The Religious Dimensions of Popular Music* (New York: New York University Press, 2002).

Eric Tamm, *Robert Fripp: From King Crimson to Guitar Craft* (London: Faber and Faber, 1991).

Joseph Tate, ed., *The Music and Art of Radiohead* (Aldershot: Ashgate, 2007).

Timothy D. Taylor, *Beyond Exoticism: Western Music and the World* (Durham, NC: Duke University Press, 2007).

David Thomas, 'Oh No, It's Yes: Where Even Irony Fears to Tread', the *Observer*, Review (8 March 1998), 5.

Graeme Thomson, *Under the Ivy: The Life and Music of Kate Bush* (London: Omnibus, 2010).

Alwyn W. Turner, *Crisis? What Crisis? Britain in the 1970s* (London: Aurum, 2008).

Steve Turner, *The Gospel According to The Beatles* (Louisville: Westminster/John Knox Press, 2006).

John Tytell, *The Living Theatre: Art, Exile and Outrage* (London: Methuen, [1995] 1997).

Gianni Vattimo, *The End of Modernity* (Baltimore: Johns Hopkins University Press, 1991).

Paul Virilio, *Speed and Politics: An Essay on Dromology* (New York: Semiotext(e), [1977] 1986).

Sheldon Waldrep, ed., *The Seventies: The Age of Glitter in Popular Culture* (New York: Routledge, 2000).

Greg Walker, 'Grand Masters of Vinyl', *Times Higher Education* (11 September 2008), 41–4.

—— 'Selling England (and Italy) by the Pound? Performing Englishness in English and Italian Progressive Rock', in *Performing National Identities: Anglo-Italian Cultural Transactions*, ed. Manfred Pfister and Ralf Hertel (Amsterdam: Rodopi, 2008), 287–306.

Michael Walker, *Laurel Canyon: The Inside Story of Rock-and-Roll's Legendary Neighbourhood* (London: Faber and Faber, 2006).

Mick Wall, *Led Zeppelin: When Giants Walked the Earth* (London: Orion, 2008).

Eric Weisbard, ed., *Listen Again: A Momentary History of Pop Music* (Durham, NC: Duke University Press, 2007).

Sheila Whiteley, *Women and Popular Music: Sexuality, Identity and Subjectivity* (London: Routledge, 2000).

—— *Too Much Too Young: Popular Music, Age and Gender* (London: Routledge, 2003).

Adrian Whittaker, ed., *Be Glad: An Incredible String Band Compendium* (London: Helter Skelter, 2008).

Mark Wilkinson, *Shadowplay* (Brusen/Fantasmus-Art, 2009).

Raymond Williams, *Marxism and Literature* (Oxford: Oxford University Press, 1977).

Richard Williams, *The Blue Moment: Miles Davis's* Kind of Blue *and the Remaking of Modern Music* (London: Faber and Faber, 2009).

Brian Wilson and Todd Gold, *Wouldn't it Be Nice: My Own Story* (London: Bloomsbury, 2002).

Deborah Withers, 'Kate Bush: Performing and Creating Queer Subjectivities on *Lionheart*', *Nebula*, 3(2–3) (September 2006): www.nobleworld.biz/images/Withers.pdf.

—— *Adventures in Kate Bush and Theory* (Bristol: HammerOn Press, 2010).

Patrick Wright, 'Resist Me. Make Me Strong', the *Guardian* (11 November 1995), 38, 42–3, 46.

La Monte Young, *An Anthology* (New York: Young & Mac Low [1963] 1970).

Rob Young, *Electric Eden: Unearthing Britain's Visionary Music* (London: Faber and Faber, 2010).

Index

305

industrial music 117, 215, 246, 261, 277
IQ 183, 185, 196–8, 199, 208
Iron Maiden 187, 260, 261
Islam 271
It Bites 159n1, 199

Jackson, Mahalia 21
Jadis 199
Jagger, Mick 36, 122
Jameson, Fredric 6, 287, 290n9
jamming 25–6, 127, 205
Janáček, Leoš 26
Jane's Addiction 280
Jansch, Bert 29n8, 57
Jansen, Mark 268
Japan (band) 225
Japanese noise 277
Jarre, Jean-Michel 131
Jarry, Alfred 111
jazz 10, 11, 20–3, 24, 26, 50, 53, 56, 62,
    105–16, 130, 225, 251, 259, 261, 285
jazz rock 105, 108, 114, 117
Jefferson Airplane 48, 53, 203
Jenkins, Keith 184
Jethro Tull 3, 11, 24, 48, 50, 51–3, 57, 58,
    70, 74, 75, 91, 113, 122, 139, 166, 187,
    196, 242, 244
Jodorowsky, Alejandro 131
John, Elton 166, 174, 208
Jones, Elvin 259
Jones, John Paul 1, 128
Jones, Steve 164
Joplin, Janis 204
Journey 181, 184
Joyce, James 212, 281

Kaipa 202n24
Kamelot 266, 267
Kansas 181, 182, 184
Kaprow, Allan 35, 37–8, 39, 43
Karnataka 219
Kaye, Tony 184
Kayo Dot 280
Keats, John 96

Keenan, David 246
Keenan, Maynard James 277, 278
Kelly, Mark 187
Kennedy, Nigel 214
Khan, Natasha 219
Khan, Nusrat Fateh Ali 180n25
Kiefer, Anselm 153
Killing Joke 289
King Crimson 3, 9–10, 11, 14n16, 25, 50,
    57, 69, 70–3, 74, 106, 109, 124, 139, 165,
    166, 175, 176–8, 182, 184, 197, 199, 245,
    261, 262, 263, 266, 277, 279, 283
Kingdom Come 150, 160n22
Kings of Leon 237
Kinks, The 25, 66, 67, 68
Kiss 122
Klausener, Rolf 254
Klein, Yves 34
Knight, Peter 43
Kopf, Biba 153
Korner, Alexis 24, 105
kosmische (Krautrock) 10, 151, 152–3, 224,
    226, 277
Kraftwerk 118n10, 153, 170, 215, 235
Krause, Dagmar 156, 161n33, 203
Krauss, Alison 241
Krauss, Rosalind 7
Kristina, Sonja 203, 204
Kruse, Holly 209, 214

Laing, R. D. 63
Lake, Greg 1, 73
Latin musics 108, 152, 254, 280, 282
Lawes, William 247
Le Orme 91–2
League of Gentlemen 176
Lear, Edward 110
Led Zeppelin 10, 50, 92, 95, 102, 123, 125,
    127–30, 164, 181, 183, 251, 259
Lee, Geddy 90, 100, 148, 203
Leech, Jeanette 255, 257
Lennon, John 33, 35, 38, 39, 122, 195
Leppert, Richard 123
Lettrism 163